The Innovator's Way

The Innovator's Way

Essential Practices for Successful Innovation

Peter J. Denning and Robert Dunham

The MIT Press
Cambridge, Massachusetts
London, England

For information about special quantity discounts, please email special_sales@ mitpress.mit.edu

This book was set in Sabon by Toppan Best-set Premedia Limited. Printed and bound in the United States of America.

Library of Congress Cataloging-in-Publication Data
Denning, Peter J., 1942–
The innovator's way : essential practices for successful innovation / Peter J. Denning and Robert Dunham.
    p. cm.
Includes bibliographical references and index.
ISBN 978-0-262-01454-0 (hardcover : alk. paper) 1. Technological innovations. I. Dunham, Robert. II. Title.
HD45.D36 2010
658.4'06—dc22
2010002550

10 9 8 7 6 5 4 3 2

To Dorothy
To Josephina

Contents

Foreword

The Social Life of Innovation

Oh no, I first thought when I opened my email from Peter Denning asking if I would consider doing a foreword for his forthcoming book on innovation. Without even looking at the book, my mind peppered me with questions. Does the world really need one more book talking about the secrets, challenges, or myths of innovation and why it is hard or easy? Another book on product innovation, or creativity and invention? Another book that sidesteps the more complex issue of institutional innovation?

But my hesitations were quickly put to rest. This is not "another book." It is refreshing and unique. Here is a book that understands that for something to qualify as innovation, a social or work practice has to be transformed by it. And for that to happen we must consider its social life, so to speak. The innovation has to be socialized; it must enable the community to appropriate it and in so doing will often lead the community to perceive the world in a new way. Invention is the fun part of innovation. The real work is in adoption, and this book tells us how to succeed at that. And it squarely faces the issues of institutional innovation.

As someone who has lived through many exciting adventures of innovation, I have come to realize just how hard this socialization process is. I was especially happy to see that this book actually went beyond mere description of the different kinds and different stages of innovation and focused on the generative practices. These practices guide our interactions with the community so that it comes to own and shape the innovation and enact its own uses and practices around it.

Although there were many things that I resonated to as I read this book, I will mention just three of them here, namely the practices of deep sensing, envisioning, and offering. Deep sensing is closely aligned to making sense of one's own emotional reactions to a proposed new idea. I still find, even after years of being in the innovation game, that when someone approaches me with an idea that I haven't thought of, I can, at times, feel myself tightening up. Almost without fail, when that happens it is because the idea challenges something in my way of seeing the world. My first reaction is to dismiss it or find some kind of fault with it. Slowly, over the years, I have learned a new practice, a practice of noting when this happens, and then being careful not to say much and to let my whole body, not just my mind, absorb. I attempt not only to interpret the meaning of the innovation but also the meaning of my reaction to it. This takes time and often involves getting a good night's sleep. Only then do I try to articulate what might lie behind my first reaction.

This kind of sensing is, of course, just one step in the long process of helping a creator begin to mobilize the acceptance of an idea within an organization or community. The next step to acceptance and community engagement is providing a way for the community to envision how this innovation might affect them. To facilitate this, prototypes are crucial, prototypes with which a conversation can be initiated with the community. The prototypes can be physical or virtual mockups. They can be stories, videos, simulations, games. They can also be specs of a protocol or policy that can be used to request comments from the community, as was so successfully done with many of the protocols now constituting the Internet.

Z Smith, a physicist, did one of the more dramatic examples of this in my tenure at Xerox PARC in the early 1990s around a radical new kind of document machine that could scan, think/interpret, and print the document. Z's prototype not only demonstrated the vision, it also became a powerful offer. His machine's "thinking" was of many forms including summarizing, filing and distributing, and so on. It was a really cool, personal document machine that pushed the boundaries of what computing and imaging could do in those days. And it certainly pushed the concept of a printer or a copier to the extreme. We knew that getting this intelligent, multifunction device embraced within the culture of our copier company would be decidedly nontrivial. The company thought and breathed stand-alone, single-purpose devices, not devices that could actually interpret the documents they were being fed.

Z's idea for moving the internal community into adopting this idea was as ingenious as his invention. He built mockups of the machine and then designed, created, and videoed three short skits of different uses of the device. Then, at the end of the video he added a fourth skit by a professional comedian that ended with the comedian asking viewers how they might use the capabilities of the device. We then invited senior officers of the company to watch the video and to storyboard out, with some artist help, how they might imagine using this device. The three main skits were meant to act as sort of an intuition pump that would orient viewers and help them internalize what the device might mean to them. The comedian segment was designed to give some time for viewers to internalize the prior skits by providing a fun but purposeful distraction. And it provided a nonthreatening transition for them to the activity of creating their own storyboard with which we could "finish" the video. Finally, of course, the viewers' own storyboards served as the basis of new stories that they could then tell others in the company.

Z titled the video "More Than a Box," which was both what the comedic skit was about but more importantly was meant to provide a strategic nudge, suggesting that a copier could be much more than just a copier. Indeed, it was meant to nudge the company into seeing that it could be reconstituted as more than just a copier company. It could start to reimagine itself not as a company that produced and sold "boxes" but as The Document Company with the realization that documents are living, social artifacts that touch us and therein create meaning.

Z's story beautifully illustrates a virtuoso performance of the envisioning and offering practices described in *The Innovator's Way*. The offer was successful. The Xerox company set up a division to manufacture and market Z's document machine.

This account is a small example of some of the things we did in order to create a new worldview of the company, for itself, and for the world outside. This is not to claim that these things always worked. They didn't. The full story could make a book, itself. But this anecdote reveals my own discovery of some of the practices articulated in *The Innovator's Way*. The generative practices that unfold in this book are real and important. They are what you will need to master in order to become a serial innovator.

John Seely Brown
Former chief scientist, Xerox Corporation, and director of Xerox Palo Alto Research Center (PARC)

Preface

No subject commands more attention than innovation in business, government, nonprofit, or volunteer organizations. Technology leaders invest billions in a never-ending search for new gadgets, devices, and systems. Business leaders proclaim innovation as a core competency. Government leaders sponsor research and foster economic climates for innovation. Social activists push for transformation of their communities or countries. Professionals see innovation as a way to gain a competitive edge in their jobs. Popular technology magazines annually venerate top innovators with special articles and profiles of the "Top 50" or "Top 100." The online bookstore Amazon.com lists over 9,300 printed books with "innovation" in their titles; innovation books are frequent bestsellers.

Why all this interest? We human beings are constantly changing. We turn from stagnation, run from boredom, jump at opportunities. What could be more natural than change?

Innovation is the art of getting people to adopt change. We are far from mastering it. Businesses report that success rates of innovation initiatives hover around an abysmal 4 percent. Is there any way to significantly raise our success rates and lower our expenses in creating innovations? Many have pursued this question but have found no systematic way to improve success rates.

Albert Einstein is often quoted for saying that insanity means doing the same thing over and over again, expecting different results. He also said that we cannot solve our problems with the same thinking we used when we created them. We need new thinking for innovation.

We have written this book because we have been part of a community that has been thinking quite differently about how to succeed at innovation. We have found a new answer to the puzzle. Our basic premise is that innovation is a personal skill that can be developed through practice and extended into organizations, and that all successful innovation requires the skill.

It is easy to explain why innovation is hard: people are more resistant to change than they like to think. Changes alter value, status, and power. We embrace changes that increase our value, status, or power, and we resist changes that reduce our value, status, or power. Because of these mixed reactions in communities, innovators find it is a constant struggle to get others to adopt new ideas or methods. Adopters face risk, uncertainty, fracture of the familiar, incentives to preserve the status quo, and hard work to integrate the changes into their worlds. How can they be induced to do this?

Many leaders find themselves in a constant balancing act between resisting and embracing changes. Too much resistance, or even hesitation, can spell the end of a company. In *Creative Destruction* (2001), Richard Foster and Sarah Kaplan report that in 1987 only forty of the original Forbes 100 companies (from 1917) still existed, only eighteen remained in the top 100, and only two performed better than the stock market average over the seventy-year period. The new entrants to the Top 100 all offered innovations that most of the established companies could not match. In *The Innovator's Dilemma* (1997), Clayton Christenson discovered a pattern where the leaders of a company cannot decide when the time is right to respond to a low-end challenger. In *Competing for the Future* (1994), Gary Hamel and C. K. Prahalad described many world-leading companies that lost their ability to compete because they could not generate innovations. In *Warfighting and Disruptive Technologies* (2004), Terry Pierce showed the tension between conservatism and innovation in defense and security, a domain of high stakes and disastrous consequences for poor judgments.

The core of the work of innovation appears to be getting people to accept and implement change, and to sacrifice old, familiar ways in order to gain new ways. For success at innovation, we must learn to do this well.

Most thinking about innovation is dominated by invention. To many, it seems that most innovations begin with a clever invention. It seems that to strengthen our ability to innovate, we need to strengthen our inventiveness by fostering climates in which creative, imaginative thinkers can flourish. What if the supposition that invention causes innovation is wrong? What if our low innovation success rate is tied to our lack of clear distinction between invention and innovation?

Many innovation leaders have importuned us to make this distinction. In *Innovation and Entrepreneurship* (1986), Peter Drucker identified seven sources of innovation and found that "new knowledge," the only source that depends on inventions, is the least significant. In *Crossing the Chasm* (2002), Geoffrey Moore discovered that most startup business failures result from the lack of attention to inducing the majority to adopt the company's clever idea into their everyday practice. Robert Metcalfe tried to drive the point home by saying, "Invention is a flower, innovation is a weed." The beauty of the clever idea contrasts sharply with the actual, grungy work of getting people to adopt it.

Yet the notion that clever invention is the source of innovation is embedded deep into our psyche. We invest enormous energy in developing new ideas and fostering research, and too little in fostering adoption. We need a much better balance between our efforts in invention and innovation.

A simple but important step in this direction would be to agree on a precise and rigorous definition of innovation. Common notions like "innovation is new ideas" do not distinguish innovation from invention. Since the acid test of innovation is adoption, we have defined innovation in this book as "new practice adopted by a community." This simple distinction opens up a torrent of new insights into how to cause innovation.

Around 1995 we both noticed that our students and clients were really frustrated about innovation. Many were baffled that their own good ideas were not taken seriously and that other, bad ideas were more likely to work their way into products and markets. Many had tried the advice of innovation books, only to find that what worked in the author's organization failed in theirs. We found many others who felt the same.

When we started to look into ways to help our students, we naturally looked around for successful innovators to see what they do. We discovered that many of them had personal success rates far above the dismal industry average of 4 percent. We thought we could learn how to be much more successful at innovation by studying these people.

By this time we had already achieved great success at teaching our students about communication and coordination based on the groundbreaking work of Dr. Fernando Flores. It seemed natural to us that the innovator's secret would lie in the kinds of conversations the innovator started. This launched us on a long and productive quest to understand innovation as an embodied conversational skill and to design practices that would help people learn that skill.

We saw that our success at getting this notion adopted is challenged by two myths that dominate innovation thinking. The first challenge is the invention myth, a widespread belief, referred to earlier, that inventions cause innovations. We found numerous examples of inventions that caused no innovation, and numerous innovations that depended on no prior invention. We focused our approach on learning how to induce adoption. Bob Metcalfe inspired us when he quipped to a youthful admirer: "I was able to afford a house in Back Bay Boston not because I invented Ethernet, but because I spent ten years selling Ethernets."

The second challenge is the process myth, a widespread belief that innovation is a process that can be managed. The two leading models of innovation process—pipeline and diffusion—are the backbones of many organizational approaches to innovation. Many managers are trained in their methods and philosophy. Yet the successful innovators we studied performed much better than these processes.

These two myths are a toxic combination. The first lures people to focus on creating ideas rather than fostering adoptions. The second lures them to play the odds by "taking many shots on goal" rather than cultivating a skill of accurate shooting. We have concluded that most innovation failures are consequences of these myths.

To find the skill of innovation, we studied hundreds of innovators, specifically looking for the kinds of conversations they initiated and the kinds of commitments they made as they went along. Conversations and commitments are important because they generate action and are easy to observe in narrative stories by and of innovators. We found that the innovators' practices fall into eight categories:

1. Sensing
2. Envisioning
3. Offering
4. Adopting (first time)
5. Sustaining
6. Executing
7. Leading
8. Embodying

We also observed that innovators do these things skillfully in the middle of pitched action where there is not enough time to think everything through. So it was not enough to *describe* these kinds of practices and skills, we had to help our students learn to *generate* them in high-intensity environments. For this, we were guided by the work of Dr.

Richard Strozzi-Heckler, whose somatic (mind–body) approach to leadership leads to deep embodiment of the practices and the ability to perform them gracefully under duress.

We asked our students to engage with these practices and bring them to the situations where they sought innovations. We learned a lot from watching their successes and failures. Just as we found definite patterns in the successful actions of innovators, we found definite patterns in the breakdowns they faced. We designed our practices with the dual objectives of teaching which actions to take and which breakdowns to overcome.

Our design pointedly rejects a procedural approach to innovation. We offer practices, which are sets of skills that can be learned and perfected. Practices are the only way we know to connect ideas to action. Successful action in human domains does not come from rules, procedures, or prescriptions. It comes from embodied skill.

This book is built around everything we learned about innovation as a personal and organizational skill. We have organized this book into three parts.

Part I: Foundations of Innovation

In chapter 1 we lay out the main theses of this book, beginning with the definition of innovation as the adoption of a new practice in a community, and culminating with the claim that the eight practices can bootstrap an innovator well into the thick of the successful innovation game. In chapter 2 we meet seven innovators, and show how each engaged in the eight practices. In chapter 3 we classify and critique the common models of innovation, showing that there is no one, good process model for innovation; the observed stages of innovation are generated by human action, not unseen economic forces. Whereas the common models describe desired outcomes, the eight-practices model of this book generates the desired outcomes. In chapter 4 we introduce the observer, referring to how the innovator listens and interprets events; the successful innovator is a keen observer of practices, habits, disharmonies, customers, concerns, assessments, trust, value, satisfaction, and struggles.

Part II: The Eight Practices

Chapters 5 to 12 examine the innovation practices overviewed in chapter 1. Each chapter develops its practice in five stages: (1) defining the outcome the practice produces, (2) presenting the anatomy of the practice when it is successful, (3) presenting the breakdowns most commonly encountered while doing the practice, (4) offering guidelines on what to practice, and (5) offering guidelines on coping with the common breakdowns.

Part III: Journey to Mastery

In chapter 13 we claim that innovative organizations practice the eight practices and cultivate teams with higher levels of innovation skill than those of individuals. Business models that do not support the eight practices inhibit innovation. We find that organizations constituting themselves as learning networks will be most successful. In chapter 14 we extend the practices to strategies for making innovations with "wicked problems"—problems in large social systems for which there is no obvious answer and no consensus on approach. In chapter 15 we extend the practices to social networking, a new paradigm of conversations supported by the Internet. In chapter 16 we examine how master innovators acquire their tacit knowledge from local interactions while immersed in a community and cultivate certain "dispositions" that lead them toward mastery.

Appendix 1 is a table summarizing the purposes, anatomies, and breakdowns of each practice. Appendix 2 provides an assessment tool for organizations and individuals. The assessment process described there can help you evaluate your strengths and weaknesses in the eight practices. You can review your "innovation engagements," looking for areas where your actions were effective and areas where they need work. Appendix 3 gives more details about levels of performance at innovation considered as a skill. Appendix 4 gives more details about exercises that coaches can use to teach aspects of the eight practices.

Our main objective in this book is to help you develop a sensibility to how innovation is generated and to show you how to attain the skillful levels through practice. Even if you use the book only to be aware of the practices, simply having this sensibility is an important step toward becoming skillful at it. You will become aware of new aspects of familiar situations and pay attention to them differently. We also want to reveal some of the more advanced practices of masters that underlie the apparent uniqueness of their mastery.

The path to innovation is both challenging and rewarding. Innovation practice is full of complexities; we cannot make it simpler. But we can distinguish recurring regularities in the practices of innovation, thereby enabling practice and learning. You do not need to master everything in the eight practices to see results. We believe that, as you become more proficient at each practice, you will find yourself getting better and better at innovating.

This book will help you shift your interpretation of innovation from a high-risk mysterious process to a skill set of eight universal practices that can be learned and trained. Those practices will enable you to increase your success rate at innovation. And they are the launch point for a journey to innovation mastery.

The eight practices are a revolutionary approach to innovation. They offer effective and practicable means to improve innovation success by developing the right skills at both the personal and organizational levels. Our eight-practices model concentrates on the reality that an organization's real competitive advantage is in innovation practices, not just inventions. It offers a generative approach that applies in many situations where the standard models do not seem to fit. We hope that this book can help ignite a revolution.

Peter Denning, Salinas, California
Robert Dunham, Boulder, Colorado

Acknowledgments

We are indebted to many people for their inspiration and help in learning and testing what is written here.

First and foremost, we are grateful to Dr. Fernando Flores, who in the late 1970s created a theory of management communication as language-action and demonstrated the practical use of his theory in a very successful international business consulting practice. He shared his theory with hundreds of students in his original and unique three-year Ontological Design course, and he published his major findings in three groundbreaking books (*Understanding Computers and Cognition*, with T. Winograd, 1986; *Disclosing New Worlds*, with C. Spinosa and H. Dreyfus, 1997; and *Building Trust*, with R. Solomon, 2003). Dr. Flores taught us many of the basic distinctions and intuitions that have proved so valuable in our work and has offered us many encouragements to move forward with it. He also gave Robert Dunham the opportunity to develop and teach a course, Management in Action, which was the basis of Bob's later course for management students through his company, The Institute for Generative Leadership.

We are grateful also to Dr. Richard Strozzi-Heckler, whose pioneering work in coupling somatics to effective leadership has been decisive in enabling us to show the path to higher levels of skill as an innovator. Peter Denning studied for several years with Richard and was certified as Master Somatic Coach in 2002. Bob also studied somatic leadership with Richard; in addition he studied Aikido with Richard and has used modified Aikido techniques to teach somatic interpretations of management and leadership.

We are grateful to our many students who have learned our practices and given us detailed feedback on them. Peter worked with engineering students at George Mason University starting in 1993, and with graduate students and faculty colleagues at the Naval Postgraduate School starting in 2003. He especially thanks Frank Barrett, Dan Boger, Richard Elster, Leonard Ferrari, Sue Higgins, John Hiles, Craig Martell, Terry Pierce, Nancy Roberts, Kevin Squire, and Roxanne Zolin at the Naval Postgraduate School. Peter also thanks Kevin Suboski for great feedback on draft chapters, David Schwaderer for many insights into how innovators do their work, Danny Menascé for encouragement to persevere in unappreciative environments, and to Erol Gelenbe and Jeff Buzen for undying faith in his own abilities as an innovator. Bob worked on our innovation approach with students of management and leadership in his Generative Leadership Program, in the MBA in Sustainable Management program and the executive certificate program at the Presidio School of Management in San Francisco, and with professional coaches in his Coaching Excellence in Organizations (CEO) program offered jointly with Newfield Network. He especially thanks Marcos Polanco for his continued feedback. Both Bob and Peter are grateful to the Company of Leaders for their feedback throughout the entire book process, especially Brian Branagan, Bill Maclay, Jim Bayuk, Ed Huling, and Ruth Otte.

JanIrene Miller was extraordinarily generous in reviewing manuscripts and asking hard questions that helped us hone the connections between our ideas and the everyday work of people seeking change.

Michael Schrage was unfailingly generous with his ideas and encouragement. We'll never thank him enough for pointing us to Robert Metcalfe's masterwork, "Invention is a flower, innovation is a weed."

John Seely Brown was equally generous in discussing ideas about innovation and giving us crucial inspirations at key points. He insisted that invention is the fun part of innovation, and adoption is where the real work is. He encouraged us to write as much as we could about how to succeed at adoption.

Peter is grateful also to his wife Dorothy Denning for her constant insistence on clear logical flow and compelling grounding, and to his daughters Anne Denning Schultz and Diana Denning LaVolpe for various inspirations and for their patience and support. Bob is grateful to his life partner Josephina Santiago for her unflagging support and for the patience of Josephina and his daughter Kymberlee through this demanding project.

Prologue: Pasteur and the Dying Cows

In the 1870s, a strange disease was decimating the French sheep and cattle industries.[1] The French farmers were completely baffled by the mounting toll of dead cows and sheep; the cause, *anthrax bacillus*, had not yet been identified and named. Without effect, the farmers tried every conventional method to protect their animals, including quarantine of the sick and immediate burial of the dead. France's economic position was in grave peril.

The French Department of Agriculture encouraged Louis Pasteur to become involved. Pasteur was already well known in France for his work in the science of microbes. He had previously demonstrated that wine ferments not from a chemical process but from the action of yeast, and he had shown how to prevent spoiling by mildly heating the wine after bottling. The same technique, which came to be called *Pasteurization*, worked for milk. Pasteurization improved quality and consistency, and saved the wine and dairy industry millions of francs. He had also demonstrated that a microbe caused the decimation of French silkworms, and he saved the silk industry by showing how to block the microbe. The authorities therefore had good reasons to believe Pasteur might be able to shed light on the dying-cows mystery, and perhaps even to save the cattle and sheep industries.

As was his custom, Pasteur took his laboratory to the field and studied the patterns of how animals got sick. He observed that animals that

1. With gratitude to our friend and teacher, Fernando Flores, from whom we first heard a version of this story that he had prepared for his students. The story was inspired by Bruno Latour's book, *The Pasteurization of France*, Harvard University Press (1988). The ontological structure of the story is discussed in *Disclosing New Worlds*, by Charles Spinosa, Fernando Flores, and Hubert Dreyfus, MIT Press (1997). Here, we name that structure "the prime innovation pattern."

had grazed near burial grounds of previous victims also contracted the disease. Inspired by his work with silkworms, he wondered whether earthworms might be carrying a bacillus to the surface. He was able to confirm this. A German scientist, Robert Koch, had isolated an anthrax bacillus from the spleens of dead animals, but had not shown it to be the cause. Pasteur demonstrated it was the cause by culturing the bacillus he recovered from burial grounds through 100 generations and showing that the last generation was as deadly as the first.

Pasteur's breakthrough came from his concurrent work studying chicken cholera, a disease that could wipe out entire chicken farms in just a few days. He discovered that an old, weakened culture of cholera did not infect chickens but instead stimulated their immunity to the cholera. He hit on the idea that an attenuated microbe—a vaccine— could stimulate an animal to develop immunity. He developed a vaccine by attenuating the strength of the anthrax microbe through oxidation and aging. He successfully tested his vaccine under laboratory conditions. The news produced both intense excitement and disbelief.

Finally, in 1882, Pasteur was challenged to "put up or shut up" by the well-known veterinarian Rossignol. Rossignol proposed that Pasteur vaccinate twenty-five of a group of fifty sheep, then inject all fifty with lethal does of anthrax and see which ones survive. Pasteur's colleagues urged him to pass up this risky experiment. Pasteur did not share their reticence. He was convinced that the vaccine would work as well in the field as it had in his laboratory tests. He performed the experiment at Pouilly-le-Fort. Every one of the vaccinated sheep survived without symptoms and every one of the unvaccinated sheep died within three days. Pasteur became a national hero. Within ten years, anthrax was virtually eliminated from the French cattle and sheep industry. Germs were no longer a theory; Pasteur's methods produced dramatic results.

The moral of his story is this: Entrepreneurs, if you want to make an innovation that people will care about and value, look for dying cows. Show the people how to keep their cows healthy.

This grand story decisively illustrates the central theme of this book: innovation means the adoption of an idea or technology into new practices that produce new outcomes. People will not adopt unless they see value; the greater the value, the more people will adopt, and the faster they will adopt. People are often most receptive to a new technology when they are in the midst of a major breakdown that is causing severe economic or other distress.

This story also exemplifies a pattern that recurs in innovation stories. The innovator becomes bothered by a disharmony, puzzles over it for a long time, discovers limitations of the current common sense that produce it, proposes a new common sense that generates a solution, and commits to making it happen. We call this the "prime innovation pattern."

Pasteur's own career was a succession of major innovations, each following the prime innovation pattern. He produced them in the French wine, dairy, silk, and chicken industries. In each case he took his laboratory to a primary site of a major problem; he demonstrated that the problem was caused by a microorganism; he devised a way to control the microorganism; and he conducted a dramatic experiment to demonstrate his solution and win powerful allies who became supporters of his science. By the time of his involvement with anthrax, he already had considerable credibility and many allies. He went on to create a vaccine for rabies, the first vaccine for human use. He founded the Pasteur Institute, which ever since has continued his tradition of conducting laboratory science for the benefit of humankind. On his death in 1895, Louis Pasteur was called a "benefactor of humanity."

Bruno Latour, a philosopher of science who has studied Pasteur at length, asked whether it was luck or skill that made Pasteur an historic figure. Why not other scientists as well? How can one man deserve so much credit? Latour concluded that Pasteur had a real skill for sensing how he could advance his science by solving major problems in industry and society. Over time, he accumulated considerable power in support of his science. Latour says that Pasteur was a master at the "theater of experiment."

During the investigation of the U.S. Space Shuttle *Challenger* explosion in 1990, physicist Richard Feynman performed in a televised public hearing his dramatic demonstration of how an O-ring—a gasket in the shape of a flat, flexible ring used to seal a joint against high pressure—becomes brittle in a glass of ice water. He galvanized an entire nation behind the theory that O-ring failure caused the disaster. He showed himself also to be a master in the theater of experiment.

We set out to discover the skills that Pasteur, Feynman, and other master innovators have used to achieve their innovations. We believe we have succeeded in our quest: we found eight essential skills. We will show you what they are and how you can acquire them. You can accomplish significant and surprising things when you become competent at them.

You can become a Pasteur.

I

Foundations of Innovation

1

Invention Is Not Enough

Innovation is not simply invention; it is inventiveness put to use. Invention without innovation is a pastime.
—Harold Evans

Every revolutionary idea seems to evoke three stages of reaction: It's completely impossible. It's possible, but it's not worth doing. I said it was a good idea all along.
—Arthur C. Clark

Innovation is one of the most vexing challenges of our time. According to *Business Week* in August 2005, our overall success rate with innovation initiatives is an abysmal 4 percent. Many people have grown impatient with the staggering waste of energy and resources invested with such a poor return. We cannot hide from this problem because innovation is essential for personal, business, and economic success.

Our collective effort to meet this challenge has been prodigious. In September 2009, Amazon.com reported 9,300 printed books with innovation in their titles. Yet all our effort and ingenuity has not lifted us to a success rate better than 4 percent. What are we missing?

Those books tend to look for answers in just four categories: talent, creativity, process, and leadership. These categories have yielded few useful new answers. The authors have not escaped the box, merely repackaged it with new paper and a fresh ribbon.

In puzzling over the nature of the box, we noticed two exceptions to the 4 percent success pattern. One is "serial innovators," who produce one innovation after another, often with success rates over 50 percent. The other is "collaboration networks," volunteer groups with little management and light leadership; the Internet, World Wide Web, and Linux operating system are examples. In both cases, personal skill seems to play an essential role.

Here, in this book, we explore a new category—personal skills—and we find promising new answers. Our fundamental claim is that by developing their skills in eight practices, individuals and groups can become competent innovators with success rates much higher than 4 percent. We identified the eight practices after extensively studying the actions of many innovators.

The eight practices are essential. They are not discretionary techniques. If you want to succeed, you need to succeed with every one of them. If any one of them fails to produce its intended outcome, the innovation will fail.

The eight practices are conversational. Their characteristic structures and failure modes are easily accessible for learning. Everything we recommend for learning is observable, measurable, and doable. Our framework offers a new way of observing both innovation practice and the consequences of innovator actions on the willingness of people to adopt.

However, success depends on more than knowing what the conversations are, it depends on your skill at executing them. Your embodied skills—your automatic habits—matter more than your ability to follow a checklist. The reality of life does not allow any other way. The pace of events in most conversations involving a network of people is too fast for your mind to think things through; your automatic reactions have to be the right ones. Your embodiment of the practices is essential to allow you to react effectively and smoothly in real time.

We realize that the claim that innovation is a skill is outside the current common sense about innovation. The notion of personal skills for innovation may sound fuzzy and nebulous. In this book, we will remove the fuzziness: With the help of language-action philosophy, we offer a rigorous treatment of the skills and show a reliable path to success with them.

The Hero, the Lucky Stiff, and the Generator

Where does success at innovation come from? When Louis Pasteur invented the anthrax vaccine, Bill Gates the Microsoft Corporation, and Tim Berners-Lee the World Wide Web, did their success come from natural talent, hard work, and determination? Or were they just lucky, happening to be in the right places at the right times? Would someone else have done these things when the times were ripe?

The standard stories about the people behind successful innovation are mainly of two kinds. The *hero* innovator is the naturally gifted individual (or organization) who brings about the innovation through talent, grit, determination, and single-minded devotion to the goal. The *lucky stiff* innovator is the individual (or organization) who happened to be in the right place at the right time, and had the good sense to seize the moment.

Malcolm Gladwell (2008) artfully analyzes the histories of well-known innovators such as Bill Gates and Bill Joy and finds that their stories can be told either way. They are simultaneously heroes and lucky stiffs. He adds that part of their good fortune was to be raised by families that valued finding and reaching out for new possibilities. However, neither form of story offers much guidance on what others can do to achieve similar successes.

This book is about a third kind of innovator, the *generator* (short for generative innovator). A generator is an individual (or organization) who senses and moves into opportunities to take care of people's concerns, and mobilizes people to adopt a new practice for taking care of their concerns. Geoff Colvin (2008) argues convincingly that many "heroes" are actually generators who got that way through sustained and deliberate practice.

This is a story of hope because, as we shall see, innovation generators all engage in the same eight essential practices, no matter what their field. We will illustrate in chapter 2 with the stories of seven innovators, showing exactly how they went about generating their innovations. It is true that they worked hard and that they were presented with unexpected, fortunate opportunities. But their success was not dependent on raw talent or pure luck; it was the product of skills that they learned.

The good news is that you can learn them too.

Rethinking How We Define Innovation

The first step in preparing to become a generator is to have a clear and rigorous definition of the outcome of innovation.

The variety of working definitions of innovation makes this a real challenge. The typical definitions say innovation is inventing something novel, introducing new ideas, making changes, or bucking traditions. So is innovation the invention, the idea, the change, or the struggle? If we pose the question that way, we are in for a lively debate but no real agreement.

Box 1.1
Innovation

Innovation is the adoption of new practice in a community.

If we pose a slightly different question, "When does an innovation succeed?" we can get to a clear, uncontroversial definition. Innovation succeeds when an idea is put into practice. The process of accomplishing this is likely to include inventions, ideas, changes, and struggles—there is no innovation until a community of people adopts a new practice. Adoption is the key to success. That leads to the definition on which this book is based: *Innovation is the adoption of new practice in a community.*

This definition is at the intersection of the notions of inventing, introducing ideas, making changes, and bucking traditions. It is rigorous and sets a strong criterion for innovation. If you want innovation to succeed, you focus on adoption.

Furthermore, this definition makes a sharp distinction between innovation and invention. Invention is the creation of new ideas, artifacts, processes, or methods. Inventions become innovations only when they are adopted into practice. Innovation does not cause adoption; it *is* adoption.

This is not a new insight; Peter Drucker (1985) made it forcefully years ago. The difficulty is that many people do not bring this distinction into their practice. Because they believe that invention is the key source of innovation, they channel considerable effort and resources into creation of new ideas. Many people also believe that innovation is more likely to result when they are organized around the right process, and they channel their resources and energy into process definition and management. While it is true that invention and process are important, they are not enough to bring about adoptions. In the next three sections, we will say why these beliefs are insufficient for innovation.

Invention Is Not Enough

There is a common, deeply held, and revered belief that inventions are the main cause of innovations. We call this belief the *invention myth*.

Those who hold this belief seek innovation by looking for ways to stimulate creativity. This is done by exercises in everything from conceptual blockbusting to design of workplaces that enhance conceptual stimulation. Adherents to the invention myth believe that if they are not cooking up ideas, they cannot innovate. They must constantly stir things up to keep the ideas flowing. They believe that this is the only way to overcome the high failure rate of innovation initiatives.

The invention myth pervades many government policies. Major reports call for more government spending on university research and for tax incentives for companies to do research.

There is an attractive and compelling logic behind this belief. If you look backward in time from when an innovation is in place, you can usually locate the key idea on which it is based and the first person to propose the idea. That person becomes the hero of the story about how the idea changed the world. However, the person who first proposed the idea did not necessarily cause the chain of events leading to the adoption of the idea. Creating new ideas is fundamentally different from getting people to adopt them.

How strong is the evidence supporting the invention myth?

It is not all that strong. Peter Drucker (1985) reported that only about one in 500 patented inventions returns more than its investment; he believed that new knowledge is the least likely source of innovation. In a study for the National Research Council of the connection between basic research and innovation, Stephen Kline and Nathan Rosenberg (1986, 288) concluded, "the notion that innovation is initiated by research is wrong most of the time." In his history of American innovation, Harold Evans (2004) analyzed seventy-five innovations and concluded that the innovators were almost always not the inventors.

Tim Berners-Lee (2000), who drove the development of the World Wide Web, spoke about how he changed his approach from inventor to innovator. He initially proposed a prototype browser with a server operating on a NeXT computer. He was surprised at how little interest others showed in his invention. He quickly abandoned his "sell-the-invention" approach and moved instead to a "get-users-to-adopt" approach. He showed his colleagues, who were his early potential adopters, how the browser readily obtained information of high value to them, especially calendars, research papers, and newsgroups. He discovered, in effect, that the invention myth would not take him to his goal.

Clearly, invention is important, but it is not enough to ensure success at adoption. An excessive emphasis on invention, rather than on adoption, is a major factor in the low success rate of innovation.

The diagram of figure 1.1 compares invention and innovation as practices. The outcome of invention practices is an idea or prototype for consideration. The outcome of innovation practices is adoption of a new practice in a community.

In a discussion of lessons for young innovators, Robert Metcalfe, the inventor of the Ethernet, compared invention to a flower and innovation to a weed (1999). He said that the Ethernet has a beautiful conceptual structure, like a flower, and offered an elegant mathematical analysis of its operation. But the actual work of adoption is quite different, weed-like as Metcalfe described: "In my picture, it's the dead of winter and I am in the dark in a Ramada Inn in Schenectady, New York. A telephone is ringing with my wakeup call at 6am, which is 3am in California, where I flew in from last night. Within the hour I'll be in front of hostile strangers selling them on me, my company, and its strange products, which they have no idea they need. . . . If I persist, selling like this for 10 years, and I do it better and better each time, and I build a team to do everything else better and better each time, then I get my townhouse. Not because of my flowery flash of genius in some academic hothouse."

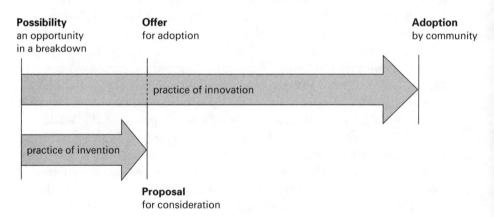

Figure 1.1
Innovation and invention are related but different.

Examples of Innovation

To drive these points home, we will illustrate the differences between invention and innovation. The examples that follow show that these two notions can show up in at least five combinations. The final two examples—innovations without obvious inventors or innovators—have become common in the Internet.

1   Inventions That Did Not Become Innovations

Eight-track stereo systems were invented in the United States in the 1950s. They were endless-loop tape cartridges with four stereo sound tracks that could play continuous music for several hours before they repeated. U.S. manufacturers pushed them hard beginning around 1965, but withdrew by 1975 when Japanese makers undercut them. The U.S. consumer market moved on to cheaper, single-play tape cartridges in the 1980s and the Japanese followed suit. This invention could not be sustained as an innovation. Sony's Betamax video tape system met a similar fate, losing to VHS in the 1970s. Toshiba and NEC's HD-DVD system likewise lost out to the Blu-Ray system in 2008.

The Betamax system for formatting video tapes was introduced by Sony in the late 1970s. Although it was offered on the market before VHS, VHS eventually won out and was universally adopted. There are many stories about why Beta lost to VHS, but the most believable one is simply that VHS was the first to offer a two-hour recording. That was more valuable to consumers than what many engineers thought was a technically superior, more error-resistant format.

The U.S. Patent Office routinely denies applications for patents on perpetual motion machines that supposedly can run forever without new energy after they are started. That the laws of entropy guarantee no such systems exist does not dampen the hopes of some inventors. The apparent discovery of cold fusion in 1990 rekindled a related hope for a process that could generate unlimited amounts of cheap energy. It also went nowhere.

2   Innovations by the Inventor

Robert Metcalfe was the inventor of the Ethernet. For much of the 1970s, the token ring network was the preferred way to connect computers. In this configuration, the computers circulate among themselves a fixed number of packets in a constant looping stream; computers insert data into empty packets on the ring and other computers remove data from full packets addressed to them. This method was the favorite of university research labs during the 1970s and had the marketing muscle of IBM behind it. But the Ethernet protocol, invented in 1973 by Metcalfe at Xerox Palo Alto Research Laboratory, eventually won out and became an international standard. Computers broadcast new packets on a shared coaxial cable nicknamed "the ether"; and they listened on the cable for packets addressed to them. The Ethernet was cheaper to manufacture and it scaled up to large sizes more readily. But the real reason it succeeded is that Metcalfe founded a company, 3Com, and spent the next decade selling Ethernets and working with international standards bodies to have them standardized. In a 1999 interview with Metcalfe about his accomplishment, the young interviewer exclaimed, "Wow, it was the invention of the Ethernet that enabled you to buy your house in Boston's Back Bay!" Metcalfe shot back: "No, I was able to afford that house because I sold Ethernets for ten years!" (Metcalfe 1999).

Edwin Armstrong was the father of modern radio. Many people do not know his name. They think that radio was invented by Marconi, RCA, Westinghouse, or General Electric. Armstrong invented four of the fundamental circuits used in radio; these circuits are used in virtually every sender and receiver today. They were the regenerative receiver (1912), the superheterodyne circuit (1918), the superregenerative receiver (1922), and the complete FM system (1933). He filed many patents on these circuits and spent many years in courts defending his patents against the big companies that wanted to use his inventions without paying the royalties.

Armstrong worked with big companies including RCA, General Electric, and Westinghouse to establish means of production for his radios. His five-tube superheterodyne radio became the standard used in nearly every home during the heyday of radio in the 1920s and well into the 1950s. In the 1930s, his friend David Sarnoff at RCA turned against him and vigorously opposed FM because it would undermine RCA's AM broadcast empire. Armstrong battled in the FCC to get approval for an FM band, against RCA's opposition; RCA wanted the same bands for TV. He finally won FCC approval and built his own FM broadcast station in Alpine, New Jersey. Starting in 1942 he broadcast crystal-clear, static-free music to a market of people who had purchased his FM receivers from General Electric. In the early 1950s, RCA and numerous other companies changed their minds about FM and started building FM equipment in violation of Armstrong's patents. He filed twenty-one lawsuits. But his financial situation became so desperate that in a moment of great despondency on January 31, 1954, he committed suicide by walking off his thirteenth-floor balcony in New York City. His widow pursued the suits in courts for the next fifteen years, ultimately winning them all and receiving millions of dollars in payments. By the 1960s, the FM system was regarded as the superior system; today almost all radio sets include FM; all microwave and space transmissions are FM. Armstrong did not witness the full impact of his innovation during his lifetime. There can be little doubt that he was not only a great inventor, but also a great innovator who spent enormous energy in bringing about the adoption of his systems.

A vivid example from centuries ago is Genghis Khan, who invented the Mongol Empire beginning in 1206 that twenty-five years later extended all the way from China to Eastern Europe (Weatherford 2004). Khan's empire was larger than the Roman Empire, which took more than four hundred years to build. Khan innovated in every battle, constantly learning from past successes and failures. He invented many new weapons and tactics, putting them immediately to the test, and retaining only those that worked well. His enemies could not keep up with him or prevent his swift advances. He also innovated in organizing and administering government.

More recent history gives another example. Abraham Lincoln, an accomplished orator, carefully crafted the 1863 Gettysburg Address to offer a new conception of the United States of America. Prior to this address *states* was the key word: the young country was regarded as a loose republic of independent states. After that time, the word *united* became the key: the United States was seen as a nation, "one arising from many" (Wills 1992). Lincoln's interpretation was adopted into the philosophy and practice of the U.S. government.

3   Innovations by Someone Other than the Inventor

Gary Kildall was the true father of the personal computer operating system (Evans 2004). In his PhD research at the University of Washington in the early 1970s, he worked with one of the best-designed operating systems of all time, the Burroughs B5500, becoming thoroughly familiar with advanced concepts such as multitasking and interactive computing. Shortly thereafter, while an instructor at the Naval Postgraduate School in Monterey, California, he acquired one of the new Intel 4004 process control chips for his lab. He soon realized that the 4004 was a general-purpose computer and not just a special-purpose chip. He designed an operating system that used a floppy disk as its memory and incorporated the advanced concepts he had learned about operating systems. This program was called CP/M, for "control program, microprocessor." Intel contracted with Kildall to develop CP/M and an associated portable programming language PL/M, for the 8008 and later the 8080 chips. He started Digital Research, Inc., in Pacific Grove, California, to market CP/M, which quickly became the operating system of choice in the nascent microcomputer market in the late 1970s.

In the early 1980s, IBM decided to start its own PC effort and visited the young Bill Gates of Microsoft for an operating system. Gates referred them to Kildall. Kildall was not willing to sign IBM's nondisclosure agreements. Miffed, IBM went back to Gates and decided to use Gates's DOS, a quick-and-dirty CP/M knockoff. Kildall was infuriated that Gates would try to copy his software without license, but Gates, flanked by a phalanx of IBM lawyers, forced Kildall to back off. It took Gates another ten years to get the quality of MS-DOS up to the original CP/M system. Many people speculate that if Kildall had been more accommodating toward IBM, he would have closed a deal with IBM and he not Gates would be the industry's magnate. Kildall was clearly an inventor but not a dedicated businessman; his invention made it into a relatively small market, the first PC users. Gates was not an inventor, but he was an astute businessman; he provided an innovative business model that eventually propelled Microsoft to a 90 percent market share of all PC operating systems. Kildall was the inventor of PC operating systems, Gates the innovator.

4   Innovations without an Obvious Inventor

In 1954 Ray Kroc opened the first McDonald's restaurant in San Bernardino, California. He built the chain to one hundred restaurants by 1959, bought all the rights from Mac and Dick McDonald in 1961, and continued to expand the chain to its present size of about thirty thousand restaurants. Kroc's innovation was an assembly-line process to prepare hamburgers, cheeseburgers, and French fries so that customers could have their tasty, fresh hot food within two minutes of placing their orders. He also focused on choice locations for the stores. Kroc innovated with food-preparation process. He thought he got the idea from the original McDonald's store, but others credit him with inventing the process. Many others imitated his business model, making fast food restaurants a way of life.

In 1971 the first Starbucks coffeehouse opened in Seattle. In 1982 Howard Schultz joined as director of retail operations and began to formulate a new vision of a coffeehouse that would offer the finest coffees from around the world, beginning with espresso and latte from Italy. He transformed coffee from its image of concentrated, vile, day-end tar to an upscale experience of the up-and-coming generation. Today there are over six thousand Starbucks Coffee stores worldwide and the number is growing. Morning latte is now a way of life.

In 1981, the National Science Foundation sponsored a project proposed by Peter Denning, David Farber, Tony Hearn, and Larry Landweber to build CSNET, a community network for computer science researchers. Throughout the 1970s, the Defense Department's research network, ARPANET, had been available only to military agencies and contractors; it had about a hundred and twenty nodes in 1980. ARPANET was the origin of the Internet. CSNET did five things: It implemented a version of the Internet protocols TCP/IP over GTE Telenet, the only public packet data network in the United States at the time. It built Phonenet, an extensive dial-in email relay network that imitated ARPANET email. It built a directory server and gateways to move traffic in and out of ARPANET. It built a network coordination center, which was the first Internet service provider (ISP). It built a governance structure so that member universities and research laboratories could pay dues to sustain the network and determine what services to include. By 1985 CSNET was fully self-sustaining and was a complete prototype of the modern Internet environment. Its 165 member organizations around the world brought upward of 50,000 students and researchers into the Internet. In the late 1980s, CSNET alumni helped build NSFNET, which became the backbone of the modern Internet and superceded CSNET in 1995. CSNET did not invent new technology. It created a social structure for an Internet community that propagated into many subsequent Internet communities. The Internet Society (2009) conferred its Jon Postel Award on CSNET for serving as a critical bridge from the original ARPANET to the Internet.

In this category, innovators typically claim that they got their ideas from someone else or that the ideas were simply "in the air." CSNET illustrates both. The innovators put into place a process that got a significant market to adopt prior inventions into standard practice. The innovators also "appropriated" ideas that were common in the research domain into operations in their community.

5   Innovations without Obvious Innovators

Wikipedia was started in 2001 by Jimmy Wales and Larry Sanger as a project to build a free-content, open-edited, online encyclopedia. Its articles are written and edited by (anonymous) volunteers. Every article has numerous authors and editors. The articles represent a distillation of knowledge from many people in the community. Sanger defined the ground rules for contributing and editing and provided the Web site. Wikipedia represents a final step in the demise of the traditional, scholarly encyclopedia. For many years, *Encyclopedia Britannica* had the unchallenged brand name and highest reputation for quality and scholarliness. When Microsoft started bundling *Encarta,* a much cheaper (and lower-quality) encyclopedia on a CD with its Windows operating system, families stopped purchasing *Britannica* and the company had to change its business. Wikipedia has major gaps, especially in technology areas where the younger contributors have no knowledge of early contributions. Wikipedia has been controversial because its policy of allowing anyone to anonymously edit anything has allowed flagrant abuses and undermines the trustworthiness of many entries. Still, most people find the quality good enough and the price unbeatable.

In the late 1990s, a new genre of Web site appeared, known as the weblog, or simply blog, which was basically an ongoing diary and commentary by its editor. A few editors (known now as bloggers) stood out because their exceptional skill at writing entertaining and informative posts drew many readers. These bloggers began to affect public opinion outside the normal news and journalistic media outlets. They came into the public eye when politicians discovered that blogs could and did influence voters. Anonymous programmers developed software kits to help those less experienced set up their own blogs and to help readers keep track of new postings on their favorite blogs. Blogging was a new practice that arose spontaneously across the Internet, providing a new channel of expression. Leaders emerged, but they were more like surfers riding waves than ships generating them.

Like the previous category, this one might seem odd because some form of leadership was needed to bring people into the new practice. However, the leadership role transferred from one person to another as anonymous people stepped forward and added something to the mix. The leadership was there, but no one person could be identified as the overall leader. The Internet has been a rich spawning ground for such innovations because it allows people who care deeply about an issue to find one another, form a special-interest community, and work together to produce a change around their issue. Sometimes the special-interest community was guided by the watchful eye of a low-key, light-touch leader (as Linus Torvalds in Linux), and sometimes the leadership passed from one unnamed person to another (as in blogging) (Tuomi 2003).

There is often no clear connection between inventions and innovations. There is often no clear pattern of an "idea that changed the world"—in fact, the "idea" was often invented as an afterthought to explain the new practice. What is clear is that, in every case, an identifiable community adopted a new practice. Examples like these gave us our focus on looking for what leads to adoption.

Process Is Not Enough

There is also a common, deeply held, and revered belief that innovations are the results of processes that can be managed. We call this belief the *process myth*.

Those who hold this belief seek innovation by looking for the right process, organizing their workplaces to facilitate that process, and closely managing it. They believe that if they are not following process, they will be derailed and their chances for successful innovation, already small to start with, will evaporate.

This process myth pervades many business innovation books. They lay out processes, the types of resources required, the risks to be analyzed, and ways of evaluating investment returns for innovation proposals. Many processes, for example, assume that ideas have sources; the corresponding management guidelines systematize the search for sources.

There is an attractive and compelling logic behind this belief. If you look backward in time from when an innovation is in place, you usually can identify a series of steps from the initial idea to the present state. The steps make sense and follow a logical order. However, what you select as the steps depends strongly on your beliefs about how innovation is produced. And the order may be an illusion: some steps do not necessarily produce the conditions needed for the next step.

How strong is the evidence supporting the process myth? Not very. In chapter 3, we will examine the main process models of innovation and find significant shortcomings in each. It is very difficult to conclude that any one model captures everything about innovation process. Moreover, the models are not easy to reconcile. Which process appeals to you depends on your biases—for example, if you believe innovation is about moving ideas into the marketplace, you will find the pipeline model attractive; and if you believe that innovation is about people making decisions to adopt, you will find the diffusion model attractive.

The combination of the invention and process myths has been toxic to success in many organizations. The only option open to them for coping with the low success rates is "taking many shots on goal." These myths are not reliable roads to innovation.

Sharpening the Definition

Having a clear definition of the outcome—meaning the adoption of a new practice in a community—is essential to our goal of formulating the practices behind skillful, successful innovation. In the next four sections, we will sharpen our definition by digging deeper into these aspects:

1. Community: the people who change their practices. How large is the community? What do its members value? What do they sacrifice to get the innovation?
2. Practices: the ways of doing things. We will distinguish the practices being changed inside the community from the innovator's practices that bring about the change.
3. Adoption: the commitment to new practices and their incorporation into the prior practices of the community.
4. Success: the goal of adoption is achieved. Three environmental factors support success: content expertise, social interaction, and movement into new opportunities. How do we cope with failure? Learn and come back for later success? Abandon when the practice is obsolete or low in value?

Community

The community is the set of people who adopt the new practice. We will examine three aspects of adoption that are defined relative to the community: fit, size, and degree of change.

The first aspect, fit, concerns the alignment of the new practice with the already existing practices of the community. Everyone in the community shares a complex set of interacting practices as they carry out their lives and work. Innovation is about introducing a new practice into the mix. Often community members have to give up another practice to fit the new one in; the value of the new practice must exceed the cost of the sacrifice they must make to have it.

When Robert Metcalfe sold Ethernets, he had to show his clients how his Ethernet would enable their companies to communicate and share information better than any of their other current methods; he had to demonstrate how his Ethernet would open doors to new possibilities valuable to the company. He had to overcome their natural reluctance to change by showing them that the sacrifice was worth it.

In the early 1980s, Fernando Flores created The Coordinator, an email client program that tracked progress in "conversations for action"—the conversations in which one person fulfills a request from another (Winograd and Flores 1986). Some organizations embraced the new email system enthusiastically and reported several-fold improvements in their productivity. Other organizations rejected it because they perceived commitment tracking as a form of surveillance. The Coordinator fit well with existing practices in the former type of organization, but the latter organizations perceived too great a sacrifice of their values.

The second aspect, size, concerns the number of people in the target community. Although the most popular innovation stories make it seem as if most innovations are very large, the truth is that the vast majority of innovations happen in small groups. There is considerable evidence that the size of innovations follows a "power law"—adopting communities of a given size are four times as numerous as communities of twice that size.[1] The big innovations catch our attention but the small ones are far more common.

In chapter 2 we will tell the stories of innovators who produced innovations that were small (family of seven), medium (small-business community), and large (the world) in size.

The third aspect, degree, concerns the amount of change required to fit the new practice into a community. A "sustaining innovation" is a small-degree change, usually involving an improvement in an existing practice to make it more productive (Christensen 1997). When Wilkinson Sword introduced the stainless-steel razor blade, they did not change shaving but rather made the experience less painful and less costly because the blades lasted longer.

In contrast, a "disruptive innovation" is a large-degree change, usually involving a change to the overall system that affects many practices besides the innovation, and often provokes resistance from those who do not want to change. Apple iTunes has been a disruptive innovation in music publishing because artists do not need a publishing house to offer their music in iTunes. Similarly, Amazon.com has been a disruptive influence in book publishing because anyone can self-publish.

Whether an innovation is considered sustaining or disruptive also depends on the time frame. Over a short period of time, Moore's Law

---

1. Private conversations with John Seely Brown. Barabasi 2003 shows that organization sizes follow a power law, and there is a correlation between the size of an organization and the size of the community it supports.

for computers (double the number of transistors for the same price every 1.5 years) can seem like a relatively modest change. But over a longer period, say fifteen years, this increases computing speed by a thousand, which completely changes the way some things are done.

Practices, Performances, and Skills

We use the terms *practice*, *performance*, and *skill* frequently in this book. People interpret these common terms in different ways. Let us take a moment to define what they mean in this book.

Practices

The word *practice* appears prominently in our definition and in several related terms used throughout this book, including "the practice of innovation," the "eight generative practices of innovators," and "communities of practice." The term *practice* has four senses:

1. A customary way or pattern of behavior
2. Exercise of a profession or discipline
3. Development of a skill by repetition
4. Name of a space of human interactions

The first three senses are standard dictionary definitions and the fourth is more generic (Spinosa, Flores, and Dreyfus 1997).

When we speak of the members of a social community changing one of their practices, we invoke the first sense. When we speak of the practice of innovation, we invoke the second sense. When we speak of the eight generative practices of innovators, we invoke the second and third senses, meaning that all innovators exercise them and develop their performance through practice. When we speak of communities of practice, we invoke the fourth sense. This sense can go quite deep and can evade our ability to describe everything involved in the practice. Consider the practice of telephony, which is concerned with people talking via telephone in order to communicate and coordinate with one another. How many people are involved in a phone call? At first glance you might think that only the two speakers are involved. But think again. All phone calls are routed through switching exchanges. Who maintains and repairs exchanges? Who maintains and repairs intercity and intercontinental cables and microwave links? Who manages the people who do these things? Who builds new exchanges and links? Who designs them? Who draws up the electrical diagrams and blueprints? Who programs the computers? Who does the research leading to the technology in the exchanges and links? Who provides operator and directory assistance? Who maintains account records? Who sends out the bills? Who processes the payments? Who sold the subscriptions to the parties who are talking? Who designed, built, and sold the telephone instruments they are using?

If that is not enough, who designed and manufactured the silicon chips used in the switching computers? Who manufactured the fiber optic cables? Who manufactured the copper wires? Who set the standards for chips, cables, and wires? Who designed the protocols for using these technologies and links? Who brought about the international standards for the protocols? Who designed telephone instruments, jacks, plugs, connectors, and closet racks? Who designed the power supplies and backup units? Who provides normal electrical power? Who pays the bills for power and equipment? Who provided the predecessors of the current telephone technology? What concerns motivated their creation? How far back in time do we need to look to find all the people whose contributions still matter today?

When you reflect in this way, you realize hundreds of people are involved in a single phone call: the two who are talking and the hundreds of others who operate and maintain the telephone system. If you consider the historical sweep of time, you see that tens of thousands, even hundreds of thousands of people were involved in the technology chains leading up to the current technology.

Suppose someone proposes downloadable ringtones for cell phones. What might it take for this to become a new practice? It will take people to design the data formats for the tones, place them on a server, modify the cell phone software to accommodate ringtone recordings, create and test new tones, build a marketing strategy for selling tones, integrate the billing of tone sales with other financial transactions, and provide enough additional bandwidth in the telephone equipment to accommodate people downloading ringtones. All these people must change what they do so that the ringtones become a new reality.

Once the downloadable ringtone practice is adopted, other parts of the space change. Many people will come to see tones as parts of their identities and as fashion statements. Many will combine the tones with caller ID, so that each incoming call rings a distinct tone identifying the caller. Many will want do-it-yourself kits that enable them to record and install their own ringtones at home. Many will want backup services so that when they buy a new phone all their caller IDs and ringtones can be transferred easily.

This is the nature of a community of practice. It goes deeper and deeper as you ask more questions about who is involved, what they do, and when they did it. There is no end. Everything is connected and interdependent. You cannot name most of the people who are or were involved, but you know they were there.

Now we see the true magnitude of the innovator's challenge. Achieving a change of practice in a community means that many people have to go along with it, changing their individual practices together and integrating the new practice into ones that already existed. It means that the change has to produce enough value to motivate each person. It means that those who see insufficient value will resist. It means that the change must be consistent with historical concerns in the community.

In this book, our use of the word *practice* draws on all four senses we have described. These statements capture what we mean when we discuss practices in this book. They (are):

- Recurrent actions that have outcomes
- Performed by individuals or groups
- Performed at different skill levels
- Cope with breakdowns[2]
- Embodied (they are not rule sets)
- Include mental processes, emotional states, and body reactions
- Embedded deeply in the context and history of communities

This is why innovation is complex and there is no easy answer to the question, "what does the innovator do?"

Notice that the "eight practices of innovators" refer to what the innovator does and "change of practices in a community" to what the innovator accomplishes.

Performances

Innovation is a performing art. Its quality, impact, and extent depend on the performance skills of the innovator. We distinguish three levels

2. The word *breakdown* is used by linguistics scholars for any event that interrupts the flow of action toward the desired outcome. It does not refer to a psychological or nervous condition, or to equipment breakage. For example, a flat tire is a breakdown for someone trying to drive to an important meeting on time.

of performance at innovating: novice, skillful, and masterful.[3] Novice innovators act in accordance with their understanding of the rules and steps of innovation processes. Skillful innovators act from their embodied skills in the key areas covered by the eight practices. Masterful innovators act from an embodiment so deep that their actions seem intuitive and unique as they mobilize entire communities to think, believe, and value differently. In addition, we tend to expect masterful innovators to be able to deal with large, complex, heterogeneous communities, and novice innovators relatively small, homogeneous communities.

A person can advance through these performance levels with practice and immersion in the communities to be changed. The novice can use this book as a guide to the rules of action in each of the eight practices. After a while, the novice becomes skillful, embodying the eight practices enough to do them well without much conscious thought. From our experience with our students, we believe that serious learners with help from good mentors or coaches can become skillful innovators within a year. After a much longer timeframe, perhaps a decade, the skillful innovator becomes masterful, with substantial experience, deep embodiment, and a unique style and intuitive ability to effect change. The third part of this book explores the journey of mastery.

Skills

In addition to practices and performances, we refer frequently to skills in this book. It appears in phrases such as "skill at the eight practices" and "skill levels of innovators."

A skill is an individual ability or capability to perform a practice acquired or trained by repetition. A skill is not the same as a practice—the practice is the context for the skill. There are numerous "communities of practice," but no "communities of skill."

The term *skill* often carries the connotation of capabilities that are relatively easily transferred from one domain to another. Transferability assumes that the new domain already hosts a practice in which the skill makes sense. Thus, one can learn the skill of debate in college and then put it to use later in the courtroom (as a lawyer), the boardroom (as an executive), or the Congress (as a legislator). One can modify a skill

3. Hubert Dreyfus (1992) uses a performance scale with more gradations. His beginner and advanced beginner correspond with our novice, his competent and proficient with our skillful, and his expert and master with our masterful.

learned in one domain for another domain; a mechanic who specializes in Volvos can transfer to a shop that repairs Toyotas.

We will shortly introduce the eight practices of innovators. Since all domains host innovation, it is possible for an innovator to learn the skills of doing the eight practices in one domain and transfer them effectively to other domains.

While innovation is commonly accepted as a process, there is a long history of skepticism toward innovation as a skill. An important reason for the skepticism is that masterful innovators rely on much tacit knowledge for which no "training" regimen is known. Our contribution in this book is to reveal eight essential practices that are not heavily dependent on tacit knowledge. Learning them will greatly improve one's success rate at innovation without requiring full mastery.

Adoption

When a community adopts a new practice they make three key commitments: considering it, adopting it for the first time, and sustaining it over a period of time. The first commitment is to discuss the new possibility; many proposed innovations have died because their purveyors could not engage others in conversation about them. The second commitment is to an initial adoption—to try out the new practice, idea, product, or approach and see how it works. And the third commitment is to a continuing adoption—to take on the new practice, learn it, and integrate it into existing practices.

While working to elicit each of these commitments, the innovator will be challenged to demonstrate the value of the innovation. Each challenge entails costs, time, and energy. Each presents breakdowns and obstacles that an effective innovator must be able to deal with to prevent failure. Adoption is not the natural outcome of clever ideas or effective marketing; it is the result of innovators successfully demonstrating value and drawing people deeper into commitments to the new practice.

Success

An innovator is most likely to be successful when three factors converge (see figure 1.2). The first factor, *domain expertise*, is your skill in the community of practice you aim to change. The greater your expertise, the more you know about deep concerns and subtleties, making you more likely to offer high-value proposals that fit your community.

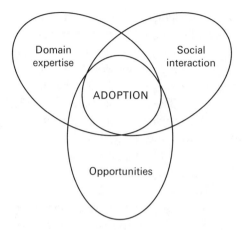

Figure 1.2
Success at innovation lies in the intersection among the innovator's domain expertise, social interaction skills, and ability to recognize and move into opportunities (realizable possibilities).

Gladwell (2008) reports studies showing that the greatest chances of success occur for people who have achieved mastery by putting in at least ten thousand hours of practice. He is not saying that anyone who accumulates ten thousand hours of practice will be a master, but rather that mastery takes a long time: ten thousand hours equals ten years at three hours of practice per day, or three years at nine hours of practice per day. We focus in this book on the path to mastery, but not on how to gain experience in your particular field.[4]

The second factor, *social interaction practices*, is your skill at influencing others. John Seely Brown says that the point of the innovation practices is to mobilize action around one's idea. Mobilizing other people around your ideas requires certain social interaction skills. Gladwell (2008) illustrates with examples of people of high expertise but low social interaction skills, who were ultimately unsuccessful. The eight innovation practices at the core of this book are all essential social interaction practices whose outcomes are all necessary for innovation.

4. The learning process can be accelerated greatly by a good ontology (conceptual framework revealing action and coordination). A simple example is the conversation for action loop discussed by Winograd and Flores (1986). Many people do not realize that these loops need to be closed and are baffled by the resulting breakdowns. Once they learn about the loop, they quickly start to pay attention to closing all their loops.

The third factor, *opportunities*, acknowledges that you cannot control your environment but you can control how you engage with it. Successful innovators have a high sensitivity to people's concerns and breakdowns, an ability that might be called "reading the world." Once they sense opportunities, they are good at moving toward them by making offers to the members of the community. The story of Pasteur (see this book's prologue), who discovered germs and developed the first vaccines, illustrates a man with extreme sensitivity and an ability to tell when something is about to become important. He engaged with flair and drama to catch people's attention when they were the most ripe for change—in the middle of a big breakdown.

The eight practices of this book—discussed next—foster your ability to sense opportunities in the world and effectively mobilize change. There is no reason to be stuck at the 4 percent success rate. You can go much higher.

Overview of the Eight Practices

In *Disclosing New Worlds* (1997), Charles Spinosa, Fernando Flores, and Hubert Dreyfus analyzed innovations in business, social, and political domains. They identified a common pattern in which the entrepreneur, social activist, and virtuous citizen engage. They called the pattern "history making" because in each case the person intervened in the practices of a community and changed its course of history. We call this the *prime innovation pattern* and summarize it in box 1.2.

When we studied innovation stories and interviewed serial innovators and volunteers in collaboration networks, we were struck by the universality of this pattern. It gave us a way to look beyond these individuals' personalities, virtues, and vices, and to examine the types of commitments they made and fulfilled. We discovered that each commitment was directed at one of the outcomes listed in box 1.3. We named the eight practices after these outcomes.

We also discovered that each practice has a *somatic* aspect as well as its conversational aspect. Somatics is a discipline that deals with the integration of mind and body: the somatic aspect of the eight practices accounts for body reactions and emotions that accompany language. The somatic aspect takes a role front and center in the eighth practice (embodying).

The structure of the eight practices is summarized in table 1.1. The first two are the main work of invention and the next three the main work of adoption. These five tend to be done sequentially. Each of the

Box 1.2
The Prime Innovation Pattern

1. Innovators find in their lives and work something disharmonious that common sense overlooks or denies.
2. They hold on to the disharmony, allowing it to bother them; they engage with it as a puzzle.
3. Eventually they discover how the common-sense way of acting leads to the disharmonious conflict or failure.
4. They design or discover a new practice to resolve the disharmony. The new practice comes from one of three sources:
a. It is already a background practice of the community, but has been dispersed and nearly forgotten. Recovering it is called *articulation*.
b. It is a marginal practice on the fringe of the community's awareness, usually resulting from an invention. Bringing it to the center is called *reconfiguration*.
c. It is a standard practice of another community, which can be mapped and adapted into the current community. Importing it is called *cross-appropriation*.
5. They make a deep commitment to getting the new practice adopted in their community.

Box 1.3
The Outcomes of the Innovation Practices

1. Sensing: Bringing forth the new possibility that would bring value to the community.
2. Envisioning: Building a compelling story of how the world would be better if the possibility were made real.
3. Offering: Presenting a proposed practice to the (leaders of the) community, who commit to considering it.
4. Adopting: Community members commit to trying out the new practice for the first time.
5. Sustaining: Community members commit to staying with the practice for its useful life.
6. Executing: Carrying out action plans that produce and sustain adoption.
7. Leading: Proactively working to produce the outcomes of the previous six practices, and overcoming the struggles encountered along the way.
8. Embodying: Achieving a level of skill at each practice that makes it automatic, habitual, and effective even in chaotic situations.

Table 1.1
Structure of the Innovation Practices

The main work of invention	1	Sensing
	2	Envisioning
The main work of adoption	3	Offering
	4	Adopting
	5	Sustaining
The environment for the other practices	6	Executing
	7	Leading
	8	Embodying

final three practices creates an environment for effective conduct of all the other practices. Although executing, leading, and embodying are fundamental to many domains of practice, they are special for innovation: we have to execute innovation commitments, proactively promote the innovation, and be sensitive to how other people listen and react.

In reality, the eight practices we set forth are not sequential at all. The innovator moves constantly among them, refining the results of earlier ones after seeing their consequences later. It is better to think of them as being done in parallel rather than in numerical order.

These eight practices are special in that their structures are completely observable in both their conversational and somatic aspects. This fact enabled us to specify how to teach, train, and coach individuals in the practices. The overall effectiveness of these practices depends on the innovator integrating them into a single, coherent style. The practices affirmatively answer the question, "Is innovation a learnable practice?" They define what it means to be a skillful innovator.

The specification of each practice has two parts. The *anatomy* describes the structure of the practice when it goes well and produces its outcome. The *characteristic breakdowns* are the most common obstacles that arise in the effort to complete the practice. Within the practice, the innovator steers toward the desired outcome and copes with breakdowns that may arise. We specify each practice this way in its own chapter in part II of this book. A summary of the specifications is included as appendix 1 of this book. In appendix 2 we have included a self-assessment tool to help you evaluate your level of skill at each of the practices, and your overall level of coherence among all eight.

After much study of successful and unsuccessful innovations, we demonstrated these features of the eight practices:

1. They are fundamentally conversations. Each practice is manifested as a conversation that the innovator engages with and moves toward completion.
2. They are universal. Every innovator, and every innovative organization, engages in all of the practices in some way.
3. They are essential. If any practice fails to produce its outcome, the entire process of innovation will fail.
4. They are embodied. They manifest in bodily habits that require no thought or reflection to perform. Thought is directed to strategic issues, not to the performance of the practices.

We will discuss and ground all of these claims in the remainder of the book.

Embodiment

To his observers, World Wide Web innovator Tim Berners-Lee has an uncanny ability to zero in on the right conversations, connecting with his audience and addressing concerns. He maintains a strong focus even when surrounded by chaos. He is able to forge consensus in the midst of seemingly intractable disagreement. His ability is actually a high level of embodiment of the eight practices. We know this because we have analyzed the conversations he engaged in during the formation of the Web (Berners-Lee 2000). He demonstrates the power of embodied, habitual skill in conversations and interactions with others.

A practice is embodied when its performance is transparent, automatic, and habitual. You can put an embodied skill into action immediately without thinking about it. In working with our students, we discovered that teaching the basic practices purely as conversational patterns was not enough to achieve the embodiment for coping with breakdowns. Even though they had strong command of the linguistic patterns, many students still had difficulties inspiring trust, connecting with their audiences, listening for deep concerns, and responding well in chaotic situations. They tended to react defensively to breakdowns. When defensive, they wound up focusing mainly on themselves, not on listening to others.

This is why we identified the eighth practice: embodying. It is concerned with the question, "How did the innovator integrate language, emotion, and body to enable the other seven practices to become automatic, habitual, and effective?" This more-advanced practice is founded in the discipline of somatics, which is the key to reaching the higher levels of performance in the other practices.

The eighth practice develops the capacity to listen well, connect, accept, show compassion, and produce receptive listening in the community. It helps read another's presence and energy, modify one's own presence, sense how others experience their surroundings, blend with others in moving them toward adoption, and retrain one's own habitual (conditioned) tendencies.

The process of learning and embodying a new practice may not be as easy as our descriptions in the following chapters might make it seem. Our brains feel safe and comfortable with embodied practices. Our brains may respond to our attempts to change our practice by making us feel uncomfortable, often the point of backing off from the change. The only way around this natural resistance is to stick with the practice until gradually the discomfort disappears.

We will give descriptions of the innovator's practices. Descriptions are *about* a practice, but they are not the same as *doing* the practice. It will be important to do the practices, moving toward the embodiment that will get the value they offer.

Conclusions

Our main objective in this book is to help you develop an understanding of innovation that guides effective action, and then show you how to attain the skillful levels through practice. Even if you use the book only to discover the eight practices we identify, that alone is an important step toward becoming skillful at innovation. You will become aware of new aspects of familiar situations and pay attention to them differently. We also reveal some of the more advanced practices of masters even though we cannot formulate definitive ways of learning them.

The path to innovation is both challenging and rewarding. The innovation process is full of complexities; we cannot remove these complexities, but we can provide you with a map to success, guidance on where to focus your attention, and practices for developing your skill at innovation. You do not need to fully master the eight practices to see results. As you become more proficient at each practice, you will find yourself getting better and better at innovating.

This book will help you shift your interpretation of innovation from a high-risk, mysterious process to a skill set of eight universal practices that can be learned and put to work. From our experience with students, we believe these eight practices will enable you to increase your success rate at innovation, often significantly. And they are the launch point of a journey to innovation mastery.

Bibliography

Barabasi, Albert-Laszlo. 2003. *Linked*. Plume.

Berners-Lee, Tim. 2000. *Weaving the Web*. Harper Business.

Bush, Vannevar. 1945. *Science: The Endless Frontier*. Available as a historical document from the National Science Foundation, http://www.nsf.gov/about/history/vbush1945.htm.

Christensen, Clayton. 1997. *The Innovator's Dilemma*. Harvard Business.

Colvin, Geoff. 2008. *Talent Is Overrated: What Really Separates World-Class Performers from Everybody Else*. Penguin Group.

Denning, Peter J. 2004. The Social Life of Innovation. *ACM Communications* 47 (4):15–19.

Denning, Peter J., and Robert Dunham. 2006. Innovation as Language Action. *ACM Communications* 49 (5):47–52.

Dreyfus, Hubert. 1992. 1972. *What Computers Still Can't Do*. Repr. with new introduction. MIT Press.

Drucker, Peter. 1993. 1985. *Innovation and Entrepreneurship*. Repr., Harper Business.

Dunham, Robert. 1997. Self-Generated Competitive Innovation with the Language-Action Approach. *Center for the Quality of Management Journal* 6 (Fall):2.

Evans, Harold. 2004. *They Made America: Two Centuries of Innovators from the Steam Engine to the Search Engine*. Little Brown.

Gladwell, Malcolm. 2008. *Outliers: The Story of Success*. Little Brown.

Internet Society. Newsletter (July 2009), http://isoc.org/wp/newsletter/?m=200907.

Kanter, Rosabeth Moss. 2006. Innovation: The Classic Traps. *Harvard Business Review* 84 (11):72–83.

Kline, Stephen J., and Nathan Rosenberg. 1986. An Overview of Innovation. In *The Positive Sum Strategy: Harnessing Technology for Economic Growth*, 275–305. National Academy Press.

Metcalfe, Robert. 1999. Invention Is a Flower; Innovation Is a Weed. *Technology Review* (November), http://www.technologyreview.com/web/11994/?a=f.

Searle, John. 1969. *Speech Acts: An Essay in the Philosophy of Language*. Cambridge University Press.

Searle, John. 1985. *Expression and Meaning: Studies in the Theory of Speech Acts*. Cambridge University Press.

Spinosa, Charles, Fernando Flores, and Hubert Dreyfus. 1997. *Disclosing New Worlds*. MIT Press.

Tuomi, Ilkka. 2003. *Networks of Innovation*. Oxford Press.

Weatherford, Jack. 2004. *Genghis Khan and the Making of the Modern World*. Three Rivers Press.

Wills, Garry. 1992. *Lincoln at Gettysburg: The Words That Remade America*. Touchstone of Simon & Schuster.

Winograd, Terry, and Fernando Flores. 1986. *Understanding Computers and Cognition*. Addison-Wesley.

Yager, Tom. 2004. Innovate, or Take a Walk. *InfoWorld* (April 19):69.

2

Generative Innovators in Action

Ideation is NOT the real problem in innovation; it is how to mobilize action around an idea.
—John Seely Brown

We introduce seven innovators who are mentioned frequently throughout this book. They are exemplars of the eight practices in action. For quick reference, we display the eight practices on the wheel shown in figure 2.1. This picture suggests that the practices are all integrated into a nonsequential, coherent whole and style in the person of the innovator. In our presentations that follow we will focus on how our innovators performed the first seven practices, leaving the discussion of the eighth practice for chapter 12.

Here is a summary of the seven innovators and what they did. Tim Berners-Lee invented the World Wide Web in 1989 and brought about its universal adoption in the 1990s. Candace Lightner and Cindi Lamb cofounded Mothers Against Drunk Driving (MADD) in 1980 to realize their vision of a nation of low tolerance for drunk driving and high respect for individual responsibility while drinking. Coleman Mockler initiated a series of major innovations with razors, a remarkable accomplishment with a settled technology, and staved off a corporate takeover. James Denning reorganized the way his family operated, replacing a disorganized group with a united family. William Sims transformed the U.S. Navy after 1908 by introducing continuous aim gunnery. Bill Maclay, a small business architect, produced new global standards for sustainable buildings.

Berners-Lee gave us a technology innovation, Lightner and Lamb a social innovation, Mockler a product innovation, Denning a family innovation, Sims a military innovation, and Maclay an architectural innovation. While it might seem that these innovators are worlds apart,

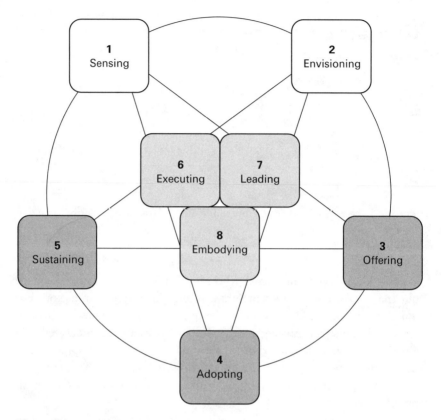

Figure 2.1
Summary of the eight practices.

remarkably, they all engaged in the same foundational practices. The eight practices are universal, appearing in every successful innovation across diverse domains.

We will present each innovation and summarize how its innovator(s) engaged in each of the first seven practices. These examples will establish the fundamental structure of personal skills for innovation. In subsequent chapters we will examine each practice in detail, showing how to develop the personal skills and how to address the common breakdowns associated with them. We will often refer back to these innovators for examples.

Tim Berners-Lee, Web Innovator

Tim Berners-Lee is widely known for creating the World Wide Web (WWW), considered one of the great innovations of the twentieth century. How did he do it? Did he exercise certain key skills? Or was he just lucky—the right guy in the right place at the right moment? We are particularly fortunate that Berners-Lee has written, in *Weaving the Web* (2000), his own account of what he said and did as the Web unfolded.

Berners-Lee grew up in a computer-savvy family. His parents were both part of the design team of the Atlas computer system project at the University of Manchester in England in the 1950s. He earned a graduate degree in physics in 1976 from Queen's College, Oxford. He worked as software engineer at Plessey Systems, a telecommunications company, and then at D G Nash, were he wrote text-processing software for intelligent printers and a multitasking operating system. He was fascinated by the question, first raised by his father, of whether computers could be used to link information rather than simply compute numbers. This question was on his mind in 1980 when he went to CERN, the European high-energy physics research laboratory.

Berners-Lee was increasingly bothered in the 1980s by the way the Internet was developing. It seemed to be good for email and limited file exchange, but not for information sharing. In fact, information sharing was tedious and cumbersome. To him, the Internet was diverging far from the visions for global information sharing first articulated by its pioneers in the 1960s. He felt a burning desire to do something about it. Given his dream about information sharing through linking, the esoteric world of hypertext was an obvious place to look for a key to an information-sharing Internet.

In his spare time, Berners-Lee worked on a program called Enquire that could link information on any computer with any other computer. He began to envision CERN not as a network of separate computers, but as a single information space consolidated across many computers. In 1989 he wrote "Information Management: A Proposal" to create a hypertext system at CERN linking all its computers and documents into a single web from which information could be quickly retrieved from anywhere in CERN. Scientists at CERN were already looking for a technology to facilitate document sharing with internal and external collaborators. At first Berners-Lee's proposal was ignored; but with help from Robert Cailliau, he got the attention of CERN's leadership. In 1990 they gave him the go-ahead to make a prototype, which he built on a NeXT computer.

The prototype included HTML, a new markup language for documents containing hyperlinks; HTTP, a new protocol for downloading object designated by hyperlinks; URL, an Internet-compatible scheme for global names; and a graphical user interface. He drew on well-known ideas and practices including Gopher (University of Minnesota's file-fetching system), FRESS and ZOG (hypertext document management systems), SGML (the digital publishing markup language), TCP/IP and FTP (standard Internet protocols), operating systems (the global identifier concept of capability systems, which had been on the Plessey System computers), and Usenet news and discussion groups.

He envisioned this prototype as the backbone of a universal hypertext linking protocol for all Internet computers. He put up the first Web page at CERN in November 1990. He released and tested browser prototypes at CERN in 1991. He gave his first external demonstration at the Hypertext 1991 conference, a natural audience for this idea. It was an immediate success and inspired others to build Web sites. The first non-CERN Web site went up at SLAC (Stanford Linear Accelerator Center) in December 1991. Web sites began to proliferate; there were 200 in 1993. With the universal free browser, Mosaic, released by Marc Andreesen at the University of Illinois in 1993, the WWW took off exponentially. During the 1990s, many new businesses and business practices formed in the Internet, including e-commerce (selling by online stores via Web interface), publishing, digital libraries, eBay, Google, Amazon, and Yahoo. The Internet even had its own business boom (and bust in 2002).

Berners-Lee had no master plan, business plan, or any other formal document outlining a strategy for the Web. Instead, he insisted that all programmers working on Web software adhere to a small set of simple core principles: no single controlling authority, universal identifiers, a markup language (HTML), and a protocol (HTTP). He steadfastly maintained that these principles were the essence of the WWW; all else would be a distraction. He analyzed all new proposals to make sure they were true to these principles.

Building support for the Web while advancing related technology became Berners-Lee's central passion. Robert Cailliau helped him build support within the CERN political system. In 1994, he worried that commercial companies might get into a competition over who owned the Web, in violation of his core principle of openness to everyone.

Michael Dertouzos at MIT helped him establish the World Wide Web Consortium (W3C), modeled after the successful MIT X Windows consortium. This consortium eventually attracted over four hundred companies, which collaborated on development of Web standards and tools; it became an engine of innovation for the Web. The W3C was an opensoftware, consensus-based organization that issued nonbinding recommendations. The recommendations become de facto standards because consortium members adopted them.

Berners-Lee refused to set up a private company so that he could benefit financially from his technology. It belongs to the world, he said.

Here is a summary of how Berners-Lee engaged in the first seven practices.

• *Sensing*   In the 1980s, he saw a disharmony between the actual direction of the Internet (email and file transfer) and its promise (semantic web of all human knowledge). This bothered him. It moved him to do something about it.

• *Envisioning*   He envisioned a system of hypertext-linked documents; any one could link to any other. Mouse-clicking a link would cause the system to retrieve the target document. The system architecture would consist of HTTP, HTML, URLs, and a browser. Common tasks such as scheduling meetings, looking up citations, and getting mail and news would be easy in this system.

• *Offering*   In 1989 he offered to build such a system at CERN. At first his offer was spurned, but with advice from colleagues he reformulated his offer around CERN document retrieval needs and got permission to build a prototype on a NeXT machine. He demonstrated the prototype at the 1991 Hypertext research conference, got strong positive responses, and solicited implementations of Web servers.

• *Adopting*   He visited many places and attended many conferences to tell people about his system, always soliciting new servers, software, and browsers. Mark Andreesen, student at the University of Illinois, in 1993 launched Mosaic, the first universal, easy-to-install graphical browser. After that users adopted the Web like wildfire.

• *Sustaining*   In 1994, he founded the World Wide Web Consortium, hosted by MIT and CERN, to preserve the WWW in the public domain by creating open software and Web standards. Over four hundred organizations eventually joined W3C; it became an engine of innovation for the Web.

• *Executing* He put together programming teams and solicited others to do the same, so that good Web software was developed and made available for anyone to use. He set clear principles for the design and implementation of all Web software.

• *Leading* At every opportunity, he recruited ever-larger numbers of followers and Web supporters. He articulated a small set of guiding principles for Web development and stuck with them. He refused to let the Web "go private" or to become wealthy from his own invention. He said the cause was too important and too big for his personal considerations to influence.

Candace Lightner and Cindi Lamb, MADD Founders

In May 1980 Candace Lightner's thirteen-year-old daughter was killed by a drunk driver as she walked to school. On top of her loss, Lightner was outraged to learn that the judicial system would probably let the driver, a repeat offender, off with a light sentence. She vowed to start an organization that would change all this.

Just a few months before, Cindi Lamb's five-month-old daughter was made permanently paraplegic in a head-on collision with a drunk driver. Lamb was outraged that the driver was still on the road and would probably get off with a light sentence. She started blanketing politicians and lawmakers with her daughter's story and entreaties to change the laws.

Lightner and Lamb soon joined forces and formed Mothers Against Drunk Driving (MADD). They held a news conference in October 1980 attended by members of Congress and the National Highway Traffic Safety Administration. The two mothers told the stories of their daughters and brought the drunk-driving issue into national awareness. Lamb's photogenic paraplegic daughter drew media attention on popular shows such as *Today*, *Good Morning America*, and *20/20*. Lightner, MADD's first president, wanted other leaders to take over after her term, and MADD has been blessed with a succession of effective leaders. Lightner also spoke in a voice of universal appeal: "We're dads and daughters, sons and uncles, friends, and neighbors. And mothers. We're all ages and from all walks of life. We are many colors with one voice" (madd.org).

By 1983, MADD had 100 chapters and the states had passed 129 anti-drunk-driving laws. By 1988 all fifty states had conformed to the new MADD-inspired federal law making twenty-one the minimum legal drinking age. By 1990, four states had lowered the permissible blood alcohol levels from 1.0 to 0.8 percent, and by 2003 forty-five states had followed suit. By 1997, MADD announced that its goal to reduce drunk-driving deaths by 20 percent was achieved, when the drunk-driving death rate dropped below 40 percent.

Today, the MADD organization has over two million members, six hundred chapters, and thousands of volunteers in its victim assistance programs. MADD is a powerful force for public awareness, victim assistance, public policy, and grassroots activism. It is one of the one hundred most admired public charities.

Here is a summary of how Lightner and Lamb engaged in the first seven practices.

• *Sensing* On learning that the drunk driver who killed her thirteen-year-old daughter would probably get a light sentence under the law in effect at that time, Candy Lightner vowed to start an organization to campaign for driver responsibility and laws to encourage it. Similarly, on learning that the drunk driver who caused her five-month-old daughter to become paraplegic would get a light sentence, Cindi Lamb blanketed lawmakers and politicians with letters demanding changes to toughen drunk-driving laws. The two mothers banded together in 1980 to seek changes in these laws.

• *Envisioning* Lightner and Lamb envisioned a transformed nation whose citizens would take full responsibility to not drive and drink at the same time, would support laws with tough penalties for drunk driving, and would provide services to victims of drunk drivers.

• *Offering* In October 1980, Lightner and Lamb held a news conference about their new organization. They told the stories of their daughters and of their outrage over the willingness of people and the legal system to excuse drunk drivers for their irresponsibility. They invited people to join them in MADD to work toward these ends. Lamb's paraplegic daughter was a news sensation; she appeared on *Today, Good Morning America, 20/20,* and in many news articles, capturing the nation's sympathies and appealing to the indignation of many other families who had lost children to drunk drivers.

• *Adopting* The new social practices sought by MADD were widely adopted—lower limits on blood alcohol, designated drivers, help for victims of drunk drivers, and heightened public awareness and intolerance of drunk driving.

• *Sustaining* By 1997 MADD achieved goal of lowering drunk-driver-caused deaths from 60 percent of accidents to less than 40 percent. By 2003, forty-five states had lowered their legal standard for blood alcohol limits from 1.0 to 0.8 percent. "Get a designated driver" became a national motto. Today MADD has millions of members, thousands of volunteers, 600 chapters, and a proactive headquarters staff.

• *Executing* By 1982 MADD had expanded to 100 chapters, was a member of President Ronald Reagan's national commission on drunk driving, was active in every state working for improved drunk-driving laws, and had established itself as an information source for drunk-driving statistics. Over the years MADD chapters have expanded their services in public awareness, victim assistance, public policy, youth outreach, and grassroots activism.

• *Leading* Lightner and Lamb established a tradition of strong, active leadership from the beginning. The vision of a transformed nation with low tolerance for drunk driving drove the two women and was carried on by a long succession of MADD leaders.

Coleman Mockler, Razor Innovator

Colman Mockler was CEO of Gillette from 1975 to 1991. It is remarkable that his innovations in razors generated so much new value for a mundane technology that everyone else, including corporate raiders, had written off. He faced down two takeover attempts of Gillette by raiders who promised better-than-market rates by liquidating Gillette. By 1996 his innovations had tripled Gillette's stock price relative to what the takeovers would have yielded in 1986.

At the time of the takeover bids, Gillette introduced the Sensor razor and then later the Mach3 razor. The Mach3 razor offered new features that did not exist in previous generations of blades: triple blades with separate floating suspensions to adapt to any facial contour, thereby eliminating almost all nicks and abrasions and the need for shaving cream; special coatings that reduce blade and holder friction on the skin; an indicator strip that tells when it's time to load a new blade; and cartridge architectures that facilitate cleaning and replacement.

Gillette was not the first to innovate with razors. In the 1960s, the Wilkinson Sword company introduced a stainless-steel, extra-sharp coated blade that lasted much longer and gave closer shaves than conventional blades. Even before the takeover bids, Gillette had already invested in research that led to the Sensor razor and Gillette's move ahead of Wilkinson in the market. In *From Good to Great*, Jim Collins (2001) said that Mockler did not capitulate to two hostile takeover bids but instead reached out to many individual investors and asked them to block the sale. Mockler's bet paid off. Collins says that someone who was an investor in 1986 made three times more by sticking with the company than by taking the buyout bid. Gillette (2006) complemented its improved technology with a canny marketing campaign that appealed to many men and women.

Here is a summary of how Mockler engaged with the first seven practices.

• *Sensing*   In 1975 he believed that advances in materials technology enabled the development of multiple-blade razors that shavers would prize and would propel Gillette to greatness. He spent 1975 to 1977 installing an executive team whose members would see the same opportunity, and replaced thirty-eight of the top fifty executives.

• *Envisioning*   He and his team envisioned razors built of multiple coated blades with individual suspensions. They envisioned selling this to men and women as a must-have advancement for an extraordinary shaving experience, without cuts and nicks, that would enhance masculinity and femininity.

• *Offering*   He offered a business plan to his board that envisioned breaking away from the disposable razor market with substantial margins. He then offered the marketplace a new and substantially higher-quality shaving experience that would be well worth the higher price.

• *Adopting*   The users adopted the new razors and propelled Gillette to the top spot in the razor market.

• *Sustaining*   The new product lines were a mainstay of Gillette's performance. From 1986 to 1996, Gillette's stock outperformed the stock market average by a factor of seven and the offered buyout value of the takeover company by a factor of three.

• *Executing*   He coordinated the R&D team, which developed the Sensor, Sensor for Women, and the Mach3, and the marketing team, which developed the marketing and sales campaigns based on improved self-images for customers aided by the new technology.

• *Leading*   In Collins's *From Good to Great* (2001) Coleman Mockler was listed as a "Level 5" (most accomplished) leader—modest, humble, willful, and fearless, who puts the greatness of the company ahead of personal considerations, and who led a highly effective team without seeking celebrity. He produced trust with his board, high performance with his team, and high market value.

James Denning, Head of Household

James Denning was Peter's father. In 1953, when Peter's mother Catherine was pregnant with the fifth child, she was overwhelmed by the work of maintaining order among four feisty children, who had become sloppy about their personal spaces and ornery about doing chores. The stress had become intolerable for both parents and was threatening Catherine's health.

James declared a breakdown and called an important family meeting. He laid out the problem in detail and asked for a change of attitude and action to restore family solidarity and help Catherine. He created a rotating system of chores and tied allowances to their on-time and quality completion. He created a system of "extra jobs" that offered extra allowances. After a few months of carefully tending to the new system, praising all behaviors that made it work, and prodding all behaviors that didn't, he transformed the household into a smoothly running organization with a healthy mother and strong sense of solidarity.

This example illustrates a small innovation: a group of six. Even at this small size, James acted in all the basic practices to achieve the adoption of a new family practice in the group. Here is a summary of how he engaged with the first seven practices.

• *Sensing*   In 1953 he became dissatisfied with the family discord being caused by his four children's sloppiness in their own rooms and in the shared family areas. He was distressed at the toll this was taking on his pregnant wife, who could not cope with disorganization or keep everything neat through her own efforts. It would only get worse when the fifth child arrived.

• *Envisioning*   He envisioned a household in which the children kept their rooms neat and contributed to the maintenance of shared areas; they each did a fair share of the chores. There were no more messes and his wife's workload was not burdensome. Each family member engaged the others with love, respect, and kindness.

• *Offering*   He called a family meeting. He declared the breakdown and his determination to rectify it. He described his vision of a harmonious household and a healthy mother for all the children. He offered a new household management system to achieve this. He asked the children to adopt a more inclusive attitude toward the family as a unit. He asked them to embrace a new system of chores, weekly allowances, and periodic family meetings to monitor progress.

• *Adopting* By a combination of cajoling and authority he got the children to accept the new system and begin by cleaning their rooms. He did not want to use the full weight of his fatherly authority because he wanted the children to buy in and keep the system going because it made life easier.

• *Sustaining* He and his wife gave constant feedback, praising when chores were done on time and impeccably, prodding when they were late or performed half-heartedly. As the overall family mood improved, he gave public thanks for everyone's contribution. Eventually the children policed each other to keep the chore schedule. And they offered to do new "extra jobs for extra pay" when they saw opportunities.

• *Executing* He wrote down a definition of four sets of chores such as emptying trash, washing dishes, dusting, and vacuuming. He created a rotating schedule and posted it on the wall showing which set each child was responsible for each week. He raised allowances but made them contingent on completing all chores. He defined *extra jobs* and established the amount of extra allowance to be earned from those jobs.

• *Leading* Once he realized there was a problem, he faced it squarely and moved into it in search of a solution. He created a solution that drew on each child's talents and took care of individual concerns while contributing to the common good. He carefully tended the system so that everyone kept the objective in mind and never wandered far off the path, giving feedback to guide behaviors.

William Sims, Naval Gunnery Innovator

William Sims retired as an admiral of the U.S. Navy in 1922. Through his leadership in the early 1900s, when he was still a lieutenant, the Navy adopted continuous-aim gunnery, a major innovation. He exercised considerable leadership in World War I protecting sea-lanes for shipping. Several ships and many buildings on Navy bases are named in his honor.

Prior to about 1898, gunners on naval ships faced a serious problem when aiming at enemy ships: the gun could be aimed at the target only for a small portion of the interval between the crests of the waves. The individual gunner had to guess the precise moment to fire so that the shell would hit the target. In the U.S. Navy, fewer than 1 percent of shots hit their targets.

In 1900, William Sims, then a lieutenant, met Admiral Percy Scott of the British Navy, who had introduced a new system of gunnery on his ship, the HMS *Scylla*. Scott had noticed that one of his gunners continuously adjusted the gears controlling the angle of the gun, achieving a much higher accuracy than anyone else. He retooled his guns with better gears and with telescopic sights. His men routinely achieved targeting accuracy exceeding 10 percent. Lieutenant Sims persuaded his own captain to try the new method and demonstrated impressive improvements in accuracy. He wrote a detailed report full of supporting data and sent it to the Naval Bureau of Ordnance (NBO) with a recommendation to adopt in the Navy. NBO bureaucrats did not find Sims's concept credible and filed his report away without comment.

Sims sent more reports with more data and still got no response. He became increasingly feisty and combative in his language in an effort to get their attention. He sent copies of his reports to fellow officers around the Navy. He finally elicited responses to the effect that continuous-aim gunnery was not feasible according to tests sponsored by NBO, that the new technology would be unnecessarily disruptive to the established social order of a ship, and that better training of the men would close the gap between British and U.S. naval gunnery performance. He persisted, but only managed to elicit the ad hominem response that he was a crackbrained egotist and falsifier of evidence. After thirteen reports, Lieutenant Sims took the extraordinary step of breaking his chain of command. He sent a letter to President Theodore Roosevelt telling of the gap, and the U.S. Navy Department's refusal to act. Roosevelt, who liked responding to such appeals, recalled Sims to Washington in 1902 and appointed him Inspector of Target Practice. From that position, Sims was able to commission new gunnery and field tests and bring about the adoption of continuous-aim gunnery as a standard practice of the U.S. Navy. When he left this post at the end of Roosevelt's administration in 1908, he was hailed in the navy as "the man who taught us how to shoot."

Some of the authors' students are military officers at the U.S. Naval Postgraduate School. They are fascinated by this account because they see their own struggles in Sims's story: persisting in the face of continued strong opposition, and being willing if necessary to buck the chain of command. Some of our students wonder if they could follow Sims because breaking the chain of command can be a career-ending move.

Here is a summary of how Sims engaged in the first seven practices.

• *Sensing* In 1900 he met Admiral Percy Scott (British Navy) and observed that the continuously adjustable guns on British ships allowed hit rates on rolling seas of up to 10 percent. U.S. Navy gunners achieved hit rates of less than 1 percent. Sims thought this was unconscionable and launched a campaign to adopt the British method.

• *Envisioning*   Sims envisioned all U.S. Navy ships outfitted with continuous-aim guns and all gunners trained in their use. Such ships would be hard to beat in battle and could engage enemies much longer with the same amount of ammunition.

• *Offering*   He wrote thirteen reports detailing the results of tests of the gun system, showing the British method's obvious superiority. He circulated them to high-level Navy officials and fellow officers. His proposals were rejected for various reasons, including a belief that continuous-aim gunnery was impossible and that he was a troublemaker. In 1902 Sims took the extraordinary step of writing directly to President Roosevelt to tell him of Scott's success and the refusal of U.S. Navy officials to adopt the technology. Roosevelt called him to Washington and appointed him inspector of target practice.

• *Adopting*   As inspector, Sims organized numerous field tests, commissioned prototypes of new gunnery systems, and developed deployment plans. The results were propagated to Naval commands from Washington.

• *Sustaining*   By 1908 all U.S. Navy ships were outfitted with the new gunnery. They increased their accuracy by a factor of 150 compared to six years before. Sims was now called "the man who taught us how to shoot."

• *Executing*   The Navy continued the practice of studying weapons and promulgating innovations such as automatic aiming and range finding.

• *Leading*   Sims was intolerant of bureaucracy and stonewalling by chains of command. He frequently criticized his superiors and broke the chain of command to get done what he believed was right. He prevailed because of his dogged persistence and his irrefutable data and because he successfully appealed to the president. He went on to become a great admiral.

Bill Maclay, Sustainable-Design Architect

As a student in the 1960s, Bill Maclay was angered by social injustice, gender inequities, environmental pollution, and powerless of individuals to effect change. In 1971 he attended a lecture about buildings heated by the sun, which inspired his interest in architecture as a means for individuals to make a difference in energy use and pollution. After completing his architecture degree in 1977, Maclay designed single-family, energy-neutral, and pollutant-free homes. Over the years he perfected his methods and turned his attention to larger-scale projects: commercial buildings and entire communities. In the mid-2000s he completed a design of a 46,000-square-foot manufacturing and office facility in Vermont with annual energy costs of less than $15,000. By 2010 this facility was fully powered by renewal energy. It has attracted thousands of visitors wanting to see firsthand how an energy-neutral building can also be healthier and more satisfying to occupy than most office facilities.

Maclay attracted a following through his published research and courses on indoor air quality, materials, and sustainability. He also lectured extensively, showing many people how it is possible to create pleasing and pleasant buildings with no net energy draw. He served as president of the Vermont chapter of the American Institute of Architects, board member and policy chair of Vermont Businesses for Social Responsibility, and faculty member at the Yestermorrow Design Build School in Vermont. He is a leading authority on sustainable architectures that do not depend on fossil fuels.

Maclay also exemplifies how a small firm can eventually influence global change. Here is a summary of how he engaged with the first seven practices.

• *Sensing*   In the 1960s, Maclay observed upheaval in U.S. political, social, and environmental protection systems and determined to do something about it. A 1971 lecture on solar-heated buildings convinced him that buildings, and eventually civilization as a whole, could be completely powered by renewable, nonfossil fuels.

• *Envisioning*   He envisioned a world powered by renewable energy with no use of fossil fuels. He described how individual buildings, and later entire communities, could be energy neutral. Real buildings that implemented his ideas had striking reductions in energy usage and were distinctively pleasing to their occupants. He added urgency for the adoption of these building principles by ferreting out data showing that world petroleum consumption has increased faster than production and that energy prices may escalate by factors of ten by 2025.

• *Offering*   He developed progressively more powerful proposals for green buildings over the years. His first designs were for single-family homes. Later he expanded to office and manufacturing facilities and recently to entire communities. He maintains a portfolio of his work to ground his proposals to new customers. He also began to design materi-

als to help other local communities design their own sustainable infrastructures and buildings. He has been an activist in his local community
advocating for and implementing farm, forest, and wildlife conservation,
and improved environmental, health, and resource conservation in buildings and his local valley and state.

• *Adopting*   Maclay and his firm have developed novel principles and
practices for environmental design. They provide customers with detailed
analyses of energy savings and returns on investment. They consistently
deliver, even over-deliver on all their promises. They built considerable
customer trust in their reliable performance, propelling steady growth in
the firm's revenue as well as in the size, complexity, and significance of
projects.

• *Sustaining*   Sharply rising energy prices and a new political climate
favorable for environmental sustainability have made Maclay's numerous novel designs of energy-saving features increasingly valuable and
attractive. More companies have turned to his firm for energy-neutral
designs, and other architects have adopted his methods for their own
customers.

• *Executing*   To provide an atmosphere in which sustainable building
principles could flourish, Maclay helped pioneer building-rating systems,
such as LEED (Leadership in Energy and Environmental Design) and
Energy Rated Homes. He has also worked to change building codes to
meet stricter environmental requirements.

• *Leading*   Maclay recognized that his success over the long run
depended on developing a high level of trust in his methods and in his
firm's ability to deliver. He established his firm's reputation as the north-
east region's most experienced and reliable environmental design firm.
His leadership has been recognized in awards, articles, exhibitions, television appearances, radio interviews, and appointments to boards and
committees. He holds the Terry Ehrich Award from Vermont Businesses
for Social Responsibility for his leadership. He is a former president and
board member of the Vermont chapter of the American Institute of
Architects.

Conclusions

Our six examples of innovations reflect diverse personalities, styles,
virtues, vices, timeframes, and communities among their innovators. The
innovations were radical (the World Wide Web), sustaining (Gillette),

disruptive (naval gunnery), social (MADD), small-scale (family), and small business (architecture). These innovators all understood that getting people to adopt the new idea was the key to their success. They accomplished their innovations by engaging in the eight practices. These practices are not discretionary—they are essential for successful innovation in any domain.

While writing this book we sought additional examples of innovative companies that were famous in the early 2000s—with names like Facebook, LinkedIn, Second Life, World of Warcraft, Twitter, and Google. (Google's innovation culture is discussed in chapter 13.) These companies are targets for further research in how these eight practices have enabled their innovations.

That most of these young companies were not public entities made it difficult for us to get enough information about their workings to build case studies. Most of the public and media-reported information about these companies focused on issues such as how the technology worked, how the innovators first came up with their ideas, and what markets were making money for them—the common concerns of the interviewers and reporters. Few and far between are those observers who ferret out how companies actually engage with the practices of adoption.

As an example, we located video recordings of interviews with Twitter CEO Evan Williamson. We were able to understand how he sensed the opportunity and envisioned Twitter's future. He had little to say, however, about his strategies for adoption, sustainment, execution, and leadership. It struck us that his perception of adoption was that it is a matter of luck, and he was grateful that so many celebrities had chosen to use Twitter. He said that the current business plan (free service) was unsustainable but offered no alternative plan. He exhibited a great deal of somatic presence and centeredness, which in our view were major factors in his success. However, because of the lack of a sustainment plan, we cannot offer Twitter as an example of a successful innovation. The company may well become successful—we just cannot tell yet.

Nonetheless, throughout the book we have included many other examples, in addition to the six presented in this chapter, to illustrate particular points about successful practice. Furthermore, many other fascinating innovator stories can be found in the great books by David Billington (1996), Harold Evans (2004), and Richard Tedlow (2001).

Bibliography

Berners-Lee, Tim. 2000. *Weaving the Web*. Harper Business.

Billington, David. 1996. *The Innovators: The Engineering Pioneers Who Made American Modern*. Wiley.

Collins, Jim. 2001. *From Good to Great*. HarperBusiness.

Evans, Harold. 2004. *They Made America: Two Centuries of Innovators from the Steam Engine to the Search Engine*. Little Brown.

Gillette Corp. 2006. http://www.gillette.com/products/grooming_men.asp.

Tedlow, Richard. 2001. *Giants of Enterprise: Seven Business Innovators and the Empires They Built*. Harper Business.

3

Frames of Mind

Failure of existing rules is the prelude to a search for new ones. . . . The significance of crises is the indication they provide that an occasion for retooling has arrived.

—Thomas Kuhn (68, 76)

Thomas Kuhn, author of *The Structure of Scientific Revolutions* (1962), showed us that we are all members of communities of practice. A community has a shared belief system—its way of interpreting the world and associated practices—that Kuhn called its paradigm. Sooner or later, he said, we encounter events or phenomena that our accepted paradigm cannot explain or respond to. He called such events anomalies. As long as the anomalies are not too common or troublesome, we tolerate them. But when faced with an accumulation of anomalies too big to ignore, we become open to the possibility that we need a new paradigm. The change to a new paradigm is a revolution.

In our review of innovation literature, we found four paradigms for thinking about innovation: mystical, process, leadership, and generative. The anomaly of low success despite high effort arises in the mystical, process, and leadership paradigms. That anomaly motivates our interest in the generative paradigm, which is a new approach to innovation.

Within the four paradigms, we found seven major models of innovation: inspirational stories, pipeline, diffusion, sources, traits and virtues, learning networks, and history making. The first five models dominate most thinking about innovation. They sustain the invention and process myths discussed earlier. We will discuss these models in this chapter to see how each shows the world differently to the innovator, and what possibilities each opens and closes.

Models of Innovation

In our analysis of the innovation literature, we found four paradigms of innovation:

1. *Mystical*   Innovation is seen as the result of a special talent, good genes, good luck, serendipity, and, occasionally, magic.
2. *Process*   Innovation is seen as the result of manageable processes with definite states, behaviors, and transition rules.
3. *Leadership*   Innovation is seen as the result of leaders applying strategies to build cultures of innovation and persuade people to adopt new products or services.
4. *Generative*   Innovation is seen as the result of individuals listening, articulating value, and observing and executing commitments in conversations that produce effective actions for the adoption of new practices.

These four paradigms are also levels of development in the approach to innovation. They mirror the traditional notion of developmental levels for children as they grow (Piaget 1954; Harris 2002). Each level is a distinct way of understanding and interacting with the world. At some points, individuals discover anomalies and breakdowns that they cannot resolve until they expand their perspectives and gain new ways to understand and interact. The expanded perspective is a new level of their development. Although they generally prefer not to, they can still understand and interact at any of the lower levels. We have found that innovators move through levels 1 to 4 as they discover limitations in their understandings and mature in their experience. Of course, some innovators get stuck at one of the levels and do not move up at all.

Someone at level 1 attempting to understand how Tim Berners-Lee brought about the World Wide Web would say that he exercised a rare talent at innovation and benefited from several strokes of good luck. Someone at level 2 would say that Berners-Lee followed one of the processes such as pipeline or diffusion. Someone at level 3 would say that he exercised leadership by targeting high-leverage communities first, and by following strategies such as simplicity of core design. Someone at level 4 would say that he displayed mastery of the essential conversations of the eight practices of innovation.

These levels also carry different perspectives on how value is created for adopters. Someone at level 1 would say that value is created by luck and by natural talents of innovators; to get innovation, you hire good talent. Someone at level 2 would say that value is created by the process; to get innovation, you hire good managers. Someone at level 3 would say that value is created through the actions of the leader and the followers; to get innovation, you hire good leadership. Someone at level 4 would say that value is created by commitments made and fulfilled in conversations; to get innovation, you develop competence in the conversational practices and in coping with their breakdowns.

Let us head off possible confusion around the word *level* in this book. We have used the word in two ways:

1. Level of performance (novice, skillful, masterful)
2. Level of development (mystical, procedural, leadership, generative)

These two kinds of levels are not independent—for example, people in each level of development will exhibit different levels of performance, and people at each level of performance will interpret their performance according to their current level of development. Table 3.1 compares these two notions of level. In most of this chapter, the word *level* will refer to development.

A Taxonomy of the Literature

In September 2009, Amazon.com listed 9,300 printed books with the word *innovation* in their titles. In sampling this literature, we discovered seven models of innovation. By *model* we mean a representation of the key elements of a way of thinking about innovation. We classified these models, along with the eight practices, among the four paradigms (developmental levels) of innovation, as shown in table 3.2. With each model we have shown the names of authors who exemplify the model. We will discuss these models in the sections following and will give full citations of the works of those authors.

The models of the process and leadership levels dominate conventional thinking about innovation. Most business case studies analyze leadership but with inconsistent conclusions. For example, some case studies suggest that a charismatic, fiery CEO increases the chances of success (e.g., Steve Jobs at Apple); but others suggest that low-key CEOs (e.g., Eric Schmidt at Google) can be equally successful.

Generative works are most common in the personal development literature. They tend to focus on practices that build skill at leadership, goal setting, and goal achievement—but not innovation skills. Leading examples are:

Table 3.1
Development and Performance

Performance		Development				
		Mystical	Procedural	Leadership	Generative
Novice		Admire talent	Follow rules	Imitate behavior	Organize to learn the EIGHT practices
Skillful		Imitate talent	Manage competently; analyze risks and returns; customize process to situation	Cultivate personal qualities; inspire; mobilize; create serendipity	Competent at all eight practices
Masterful		Identify, attract, and hire talent	Manage large organizations; produce "happy accidents"	Develop leadership presence; foster culture of innovation	Acquire advanced skill through immersion and development of a unique way of observing

Table 3.2
Models of Innovation

Level	Innovation as . . .	Models		
1 Mystical	Special talent, good fortune, luck serendipity, magic	Inspirational stories of individual innovators (Billington, Evans)		
2 Process	Process that can be managed	Pipeline (Bush, Kline)	Diffusion (Rogers)	
3 Leadership	Change of practice brought about by leadership strategy and action	Sources (Drucker)	Traits and virtues (Gilder, Deschamps)	Learning networks (Schon)
4 Generative	Individual skill of achieving adoption of new practice in a community	Eight practices	History-making (Spinosa, Flores, and Dreyfus)	

- Thomas Armstrong, *The Seven Kinds of Smart*
- Marcus Buckingham, *Go Put Your Strengths to Work*
- Stephen M. R. Covey, Stephen R. Covey, and Rebecca Merrill, *The Speed of Trust*
- Stephen R. Covey, *The Seven Habits of Highly Effective People*
- Daniel Goleman, *Emotional Intelligence and Working with Emotional Intelligence*
- Richard Strozzi-Heckler, *The Leadership Dojo*
- Marcie Hughes and James Terrell, *The Emotionally Intelligent Team*
- Robert Kelley, *How to Be a Star at Work*
- Allen Weiner, *So Smart But . . .: How Intelligent People Lost Credibility—And How They Can Get It Back*

In *Disclosing New Worlds* (1997), Charles Spinosa, Fernando Flores, and Hubert Dreyfus compiled an overview of three main schools of thought in the innovation literature, which they named theoretical, empirical, and fundamental practices. They cited Peter Drucker (1985) as an exemplar of the theoretical, Karl Vesper (1980) as an exemplar of the empirical, and George Gilder (1992) as an exemplar of the fundamental practices. They proposed that the fundamental generative practice of all entrepreneurs (business innovators) is "history making." History making is behind the prime innovation pattern discussed in chapter 1. It means the ability to change the way people see the world and how they act to create a future different from the past. This notion is the basis of the eight practices. At its most advanced, it is the defining characteristic of innovation mastery.

What or How?

In the end, all innovations depend on the actions of individuals: innovators offer new products and services, and adopters commit to learn them, use them, and integrate them into their existing practices. Therefore, how individual innovators and adopters make their commitments and cope with breakdowns is directly connected with an innovation's success.

Unfortunately, the models at the levels of mystical, process, and leadership do not tell us how individual participants achieve success; they tell us only what certain individuals did (mystical level), what happened at different stages of a process (process level), and what strategies their leaders followed (leadership level). They emphasize the "what" and not the "how."

There is a big gap between "what" and "how." Experts in many fields can tell us what they did but they cannot tell us how they did it (Polyani and Keegan 1966; Dreyfus 1972, 2001). Whatever rules we can tease out from these experts still do not tell us how they do their work. Tiger Woods has the most admired and measured golf swing of all time; yet all the videos and tips gleaned from his game do not help other golfers improve their games. Woods can describe what he does but not how he actually does it. None of his rules, tips, techniques, and guidelines helps others play golf as he plays golf.

We have chosen the term *generative* for level 4 precisely because it focuses on how individuals generate the outcomes that make up an innovation. Generative acts are observable and executable means to produce the desired outcomes. In contrast, the other levels are "descriptive"—they name what individuals might do, but not how they can do it effectively.

We actually use the term *generative* as shorthand for *generative interpretation*. Individuals at the generative level have an interpretation of the world that allows them to observe and execute actions that produce adoption of new practices. Their generative interpretation includes practices that cultivate the tacit knowledge required for them to be effective. A descriptive interpretation is abstract and rule oriented. The abstraction usually is too far removed from the reality to offer useful guidance in the real world, and the rule orientation conveys none of the tacit knowledge needed for effective performance.

Planning is an example. Planning is done to prepare a process description along with analyses of risks and costs and other activities and deliverables. But these analyses and deliverables do not describe how to produce the shared commitment that enables a plan to produce its outcomes. A generative interpretation provides this. A generative plan addresses a team leader's *offers* of specific *promises* for team outcomes, along with subsidiary *promises* by team members for their contributions *negotiated* in specific *conversations* with the leader. The italicized words specify acts that can be observed and executed. The planner can become skillful at them with practice.

Level 1: Mystical Models for Innovation

There are numerous books of stories of individual innovators; Billington (1996) and Evans (2004) are fine examples. Their stories have served wonderfully as inspirations that motivate other innovators to take risks, work hard, and be persistent. Because it is hard to find consistent correlations between the personalities of these innovators and success at innovation, these stories have never formed the basis of business approaches to innovation.

We have found the inspirational stories helpful in our research because they reveal the conversations those innovators engaged in. The eight practices emerged from our studies of these stories.

Level 2: Process Models for Innovation

The pipeline and diffusion models are the two main process models. They are widely accepted and respected and have influenced the business processes of many organizations. They emphasize different parts of the innovation process: pipeline emphasizes the creation aspect, diffusion the adoption aspect. We will discuss them in the next two sections.

The Basic Pipeline Model   The pipeline model is the most popular, and certainly the simplest, framework for innovation. It says that all innovations (1) originate as ideas that (2) flow through a series of defined stages as they are transformed into (3) products of economic value in the marketplace (figure 3.1).

This model has an attractive logic if you work backward to identify the chain of events leading to a successful product. The chain of events can be modeled as a pipeline that transforms the inventor's idea, step by

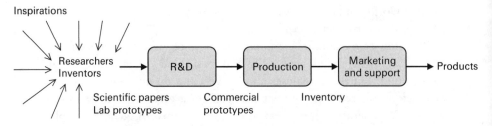

Figure 3.1
Pipeline model of innovation holds that innovations form as ideas generated by researchers and inventors flow through a pipeline to the market. Many ideas are filtered out by the pipeline; only the best make it to market. The model is sometimes called "funnel model" because each stage takes in many inputs for each output. Hundreds of ideas may flow in for every product flowing out.

step, into a commercial product or service. The flow through these stages is driven by two economic forces largely beyond human control:

1. Pull: the market draws ideas with economic value down the pipeline.
2. Push: the players along the pipeline proactively promote and adapt their ideas to seek market acceptance of the innovation and ultimately achieve a return on their investment.

The pipeline model has a rich history tracing back to nineteenth-century industry. The research lab was one of the most successful structures for innovation in the industrial age. General Electric, Westinghouse, Dow Chemicals, IBM, and Bell Labs were the envy of many other organizations and the career aspiration of many professionals. The archetype was Thomas Edison's laboratory in the 1880s. Edison's French contemporary, Louis Pasteur, also an ardent advocate of laboratories, made a string of astonishing discoveries in his mobile field laboratories and later at the Pasteur Institute. To reap similar benefits corporations created their own laboratories, enclaves where scientists and engineers explored new technologies, then passed the most promising prototypes on to the manufacturing and marketing arms of the company. The flow from lab to market was called the "innovation pipeline" and the innovator was the person in the lab feeding the pipeline.

At the end of World War II, Vannevar Bush, President Franklin D. Roosevelt's science advisor, advanced a novel and far-reaching policy proposal based on this model (Bush 1945). He proposed that universities form an extensive network of research laboratories that would generate large numbers of ideas that could be pushed into the pipeline, thus leading to great advances in U.S. innovation. In the long term, the investment would be paid off with significant benefits to the nation's defense, health, and economic well-being. The U.S. government created the National Science Foundation to sponsor research in university labs.

Because the labs had few direct links to corporate manufacturing and marketing facilities, their output went mostly into scientific publications. Today, there are over sixteen thousand scholarly journals. The publications "network" has replaced the "pipeline" as a larger and wider conduit from idea generators to industry. In the churning froth of networking, the laboratory is joined by other modern sources of ideas including startups, open software movements, online journals, blogs, and open consortia. The push and pull assumptions still hold; the medium of propagation is different.

An important assumption of the model is that new ideas are the ultimate source of innovations. Although various experts have challenged this (comments follow), it remains very popular. A recent illustration of the model's popularity is the report of The Council on Competitiveness (2004), signed by twenty-one presidents and CEOs. The report warned that without more government support of research, the source of ideas to drive U.S. innovation will dry up.

The Quadrant Pipeline Model   In the 1990s, numerous complaints arose about the effectiveness of the pipeline as a model for public policy (Likins 1992). According to U.S. congressional critics, the system was not producing a return on investment in health, defense, and economic development. Kuhn tells us that the first reaction of a paradigm to an anomaly is to patch itself; for example, Ptolemaic astronomers explained retrograde planetary motions as planets moving on small spheres attached to the large celestial sphere. A similar reaction happened with the pipeline paradigm.

Donald Stokes (1997), a fellow at the Brookings Institution, challenged Vannevar Bush's claim that there are just two categories of research—basic and applied. Bush defined basic research as a quest for fundamental understanding without regard to potential utility, and applied research as technology development on near-term problems. Successful results of basic research are likely to take twenty to fifty years until adoption; for applied research the lag is more like two to five years. Bush argued that, because the return on investment of basic research is so far in the future, the federal government should be its main sponsor; and because the return on applied research is fairly immediate, industry should be its main sponsor. In fact, Bush argued that federal sponsorship of applied research would drive out basic research.

Stokes proposed a revised framework for understanding research by removing the dichotomy between basic and applied. He defined a new way to categorize styles of research as quadrants in a plane (figure 3.2). He named three of the four quadrants after Louis Pasteur, Niels Bohr, and Thomas Edison, reflecting the well-known research styles and public statements of these great men. He argued that an important category of research (Pasteur quadrant) got lost in Bush's artificial distinction between basic (Bohr quadrant) and applied (Edison quadrant).

Stokes believed that greater emphasis on the neglected Pasteur quadrant would reverse the public perception that research yields little tangible value. With a new emphasis, he speculated, public support for research would return.

Stokes defined new ways to classify the idea sources at the start of the pipeline, but he did not challenge the idea of a pipeline.

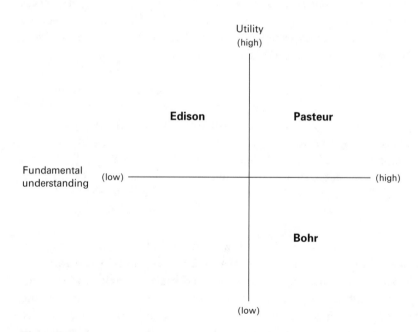

Figure 3.2
Stokes's models three categories of research by the styles of great scientists by assigning them quadrants in the plane. The fourth (unnamed) quadrant is the home of junk science and pointless investigations. The Bush model associates basic research with the Bohr quadrant and applied research with the Edison quadrant.

Pipeline with Feedback   In a report from the National Research Council, Stephen Kline and Nathan Rosenberg (1986) wrote a detailed critique of the pipeline model. They believed that the model misleads people into thinking that innovation is an orderly, well-structured process when in fact it is disorderly, complex, and uncertain. They argued that feedback loops dominate real innovation processes (figure 3.3). The most important of these feedbacks are "demand signals" from actual markets to those looking for potential markets. Three-quarters of successful innovations are inspired by market needs, not by technological opportunity or research results. Kline and Rosenberg concluded, "The notion that innovation is initiated by research is wrong most of the time" (288). This mirrors Peter Drucker's (1985) conclusion, discussed shortly, that new knowledge is the least dominant of innovation's sources.

Comments on Pipeline Models   Our main criticism of the pipeline models is their assumption that ideas are the main source of innovations.

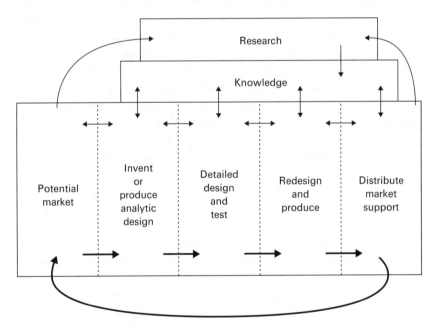

Figure 3.3
Kline-Rosenberg model says that there is a main flow from left to right among the stages shown, but there are numerous feedbacks among all the stages. All the stages, not just the first, draw on knowledge and research. The most important feedback is from market (right end) to potential market (left end).

Drucker (1985) identified seven sources of innovations, only one of which relied on the creation of ideas; he put that source near the bottom of his list. Kline and Rosenberg (1986) said that three-quarters of innovation arise from "market needs," not research ideas. They concluded that generating ideas is not a reliable way to generate adoptions.

In *The Innovator's Dilemma* (1997), Clayton Christenson offered a major challenge to the pipeline model. He studied "disruptive technologies," a pattern whereby a new company could take over an older company's low-end market by offering a cheaper version of a product, and then gradually erode the rest of the older company's market by moving to other products farther up the chain. For example, floppy disks were invented because mainstream hard disks were too expensive for early personal computers. After a while, floppy and Zip drive disks and other low-end portable storage technologies started competing with mainstream storage devices. By then it was too late for the mainstream storage companies to hold their original markets.

Another example of this pattern is in book publishing. Amazon.com has encouraged self-publishing so that authors do not have to deal with slow, labor-intensive publishing houses. Facilitator companies such as booksurge.com and booklocker.com offer inexpensive packages that allow authors to publish quickly and offer books (printed on demand) through Amazon.com. Publishing houses ignored this phenomenon, but according to the *New York Times* (January 16, 2009), self-publishing is becoming a serious threat to traditional publishing.

Whereas the pipeline suggests an orderly process of moving from idea to product, Christenson says that many innovations come as surprises from the edges and margins of awareness. They disrupt the established pipelines of production. None of the pipeline models recognizes the possibility that events outside our immediate awareness can be important sources of innovations.

Another serious challenge to the pipeline model came from Dennis Tsichritzis (1997), then chairman of GMD, the German national laboratory for informatics. Tsichritzis concluded that the popular idea-oriented pipeline model inclined GMD researchers to choose projects that GMD's sponsors did not value. He said: "Research is not the goal but the means. Searching for something cannot be the goal; finding it is the goal. Research, like any other activity, is measured by its results." In addition to idea innovation (the focus of pipeline models), he said that people come to adopt new practice from education, from use of new products, and from establishment of new businesses. He remade GMD's business model into a portfolio dedicating approximately 15 percent of projects to idea innovation, 50 percent to cooperative projects with industry to support product innovation, and the remainder to various education and training activities.

Still another challenge came from Peter Likins (1992), then president of Lehigh University. He indicted the assumption behind public policy that improvements in health, defense, and economics flowed from an idea pipeline originating in the research universities and laboratories. He said that this policy, in place since the 1950s, has cost billions of dollars and not delivered on its promises. It remains a popular policy (Council on Competitiveness 2004).

We conclude that the pipeline model may explain a few innovations, but it falls far short of explaining the majority. Through its abstraction, it draws attention away from the real drivers of action—customers, value, concerns, offers, promises, and practices. It is an unreliable guide to innovation.

The Diffusion Model   The diffusion model, first proposed by social scientist Everett Rogers in 1962, overcomes many of the shortcomings of the pipeline model. It is concerned with how proposed innovations are communicated and adopted by members of a social system. Rogers did not believe in mysterious forces such as technology push or market pull. He used the word *innovation* where we would use *innovation offer* in this book.

Rogers defines diffusion as: (1) a proposed innovation that (2) is communicated through certain channels (3) over time among (4) the members of a social system, some of whom (5) decide to adopt. The diffusion rate of a proposed innovation depends on its perceived relative advantage, its compatibility, its complexity, its ability to be tried out, and its ability to be observed and measured. His model is summarized in figure 3.4.

Rogers began his forty-year career by studying how farmers in Iowa adopted pesticides. He interviewed many farmers and kept statistics on everything they told him. He formed hypotheses about how receptive they were to new technology, how they decided to adopt, how long it took them to decide, and whether they changed their minds later. He postulated the diffusion model. He found that the same pattern appeared in the adoption statistics for other innovations. Beginning in the 1950s, his model was extensively validated not only for agricultural development, but also for medical technology and numerous industries. It

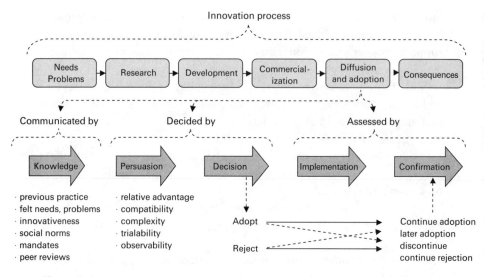

Figure 3.4
Rogers's overall model of innovation process contains diffusion and adoption as key elements. Diffusion refers to the somewhat slow social process of spreading the adopted practice throughout a community. Diffusion can be divided into five parts. (1) Knowledge refers to knowing not only the proposed innovation but also the adopting community. (2) Persuasion refers to getting individuals the information they need to decide—salesmanship is key, and different subgroups take different times to reach affirmative conclusion. (3) Decision refers to the act of committing to (or rejecting) the innovation. (4) The decision is implemented with help from vendors, installers, service centers, help lines, and other infrastructure. (5) Confirmation refers to later evaluation that either affirms or abandons the innovation. These five diffusion elements are connected to the practices of this book. The first (knowledge) overlaps between the offering and adopting practices of this book. The next three (persuasion, decision, and implementation) are part of the adopting practice. The fifth (confirmation) is part of the sustaining practice. (This figure is adapted from Rogers's book by merging his stages of innovation process with his stages of diffusion, and adding the interpretations communication, decision, and assessment.)

strongly influenced the principles of marketing and is taken as a classic in many marketing departments.

Diffusion shares two aspects with the pipeline models: ideas are the source of innovation and there are definite stages of progress toward adoption. However, its three main differences are far more significant.

First, diffusion emphasizes the dynamics of communication and commitment in a social system. The pipeline model includes no social system.

Second, diffusion allows for innovations to be abandoned, for example, if they become obsolete or produce negative value.

Third, time plays a critical role in diffusion: (1) the time period of observation influences how much change is seen; (2) the overall speed of adoption depends on the perceived advantage of the innovation; (3) individuals adopt at different rates according to their temperaments. The idea of individual adoption rates is especially important. Rogers measured the times individual take to adopt and found they follow a Bell curve (figure 3.5).

Rogers believed that the major segments of the Bell curve represent five kinds of temperaments among potential adopters:

• *Innovators* are creators of new ideas. They are venturesome. They will be the first to adopt even if the implements of the new ideas are still shaky.
• *Early adopters* are visionaries who grasp the future implications of a new idea. They are opinion leaders in the community and help persuade others to come in.
• *Early majority* individuals value the products and services based on the new idea, but want assurances of stability before coming in.
• *Late majority* individuals are skeptics. They want to be sure idea is well tested and that most other people are satisfied before coming in.
• *Laggards* are traditionalists. They often see no value in the new idea and prefer the old ways.

In *Crossing the Chasm*, Geoffrey Moore (2002) embraced Rogers's time model and explained the large number of business failures in

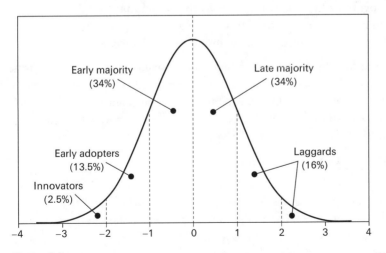

Figure 3.5
Lengths of time intervals to adoption follow a normal distribution. The vertical lines are one standard deviation apart. They divide the curve into regions corresponding to different temperaments of adopters.

California's Silicon Valley. The founders of startups are usually innovators and early adopters. Their ultimate success depends on communicating to the majority, whose concerns are quite different from theirs. Not appreciating the magnitude of this communication problem, they set aside too few resources to address it in their business plan. They meet their early objectives within their affinity group and among innovators and early adopters; but they fail miserably in selling to the majority. Moore's "chasm" is not a discontinuity in the data of adoption times; it is a gap of understanding between the standards of the early adopters and those of the majority.

The median time to adoption varies widely by innovation. Electricity and telephony each took nearly fifty years to reach half the U.S. population. The Internet took thirty years and the World Wide Web ten years. When the rate of adoption is slow, people may not even notice that they are part of a process of adoption; only when they compare the present with a time many years before do they see the magnitude of the change.

Comments on Diffusion Models   We like Rogers's emphasis on adoption and the use of language to communicate innovations. He shows clearly that adoption is a social phenomenon, not the mysterious pushes and pulls of economic forces. Still, the model has significant limitations. Donald Schon (1971) challenged its four key assumptions:

1. Innovations start as new ideas.
2. Innovations flow from a source to the community.
3. Communication is a good model for adoption of practices.
4. The social system responds with inertia to change.

He based his objections on the behavior of dynamic learning networks, which modeled social networks. These limitations have become more pronounced as the world has become more connected by modern Internet (Tuomi 2003). We will give some modern examples where these assumptions fail.

Assumption 1: Innovations start as new ideas.

The same criticisms as for pipeline models apply here. Many new practices are spontaneous reactions to breakdowns: people do them first and call them ideas later. Open software movements, such as Linux, arose from reactions to high software license fees.

Moreover, practices tend to evolve over time, making it hard, even in retrospect, to identify the "idea behind the practice." For example, the early adopters of the Web had to install their own Web servers and hand-code their own HTML documents. Ten years later, adopters subscribed to Web service providers and used sophisticated editing programs to generate Web pages. The "idea of the Web" perceived by adopters in 2003 was not the same as the "idea of the Web" in 1993. The later adopters were not adopting the same Web that Berners-Lee introduced originally.

Assumption 2: Innovations flow from a source to the community.

Many innovations seem to arise spontaneously without a definite source. Various leaders pop up, advance the innovation, then disappear. Blogging is a modern example. The idea of a blog (short for "weblog") started around 1994 when someone started a "personal newsgroup" on a Web page. No one knows for sure who was the first blogger, and no one seems to care. Others copied the practice. When it was apparent that there was strong interest in blogs, more unnamed individuals responded with free blog software, allowing nonprogrammers to set up their own blogs. Then other individuals set up Web services that allowed subscribers to set up their own blogs without installing software. Then news media discovered that significant numbers of people were being influenced by bloggers' opinions, outside the mainstream; so the media publicized blogging and started their own blogs. By the mid-2000s there were many millions of blogs; Google and others set up search services to allow people to locate blogs and subscribe to them. This process involved a lot of bubbling and churning in the Internet community, without any organized leadership.

Web searching is another innovation without a definite source. In the 1980s various researchers proposed search engines to locate Web pages given keywords that they contain. Several search engines were set up even before Web sites: these include Archie (short for "archive") in 1990, Gopher in 1991, Wandex in 1993, Aliweb in 1993, WebCrawler in 1994, Lycos in 1994, AltaVista in 1995. Google appeared around 2001 with the fastest response time and a very good ranking algorithm for presenting the search-matching Web pages. Google joined late in the game, but became a primary supplier of search services and many other tools for organizing information. Prior to Google, market leadership bounced around from one search engine to another.

Assumption 3: Communication is a good model for adoption of practices.

The community embodies the new practice by performing it repeatedly until it becomes an integral part of its members' world. The process of embodiment involves coordination, engagement, imitation, repetition, education, and modifications of the rules of interaction (Carse 1986). Communication of messages is not the most important part.

Assumption 4: The social system responds with inertia to change.

Schon thought that inertia is the wrong way to describe social resistance to change. Inertia of physical objects is overcome by applying constant force in the new direction. Social systems, however, tend to prefer the status quo over change. They actively resist change in a process Schon called "dynamic conservatism." Often, the greater the force, the greater the resistance. Active resistance can be overcome only by adaptive strategies that defuse the resistance.

A prominent modern example is the Napster company, which released its peer-to-peer (P2P) music sharing software in 1999. Napster directly challenged the principle of paying fees to music copyright holders. Within a year music groups started filing suits for copyright infringement, and in 2001 A&M records got an injunction against Napster. Napster was out of business a few months later. Apple quickly moved in with its iTunes service, a paid service that gives royalties to the copyright holders. Although the social system was generally supportive of music sharing, music publishers strongly resisted, and quashed, the free service (Napster) and supported the paid service (iTunes). Apple displayed considerable canniness by recruiting potential resisters into its enterprise, thereby defusing the resistance.

Level 3: Leadership Models for Innovation

There are the four main complaints against the pipeline and diffusion models:

• In the thick of the action, it is very hard to know which model stage best reflects the current situation, and therefore to figure out an appropriate action. For example, if customers seem apathetic toward our product, should we find a better marketing story or be patient because the majority has a slower adoption rate?
• Knowing the model stage usually is not helpful because the model does not advise on the specific actions to take in the stage.
• The models feel too mechanical. They seem to say, follow the steps and the desired innovation will be produced. Real life is not that easy. Relationship problems, tradeoffs, lack of data and clarity, improvisation, solidarity, trust, commitments, listening, resistance, and finding value are not part of the model, yet are a regular part of real innovation.

• The models feel abstract. They are purposely disconnected from the context of the real process. Without knowing the context, it is very hard to evaluate the value of individual actions. What if some group opposes our innovation? The models do not say what happens in the face of organized opposition.

In other words, when engaged in the actual work of innovation, people seeking to use these models are frequently left hanging when they come to the question, "What do I do now?"

The next three models attempt answers to this question by looking at leadership.

The Sources Model   In 1985, Peter Drucker published *Innovation and Entrepreneurship*, a definitive work based on more than thirty years of working with innovators. He said innovation is a discipline, having a theory and definite practices. Entrepreneurs are the most obvious practitioners of the discipline; but most professionals and many amateurs also practice it. He bucked the conventional wisdom of pipeline adherents by claiming that business executives or managers produce innovations through their professional leadership skills. He said they employ five principles:

1. *Opportunity*   Noticing an opportunity in one of the seven innovation sources
2. *Analysis*   Developing a project or business plan, identifying costs, resources, and people, analyzing risks and benefits
3. *Listening*   Going out into the community, listening for concerns, finding what community members are receptive to; adapting the proposal to match
4. *Focused execution*   Carrying out actions to effect the change, all the while maintaining a simple articulation of the central idea and sticking to it despite temptations to embellish or extend prematurely
5. *Leadership*   Positioning the technology to be the best of breed; mobilizing people and markets for it

Drucker devoted more than half of his book to the search for opportunities, which he believed to be the hardest problem for innovators. He grouped opportunities into seven categories or sources (table 3.3), which he listed in the order of decreasing reliability for producing innovations. The point is to look for opportunities in breakdowns, problems, changes, threats, and challenges. Many people are not accustomed to looking for

Table 3.3
Drucker's Seven Innovation Sources

Unexpected events	Unexpected successes or failures; outside events
Incongruities	Gaps between reality and common belief; aspects that do not fit together
Process need	A bottleneck in a critical process
Change of industry structure	New business models, distribution channels, modes of business.
Demographics	Changes in groups by age, politics, religion, income, etc.
Change of mood or perception	Change in the way people see the world (e.g., post 9/11 terrorism), in fashion, convention, etc.
New knowledge	Application of new knowledge, often involving scientific advances and convergence of different areas

opportunities in these areas. They see only problems, and when they do see opportunities, they do not hold on to them long enough to act.

Unlike proponents of the process models, Drucker believes innovation is a skill: the "stages" of a pipeline or diffusion are actually arenas in which executives and managers act. He believes that the core of the skill is sourcing opportunities for the business to commit to and then keeping everyone focused on those commitments. He dismisses the notion that clever ideas are behind most innovations and says that, except when new knowledge is the source, most innovations do not even exploit new knowledge.

Drucker's model is based on the practice of noticing breakdowns in seven preset categories and initiating changes to overcome them. Spinosa, Flores, and Dreyfus (1997) say that Drucker's formulation leads to formulaic methods for responding to known kinds of breakdowns, but not to a skill of responding to new kinds of breakdowns or anticipating future breakdowns.

Drucker's model also assumes that the innovator has time for a systematic search and analysis. This makes sense for a business, where decisions to commit the business to a course of action must be taken with care. Quite often, however, innovators are confronted with many possible alternatives and must act quickly before the window of opportunity closes. Skillful innovators sense opportunities even before they can be put into words; Drucker's model does not account for this common case.

Drucker's model shares with the process models a tendency to recommend analytic approaches. Many executives create formal processes to create opportunity checklists, build spreadsheets that calculate return on investment for each opportunity, analyze effects on supply and value chains, assess customer receptivity through market research, and reengineer business processes for efficient production. The analytic processes are often overemphasized, drawing attention away from human interactions, relationships, connections, trust, influence, intuition, sensitivity, negotiations, building political support, or neutralizing opposition.

The Learning Network Model   Donald Schon (1971) was probably the first to challenge the diffusion model over the limitations we have noted. These limitations show that adoption is not simply a process of people deciding to join the adopting circle based on information spread to them via various channels in their social system. It is a learning process of a social network. Innovators need to interact with those systems not as informers, but as teachers, coaches, and leaders. The innovator's objective is that the system learns and embodies the new practice.

Schon said that every social system has three aspects:

• *Structure*   The set of roles of people in the community and relationships among them; its organization chart, information connections, and social network
• *Conceptual framework*   Its belief system, value system, standard practices, and deeply held principles
• *Technology*   The set of tools, equipment, techniques, and methods that support the system

These three aspects evolve together and are deeply entangled. A change in any one incurs a change in the others. When a system "learns," it changes in all three aspects.

The learning network model replaces the four limiting assumptions of the diffusion model with these:

1. Innovations are new practices in a social system.
2. Innovations can arise spontaneously without an identifiable source.
3. Communication, coordination, imitation, education, and changing the "game" (rules of interaction) are effective means to spread a practice.
4. The social system is likely to actively resist change.

Schon's great insight was the nature and dynamics of resistance to change. Social communities tend to strive for equilibrium and actively push back when someone proposes to change the system. Innovators must lead them past their natural resistance to change.

When William Sims proposed continuous-aim guns on U.S. Navy ships in the early 1900s, he thought he was offering a technology improvement. To him, it seemed that increasing accuracy tenfold and reducing recoil injuries to gunners was a no-brainer decision for the Navy. He was surprised and baffled by the Navy's resistance. The resistance is easy to understand within the learning network model. Sims's technology challenged the concept of the ship's society. Weaponry is a core concern of the Navy, and the gunners were a well-trained, highly coordinated, elite corps. A technology that requires little training disrupts that corps. The natural reaction of ship commanders was to resist something that would apparently undermine the ship's society. Sims eventually got his way because he got the ear of President Theodore Roosevelt, who forced the ship commanders to go along.

One way to understand the tendency toward resistance is that proposed changes alter the configuration of power in the network. Power refers to someone's capability to influence or affect action. Power can come from authority of an office, personal respect, and even fear. Smart innovators recruit "thought leaders," who already have power in the network, to speak on their behalf. Smart innovators also pay attention to whoever will gain or lose power if the innovation is adopted. Gainers will tend to support the innovation, losers to resist. If they stand to lose a lot of power, losers may organize stiff resistance to the proposal. It is important to anticipate where opposition will come from and make moves to neutralize it—for example, recruit the leaders to the cause, contain the resistant groups, or position the innovation as something they can live with.

Power shifts explain many but not all forms of resistance. People who feel that important principles or standards are being violated can mount stiff resistance. For example, privacy advocates resist all technology changes that they perceive would undermine privacy. They react swiftly to proposals and rumors. They simply do not want to be part of a society that does not uphold basic privacy principles.

The degree of resistance depends on the depth of the proposed change. Changing something peripheral usually is easy; changing a core principle is hard. Gillette found it easy to sell its razor innovations because those changes gave better shaves without challenging the principle that men and women shave. Candy Lightner found much more resistance in promoting Mothers Against Drunk Driving (MADD) because she was challenging a core belief that drunk driving was a tolerable aberration; she had to recruit political and media big guns to overcome that resistance and change people's conceptual framework around drunk driving.

Schon's model provides considerable insight into how and why social systems respond to change. Although a change will ultimately affect the structure, theory, and technology of a social system, an intervention to produce the change can begin in any of the three components. Schon's model is particularly helpful to innovators seeking to understand the resistance they will face.

Traits and Virtues Models   George Gilder (1992) was one of the earliest to claim that the ability to innovate flows from certain leadership virtues the innovator can cultivate. He specifically cited the virtues of giving, humility, and commitment. Giving refers to a spirit of generosity and optimism; humility to a willingness to get involved in the nitty-gritty issues of one's enterprise and to a capacity to learn from others through deep listening; and commitment to a faith that the innovation will ultimately succeed, feeding a tenacious persistence to stick with it until it does so. Gilder believes that these three virtues help generate effective entrepreneurial action.

Since that time, more people have accepted the basic claim and have studied what leadership traits an innovator must develop. Jean Philippe Deschamps (2008) says that innovation is a special form of leadership with these traits:

· Insatiable urge to try new things
· Passion for the mission
· Obsession with customer value
· Tenacity
· Courage to take risks and the urge to learn from failures
· Speed in spotting opportunities and then executing
· Ability to choose good people

Welter and Egmon (2005) say that successful leaders have developed eight mental practices, which they call observing, reasoning, imagining, challenging, deciding, learning, enabling, and reflecting. Drucker (2004) similarly says that effective executives have developed eight conversational practices: they ask what needs to be done, they ask what is right for the enterprise, they develop action plans, they take responsibility for decisions, they take responsibility for communicating, they focus on opportunities rather than problems, they run productive meetings, they think and say "we" instead of "I."

There is no question that leadership is one of the major breakdowns in innovation. But leadership is only one of eight practices. The other seven deal with breakdowns in other parts of innovation process. The traits and virtues are skills that guide in the right direction during times of intense action and help cope with breakdowns, but there is much more to the story.

It is easy to think of people who are giving, humble, committed, insatiable, passionate, obsessed, tenacious, courageous, speedy, and choosy, and who are still not successful entrepreneurs. Therefore, something is missing from Gilder's formulation. Spinosa, Flores, and Dreyfus say it is this:

We contend that it is the product or service, not the virtuous lifestyle of the entrepreneur, that makes the world change; it is the entrepreneur's practices for innovating and forming a company to market products and services that should be examined. Here we shall find practices that do not easily fall under the headings of giving, humility, or commitment. (1997, 45)

In other words, the traits and virtues do not guarantee that innovators will either observe or produce the eight essential outcomes. Which of these traits guarantee that the innovator will tell compelling stories, make attractive offers, execute to produce customer satisfaction, or convince people to adopt and embody their adoption through practice?

As for practices that leaders have developed, it is hard to tell which items listed by Welter and Egmon and by Drucker are essential or optional. Some entries on one list do not appear on the other. We do not doubt that many leaders exhibit these practices. But whether they guarantee an ability to innovate is more problematic. For example, the Welter–Egmon list does not account for body as well as it does for mind, for listening and discerning value, and for mastery that goes beyond skill.

Level 4: Generative Models for Innovation

Generative models distinguish practices from descriptions, and look to practices as the prime source of effective action. With a generative interpretation, we become observers of how we generate action from commitments made in conversations, giving us access to powerful ways of generating innovation actions that are not observable in the other paradigms.

The distinction between descriptions and practice is deep and fundamental. These examples illustrate:

- A menu is not the same as the meal.
- A map is not the territory.
- A simulation of digestion is not digestion.
- The sports journalist's account of what the quarterback should have done does not help the quarterback.
- A description of finger positions on a QWERTY keyboard does not make one a good typist.
- A description of violin technique does not enable one to be the concertmaster.
- A description of Winston Churchill's rhetorical devices does not make one a master orator.
- A description of jazz improvisation does not help one become a good improviser.
- A description of Tiger Woods's golf swing as a free-swinging pendulum attached to a rotating arm does not help others hit balls like Woods.

The point of these examples is that descriptions are important but do not empower competent action. They do not teach tacit knowledge. People engaging in relevant practices produce the action and gain the tacit knowledge. To be effective, one must understand the relevant practices and develop an appropriate level of skill.

Models at the generative level of innovation focus on practices that produce (generate) the desired outcomes. The practices of interest in innovation are primarily conversational: they involve making certain commitments, which shape the actions leading to the desired outcomes when completed.

The first generative model of innovation was the history-making model of Charles Spinosa, Fernando Flores, and Hubert Dreyfus (1997). We summarized their insight in chapter 1 as the prime innovation pattern. The innovator senses a disharmony, struggles with it until able to articulate it, finds ways to transform the community's thinking and practices to eliminate the disharmony, and commits to making the necessary changes happen. Spinosa, Flores, and Dreyfus called it history making because the innovator gets the community to adopt and embody new ways of thinking—thereby changing the course of its history, opening new future actions for members, and altering how they perceive the world.

Chauncy Bell (2008) offers another view of history making tailored for designers.

Conclusions

We have reviewed these seven models of the innovation process:

1. The inspirational stories model interprets innovation as the work of individuals gifted with the right talents, often benefiting from good luck.
2. The pipeline model interprets innovation as a linear sequence of steps that transform ideas from researchers into market-adopted products. Despite its attractive logic, it represents no more than a fraction of all innovations.
3. The diffusion model interprets innovation as the decision to adopt an idea through communication within a social system.
4. The sources model interprets innovation as a skill whose core is discovery of ideas. It offers a systematic way to search for ideas and analyze them before committing a business to them. It can be seen as an idea feeder for the process models.
5. The virtues model interprets innovation as practices that are generated from the leadership virtues of giving, humility, and commitment.
6. The learning network model interprets innovation as a change in structure, principles, and technology of a social network. The network must learn and embody the change, and it is likely to actively resist the change.
7. The history-making model interprets innovation as the resolution of a disharmony by adopting a marginal practice into the central, embodied practices of a community.

Pipelines and diffusion are widely used to guide organizations, set public policy, and teach parts of business curricula. They are the most common frameworks for thinking about innovation.

This book adds individual skills to the paradigms of innovation. The skills of the eight practices must always be present for successful innovation no matter what other interpretations are involved. The eight practices enable people to become competent at the history-making pattern by practicing in, and embodying, eight essential conversations. It belongs to a new tradition that interprets knowing as action, and learning as embodiment.

In the coming chapters, we will formulate each practice in terms of what you must pay attention to and what actions you can perform based on what you see. The more you engage in those practices until you can do them well, the greater will be your success at generating innovations.

Bibliography

Armstrong, Thomas. 1999. *The Seven Kinds of Smart*. Plume.

Bell, Chauncey. 2008. My Problem with Design. *ACM Ubiquity* (September), http://www.acm.org/ubiquity/volume_9/v9i34_bell.html. Accessed September 2009.

Billington, David. 1996. *The Innovators: The Engineering Pioneers Who Made American Modern*. Wiley.

Buckingham, Marcus. 2007. *Go Put Your Strengths to Work*. Free Press.

Bush, Vannevar. 1945. *Science, the Endless Frontier. A Report to the President*. U.S. Government Printing Office.

Carse, James. 1986. *Finite and Infinite Games*. Random House.

Christenson, Clayton. 1997. *The Innovator's Dilemma*. Harvard Business.

CNRI (Corporation for National Research Initiatives) series on infrastructures (railroads, telegraph, telephone, power, banking, and radio), http://www.cnri.reston.va.us/series.html.

Covey, Stephen M. R., Stephen R. Covey, and Rebecca Merrill. 2006. *The Speed of Trust*. Free Press.

Covey, Stephen R. 1990. *The Seven Habits of Highly Effective People*. Free Press.

Council on Competitiveness. 2004. *Innovate America: Thriving in a World of Challenge and Change* (December), http://www.compete.org.

Deschamps, Jean-Philippe. 2008. *Innovation Leaders*. Jossey-Bass.

Dreyfus, Hubert. 1992. 1972. *What Computers Still Can't Do*. Repr. with new introduction. MIT Press.

Dreyfus, Hubert. 2001. *On the Internet*. Routledge.

Drucker, Peter. 1993. 1985. *Innovation and Entrepreneurship*. Harper Perennial. Repr., Harper Business.

Drucker, Peter. 2004. What Makes an Effective Executive. *Harvard Business Review* 82 (June):58–63.

Evans, Harold. 2004. *They Made America: Two Centuries of Innovators from the Steam Engine to the Search Engine*. Little Brown.

Gilder, George. 1992. *Recapturing the Spirit of Enterprise*. ICS Press.

Goleman, Daniel. 1997. *Emotional Intelligence*. Bantam.

Goleman, Daniel. 2000. *Working with Emotional Intelligence*. Bantam.

Harris, Bill. 2002. *Thresholds of the Mind*. Centerpointe Press.

Hughes, Marcia, and James Terrell. 2007. *The Emotionally Intelligent Team*. Jossey-Bass.

Kelley, Robert. 1999. *How to Be a Star at Work*. Three Rivers.

Kline, Stephen J., and Nathan Rosenberg. 1986. An Overview of Innovation. In *The Positive Sum Strategy: Harnessing Technology for Economic Growth*, 275–305. National Academy Press.

Kuhn, Thomas S. 1970. 1962. *The Structure of Scientific Revolutions.* Repr., University of Chicago Press.

Likins, Peter. 1992. A Breach of the Social Contract. *ACM Communications 35* (11):17–19.

Moore, Geoffrey. 2002. *Crossing the Chasm.* 2nd ed., Harper Business.

Piaget, Jean. 1954. *The Construction of Reality in the Child.* Basic Books.

Polyani, Michael, and Paul Keegan. 1966. *The Tacit Dimension.* Routledge.

Rogers, Everett. 2003. *1962. Diffusion of Innovations.* 5th ed., Free Press.

Schon, Donald. 1971. *Beyond the Stable State.* Norton.

Spinosa, Charles, Fernando Flores, and Hubert Dreyfus. 1997. *Disclosing New Worlds.* MIT Press.

Stokes, Donald. 1997. *Pasteur's Quadrant: Basic Science and Technological Innovation.* Brookings Institution.

Strozzi-Heckler, Richard. 2007. *The Leadership Dojo.* Frog.

Tsichritzis, Dennis. 1997. The Dynamics of Innovation. In *Beyond Calculation,* ed. P. Denning and B. Metcalfe. Copernicus Books, 259–265.

Tuomi, Ilkka. 2003. *Networks of Innovation.* Oxford Press.

Vesper, Karl. 1980. *New Venture Strategies.* Prentice-Hall.

Weiner, Allen. 2006. *So Smart But ...: How Intelligent People Lost Credibility— And How They Can Get It Back.* Jossey-Bass.

Welter, William, and Jean Egmon. 2005. *The Prepared Mind of a Leader: Eight Skills Leaders Use to Innovate, Make Decisions, and Solve Problems.* Jossey-Bass.

4

Observing

The world is full of obvious things which nobody by any chance ever observes.
—Sherlock Holmes (Arthur Conan Doyle)

Everything that is said, is said by an observer.
—Humberto Maturana

You don't know what you have until it is gone. And you don't know what you're missing until it arrives.
—Anonymous

You can observe a lot just by watching.
—Yogi Berra

When the innovator's work is done, it is said, people see things differently than they did before. This niblet of folk wisdom holds the key to the innovator's skill. The innovator sees things differently before starting to work. The key is in how the innovator observes.

Practitioners in every field have acquired the skill of looking at the world in a particular way that empowers them to make distinctions and take actions. A physician is trained to see things in human bodies that signal illness, diagnose the illness, and prescribe a treatment. A construction engineer is trained to see things in structures and soils that signal weakness in structures, then diagnose the weakness, and prescribe reinforcement. A police officer is trained to watch human behaviors, see signs of criminal intent, and intervene when necessary to prevent crimes. In the same way, every profession has a characteristic way of seeing the world, which we call its "observer"; each practitioner is an embodied variation of the profession's observer.

Innovators must be an observer who can sense disharmonies, articulate them, and take action to resolve them. The prime innovation pattern discussed in chapter 1 summarizes the essence of the innovation observer. The eight practices build one's capacity to be an innovation observer and actor. To be that observer, the skilled innovator continually observes these seven things:

- The *cares* and *concerns* of people
- The *practices* people have for taking care of those concerns
- The *value* and level of *satisfaction* people place in their practices, current and future
- The *breakdowns* and *struggles* people are experiencing
- The *disharmonies* revealed by the breakdowns and struggles
- *New practices* that, if adopted, would resolve the breakdowns and bring harmony
- *Resistance* from people who see a net loss of value in the change

How does the innovator go about observing and acting on these things? This chapter investigates this question as follows:

- We all have internal brain processes that constantly interpret sensory input. We will explain the structure of those processes and how they lead to the principle of "action follows attention." The innovator exploits the principle by getting the adopting community to focus members' attention in a new way, whereupon the new practice follows naturally. Innovation is a learning process and the innovator is a teacher.
- We will explain what it means to be an innovation observer, which includes the capacity to see what is going on for potential adopters and to see opportunities to move them closer to adoption. The eight practices build this embodied observer and enable the innovator to generate effective action.
- We will explain why assessment is an integral part of observing and offer a practice for learning to effectively "ground assessments."
- We will explain why "observing the observer" is a foundational skill for all innovators and offer a practice for learning it.

Because these observation skills are required by all eight practices, we have not designated "observing" as a separate practice. Observing is a fundamental skill for innovation.

The Learning Cycle

A powerful learning practice is a continuing cycle of practice and reflection. During practice, we engage in action with others. During reflection, we step back and become an outside observer of the consequences of the action, and then we plan new actions for the next round of practice. The process can be significantly accelerated under the guidance of a teacher (or coach) who is familiar with the domain. The cycle builds a new observer and capacity for action in the learner, enabling the learner to perform effectively independent of the coach.

The reflection phase does most of the cultivation of the observer. You build a new observer who goes back into the action and plays differently. The innovator learns the eight practices most effectively by engaging with them in this cycle. Moreover, the adopting community of an innovation goes through a similar learning cycle where the innovator is the coach.

This simple cycle works well because the brain is very good at implementing the principle of *action follows attention*. Our actions tend to move us toward the targets of our attention. Richard Strozzi-Heckler (2007) and Bill Harris (2002) emphasize this in their discussions of how to train for leadership. They also warn that focusing attention on avoiding something is likely to be counterproductive because focusing on the unwanted outcome may draw us toward it and achieve the unwanted rather than the desired outcome.

Defining the Observer

Let us refine what we mean by *observer*. There are many definitions depending on whether we observe individuals or communities, and internal or external aspects. Ken Wilber (1996) uses quad charts like the one in table 4.1 to integrate these different kinds of observers into a single framework.

The innovator's path from self-learning to community change can be viewed as a traversal of the four quadrants: the innovator (1) trains his or her observer to be self-aware of internal experience, and then (2) to observe others in a community so as to (3) infer their social observers and then (4) produce for them new practices more aligned with their concerns. The traversal may not be linear because the innovator can backtrack to any previous stage at any time.

Table 4.1
Four Kinds of Observers

	Observer of the internal (subjective)	Observer of the external (objective)
Observer of individuals	1 Observing one's own internal states and interpreting them in one's perceived worlds (self-observer)	2 Observing external behaviors of themselves and other individuals (behavioral observer)
Observer of collectives	3 Experiencing a collective "we" and interpreting the world in terms of community values, care, and truth (social observer)	4 Behavior of social systems, scientific theories, community paradigms (observing the world)

The eight practices aim to open this path and increase the success rates of those following it. Through the practices, the innovator comes to embody an observer and actor capable of doing this well.

Observing Individuals

Humberto Maturana, a biologist, was one of the first to call attention to the importance of the observer in generating action (1989, 2004). He developed a biological theory of cognition based on the notion that every organism reacts to the world in ways conditioned by the organism's structure and history of experience. He said that all biological organisms react to external stimuli only in accordance with their internal structure, which is set up genetically and, within limits, modified by previous experience. The only actions available to an organism are those allowed by its structure.

According to Maturana, part of our structure as human beings is our linguistic capability: we couple with the world through our interpretations. The language we live in, and our past experiences with it, biologically structures what we can see and pay attention to. Anything we say about the world is said by our observer. Anything we do in the world is enabled by our embodied capacity for action—our actor.

We cannot overemphasize how much our biological structure conditions our actions or reactions in response to perturbations from our environment. We can act only as we are structured to act. Learning is biological restructuring. When we are novices, we use our brains to override our current structural conditioning and imprint new behavior patterns. When the new behavior is integrated into our biological structures—embodied in our limbic system (Lipton 2005)—we no longer need to use our thinking brain to get the behavior; it happens automatically.

Many authors have sought to explain how our internal observers work so that we might be able to overcome our blindness and train ourselves to see better and act more effectively. Stephen Covey (1990) and later Bill Harris (2002) said that we organize our knowledge into an internal "map of reality" and then try to navigate the world based on our map. The map is actually a metaphor for our biological cognitive structure. When we learn something, we do not rewrite our map, we shift our biological structure and our way of coupling with the world. Covey and Harris point out that, if our map is an inaccurate representation, we will encounter frequent breakdowns. Covey designed the "Seven Habits" to help people develop more realistic maps and thereby increase their success at reaching their own goals.

We can summarize these findings in the following statements about what our observer does (the term *biological structure* refers to the current configuration of sensors, neural pathways, and brain). Our observer:

• Reacts only to perturbations from the environment that our biological structure is prepared to receive
• Interprets and interacts with the environment based on our current biological structure
• Stores memories of perturbations and actions by restructuring our neural and brain connections
• Generates moods, emotions, concerns, perspectives, and interests that color our interpretations and filter sensory inputs
• Gives a reference frame to evaluate the consequences of previous actions
• Gives a reference frame to imagine future actions and their consequences
• Gives the ability to focus on a portion of our interpretation of the world
• Enables the actions, if any, we can take

Notice how dynamic and active our observers are! They are constantly perceiving, evaluating, and conditioning the actions we can take, and constantly modifying our biological structures (learning) in the process. This is why the choice of practices is so important. We are always observing and practicing something. If we observe and practice the wrong things, we will be unsuccessful at generating the outcomes we want. If observe and practice the right things, we will be successful. The eight practices teach the right things that lead to successful innovation.

Observing Social Groups

How we observe individuals can be scaled up to communities. The members of a community experience a world in their shared practices, conversations, culture, and memories. In their conversations together, they collectively share perceptions, propagate moods, evaluate consequences, imagine the future, focus on things, and shape their commitments and actions.

There can be many social observers in a community. These include religious, ethical, moral, political, and corporate belief systems as well as fads, fashions, and group moods.

Science is one of the most discussed and dominant social observers of our era. Science is an induction process by which a hypothesis about the world is formulated as a generalization of observable evidence and then is tested for consistency with new evidence. Francis Bacon (1521–1626) is often credited with being one of the first to articulate the nature of science as a social process. A scientist is expected to document every experiment with sufficient detail so that any other scientist in the field could repeat the experiment with the same results. Because the documented experiment defines a standard method of making an observation, science has been called a "process of constructing standard observers" (Latour 1987). A claim becomes a scientific fact only when everyone in the community comes to believe it. Because it insists on validation with evidence, the "scientific observer" has a reputation of impartiality. Scientists also know that scientific observers may be blind to phenomena that were not visible in the initial evidence behind a scientific theory. Thomas Kuhn (1962) used the term *paradigm* for widely accepted scientific belief, and pointed out that accumulations of unexplainable anomalies lead to scientific revolutions.

Since Kuhn's time, the term *paradigm* has come to mean any belief system and its associated practices in a community. Kuhn uses the term *anomaly* for any event that is inconsistent with the paradigm. Innovators often use anomalies to alert them to opportunities. The innovator's challenge is to alter the community's belief system and its practices—to change its observers and its actors.

Levels of Observation

Observers make distinctions. When we see that two things are not the same, we have made a distinction between them. Philosophers say that our ability to be aware of an entity comes from our ability to distinguish the presence of the entity from its absence. They apply the term *distinction* to anything observed that can be used to focus attention and action.

For example, the eight practices are distinctions about what an innovator can learn and do to produce adoption of new practices in a community. We have found no cases of successful innovation where any of these distinctions was missing. It is hard for someone who does not embody these distinctions to innovate.

There are four levels of observation that correspond to how we interact with distinctions:

1. *Not noticing*   This can happen if we are blind (we have no distinctions) or inattentive. We will discuss the problem of blindness in chapter 5, as it is an important limitation on our ability to sense possibilities for innovation.
2. *Being aware*   We are able to see with our distinctions and describe what we see to others.
3. *Practicing and attending*   We are immersed in our distinctions and can observe with them without being aware of them. The eight practices aim to do this for the innovation distinctions.
4. *Observing the observer*   We are able to see how other observers work, at both an individual level and social level, and we are self-aware of our own observers. Innovators must be able to do this in order to develop stories about the value of proposed innovations.

Strengthening the Observer

We know that skill can be deepened by recurrence. This means that we repeatedly engage with a practice, each time being mindful of how it feels and how well it is working compared to previous times. Recurrent practice is a process of learning. Richard Strozzi-Heckler (2007) says that 30 recurrences confer familiarity, 300 muscle-memory, and 3,000 embodiment.

But recurrence is not the whole story. Just as we deepen the practice by recurrence, we sharpen the observer by reflection. Reflection is a process of stepping back from the experience of the practice and asking questions: What did I observe? What did I experience? Anything new? What worked well? What did not work? What adjustments can I make the next time? Writing about this cycle between practice and reflection, Angeles Arrien says:

Practice is meant to be active, rigorous, and dynamic. While it builds upon reflection and allows you to see what works and what does not work, it is not merely reflective, nor is it an exercise in intellectual understanding. To practice is to take daily action that supports change and provides a discipline for incorporating and strengthening new values, skills, and character qualities. Both reflection and practice are essential to cultivating and embodying wisdom. (2005, 25)

The Innovation Observer

We noted earlier that the innovation observer constantly looks for concerns, breakdowns, struggles, practices, value, resistance, and opportunities. This observer operates at two levels simultaneously:

• *Social*   What is going on in the potential adopter's world where I can help? (Table 4.2 lists six aspects.)
• *Individual*   How can my response from within one of the eight practices help?

There are at least three advantages to cultivating this observer. First, this observer directs attention to the generative acts that produce an innovation; in contrast, the dominant paradigms of innovation (pipeline, diffusion) direct the observer to managing processes. Second, this observer sees the adopter's world and what is of value in that context. Third, this observer sees the breakdowns and helps the adopter cope.

Marketing guru Jack Trout (2008) says that when these observers are working well, the innovator's proposals meet the *obviousness test*— people in the community see the proposal as simple, easy to understand, and evident.

Figures 4.1 and 4.2 illustrate the innovation observer in an elemental interaction between an innovator (Alice) and a prospective adopter (Bob). The first figure takes them through the offer, and the second through adoption after the offer.

Sports coaches like to counsel: "watch the footwork." In a martial arts demonstration, for example, you witness a wide variety of tech-

Table 4.2
Observing the Adopter's World

Care and concerns	All the issues that drive people to action and occupy their attentions. People are not open to innovations on issues they do not care about.
Offers	The conditions the innovator asks people to commit to in order to have their concerns taken care of. People are always making choices; can the innovator offer better ones?
Customers	In making their choices, people are looking to satisfy themselves and take care of what they care about. As customers for the choices they make, they will be satisfied or dissatisfied with the outcomes.
Assessments	People make their choices based on opinions, evaluations, or judgments they have about their situation, their future, the actions available to them, and the possibilities they have. They make three key assessments when considering offers that might provide a better future: • Value—they see sufficient new value and opportunity that they are willing to change to get it. • Trust—they are willing to make the bet that the future will turn out all right. • Satisfaction—they expect that the outcome will meet or exceed all agreed-on standards and expectations.
Practices and Learning	In taking on a new possibility, innovation, product, or service, what does the person have to learn to get the benefit? What habits need to change? Is the learning process difficult or easy?
Breakdowns and struggles, and resistance	What events might occur that will prevent the person from attaining the result? If they occur, how will the person respond? Who can help?

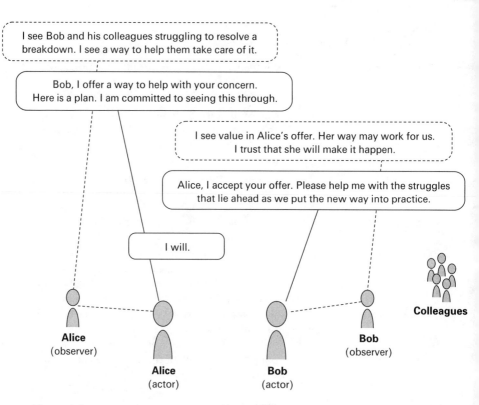

Figure 4.1
Alice (innovator) interacts with Bob (prospective adopter) to make an offer that Bob is willing to accept. The dotted balloons and lines are observations (assessments in this case) and the solid balloons and lines are actions.

niques for attacking, defending, avoiding, and gaining advantage. You can easily wonder how students successfully learn all those moves. The instructor tells them it is not as hard as it seems: "Don't watch my head, my hands, my arms, or my hips. Watch my feet. If you can imitate my footwork, you will with practice learn all the other moves. You can properly move your head, hands, arms or hips only if your feet are in the right place." Golf instructors, dance instructors, and coaches in baseball, football, soccer, and tennis, among other sports, all use the same principle.

The eight practices are the footwork of innovators. Practice the footwork, and the rest of the moves will come naturally.

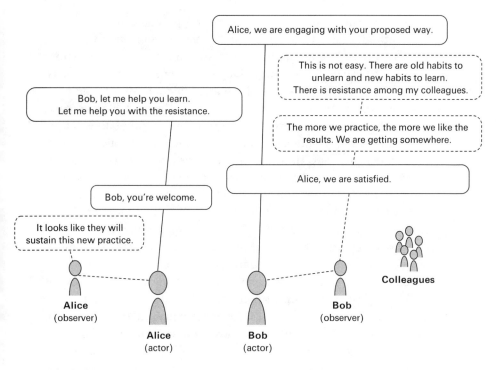

Figure 4.2
Alice and Bob continue their interaction through adoption.

Grounding Assessments for Acceptance

Innovators and adopters make crucial assessments at every stage of the process. When is a possibility an opportunity worth pursuing? What would be an effective plan to realize it? To whom should the plan be addressed? Can the offer be trusted? What expertise is needed on the team? Which feedback from prospective adopters is valuable? What are the consequences of adoption? Is the adoption worth sustaining?

Perceiving and assessing (evaluating) are integral functions of an observer. Our assessments will be more effective if we learn to "ground" them well. That means to provide relevant and compelling evidence that convinces our listeners to accept our assessments. We will examine this practice now.

The basis for our treatment is the work of Fernando Flores (1997), who articulated a theory of assessments and their grounding in the middle 1980s and applied it successfully in business. He made the following claims. The purpose of an assessment is to set a context, orientation, or attitude that motivates people to act on something they care about. The core skill of grounding an assessment is to provide assertions that inspire the listener's trust. Assertions are statements of relevant facts; they produce confidence that we share a reliable and observable basis for our interpretation of the situation. We will extend Flores's basic framework by paying extra attention to grounding that mobilizes action.

It is important to distinguish assertions from assessments. An assertion is a statement that claims something is true about the world. Assertions can be substantiated or refuted through observation and evidence.

An assessment is a statement of evaluation, opinion, or judgment. Assessments are neither true nor false. Instead, they can be *grounded* (supported by evidence) or *ungrounded*. The grounding answers a set of questions that require clarification before the listener can accept the assessment. These questions concern care, standards, domain, and evidence.

Grounding assessments is a complex skill. Its purpose is to allow us to assess whether an assessment is trustworthy for action, enabling the listener to trust that the original assessment will, if acted on, lead to outcomes of value. Many people are not good at grounding. The most common errors include trying to base the grounding on more assessments rather than on assertions, offering insufficient or irrelevant assertions, and not honoring the listener's standards of acceptance. We will discuss these errors shortly.

Assessments are our primary way to prepare for action. Our leadership will fail when we ask our listeners to act based on ungrounded or weakly grounded assessments. If we operate only from feelings, without rigor or clear standards, we will gain a reputation of being "flaky," "insubstantial," "airy," and "ineffective."

It is very important to notice that listeners, not speakers, decide whether a statement is grounded. No matter how hard the speaker works to convince, nothing will happen unless the listener accepts the speaker's grounding arguments. To be good grounders, we have to be good listeners.

What Makes Assessments So Important?

On January 28, 1986, the Space Shuttle Challenger exploded thirty-nine seconds into its flight, killing all seven astronauts aboard. President Reagan quickly convened the Rogers Commission to determine the cause of the accident and to recommend changes that might prevent similar accidents in the future. The commission moved rapidly and issued its report in June 1986.

The investigators heard many theories about the cause and who would be to blame. The most credible theory was that an O-ring, which sealed adjacent stages of the booster rocket, failed because it lost its resilience on that exceptionally cold, frosty Florida morning. There was much argument and finger pointing between NASA managers and engineers of the Morton-Thiokol company about whether engineers had properly warned of the possibility of O-ring failure and, if they had, whether NASA managers ignored the warning in their rush to launch the shuttle. In one of the televised public hearings, physicist Richard Feynman quizzed witnesses about their claims that O-rings remained resilient at 32 degrees. As they maintained their claims of resilience, he casually dropped a sample of O-ring material clamped in a small vise into a glass of ice water. A few minutes later he removed it and showed it did not regain its shape after the clamp was removed. That demonstration demolished the claims and clinched the O-ring theory. The Rogers Commission handed NASA a stinging rebuke for its failure to heed engineers' warnings about O-ring failure in cold weather.

Feynman's demonstration was a brilliant, well-grounded assessment. The brilliance was not in his genius as a physicist, which everyone accepted, but in his mastery of communication. He sensed that everyone was confused by the complexity of all the arguments. He chose a high-school experiment that would crumble all that complexity and place a stark, simple truth before his audience. His timing was perfect. He created suspense and tension in his preamble and heightened the "aha!" moment many people experienced when he suddenly created a new observer for them. Like Louis Pasteur, he was a "master of experimental theater" (Latour 1988).

If you were one of those engineers and you were convinced that O-ring failure was the cause, how would you communicate your conclusion in a way that NASA managers could not ignore? Would you have thought of Feynman's experiment? Or would you have thought, as did the Thiokol engineers, to offer mathematical models showing failure probabilities at various temperatures? Feynman's approach was direct, clear, and compelling. The modeling approach did not require the engineers to take a stand; it left the NASA managers to decide what failure probabilities they might accept. Might the outcome have been different (launch aborted) if the engineers had offered different grounding for their assessments?

We cannot know because, as the Rogers Commission found, NASA managers might not have been open to Feynman's conclusion. But if you, as one of the engineers, were skilled at grounding assessments, maybe they would have listened to you and you might have averted the disaster. Would you want to be without that skill?

You do not have to imagine yourself as an engineer supporting NASA. Think of a situation in which your manager or a member of your team turned to you at a key moment and asked for your evaluation of the situation. Your ability to provide a well-grounded assessment of the facts and the risks at that moment can easily make the difference between whether your opinions guide your group's actions and whether you will be taken seriously by the others.

Think of yourself in a group while a manager is putting together a team that you really want to join. The manager is going around the table asking each of you to state your expertise, what you have to offer to the team. Based on what you say, he either selects you or bypasses you. Can you claim your expertise in a way that compels him to trust you? Do you sound confident and knowledgeable? Or do you sound puffy and pretentious?

Think of yourself standing before a group to make your offer of innovation. You will want your audience to accept five key assessments, concluding that:

- The new practice brings great benefits to the group;
- Each member of the group gets a personal benefit;
- The benefits are enough to warrant costs of time, energy, and resources to achieve them;
- The action plan is achievable; and
- You have the expertise and can be trusted to help them accomplish it.

You are likely to find the fifth assessment to be the most challenging because it is the most personal for an innovator. Can you do it?

These are strong reasons for all of us to be competent at grounding assessments. Other people's lives or livelihoods can depend on our assessments. So do our own. Let's take a closer look. What constitutes a well-grounded assessment? What do we practice so that we can do it every time?

Anatomy of Assessments

Grounded assessments do directly produce action. They set a context for consideration, negotiation, and commitment. The commitment produces the action.

Let us examine in detail the structure well-grounded assessments that enable acceptance. Table 4.3 summarizes: An assessment grounded for acceptance is (1) believable (2) toward a purpose (3) in a domain (4)

Table 4.3
Anatomy of an Assessment Grounded for Action

Frame	Does the assessment fit with listeners' beliefs?
Domain	To what community, discourse, discussion, situation, or event does the assessment apply?
Purpose	What is the point? What are the concerns? Does anyone care?
Supporting assertions	What assertions (facts) are offered to support the assessment? Are they relevant to the domain and purpose? Are there enough of them to make the case?
Standards	Are the supporting assessments consistent with common criteria of the domain?
Somatic aspects	Does the speaker display confidence? Authenticity? Centeredness?

supported by assertions (5) whose number and relevance satisfies the standards of the listener and are (6) consistent with nonverbal behavior of the speaker. Each of the six aspects is an area about which your listener will have concerns. If you do not provide the answers, your listeners will fill in the blanks and you probably will not like their answers. We will explore these aspects below.

Frame   Suppose that you construct a well-grounded assessment that meets all the criteria we have listed. Will your listeners accept it? Acceptance is ultimately up to the listener. Even if your assessment has a purpose the listener cares about, applies to the listener's domain, and has a sufficient, relevant set of supporting assertions, it's still possible that your listener will not accept it.

Perhaps the single most important reason a listener will reject a well-grounded assessment is that the listener's belief system does not accommodate your assessment or its consequences. Thomas Kuhn (1962) claimed that members of a scientific paradigm are likely to resist anomalies. Accepting the anomalies would disrupt the system. The members would rather ignore or tolerate the anomalies than disrupt their beliefs. A well-grounded assessment of an anomaly can meet this fate.

Cognitive scientist George Lakoff (2003) uses the term *frame* for the same issue. In political debate, he says, one's ideological frame easily prevails over contradictory evidence. Innovation expert Terry Pierce (2004) says that a proposed innovation can be rejected because it offends too many beliefs. Pierce notes that many successful disruptions started out in disguise—appearing to be compatible with the existing system but ultimately changing it.

Domain If you are not clear about the domain of your assessment, your listeners will be forced to guess what domain you are talking about. If they guess wrong, they may dismiss your apparently irrelevant assessment. Clarity avoids such interpretations.

World Wide Web creator Tim Berners-Lee's original assessment was that the Internet had fallen far short of its promise to facilitate information sharing (Berners-Lee 2000). He was explicit that "Internet" meant all the computers worldwide served with Internet protocols, and "information sharing" meant access to all files and documents made public by their owners. He focused his proposal for hyperlinks on file sharing in the Internet. He was not interested in more general uses of hypertext systems and editors.

Purpose With a clear purpose, your listeners are less likely to become confused about what the point of your assessment is, or what you want them to do. If they do not see the point, they will ignore your assessment.

Tim Berners-Lee's assessment about the Internet led him to focus on file sharing because files were the main containers of information. At the time, file sharing was cumbersome and difficult. With his assessments he created a sense of urgency to provide a way to download any file simply by clicking on a hyperlink pointing to it.

Supporting Assertions Assertions are claims about what is observable in the world. They take the form of facts, evidence, propositions, and true–false statements. They can be verified by witnesses.[1]

1. The "detective exercise" is a simple but effective practice to train for assertions. Put a set of objects on a table. Write down a description of what you see on the table. Ask other people in your group to do the same. When everyone is done, each person reads his or her statement; the others critique by saying which statements were assertions and which were assessments. When many people first try this, they discover that half their statements contain assessments. For example, you might say, "The pen was placed neatly near the pad," instead of "the pen was laid parallel to the edge of the pad about two inches away on the left." It takes real practice and discipline to write down only assertions about what you see on the table.

On the one hand, for example, the statement "Bob received an award for his work" is either true or false and can be verified by someone who was present at the ceremony. On the other hand, a report of one's internal state, such as "I am elated by my award," is not an assertion by this definition because there is no way another observer can verify one's private state.

Standards of Acceptance   Under what conditions do listeners accept a speaker's grounding? There are three:

1. *Supportive assertions*   Only assertions count as supporting statements. Other assessments do not. It pays to be rigorous in distinguishing facts from opinions when supporting your assessment.

2. *Relevant*   The supporting assertions are in the same domain as the assessment. Listeners often characterize relevant assertions as concrete, direct, specific, and clearly related to the purpose of the assessment.

3. *Sufficient*   The supporting assertions all meet community standards. This means that you have supplied assertions for each standard, and you have supplied enough assertions to meet expectations about the quantity of evidence. For example, the standards for expert performance are higher than for beginners; you will have to offer more evidence to support a claim of expert performance.

Here is an example where an assessment fails to persuade the listener because the assertions are not supportive or relevant:

"I think you should choose me as the new software project team leader."
"Why?"
"I am very smart. My IQ was measured at 160."
"Why else?" ·
"I work hard. I got A's on all homework assignments in college."
"Why else?"
"I am a leader. I was chosen as captain of my football team."
"Sorry."

These claims are all assessments, not assertions; it is not obvious that a high IQ, all A's, and the football team captainship qualify one to be a software team leader.

Here is an example where the grounding is relevant but is not sufficient to convince the listener:

"I think you should choose me as the team leader for the new software project."

"Why?"

"I was team leader for three other projects, all of which delivered on time, within budget, and satisfied the customer."

"How big were the systems you built?"

"About ten thousand lines of code each."

"Sorry, but the system we are trying to build will have over a million lines of code. Large systems are a different ball game and I don't have confidence you can deliver what I want with your current level of experience."

The listener sees a qualitative difference between a ten-thousand-line system and a one-million-line system. The speaker has provided no evidence that he can deal with larger systems.

Somatic Aspects   Even if you have been careful about the frame, purpose, domain, supporting assertions, and standards, your listeners may still not accept your assessment. The reason is that your listeners also make judgments based on your nonverbal communications. Based on your behaviors, they silently make several assessments about you, notably with regard to:

1. *Commitment*   Do you believe deeply in your purpose and the assessments you are making? Are you prepared to go to great lengths to achieve your purpose? Will you find ways to deal with obstacles?

2. *Authenticity*   Do you speak without pretension about your purpose and what you can and cannot do? Do you speak sincerely from the heart? Do you genuinely care about your purpose?

3. *Centered*   Do you have great clarity and focus? Do you bring the necessary skills and resources to do it? Are you confident that you can achieve your purpose?

You communicate these aspects through your behavior. For example, if you keep sliding into tangents from your main story, your listeners may wonder about your commitment. If you avoid eye contact, or if you do not seem fully present and engaged, they may wonder about your authenticity. If your shoulders are hunched up and your neck stiff, or if your breath is shallow and your voice squeaky, they may wonder about your centeredness because your words and body are not sending the same signals.

As part of your practice, therefore, you may want to get another person to observe you and share their assessments of you in these aspects. It is often very hard for you to tell by yourself what nonverbal cues you are sending and how others are responding to them.

Example: Claim of Expertise

You claim expertise whenever you say can perform at a certain level of skill in a domain. For example, you might claim to be a novice at chess, a competent programmer, a violin virtuoso, or a master of graphic design. Each of these claims is an assessment. Can you ground a claim of your own expertise and get others to accept it?

Claims of expertise are important throughout the innovation process. When you make your offer or work for adoption, you want your listeners to accept that you have the expertise to deliver the result. When you form a team, you want your team members and customers to accept that the team has the competence to achieve its mission.

In any domain you can claim at least seven levels of skill (Dreyfus 2001; Denning 2002). In the innovation framework, we have distilled them into three levels: novice, skillful (competent), and masterful. Let us consider the last two here. In proposing innovations, you want to appear to be at least competent, if not expert. What does it mean to ground assessments of competent or expert performance? Commonly accepted criteria for these two levels are:

• *Competent* The competent person has the skill to accomplish standard tasks properly according to generally accepted standards for competence in the domain. This person is familiar with all the standard situations and knows how to act without having to figure them out. When faced with a new situation, this person invokes the basic ground rules and figures out an appropriate course of action. This person can be relied on to interact well and responsibly with customers, leaving them satisfied without the intervention of a supervisor.

• *Expert* The expert has a high degree of problem-solving skill honed with considerable practice and many varied experiences. Others admire the expert's style of performance. The expert's way of speaking and observing seems to dispel the fog of complexity. Competent performers come to the experts for advice with nonstandard situations. The expert can solve many problems that people of less skill find difficult or impossible. The expert's intuition leads immediately to appropriate and rapid action without having to "figure things out." The expert can design new practices that help people avoid problems in the future (innovation). The expert copes with new situations though improvisations and is as likely to rewrite the basic ground rules as to try to figure out how to apply them in the new situation. The expert is recognized as such by members of the community and in particular by other experts.

Consider the examples of Alex and Barbara, both claiming to be expert programmers.

• *Alex*   I am an expert programmer. I have been writing programs for over fifteen years. I have worked in several kinds of environments including database services, financial services, transportation, and university computing centers. I have written code for DoD [U.S. Department of Defense] applications. I am thoroughly familiar with the modern languages Java, Ada, and C++, as well as assembly code. I follow good programming practice such as proper indentation, structured comments, and user-friendly documentation. I graduated from college with straight A's and scored very high on the programming aptitude test.

• *Barbara*   I am an expert programmer. I have been programming for fifteen years. Over the years I have used every major programming language and have written thousands of applications ranging from tens of modules to several thousands of modules. Among my major accomplishments is a database system for Citibank, a traffic control system for Philadelphia, and an air traffic control system for the FAA. I have been named chief programmer for every programming team I've been on for the past five years. Many people in my organization come to me to help solve problems they are having trouble with; I can usually help them in a jiffy. Some of my programs are included in standard distributions with Unix and Oracle systems. My customers frequently send letters of commendation to my bosses. I receive frequent speaking invitations to discuss risks of programming and methods to assure safe programs for critical applications. I received two awards for programs I wrote, including the ACM software system award.

Most people react that Barbara is an expert, but not Alex. Alex has not met the stringent criteria for expert. He is vague about his accomplishments. He offers no evidence that anyone thinks his work is good or that anyone recognizes his expertise. He offers some assertions that have no relevance to the claim (getting A's in college). While Alex refers to his activities, Barbara focuses on the outcomes of her work and how they are regarded, used, and recognized.

We have designed a powerful exercise that gives students practice with grounding assessments in the context of claiming expertise. We ask each student to stand before the group, make a claim of expertise (competent or expert), and ground the claim. After some questions and answers we take a poll to see how many listeners accepted the claim. We then ask the listeners to give feedback about what aspects of the presentation and discussion were most and least persuasive.

Our students find this to be a challenging exercise because it is very personal. They want to discuss an area of great competence without appearing to be pretentious or self-promoting.

The exercise reveals a gap between our students' theoretical understanding of a grounded assessment, and their own ability to actually *perform* it. They understand the concept of grounding but do not embody the practice. This exercise demonstrates how easily one can be sloppy about domain, purpose, supporting assertions, and standards of acceptance. It reveals how often we do not listen to how our listeners are reacting—we do not notice that we are not addressing all their criteria, that we are offering assessments instead of assertions, or that our assertions are not relevant to their concerns.

Here are examples of what some of our students learned in the claim-of-expertise sessions.

• *Stefan*   A Marine captain, he claimed to be an expert marksman. His grounding was simply that the Marines had run him through a rigorous training course and he passed the expert-qualification tests. To his surprise, many others in the room did not accept his claim. He defended it vigorously and the discussion started to get heated. Finally one of his classmates asked, "What are the standards for expert marksman in the Marines?" Stefan then listed them and showed how he had met each one. Now there were many nods of approval and his classmates changed their minds. In the debriefing at the end, he concluded that he was mistaken in assuming that his classmates understood the Marine criteria and their rigor. Once his classmates learned about the criteria, and accepted them, it was easy for them to accept him as the expert.

• *Judith*   Judith claimed to be competent at mathematics. She was disarmingly shy and started slowly and tentatively. Then she started to recite a long list of awards she had received, contests and scholarships she had won, and special invitations from math experts for her to help them. Her voice became strong and her posture straightened. When she finished, there was pure silence in the room. Someone finally broke the silence, saying, "You claimed competence. I don't accept your claim." Her face went white. He smiled and said: "I would easily accept a claim of virtuoso. You undersell yourself. I wonder how many opportunities you have missed." Judith knew she was good at math, but she did not realize others might see her as virtuoso. She had a self-characterization that might be holding her back. After that time, she did not hold back with her classmates and they always deferred to her on questions about mathematics.

• *Jenny* An extremely shy Asian student, she was so quiet that the other members of the class knew nothing about her. After we announced the exercise, she came up after class and asked if she really had to do this. When she finished her degree, she explained, she would be returning to her home country where a job already awaited her. We assured her that grounding assessments will be useful to her at home and asked her to do her best. She shrugged and said, "OK." The next week, members of the class presented their claims of competence. Well over half of the students were surprised to find that their classmates did not accept their claims. Jenny spoke last. By that time she was shaken by the difficulties her predecessors had with getting their claims accepted. Jenny claimed to be a competent schoolteacher. She listed teaching experiences she had in her home country and an award she had received for teaching. She gave numerous factual statements of accomplishment. One by one, the jaws of her classmates dropped open in amazement. They said they had no idea that a gifted teacher was in their midst. They wanted to hear her stories about her experiences and what she had learned from them. From that moment on they granted her great respect.

Jenny taught them, through her own example, what a grounded assessment looks like and how powerful a leadership move a grounded assessment can be.

When we do the claim-of-expertise exercise, we find that many students do not make the immediate "sale"; often as many as half of their listeners are skeptical. The Q&A sessions help resolve many of the skeptics' questions and result in a high acceptance rate. It is evident that being willing to engage in a conversation to answer questions can go a long way toward providing grounding that is sufficient and relevant.

A well-grounded assessment is not a PowerPoint slide with proper bullets; it is the result of a conversation between the speaker and listeners. Grounding assessments is an art of producing listening in others.

Assessments of Value, Trust, and Satisfaction

In discussing the adopter's experience of innovation at the beginning of the chapter, we said that adopters make frequent assessments of value, trust, and satisfaction (table 4.2). All three assessments are crucial to the success of the innovation. Innovators must generate positive assessments from their adopters in all three categories.

These assessments correspond to the beginning, middle, and end of a series of actions. The series begins with our seeing value in a desired outcome; at that moment, we can commit to the actions to produce the outcome. In between, we persevere because we trust that the desired result will be achieved. The series ends when the outcome is produced and we commit to accept it; at that moment, we register satisfaction with the outcome. Value gets us started, trust keeps us going, and satisfaction allows us to complete.

• *Value*   We judge that an outcome is valuable if it provides something that we care about and want to have. Value can take many forms: money, professional reputation, recognition, advancement, or self-esteem. There are often many ways to generate value. Value can be immediate (a short-term gain) or deferred (a long-term gain). Because perceived value is individual, the innovator may have a challenge to find how to shape the offer so that the target community will collectively perceive value.

• *Trust*   Trust is a belief that the future outcome will be valuable and satisfactory. Without some degree of trust people will not enter a transaction in the first place. Extreme distrust can degenerate into conflict, perhaps, in a broader public context, even war.

• *Satisfaction*   We judge that an outcome is satisfactory if it meets our expectations. Innovators must pay attention to what expectations they generate. Satisfaction is assessed after the action is complete. It is fundamental in every interaction between a provider and a customer (Denning and Dunham 2003). An innovation process that produces unsatisfactory adoptions will not be sustainable.

Trust is the most complex of the three assessments. You will not get very far unless potential adopters and teammates trust you. You will want to organize yourself so that people will trust you and your assessments and offers.

One of the first treatments of trust from a language-action perspective was by Robert Solomon and Fernando Flores (2001). They said that trust is an assessment of a person's competence and sincerity, coupled with an expectation that the person will take care of our interests and an acceptance of the possibility that the person will betray us. They say that trust can be earned (when the person's actions demonstrate these criteria) or simply granted.

Sociologist Piotr Sztompka offers a richer analysis (2000). He says trust is more than a set of assessments; it is a bet that the person will deliver an expected outcome and a willingness to commit based on the bet. It is never a sure bet. It is a commitment to action based on the assessments that the person is:

- Competent and skillful
- Sincere
- Reliable
- Efficient and cost effective
- Respectful of one's interests
- Caring
- Honest
- Fair
- Just

There can be no innovation without trust. Because they are asked to take risks, adopters need to trust that the outcome will be positive and that the innovator brings the right qualities to make it happen. Trust mobilizes the adopters' actions. As an innovator, you have a lot to live up to, to earn the trust of your potential adopters.

Common Breakdowns around Assessments

There are numerous ways for an assessment to fail. Table 4.4 lists the most common. The first six are direct violations of the anatomy of an effective assessment. The last three are additional issues that often arise even if the anatomy is intact; we describe them briefly in the next paragraphs.

- *Permission* People are not always open to receiving assessments. Unless you have a relationship with them in which you are entitled to make assessments, it is better to ask for permission before giving your assessment. Examples of implicit permission include bosses assessing employees, coaches assessing players, spouses assessing each other, parents assessing children, and consultants recommending new actions for a company. In most others, permission is not implicit.
- There is a curious flip side to permission. We often uncritically grant permission to others to make assessments of us. Strangers can offer ungrounded negative assessments that will stop us in our tracks or side-track us to actions that do not serve our purposes. They can also offer ungrounded positive assessments and lure us into actions that do not

Table 4.4
Common Breakdowns around Assessments

Frame	Failure to understand that an assessment is disharmonious with the listener's belief system
Purpose	Lack of clarity about the purpose of the assessment. Not noticing that the purpose is not a concern for the listener.
Domain	Lack of clarity about the applicable domain of the assessment
Supporting assertions	Failure to provide relevant facts and evidence. Attempting to use assessments as ground.
Standards	Failure to acknowledge and respect community standards, e.g., substituting one's own standards Failure to interact with people to find out what standards they apply
Somatic aspects	Failure to act on discrepancies between spoken and nonverbal cues
Permission	Failure to get permission to give or receive assessments
Characterizations	Automatically accepting assessments (about oneself or others) to be permanently true or applicable in all domains
Meta-assessments	Making assessments about assessments, thereby getting farther from acting on the original ones

serve our purposes. In the best case, these ungrounded positive or negative assessments are distracting, and in the worst case, are manipulative.
• *Characterizations*   Assessments that we believe to be true in all situations or at all times are characterizations. These are always ungrounded because assessments cannot be valid in all domains, and they cannot be valid and unchanging for all time. For example, I might believe I am not good at management, or that you are unreliable, or that the organization cannot be changed. Maybe I am a good manager in some domains, you are reliable in some domains, and the organization can be changed. Characterizations deny us, other persons, or organizations the opportunity to change. We think they are always the same, and that is that.[2]

2. Many people have inflated self-characterizations. The Educational Testing Service, for example, once found that 70 percent of people taking SAT and GRE exams believed themselves to be in the top 50 percent! Ungrounded, inflated characterizations about your own capabilities can lead to costly failures when a project you thought you can do is beyond your actual capabilities. Rather than learning from the experience by reevaluating your characterization, you blame it on external factors. Thus you remain trapped in your characterization and cannot change.

• *Meta-assessments*   Assessments about assessments often distract from action around the original assessment. For example, when your Internet connection dies, you may find yourself diverted into an assessment that the Internet should not have failed, and then to even more tangential assessments such as that your service provider is incompetent, or Congress failed to pass an appropriate accountability law. None of these meta-assessments helps you get service restored. It takes some skill to recognize meta-assessments and let go of them.

Observing the Observer

In chapter 1, we said that an important element of the prime innovation pattern is the ability to observe the current common sense that is sustaining a disharmony or unrealized opportunity. That observation is a prerequisite for designing an innovation and, along with it, a new common sense.

Since the current common sense is the way that the members of the community are observing their world, the process of describing the common sense is a form of observing the observer. Domain mapping is an organized practice for doing this. Domain mapping yields an interpretation about the practices, organization, and tacit beliefs of a social community.[3] It constructs a social observer of a domain. It enables the design of tools that support existing practices (Denning and Dargan 1996) or the design of new practices (Winograd and Flores 1987).

For innovators, domain mapping can be a tool to help understand the nature and sources of disharmonies and to support speculations about changes to the domain that would resolve disharmonies. In most cases, achieving a desired outcome will require changes to be made simultaneously in the structure, theory, and technology of the domain (Schon 1971); the mapping process can help reveal these aspects.

Table 4.5 defines the key elements to be produced by domain mapping and illustrates them using the Internet as example.

---

3. The overall framework of what exists in a domain is sometimes called the *ontology* of the domain. An ontology is a conceptual framework for interpreting the domain in terms of recurrent actions. In the mid-1980s, Fernando Flores used the term *ontological reconstruction* for the process of articulating an ontology. It is not an easy process because many of the deeply embodied practices of a domain are difficult to observe. See Winograd and Flores (1987).

Table 4.5
Elements of Domain Mapping

Aspect	Definition	Internet Examples
Language	Nouns naming objects manipulated, including tools and equipment. Verbs naming actions on objects. Jargon. Idioms.	Link, fiber optics, encoding, packet, router, client, server, hyperlink, domain name, IP address, protocol (e.g., TCP, IP, HTTP, FTP, SSH, RSA), daemon, browser
Practices	Domain members' recurrent actions, habits, processes, roles, standards of assessment	Universal use of domain names, IP addresses, text encoding, attachment encoding, and protocols (HTTP, FTP, TCP, IP, etc.). XML data definition. Email. Remote login. Clicking on a link. Web menu in left margin. Browser standards.
Breakdowns and concerns	Breakdowns are interruptions of standard practices caused by tools breaking, people intervening, external circumstances, etc. Concerns are conditions that receive attention because they are breakdowns or opportunities.	Breakdowns include: worms, viruses, intruders, copyright violators, bandwidth hogging video files, inability to validate senders, lack of access for some people. Concerns include: access to all useful information, fast search, high availability, fast response, protection.
Moods, speculations, and controversies	Prevailing moods in the community, and their historical origins. Speculations about new possibilities. Controversies.	Resignation over whether a good solution can be found for worms, viruses, hacking, and spam. Speculations about future architectures such as "Internet 2." Controversies over privacy practices and "Net neutrality."
Belief system	Shared beliefs that drive or constrain the previous aspects. Sometimes called the behavioral "rule set" of the domain.	Anonymous transactions, no caller ID, security can be added on, information is free once posted, everyone has equal right to bandwidth, lack of connection a social injustice, bits not atoms, etc.

Belief systems often are the hardest to fully describe; yet describing them in a fair manner often is the key to designing new practices that would eliminate the breakdowns. On the Internet, for example, the lack of security can be linked to beliefs that anonymous transactions and no caller ID protect privacy.

An innovator who concludes that a key assumption in the belief system is the cause of a chronic breakdown cannot realistically expect an announcement of that conclusion to induce the community to change. People cling steadfastly to their beliefs. The innovator has to confront them with incontrovertible evidence that their belief blocks them from attaining their most cherished goals. Four examples will illustrate.

Louis Pasteur determined from his field experiments that the dead cattle and sheep all harbored the anthrax germ (see this book's prologue and Latour 1988). At the time, however, only a handful of scientists believed in a germ theory of disease; few doctors accepted the germ theory-inspired warning to wash hands regularly; and no rancher or farmer understood much less believed the theory at all. Pasteur's challenge was to demonstrate that a germ caused the disease and that a vaccine could immunize cattle and sheep against the germ. He accomplished this with his dramatic experiment in 1882, whereby the twenty-five sheep that were vaccinated were the only survivors among the total of fifty sheep injected with anthrax.

Albert Einstein resolved a paradox of physics by claiming that two apparently contradictory beliefs were in fact simultaneously true (Einstein 1916). One belief was that the motion of any object could only be measured relative to the observer's frame of reference. The other belief was that the speed of light is the same in all frames of reference. Einstein's special theory of relativity, published in 1905, postulated that both were true and then derived the equations predicting dilation of space and time under motion. Many scientists instantly rejected his theory, but by 1920 the experimental evidence confirming it had become overwhelming.

Today it is widely accepted that the original Internet has important limitations including vulnerability to viruses and hackers, bandwidth hogging by large video file transfers, fraudulent entities, and inability to guarantee deadlines for real-time applications. The debates about designing a new "Internet 2" free of these limitations have revealed significant numbers of people believe that all transactions should by default be anonymous and that there should be no postage for email. They strenuously oppose proposals for caller ID and small charges for sending email, even though they agree that these reforms would eliminate most fraud and spam. They will not budge from their beliefs. They even resist inclusive proposals such as giving people a choice of using the regular Internet or a secure subnet.

Our education system today is under fire for being a high-cost way of providing ineffective results. Much of the system is founded on the belief that practice follows understanding: school systems aim to instill mental models and procedures on the assumption that, with these understandings, graduates will fall into good practices later. Some education reformers have proposed that in fact most learning proceeds in the opposite direction: understanding follows practice. They propose school systems that include considerable immersion in domains of practice. Their proposals have not led to any widespread reform. The challenge for these reformers is to demonstrate that the prevailing belief about education process is the cause of the breakdowns in the education system.

The conclusion is that identifying the beliefs that may cause the persistent breakdowns is hard and subtle work. And when it is fruitful, the innovators still have a tough challenge in getting people in the domain to accept that they need to modify their beliefs before they can solve their problem.

We close with the observation that domain mapping is not the same as the popular practice of trend extrapolation. Trend extrapolation has two aspects: (1) a calculation of the capabilities of a technology at various points in the future, using an equation fitted to the data about the changes of the technology, and (2) a speculation about the social consequences of the extrapolated technology. For example, Ray Kurzweil (2005) reckons from Moore's Law that by 2030, we will be able to construct brain-size computers with all the power of a human brain. He contends that artificial brains will be intelligent but there is no way to tell if the robots housing them will be benevolent toward human beings. A number of people have joined him in calling for safeguards on research to minimize the chance that scientists will design malevolent intelligences that will destroy humanity.

John Seely Brown and Paul Duguid (2002) demonstrated why a whole series of Internet trend analyses of the early 1990s led to the business disasters of 2001. The 1990 predictions warned of the disappearance of libraries, universities, newspapers, and physical workplaces. These predictions failed because the entire social system adapted to, and changed, as the trends unfolded; for example, libraries went digital and online. In contrast with trend analyses, domain mapping focuses on present realities, not predictions of future realities.

Conclusions

We constantly exercise two capacities—observing and acting. Observing is the capacity to perceive and evaluate. How we observe influences what we see and therefore what actions we think are possible. And our actions have consequences that influence how we see things in the future.

The innovation observer operates on two levels simultaneously. The social observer pays attention to practices, value, habits, breakdowns, struggles, care, concerns, customers, assessments, learning, and sources of resistance in the community. The individual observer sees, moment by moment, the most appropriate actions of sensing, envisioning, offering, adopting, sustaining, executing, leading, and embodying to move the community closer to adoption.

One of the most common acts of an observer is making assessments. The assessments of value, satisfaction, and trust permeate the innovation process. Innovators must be observers of how their prospective adopters are assessing their situations and proposed innovations.

More generally, assessments are our most powerful linguistic tool for observing and communicating what we observe. A well-grounded assessment can be a powerful leadership move. Grounding can supply a basis for your listeners to feel that the situation demands action and that the action you call for has tolerable risk and acceptable return. When you are not good at grounding assessments, people are likely to ignore or resist your proposals. When you are good at grounding assessments, people will trust you and seek your advice.

Domain mapping is a practice for observing and assessing the world of concerns of our adopting community. It describes a domain as a whole by its language, practices, breakdowns, concerns, moods, speculations, controversies, and beliefs. It is a powerful first step in designing new practices for a domain.

Bibliography

Arrien, Angeles. 2005. *The Second Half of Life*. Sounds True.

Berners-Lee, Timothy. 2000. *Weaving the Web*. HarperBusiness.

Covey, Stephen. 1990. *The Seven Habits of Highly Effective People*. Free Press.

Denning, Peter. 2002. Career Redux. *ACM Communications* 45 (9):21–26.

Denning, Peter, and Pamela Dargan. 1996. Action-Centered Design. In *Bringing Design to Software*, ed. T. Winograd. Addison-Wesley.

Denning, Peter, and Robert Dunham. 2003. The Missing Customer. *ACM Communications* 46 (March):19–23.

Dreyfus, Hubert. 2001. *On the Internet*. Routledge, chap. 2.

Einstein, Albert. 1916. *Relativity*. Repr., Penguin Classics, 2006.

Flores, Fernando. 1997. The Leaders of the Future. In *Beyond Calculation*, ed. P. Denning and R. Metcalfe, 176–192. Copernicus.

Harris, Bill. 2002. *Thresholds of the Mind*. Centerpointe Press.

Kurzweil, Ray. 2005. *The Singularity Is Near*. Viking.

Kuhn, Thomas S. 1962. *The Structure of Scientific Revolutions*. 2nd ed., University of Chicago Press, 1970.

Lakoff, George. 2003. *Metaphors We Live By*. 2nd ed., University of Chicago Press.

Latour, Bruno. 1987. *Science in Action*. Harvard University Press.

Latour, Bruno. 1988. *The Pasteurization of France*. Harvard University Press.

Lipton, Bruce. 2005. *The Biology of Belief*. Hay House, Inc.

Maturana, Humberto. 2004. *From Being to Doing*. Carl-Auer Verlag.

Maturana, Humberto, and Francisco Varela. 1989. *The Tree of Knowledge*. Shambala. Revised, 1992.

Pierce, Terry C. 2004. *Warfighting and Disruptive Technologies: Disguising Innovation*. Frank Cass.

Schon, Donald. 1971. *Beyond the Stable State*. Norton.

Seely Brown, John, and Paul Duguid. 2002. *The Social Life of Information*. Harvard Business School.

Solomon, Robert, and Fernando Flores. 2001. *Building Trust*. Oxford University Press.

Strozzi-Heckler, Richard. 2007. *The Leadership Dojo*. Frog.

Sztompka, Piotr. 2000. *Trust: A Sociological Theory*. Cambridge University Press.

Trout, Jack. 2008. *In Search of the Obvious: The Antidote for Today's Marketing Mess*. Wiley.

Wilber, Ken. 1996. *A Brief Theory of Everything*. Shambhala.

Winograd, Terry, and Fernando Flores. 1987. *Understanding Computers and Cognition*. Addison-Wesley.

II

The Eight Practices

5

Practice One: Sensing

When we are presencing, our perception connects the highest future possibility with self and whole. The real challenge in understanding presencing lies not in its abstractness, but in the subtlety of the experience.
—Peter Senge

We have eyes but do not see. Ears but do not hear.
—Anonymous

It is because I cannot see what you see that I can see at all.
—James P. Carse

Every innovation begins with a new possibility. Who can not find possibilities can not innovate. Finding worthy possibilities turns out to be a challenge for many people.

How often instead of "Eureka!" have we said, "I wish I'd thought of that!" Or, "How come I can't think up new ideas?"

Is finding new possibilities the result of brainpower? Serendipity? Creativity? Luck? Circumstance? Working environment? While these things are important, they are not essential. Growing good ideas into possibilities is a practice. It is a practice of listening and observing for disharmonies and asking what is possible if the disharmony could be resolved. We call this practice *sensing*.

In our earlier discussion of the prime innovation pattern, we summarized the work of Spinosa, Flores, and Dreyfus (1997). We said: "Innovators find in their lives and work something disharmonious that common sense overlooks or denies. They hold on to the disharmony, allowing it to bother them; they engage with it as a puzzle. Eventually they discover how the commonsense way of acting leads to the disharmonious conflict or failure." The sensing practice guides innovators as they grapple with their conundrums.

Mental practices like puzzle solving, brainteasers, or conceptual blockbusting keep the brain sharp but play a small role in innovation (Adams 2001). Most successful innovators do not focus on the mind at all. The heart of their skill is their ability to hear what people deeply care about and bring forward ways to take care of those concerns. Their skill is rooted in the subtleties of listening.

Four Strategies

The sensing practice aims to generate new possibilities for innovation. We find that successful innovators employ at least one of the following four strategies to do this. Underlying all the strategies is the issue of how the future can be different and better than the past. The future might be better because of a simple process improvement, a departure from prior assumptions and designs, or a discovery of something previously unseen within the current common sense. The four strategies go from the obvious procedural approaches, to increasingly sophisticated sensibilities based on wide exposure to many approaches, and finally to cultivated openness.

1. *Source checking* Experienced innovators have compiled lists of likely sources of opportunities. By consulting these lists, you may find your attention focused in places you would otherwise miss, leading you to a possible resolution of the issue.

2. *Learning with inquiry* By reading books and articles, taking courses, attending workshops, gathering opinions, looking for anomalies, and finding teachers, you can educate yourself about the issue and come to know it well. You are then likely to discover patterns or connections that others have not seen. Those patterns may help you find a possible resolution of the issue. They may also produce a new sense of disharmony to be investigated. The search for new possibilities comes from learning as exploration rather than learning as the finding of answers.

3. *Speculating* This fundamental human practice creates possibilities that become the context for future action. Organized speculation practices such as brainstorming sessions or collaboration workshops may help you locate possible resolutions for the issue. The most powerful speculations come from identifying and questioning background assumptions, going beyond the boundaries of the current common sense.

4. *Sensing* Before articulation, an idea begins with a feeling, often a sensation of disharmony, followed by a struggle to put it into words. By learning to recognize the sensation, you can attune yourself to opportunities for resolving the issue before others become aware of them. The skill at sensing will further empower the prior three strategies.

Source checking orients mostly toward the past (what worked before?), sensing mostly toward the future (what might work next?), and learning and speculating are combinations. Source checking is mostly searching, sensing mostly awakening. Source checking requires the least experience, sensing the most.

You will almost certainly encounter two major breakdowns as you pursue these strategies. One is *inattention*, which occurs when you miss seeing something important because your focus is somewhere else. The other is *blindness*, which occurs when you have no distinctions about something: you are literally unable to see, and unable to see that you cannot see. We will discuss practices for overcoming these two breakdowns.

Why call this practice *sensing* rather than *discovering*? Discovery implies uncovering something that already exists. If, as is often the case, the possibility for innovation does not yet exist, discovery will not find it. If it does exist, someone else may discover it before you. Discovery, therefore, seems to carry an inherent competitive disadvantage. There is a definite competitive advantage to developing the skill of sensing.

As you gain in skill you will come to a point where you no longer need to remember checklists, rules, and guidelines. Your awareness will be trained to be always on the lookout, like good radar, for new opportunities. Trained, alert awareness is part of the habit of innovators and leaders.

Strategy 1: Source Checking

Various authors have identified the most common sources of innovations. Peter Drucker (1985) studied seven sources extensively. Ideation International (ideationtriz.com) perfected a discovery process based on patterns in over three million patents worldwide. Their discovery process began in Russia as the "Theory of Inventive Problem Solving," which has the acronym TRIZ in Russian. Charles Spinosa, Fernando Flores, and Hubert Dreyfus (1997) argued that a sensibility to marginal practices and disharmonies is a source of much innovation. James Womack and

Daniel Jones (2003) and Ric Merrifield (2009) demonstrated that organizations can deliver significant improvements in value and innovation
by identifying the highest-value outcomes, and focusing on them alone.
With inspiration from Bruno Latour (1988), Fernando Flores exhorted
us to imitate the practices of Louis Pasteur (see prologue). Philip Kotler
and Fernando Trias de Bes (2003) claimed that defining new games is a
major source of innovation. These twelve sources are summarized in
table 5.1 and are discussed in the next section.

Drucker's Sources

Peter Drucker said that entrepreneurs find their inspirations in one or
more of the first seven categories listed in table 5.1. The following
examples illustrate his categories.

• *Unexpected* Unforeseen failures, successes, and other surprises are
sources. It is well worth probing the reasons behind the surprises. Apple
Computer was surprised by the failure of its hand-held Newton; it took
the lessons learned into the design of the Mac OS X and abandoned its
attempts to build general personal digital assistants (PDAs). Apple was
later surprised by the wild success of the iPod, originally conceived as a
secondary line to bring great design to a small, personal portable recorder;
Apple quickly made iPod a central business line and spawned new industries of iPod accessories and imitators. Apple then built the iPhone's
success on the iPod's. Apple responded to an unexpected turn in the
marketplace—music industry lawsuits over file sharing on the Internet—
by creating iTunes, a legal downloading service for iPods.

• *Incongruities* Gaps between expectations and reality are opportunities for innovation. Tim Berners-Lee noticed that the Internet was not
living up to its promise of information sharing and proposed a way to
refashion it around hyperlinks. This book is responding to an apparent
missing link between innovation process and personal practice. Thomas
Kuhn (1962) showed that scientific revolutions begin only when the
evidence contradicting existing theory becomes too conspicuous to
ignore. Adrian Slywotsky (1996) showed that new business models
emerge when business leaders recognize that the current system is not
attracting customers as it used to.

• *Process needs* Bottlenecks and wasteful steps in existing processes are
opportunities for innovation. Dell computer company introduced a user-
driven Web interface for ordering customized computers, eliminating
delays, mistakes, and excess inventory. Around 1910, Navy Lieutenant

Table 5.1
Innovation Sources

Type	Explanation	Advocate
Unexpected events	Unexpected (unplanned) successes or failures; outside events	Drucker
Incongruities	A gap between reality and common belief; aspects that do not fit together; disharmonies	Drucker
Process need	A bottleneck in a critical process	Drucker
Change of industry structure	New business models, distribution channels, modes of business	Drucker
Demographics	Changes in groups by age, politics, religion, income, etc.	Drucker
Change of mood or perception	Change in the way people see the world (e.g., post 9/11 terrorism), current fashion, convention, etc.	Drucker
New knowledge	Application of new knowledge, often involving scientific advances and convergence of different areas	Drucker
Patent patterns	Identifying recurring patterns of invention from analyzing millions of patents	Ideation International
Value maximization	Simplifying all processes to support only the highest-value outcomes of the organization	Womack and Jones; Merrifield
Marginal practices	Adapting practice to recognize what appears marginal to mainstream thinking or practice	Spinosa, Flores, and Dreyfus
"Dying cows"	Discerning and responding to deep, strongly felt concerns within a community	Flores; Latour
New games	Defining new rules of interaction and new objectives to be achieved	Kotler and Trias de Bes

William Sims developed technology for continuous-aim gunnery, improving seaborne gunnery accuracy from well below 1 percent to over 50 percent. In the 1980s, industrial engineers exploited esoteric queuing network technology to map out and then relieve bottlenecks in manufacturing processes, creating a whole industry for performance optimization. Womack and Jones (2003) extended the lean-thinking principles of the Toyota automobile production line to general corporate processes.

• *Changes of industry structure* Customers flock to new business models that produce more value than traditional ways of doing business. In the 1960s small "mini mills" cropped up in the steel industry and turned scrap into cheap steel such as rcbar (Christensen 1997). The mini mills eventually moved into manufacturing high-grade cheap steel; the large steel mills fell on hard times after refusing to follow this trend. In the early 1980s Intel Corporation came to believe that memory chips would become worldwide commodities; as a result the company abandoned its memory chip business and focused exclusively on processor chips. In the 1980s IBM noticed that many individuals wanted to own personal computers, not mainframes; they built the IBM PC that became the industry standard. Starbucks prospered by offering a coffee "experience" to replace the standard office coffeepot.

• *Demographics* Changes in groups by age, politics, religion, or income create opportunities for innovation. The looming massive retirement of the baby boomers has created a search for new kinds of pension systems and for federal Social Security reform. The influx of Latin American immigrants has fueled a booming market in Latino goods.

• *Changes of mood or perception* Shifts of the public mood or of conventional wisdom in an industry sector create opportunities for innovation. The fall of communism in 1989 changed the public mood to cautious optimism about a world without war. The 9/11 terrorist attacks shifted the public mood to a concern for homeland security. The global financial crisis of 2008 to 2009 changed the public mood from consumption to savings. The rise of identity theft and fears of disabling attacks to the electric grid spurred a new public concern for cyberspace and critical infrastructure protection (Lewis 2006).

• *New knowledge* New scientific and technological knowledge always creates opportunities for innovation. Many organizations maintain research labs or buy startups to help them generate or discover knowledge that they can exploit during a narrow window of opportunity. The technology world is filled with such examples. The electronic word processor killed the typewriter. The electronic calculator killed the slide rule. The Internet created a new telecommunications infrastructure that is gradually replacing telephone and broadcast media.

• All these sources are about exploiting change that is already underway and can be spotted by the astute observer. Although exploitation of change is not the same as creating new change, Drucker believes that most innovation (except in the area of new knowledge) comes from early recognition and exploitation of change-making trends.

Drucker says that the first four sources are internal: they are noticeable mainly when one examines challenges to one's business or industry sector. The other three sources are external: they are noticeable when one examines the larger context in which the organization does business.

Drucker says that new knowledge is the riskiest source. It is often unpredictable how new knowledge will affect a community and which competitor will win in the end. The window of opportunity from the time the knowledge is available until the time it can be exploited is narrow: many competitors pop up simultaneously, and only the few who are lucky enough to avoid missteps succeed. Drucker cautions against thinking new knowledge is the main source of innovation. He thinks that fewer than 20 percent of all innovations come from this source.

The new knowledge category refers to the pursuit of new knowledge for its own sake, as in scientific or engineering research. An opportunity in another category pursued by applying new knowledge belongs primarily to that category; thus applying a materials breakthrough to prevent wear in a critical part of a machine counts as alleviating a process need. Drucker believes that such innovations are more plentiful, easier to come by, and less risky in the other categories.

The pipeline model cited in chapter 3 is based on the notion that innovation always starts with the creation of a new idea. Drucker challenged this notion by pointing out six other sources of innovation that are not explained in this model.

Patent Patterns
Starting in 1946, Russian inventor Genrich Altshuller began developing TRIZ (as already noted, the Russian acronym for Theory of Inventive Problem Solving). The Kishinev School in Moldova took it over in 1985 when Atschuller retired. In 1992, members of the Kishinev School moved to the United States, where they helped found Ideation International, which continues to develop and apply the method. Their method is based

on an extensive "analysis of over 3 million worldwide patents, from which approximately 1000 patterns of invention and more than 500 patterns of technological, market, and organization advancement have been extracted" (ideationtriz.com). They have encapsulated their knowledge into a software package that leads a user systematically through the patterns to find those that might become a new invention or innovation. Many users find the software an eye-opening experience because it has them look at aspects they would never have considered under any other method.

Value Maximization
Over time, organizations accumulate many processes and rules to achieve many outcomes. The sheer complexity eventually drags them down. Womack and Jones (2003) advocated "lean thinking," a philosophy of treating all low-value outcomes as waste and eliminating all actions and processes that produce them. Ric Merrifield (2009) similarly advocates periodic "rethinking" of an organization by identifying the highest-value outcomes, dropping commitments to the low-value outcomes, and simplifying all organizational processes to support the high-value outcomes well. Drucker (1985) would regard this as a form of "process needs." It is capable of producing significant innovations.

Marginal Practices
Spinosa, Flores, and Dreyfus (1997) are critical of Drucker's formulation. They say all one can do with Drucker's list is chase change but not initiate it. They are more interested in how innovators *create* changes. What do innovators notice *before* any change has occurred that signals a new possibility?

Innovators who create change begin by noticing two things: (1) anomalies that can be exploited to bring a change the community would welcome, and (2) a community's mood of receptivity to a change. The mood might be a sense of euphoria as in a rising stock market, discouragement as with rising gasoline prices, or frustration as with spam and telemarketing. The innovator fashions an offer that appeals strongly to people in the mood they are in. The offer is usually based on one of the following:

• *Articulation* Drawing attention to a valued practice that has faded into the background. Example: In 1961 President Kennedy made an appeal to the American pioneering spirit to launch the Apollo space program.

• *Cross-appropriation* Adapting some little-noticed practice from another community. Example: Hypertext became the central practice of the World Wide Web.

• *Reconfiguration* Combining existing practices in a new way. Example: Combining cell phone and digital camera appeals to a community fascinated with gadgets and desirous of sending photos to family and friends.

The common feature behind articulations, cross-appropriations, and reconfigurations is the innovator's special skill of noticing things around the "margins," the "edges," or the "peripheries." These marginal practices and disharmonies easily escape notice because they appear to most community members to have no connection with their concerns. Marginal practices are anomalies because they do not fit the mainstream.

Each of Drucker's categories can be interpreted as the consequence of some marginal practice. The innovator acts on unexpected events, incongruities, process needs, industry or demographic shifts, and changes of perception, which seem initially to be unimportant or out of place. The creation of new knowledge often reconfigures (converges) older, marginal pieces of knowledge to produce something new and useful. Many knowledge workers pay attention to the boundaries between their fields and other fields, boundaries that are often rife with marginal practices. An example is the new field of bioinformatics, a combination of biology and computer science.

This is why Spinosa, Flores, and Dreyfus see marginal practices as more fundamental than Drucker's list of seven sources.

The notion of marginal practice is linked to the notion of blindness to be discussed shortly. Blindness means that people in a community lack a capacity to see certain things that may help them. The skill of observing marginal practices is also a skill to overcome some of the blindness.

Dying Cows

This book's prologue tells the story of "Pasteur and the Dying Cows." We first heard this story from Fernando Flores in 1990. He wanted to illustrate his claims that much innovation consists of transforming practices from the margins to the center, and that the transformation happens most rapidly when it deals with a problem people care deeply about. Pasteur's practice of taking his laboratory into the field where he could analyze for microbes and make vaccines was definitely marginal in the 1880s. In fact, very few people believed in microbes or germs at all. In *The Pasteurization of France* (1988), Bruno Latour wrote that Pasteur had a genius for the "theatre of experiment." Pasteur deduced that the sheep and cows were dying of a microbe-caused disease—anthrax—and he developed an anthrax vaccine. In a famous demonstration with fifty sheep exposed to anthrax, the twenty-five vaccinated sheep survived and the other twenty-five perished. Although his associates thought the demonstration was foolhardy, as an all-or-nothing effort, Pasteur was certain that the vaccine would work and that the timing was perfect. He not only invented the new practice of analyzing for microbes and developing vaccines, he also transformed it into a central practice of science by linking it to a looming economic threat in France.

In the metaphor, dying cows represent major, costly breakdowns that people tried to live with. Dying cows probably appeared a normal occurrence in their world; the innovator's proposal to prevent their deaths may have seemed a fantasy. Pasteur overcame that appearance of fantasy through his "theatre of experiment." Within five years, anthrax vaccination was widespread.

The moral of the Pasteur story is this: innovators, if you want to make an innovation that people will care about and value, look for their dying cows. Show them how to keep their cows healthy.

Not all of Pasteur's proposals were adopted as rapidly. In 1879 Pasteur endorsed an 1840s finding of Dr. Ignatz Semmelweiss that deaths in maternity wards dropped to near zero when all the medical personnel washed their hands; but even with Pasteur's endorsement it took another thirty years before hand washing prior to surgery became widespread. Adoption can be very slow, even with well-grounded assessments, when the new practice does not seem important, or it threatens established political relationships, power structures, habits, and values.

In Flores's mind, the dying cows story is closely linked to the ability to see and exploit marginal practices. The story emphasizes the importance of community receptivity toward a new practice. Innovators are sensitive both to marginal practices and to community moods.

New Games

Some business people say that the job of managers is "innovating within the current game" and the job of executives is "defining new games." Alternate terms for these concepts are *improving a business process* and *defining a new business design*.

Game theorists use the term *game* for a social system whose rules of interaction can be stated explicitly. The game interpretation has arisen in many arenas. Psychologist Eric Berne (1964) interpreted many human interactions as games with both sides gaining or losing from individual moves; he invented "Transactional Analysis" as a way to map the games and guide clients to more productive interactions. Based on the work of linguistic philosophers John Austin (1962) and Ludwig Wittgenstein (1953), philosopher John Searle (1969) interpreted many other human interactions as language games, in which specific moves made by the two sides lead to a mutually beneficial outcome. James Carse (1986) interpreted all human interactions as finite games (played for the purpose of winning) or infinite games (played for the purpose of continuing the play).

Fernando Flores combined these ideas of games with linguistic philosophy in the mid-1980s to produce a very compact description of all games. According to a description by Guillermo Wechsler (2007), a Flores game consists of:

1. Point of the game (what players aim to accomplish)
2. Entities, including actors (the players), equipment (playing field, markers, tokens, flags, tools, etc.), and judges (referees who enforce the rules)
3. Rules of play specifying allowed and unallowed moves
4. Strategies (guidelines for winning)
5. Play

Flores (1997) wanted leaders and managers to see that social practices begin with declarations made by people and that the declarations can change.

The innovation literature frequently distinguishes between sustaining and disruptive innovation (Christenson 1997, Pierce 2004). The game interpretation clarifies the distinction:

• *Sustaining innovation*   Modify equipment, rules, or strategies of the game, in order to enable more efficient, productive, or satisfying play. The purpose of the game is unchanged.
• *Disruptive innovation*   Invent a new game—new rules with a new purpose—in order to take care of some deeper concern with a new approach.

In either case, the innovator will have to induce the community to accept and play in the modified or the new game. Disruptive innovation is harder than sustaining innovation.

The MP3 portable music player illustrates the first approach. The first of these devices appeared in the late 1990s. In the existing game of personal musical entertainment, the small MP3 player, loaded from a personal computer, was much more efficient than a CD or cassette player and the accompanying tote bag of disks or tapes.

Apple's iTunes music distribution service illustrates the second approach. With iTunes, users can access immense online libraries of individual music tracks and download them at reasonable prices without having to worry about copyright violations. Individual artists can offer their songs directly to users without having to share royalties with a music publishing house.

The Internet offers examples of both kinds. The original approach to moving data between computers was with the file transfer protocol program (ftp); the user had to issue many commands to get "ftp" to move one file. A sustaining innovation came as the shareware program "fetch," which offered a simple graphical interface for managing file transfers. A disruptive innovation came when the World Wide Web offered one-click hyperlinks that automatically initiated file transfers. The point of the original game was to transfer files, and of the new game to share information by citing it.

Marketing people refer to similar concepts. Adrian Slywotsky (1996) discussed how new business designs (new games) can disrupt older ones; for example, Starbucks made the home coffee pot obsolete and IBM's personal computer made the mainframe obsolete. Slywotsky said people migrate to the business design that gives them the greatest value. No amount of sustaining innovation will save a dying design. Philip Kotler and Fernando Trias de Bes (2003) said that traditional (sustaining) marketing focuses on differentiating within the same market to make new products as variations of existing ones. Lateral (disruptive) marketing means to define a new market by reinterpreting the point of the game. For example, a breakfast cereal manufacturer might add fruit to an existing cereal; or it could redefine cereal as a snack food for any time of the day.

Summary

Source descriptions and checklists are useful. They get you to focus attention where you may not have thought to look. They are systematic and require little or no training. They make someone else's expertise available to you such that you can use it without being an expert yourself.

Some of the source descriptions are intended by their authors to be guidelines that can be used by any innovator at any level of skill. All you need to do is fit the source description to your circumstances. Drucker's seven categories and the TRIZ database operate this way. Other source descriptions are intended by their authors to be outlines of generative skills: you do not match a pattern to your circumstance; you create the circumstance. The rethinking category brings a sharp focus on the value of an organization's every action. The marginal practices category (and its associate, "dying cows") relies on a skill of interpreting anomalies and disharmonies as signals of opportunities for change. The games category relies on a skill of interpreting a social system as a game and of designing new or modified games.

We believe that your level of skill as an innovator will determine which of these sources will be useful to you. If you are a beginner at innovation, the Drucker checklist or TRIZ software will be very helpful. If you are an expert, you'll probably find rethinking, marginal practices, dying cows, and games to be most useful.

Strategy 2: Learning

It is quite common to find yourself and those around you in chronic perplexity, turmoil, and frustration over ineffective ad hoc solutions to a costly problem. We call this situation *the mess*. Those involved in the mess have tried all the obvious simple solutions and incremental improvements; none has worked. The story of Pasteur and the dying cows discussed earlier is an example of a big mess. A mess is a terrific opportunity for innovation.

Because a mess looks intractable when you're in the middle of it, you will see no obvious path out. Learning is a powerful strategy: *become an expert on the mess*. After a while, you will know more about the mess than anyone. You will start to see patterns that others have missed. Some of these patterns may suggest paths out of the mess. We will return to this in chapter 14, Mastering the Mess.

Learning includes all the usual approaches: find and read all relevant literature, solicit opinions from many people, attend lectures and workshops, find teachers, and run experiments. The modern Internet and world of software tools offer two additional learning approaches that you may find valuable, especially when used together: following the network, and mind mapping.

Following the Network
The Internet offers many resources that can help you learn about a mess: Web pages, databases, newsgroups, discussion groups, blogs, and digital libraries. You can use search engines and follow hyperlinks to find many relevant items. When following the network in this way, you do not

know in advance where it will lead you. The objective is to get to know the network and to see its patterns.

As attractive as this sounds, it is notoriously incomplete. Only a small fraction of print literature is available online, and much of that requires access fees. Therefore, you will only find a small fraction of the literature on a subject by using search engines and following links. Moreover, many documents found by these means are untrustworthy: they are based on unverified sources, attractive rumors and myths, pure speculations, and even fraud. You will need to seek independent sources for key information. You will need to look outside the Internet, following additional connections by relationships and referrals. You can talk to people directly, and you can attend lectures and workshops. You may also need to visit the library to see articles, papers, and books that are not on the Web.

When performing these searches, people often think of a literature as a set of linked containers—files, books, articles, and so on. They see the purpose of the search as locating "interesting" containers and trying to absorb the information they contain. Around 1985, Fernando Flores offered a much more powerful interpretation: *a literature is a network of conversations.* Each text records a snapshot of conversation in the network. With these snapshots, we can deduce who talks to whom, who are the major influences, what are the major communities of thought, and whether communities are isolated or connected. Flores suggested seven questions as a way to locate each document in the network and eventually to map the network:

1. What question do you bring to this author's text?
2. What is the author's main claim?
3. What grounding does the author offer to support the claim?
4. What is the author's motivation or intent?
5. What is the author's context at the time the text was written?
6. What actions does the author implicitly or explicitly call for?
7. Did the author close or open possibilities for you relative to your starting question?

We recommend keeping notes on your answers to these questions for each key document you locate. They will help you identify patterns and compare what the different authors say.

Mind Mapping
British psychologist Tony Buzan (1991) advocated a technique he called "mind mapping" to help people organize complex information sets. The

idea is to start with a central image on a blank page, and then record main and subsidiary concepts emanating from the center in a network. Buzan maintained that the resulting picture depicts the "semantic network" stored in your brain more accurately than a linear outline can. It leads to simpler and more natural organizations of complex topics. Figure 5.1 illustrates with a map of this chapter.

The idea behind mind mapping—using visual depictions of networks—dates back to ancient Greece. What is new is that since 1991 numerous companies have offered software that lets you draw the maps with graphic tools and then incorporate them into texts and presentations.

We know many people who jot notes to themselves in the form of mind maps during meetings. They dynamically map the evolving conversation at the table. When it is their turn to speak, they are able to give coherent overviews and speak with great clarity.

It is easy to use mind mapping to organize complex information sets— such as those generated by following networks. Take each item from the set and place it on the map near other, related items. As items are added, clusters of related items will become apparent. The computer tools make it easy to move items around until groupings and the connections are satisfactory.

Mind mapping is a useful practice for sensing opportunities because it activates a new observer and brings awareness to everything you know about the topic.

Domain Mapping
A key part of the prime innovation pattern (see chapter 1) is the identification of how the current common sense may be creating the disharmony. A domain map is a useful step in identifying that common sense. Domain mapping (introduced in chapter 4) is a useful way to understand the current structure and operating rules of the community. The map can enable us to formulate statements expressing the current common sense—which helps to hold the structure in place—and then to create new possibilities for resolving community disharmonies by proposing modifications of the structure or the rules.

Domain mapping can, unfortunately, be a time-consuming exercise. Many domains are not homogeneous communities, but are interactions among heterogeneous, sometimes cooperating, sometimes conflicting communities. J. Paul Mark's (1987) description of the Harvard Business School demonstrates this with exceptional clarity.

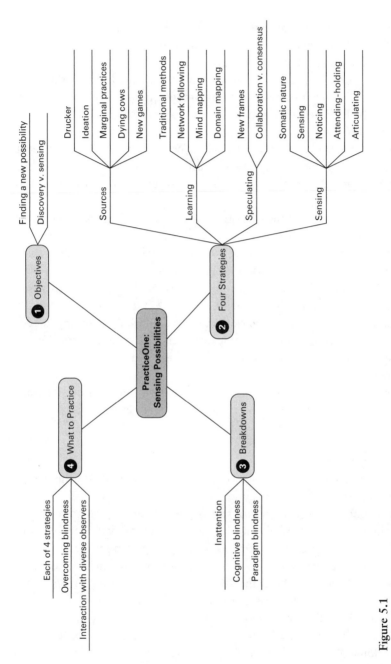

Figure 5.1
A mind map of Practice One. (Produced by ConceptDraw MindMap Pro.)

Strategy 3: Speculations

A speculation is a conversation in which the participants create new possibilities for future action, and set a context in which those actions make sense. Using the term *conversation for possibilities*, Winograd and Flores described it this way:

The key aspect of conversations for possibilities is the asking of the questions "What is it possible to do?" and "What will be the domain of actions in which we will engage?" This requires a continuing reinterpretation of past activity, seen not as a collection of past requests, promises, and deeds, but as interpretations of the whole situation—interpretations that carry a pre-orientation to new possibilities for the future. (Winograd and Flores 1986, 151–152)

The characteristics of a speculation are (1) openness to possibilities and (2) consideration of possible future action with (3) no commitments to action. The generative mood of a speculation will be destroyed if you are close-minded, you do not consider possible future actions, or you try to commit to a possibility too early.

Conversation for possibility is a very important skill for team leaders, who may use it every day, for example:

• The leader declares that some problem is stalling progress and needs to be solved before the team can move forward. The leader calls the team together for a brainstorming session.
• The leader asks a team member to speculate about ideas for resolving a problem.
• The leader (or any team member) has a proposal and wants to explore it with the team. The leader requests a "what if" conversation.

Speculations are not limited to teams and short time spans. They can involve an entire community and can last for many years. An example is the NASA-led speculation about building a space elevator (Edwards 2003, 2005). The space elevator is a vehicle that climbs a cable anchored to earth and to a geosynchronous counterweight at an altitude of about twenty-two thousand miles. Proponents hope that a space elevator would transport people, payloads, power, and gases between earth and space at a fraction of the energy and cost now required for rocket launches. The ongoing speculation involves scientific analyses, engineering prototypes, and prize competitions for components of the system such as cable material, cable installation process, and elevator car design.

Two common forms of organized speculation are brainstorming and collaboration processes.

Brainstorming
Groups frequently create new possibilities for action by brainstorming. Brainstorming is usually a structured conversation in which a facilitator makes sure the group sticks with four ground rules: (1) uncritical openness, (2) no criticisms or evaluations of ideas, (3) no interrupting a speaker, and (4) allowing oneself to be triggered by a comment from another speaker. Tools such as flipcharts and wall screens record ideas and display them for the entire group to see.

Experience with brainstorming is generally good. It works by harnessing the collective wisdom and multiple observers of the whole group. Group brainstorming often generates better possibilities than individuals working alone.

Collaboration Process
A collaboration process goes deeper than brainstorming. It is a facilitated process that aims to expose the deep concerns of stakeholders in the issue, helps them formulate actions that will take care of concerns simultaneously, and seeks their commitment to the actions. It generates a sense of solidarity. We will give more details about collaboration processes in chapter 14.

Unfortunately, many organizations have not been able to make a collaboration process work for them. The reason is that they do not distinguish between collaboration and consensus. Collaboration means working together synergistically to generate solutions to problems and execute action plans. Consensus means to make a minimally disagreeable compromise that may be unsatisfying to many but not bad enough to provoke serious opposition. Collaboration opens possibilities; consensus narrows them. Collaboration leaves everyone with a feeling of "win-win," consensus with a feeling of "win-lose" or even "lose-lose." Consensus is the enemy of collaboration.

In a collaboration process, someone with a new idea can offer to form a team to pursue it. Thus, any idea that can attract a following can be investigated. In a consensus process, competing ideas are put to a vote and only the largest vote-getters will be pursued. Proposals to explore marginal ideas are killed by lack of votes. Since marginal ideas are often the ones that end up as innovations, the consensus process is actually an innovation killer.

It is a common practice in organizational retreats to follow a brainstorming session with a consensus process. The idea is that brainstorming creates possibilities and consensus decides which ones to pursue. This is a mistake. The consensus process kills the marginal ideas produced by brainstorming. It is much better to use a collaboration process.

Strategy 4: Sensing

In many people's minds, the sources, learning, and speculation processes have a strong orientation toward exploration and discovery. It is as if the innovative idea already exists somewhere and can be uncovered by one of these methods. The notion of discovery actually hides much of what goes on when we create.

The reality is that our first encounter with a new possibility is most likely to be in the form of a bodily sensation, not an idea. The idea itself is not yet formed. Yet we can feel something. For example, prior to coming up with new ideas people say:

• Something is bothering me, but I can't put my finger on it.
• I have a gut feeling that draws me in this direction.
• This is gnawing at me, but I'm not quite sure what "this" is.
• The hairs on the back of my neck are tingling. We must be getting close.

What is going on? How often have we experienced such things and just let them go? How often have we dismissed such sensations as annoyances too insubstantial for further attention? In contrast, the most admired innovators have a capacity to latch on to such feelings and not let them go.

In his book, *Weaving the Web,* Tim Berners-Lee (2000) reports on how he came upon the idea for a web of interconnected computers. It was no "Eureka!" moment but a gradual building of a dream in a mood of wonderment over several years:

The Web arose as the answer to an open challenge, through the swirling together of influences, ideas, and realizations from many sides, until, by the wondrous offices of the human mind, a new concept gelled. It was a process of accretion, not the linear solving of one well-defined problem after another.

A computer typically keeps information in rigid hierarchies and matrices, whereas the human mind has the special ability to link random bits of data. When I smell coffee, strong and stale, I may find myself again in a small room over a corner coffeehouse in Oxford. My brain makes a link, and instantly transports me there.

One day, my father was looking for clues about how to make a computer intuitive, able to complete connections as the brain did. The idea stayed with me that computers could become much more powerful if they could be programmed to link otherwise unconnected information." (Berners-Lee 2000, 3–4)

In 2004 Peter Denning led a team that proposed to the U.S. Department of Defense (DoD) to establish the World Wide Consortium for the Grid (w2cog.org). The purpose of W2COG is to provide a collaboration forum where engineers from different agencies and military services can reach agreements on data formats, protocols, and basic services for future networks in which DoD will conduct operations. Denning describes the process of sensing the opportunity that lead to the formation of the W2COG:

Our sense of possibility that gelled into the W2COG was actually a progression of senses. The first stage began in August 2003, when I became director of the Cebrowski Institute at the Naval Postgraduate School. Our Navy sponsors urged us to focus on FORCEnet, Navy's conception of an advanced network to support naval operations. Our initial sense of possibility soon gave way to frustration when we discovered that the Navy did not yet have a reference model of FORCEnet. How could we engineers work on prototypes without the guidance of a reference model?

The second stage began in October 2003 when we teamed up with the Navy command in charge of FORCEnet to make our own reference model. Our initial optimism that we could do this quickly turned to frustration when we discovered that the FORCEnet requirements precluded a simple adaptation of the familiar Internet reference model. We lacked the resources to mount the necessary effort. Then, at the peak of our exasperation, a DoD group previously unknown to us released a reference model for all DoD networks, including FORCEnet. What a relief!

Our sense of relief gave way to more frustration when we discovered that the model had important gaps relative to key FORCEnet requirements. The DoD had no process to fill gaps in its model. It seemed that it would take a very long time fill those gaps and build prototypes for FORCEnet.

The third stage began in early 2004. We had a strong gut feeling that the DoD could learn from the open software movements in the public sector. The DoD was already committed to using commercial off the shelf (COTS) components; why not also the process that produced many of those components? With an open consensus process, the DoD could get what it wanted much faster than it could from any committee of experts. We touted the World Wide Web Consortium (W3C) as a model because of its unrivaled success as an engine of innovation for the Web. This proposal resonated strongly with senior DoD leadership. We received startup funds in September and began organizing W2COG in October. (Peter Denning, personal notes)

The two previous narratives describe the *experience* of finding the possibility that became an innovation. It is important to ferret out these stories and understand them, for their wisdom reveals the way the brain generates possibilities. Mastering such a process is essential for anyone seeking a competitive edge in innovation: generation precedes discovery, which is what most other people are trying to do.

Peter Senge and his colleagues (2004) have dug deeply into these stories and made extensive studies of how people create new possibilities by nursing dreams, gut feelings, and sensations into articulation. They call this process *presencing*. They used a "U" diagram as shown in figure 5.2 to describe its flow.

The figure suggests that the possibility, which appears as an idea in the mind, is actually the outcome of a somatic process consisting of sensing, noticing, attending, holding, and articulating. It is very important that these five elements of the process are somatic: it means we can train them through appropriate mind–body practices.

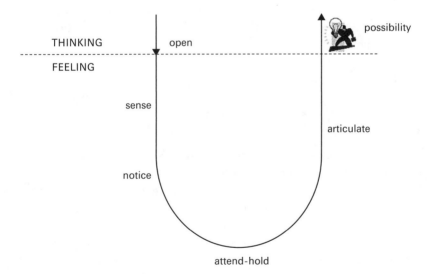

Figure 5.2
A somatic interpretation of the process of creating a possibility shows a descent into the world of feeling followed by an ascent back to the world of thinking. The process begins with our openness to the sensations that precede ideas. We move from having a sensation, to noticing the sensation, and then to attending to it and holding on to it. Attending and holding are part of a struggle to articulate the sensed possibility. Once articulated, the sensed possibility appears in the mind as an idea. In real life, the boundary between thinking and feeling is much fuzzier than this drawing suggests. *Source:* Adapted from *Presence* by Peter Senge et al. 2004.

We summarize these five elements and their supporting practices in table 5.2.

Two practices mentioned in the table are so useful they deserve further comment. One is journaling. This simply means to keep notes of what you are observing and how you interpret what you are observing; and if you make decisions, what you decide and what you expect to accomplish. Such note keeping has numerous benefits: it helps you become a keen observer of the phenomenon, it helps you trace the development of an idea, and it helps you learn where your decision making is reliable.

The other practice is daily meditation. In meditation we sit quietly, focus on something simple such as following our breath, and let go of thoughts that pass by. Meditation helps us see how much chatter fills our minds—and that we can nonetheless let go of any thought. Over time, meditation improves our ability to be more open to looking outside our current frames of reference. Meditation builds our ability to let go of distractions and to be open to subtle sensations outside our focus. Then, outside the meditative state, we can focus on such a sensation and stay with it until it is articulated. Many leaders meditate from twenty to sixty minutes daily.

Breakdowns

Many authors have spoken of many ways that we fail to see new possibilities. Here are some well-known examples:

• *Distractions and obsessions* are issues on which we focus attention at the cost of not seeing other issues.
• *Tunnel vision* is a focus on a future outcome that ignores possible ways the outcome may be disrupted; many technologists are blinded by tunnel vision (Brown and Duguid 2002).
• *Training* is ingrained, habitual response that does not require awareness and can be performed mindlessly.
• *Conditioned tendencies* are invisible, old trained responses that are not appropriate for the current situation (Strozzi-Heckler 1984; Weick 1995).
• *Extrapolations* are the extensions of current trends without regard to influences that might disturb them.
• *Personal biases* are assumptions that filter and interpret what we see.

Table 5.2
Practices Supporting Sensing Process

Stage	Interpretation	Supporting Practices
Open	Allow our senses to alert us to new possibilities.	Practice openness by declaring yourself open and relaxing all contractions in the body. Practice humility, which supports openness, by consciously pushing aside the automatic opinions of prior prejudice. Practice curiosity, which supports openness, by looking for questions to ask, then asking them in a mindset of wonder and learning.
Sense	Become aware of sensations such as a gut feeling, an anxiety, a tingling, a rush, a hot flush, an urge, an impulse. The feeling may be vaguely uncomfortable or it may be uplifting and joyful.	Meditate by sitting quietly for ten minutes or more. Focus on something simple such as following the breath, and let go of thoughts that pass by. This practice helps to still our chattering minds and teaches that we can let go of any thought. With practice, we learn to distinguish between the purely random noises of our bodily processes and the subtle sensations of something new.
Notice	Acknowledge the feelings as signs something is up.	Keep notes in a diary or journal.
Holding-on	Attend to the feeling. Do not let go. Inquire into it.	Practice allowing a bothersome feeling to be bothersome. Pay attention to it. Question it: what is the meaning? Where does it come from? Why is it bothersome? Keep notes in a diary of such feelings, questions, and answers.
Articulate	Find words for the feeling.	Practice writing down the feeling and concerns behind it. Talk with other people and let them help you find the words. Sometimes it may be a struggle to get the feeling articulated, taking days or weeks or months.

• *Structural blindness* is an incapacity to see resulting from physical or biological structure; for example, the eye's blind spot (Maturana and Varela 1987).
• *Linguistic blindness* refers to a lack of distinctions. (Distinctions are brain patterns that enable the brain to distinguish a referenced object from other things in the perceived environment. If the brain does not register a distinction, it cannot name an object or even see it.)
• *World models* are belief systems about how the world works.
• *Community traditions* are belief systems shared by everyone in a community.
• *Scientific paradigms* are belief systems about the workings of nature in various fields (Kuhn 1962).

Joseph Hallinan (2010) has compiled a wonderful book full of ways, including a few not listed above, that the structure of our brains causes us to not see things or to think we see what is not actually there. Two themes run through this list: inattention and blindness.

Inattention is not noticing what we have the capability to see. Something of value is beyond our focus. When using cell phones while driving, for example, we get immersed in the conversation and stop paying attention to the road; because we no longer see potential dangers, we become a hazard to other drivers.

Blindness is the incapacity to see. In our context, we refer not to physical blindness but to blindness resulting from the way the brain works. Two forms are of particular interest here: *cognitive blindness* refers to an individual's incapacity to see, and *community blindness* refers to an entire community's incapacity to see. The new possibility is beyond perception because we (as individuals or communities) have neither language nor embodied sensitivity to grasp it. Typical folk descriptions of these kinds of blindness are: "you cannot see, and you cannot see that you cannot see" and "you do not know, and you do not know that you do not know."

Cognitive scientist and linguistic philosopher George Lakoff (Lakoff and Johnson 2003) uses the term *frame* for a mental construct that limits what we see of the world and interprets what we do see. A frame defines an observer who can see only what is visible or meaningful within the frame. We can become different observers by switching among multiple frames. Lakoff's definition captures the meaning of the common concepts "frame of mind" and "frame of reference."

The inattention breakdown occurs when our attention is focused in a frame of our personal knowledge space that does not allow the possibility; we could observe the possibility by redirecting our attention to another frame that we already know. A striking example is the famous "gorilla video" from the Visual Cognition Laboratory at the University of Illinois (viscog.beckman.illinois.edu/flashmovie/15.php). Viewers are asked to count the number of times white-shirted players pass a basketball among them. Hardly anyone notices the big gorilla that strolls right through the middle of the action, beating its chest. In the "count the passes" frame, the gorilla is invisible.

The blindness breakdowns occur when the possibility is outside any frame we know; overcoming blindness means getting someone else to show us a new frame, or constructing a new frame on our own.

The Johari Window, invented in 1955 and named for its inventors Joseph Luft and Harrington Ingham (1955), is a famous way to expose differences of frame and to reveal frames you cannot see (figure 5.3). The window emphasizes a point of central importance about our frames: the boundaries of the known and unknown depend on the individual observer. One person's blind spot may be obvious to another. This is why, as we shall see, having conversations with other people is a powerful way to overcome blindness.

Because we have to look outside our familiar communities and belief systems, community blindness is much more difficult to break than individual cognitive blindness. When innovators look for marginal practices, they are seeking to overcome community blindness by intentionally looking to other communities and noticing practices that cannot be seen or taken seriously in their own community.

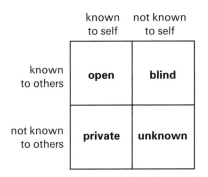

Figure 5.3
The Johari Window divides knowledge known to oneself and to others into four domains. Relationships improve when one's open domain is as large as possible, and one's blind and private domains are minimal. Blindness is relative to the observer; by sharing knowledge observers can overcome their blind spots.

When there is no other community to look to, the innovator has to puzzle over anomalies visible within the current community and invent a new frame that accounts for them. According to late-nineteenth-century physics, for example, light propagated through an unseen medium called the ether; but the most sophisticated experiments to detect the ether measured nothing. No one could explain this anomaly. In 1905, Albert Einstein (1916) offered relativity, a new paradigm in which there was no ether and the speed of light was the same in all frames of reference. He invented mathematical language to talk about space and time in the new framework. Prior to 1905, physicists could only "see" light that traveled at a speed relative to the ether. After 1905, physicists could "see" fixed light speed and no need for an ether.

What to Practice

The sensing practice emphasizes openness to disharmony. It has two parts: using one or more of the four strategies to find or create possibilities, and coping with the inattention and blindness breakdowns. Many of the strategies are practices for overcoming blindnesses (table 5.3).

A major theme underlying these practices is to find observers who see things differently from us and then to build on what they see. As demonstrated by the Johari Window, other observers see things we do not

Table 5.3
Practices for Coping with Inattention and Blindness

Type of Not-Seeing	Strategies	Practices
Inattention	(1) Switch attention within one's own frame set. (2) Enlarge awareness.	Journaling Daily meditation Use of checklists
Cognitive blindness	(1) Learn a new frame from someone else. (2) Create a new frame.	Above, plus: Speculation Learning
Community blindness	Create a new frame.	Network following Mind mapping Domain mapping Question the paradigm Get a coach Diverse teams or advisors

see. They can show us what is valued in their perspectives. The most successful innovators populate their teams (or advisory panels) with persons who see the world quite differently. They use these groups to examine interactions, agreements, disagreements, assessments, and commitments from multiple perspectives, looking for a way to codesign a plan that takes care of their shared concerns. This is the spirit of Stephen Covey's Habit 4, "Think win-win," and Habit 6, "Synergize" (1990). Engaging with diverse views is the single most important practice for coping with blindness.

Many of us find this advice difficult to implement. Interacting with someone who does not see things the way we do can be quite uncomfortable, especially if that person challenges our most cherished beliefs. But such interactions almost always lead to more innovative solutions to problems and avoid strategic or tactical errors in execution. We will discuss how to engage in productive conversations and overcome discomfort in chapter 12 on the somatics of innovation.

Conclusions

The sensing practice aims to generate new possibilities. It is rich and deep in the places it can take you and the discoveries you can make. It encompasses four main strategies.

1. You use source descriptions to direct your attention to places you may not have thought to look.
2. You engage in a learning process to find out everything you can about the community and its domain.
3. You employ conversations for possibility, including speculations and brainstorming sessions, to create synergies among different observers and find new frames.
4. You attend to the subtle sensations that signal a new possibility or a disharmony that has yet to be articulated.

The core of these four strategies is: interact with other people. Because they do not see the same way as you do, others can help you see what you cannot see. They literally perturb your nervous system so that you can see what you did not see before. The more different their observers are from yours, the more helpful they will be.

Although we dissected the practice of sensing new possibilities into four parts, the practice itself is a unified whole. Pulling them apart helps us to identify the strategies and assist coaches. How you integrate them depends on your level of skill. Novices will find the checklist to be the easiest tool. Intermediates will find learning and speculating to be the most useful. Experts will find the capacity of holding and articulating sensations to be the most productive.

Inattention and blindness are the principal obstacles to success with these strategies. To cope with them, you should build practices that help you expand your awareness and find new frames. These practices rely on interactions with other people who do not see the world the same way you do. Expert innovators have much larger networks of associates than novices.

In theory, we can separate finding of a new possibility from determining its value to people. In practice, however, we develop the ability to sense both at the same time. This is because innovation is always about adoption, and people will adopt only when they see an advantage in doing so. Therefore, you want to learn to sense ideas that people will value. The better you are at listening for concerns, the better you will be at generating possibilities that others will value.

Once you have a valuable possibility, your next task is to communicate it to the community you are trying to influence. That is the subject of the next chapter.

Bibliography

Adams, James L. 2001. *Conceptual Blockbusting: A Guide to Better Ideas.* 4th ed. Basic Books.

Austin, John L. 1962. *How to Do Things with Words.* Clarendon Press. Repr., Oxford University Press, 1976.

Berne, Eric. 1964. *Games People Play.* Grove Press.

Berners-Lee, Tim. 2000. *Weaving the Web.* Harper Business.

Buzan, Tony. 1991. *The Mind Map Book.* Penguin.

Carse, James P. 1986. *Finite and Infinite Games.* Random House.

Christenson, Clayton. 1997. *The Innovator's Dilemma.* Harvard Business.

Covey, Stephen R. 1990. *The Seven Habits of Highly Effective People.* Free Press.

Drucker, Peter. 1985. *Innovation and Entrepreneurship.* Harper Perennial. Repr., Harper Business, 1993.

Edwards, Bradley C., and Eric Westling. November 2003. *The Space Elevator: A Revolutionary Earth-to-Space Transportation System.* BC Edwards Publisher.

Edwards, Bradley C. 2005. "A Hoist to the Heavens." *IEEE Spectrum* (Aug.), http://spectrum.ieee.org/aerospace/space-flight/a-hoist-to-the-heavens

Einstein, Albert. 1916. *Relativity*. Repr., Penguin Classics, 2006.

Flores, Fernando. 1997. The Leaders of the Future. In *Beyond Calculation*, ed. P. Denning and R. Metcalfe, 176–192. Copernicus.

Hallinan, Joseph T. 2010. *Why We Make Mistakes: How We Look without Seeing, Forget Things in Seconds, and Are All Pretty Sure We Are Way above Average*. Reprint edition. Broadway.

Kotler, Philip, and Fernando Trias de Bes. 2003. *Lateral Marketing: Techniques for Finding Breakthrough Ideas*. Wiley.

Kuhn, Thomas. 1962. *The Structure of Scientific Revolutions*. Third printing, University of Chicago Press, 1996.

Lakoff, George, and Mark Johnson. 2003. *Metaphors We Live By*. 2nd ed., University of Chicago Press.

Latour, Bruno. 1988. *The Pasteurization of France*. Harvard University Press.

Lewis, Ted. 2006. *Critical Infrastructure Protection in Homeland Security*. Wiley Interscience.

Luft, Joseph, and Harrington Ingham. (1955) The Johari Window: A Graphic Model of Interpersonal Awareness. *Proceedings of the Western Training Laboratory in Group Development*. Los Angeles: UCLA.

Mark, J. Paul. 1987. *The Empire Builders: Inside the Harvard Business School*. William Morrow.

Maturana, Humberto, and Francisco Varela. 1987. *The Tree of Knowledge*. Shambhala.

Merrifield, Ric. 2009. *Rethinking: A Business Manifesto for Cutting Costs and Boosting Innovation*. Pearson Education.

Pierce, Terry. 2004. *Warfighting and Disruptive Technologies: Disguising Innovation*. Frank Cass.

Searle, John R. 1969. *Speech Acts*. Cambridge University Press.

Seely Brown, John, and Paul Duguid. 2002. *The Social Life of Information*. Harvard Business School Press.

Senge, Peter, C. Otto Scharmer, Joseph Jaworski, and Betty Sue Flowers. 2004. *Presence: Human Purpose and the Field of the Future*. Society for Organizational Learning.

Slywotsky, Adrian. 1996. *Value Migration*. Harvard Business School Press.

Spinosa, Charles, Fernando Flores, and Hubert Dreyfus. 1997. *Disclosing New Worlds*. MIT Press.

Strozzi-Heckler, Richard. 1984. *Anatomy of Change*. Repr., North Atlantic Books, 1993.

Winograd, Terry, and Fernando Flores. 1986. *Understanding Computers and Cognition*. Addison-Wesley.

Womack, James, and Daniel Jones. 2003. *Lean Thinking: Banish Waste and Create Wealth in your Corporation.* 2nd ed., Free Press.

Wechsler, Guillermo. 2007. "On Linguistic Games." Blog entry of April 20, http://guillermowechsler.typepad.com/my_weblog/games. Accessed January 2010.

Weick, K. 1995. *Sensemaking in Organizations.* Sage Publications.

Wittgenstein, Ludwig. 1953. *Philosophical Investigations.* Repr., Blackwell Publishing Ltd., 1958, 2001, 2009.

6

Practice Two: Envisioning

All things are created twice. There's a mental or first creation, and a physical or second creation.

—Stephen Covey

If you can harness imagination and the principles of a well-told story, then you get people rising to their feet amid thunderous applause instead of yawning and ignoring you.

—Robert McKee

The seedling of innovation, sprouted as a fragile possibility in the sensing practice, must be carefully cultivated in the ground of other people's consideration. We do this through the envisioning practice.

Envisioning is about crystallizing the possibility that arose in sensing into a story about how the possibility will appear and be valuable in the future of the adopting audience. In other words, envisioning practice is all about good storytelling. A compelling story captures hearts and imaginations. It diagnoses a problem or missing opportunity and shows a path to resolution. It provokes new thought and new action. It conveys a vivid, concrete, engaging, relevant, and touching depiction of a future that matters to your listeners. Your success depends on being able to generate such stories.

While this may sound relatively straightforward, many people find storytelling fiendishly difficult. For many, it is a struggle to design and tell good stories. But we cannot let this difficulty stop us: storytelling generates innovations. When creating the stories, we become generators of new actions and leaders of others who want to be players in our new worlds.

From Vision to Story

Many organizations have a "vision statement." They put it in their brochures, Web pages, and on their walls. All too often it becomes irrelevant to the members of the organization. It seems like some abstract future that might happen one day and bears little connection to everyday work. What's missing? An envisioning story.

We distinguish "vision" from "envisioning story." The vision is a simple declaration that provokes three reactions in listeners:

- They understand the future outcome clearly.
- They care about this outcome.
- They see its value.

Examples are "a world without war," "a healer in every home," and "service to one customer at a time."

The envisioning story is a compelling, relevant narrative that connects the vision to the concerns of the people and provokes their care and commitment. A good story inspires your audience

- to believe that there is a better future, well worth sacrificing what they do to gain it;
- to see that a blind spot has kept them from seeing this future sooner;
- to trust in your ability and commitment to make it happen; and
- to ask for more conversation about this future.

You build this story not by sitting in front of keyboard and grinding it out, but by engaging in conversations with people over a period of time, constantly refining the story until you find a version that works. You story does not come in a brilliant flash; it unfolds. As it unfolds, the vision may also change as it becomes more attuned to your audience. We have not encountered an example of a compelling vision story that was not refined, changed, and made more potent through the practice of getting feedback in many conversations.

With practice, you can master storytelling. We will study the structure of successful innovation stories, the main kinds of obstacles you will face in creating them, and what you must practice. We will discuss four styles of stories that have been associated with innovation: the research paper, the life struggle, the transformational event, and the manifesto. Each of these has its place. The research story is king in the domain of invention, the manifesto in the domain of innovation. The transformational event story is a powerful way to tell the history of an innovation. The life struggle story is an ambassador in the middle.

Let us turn now to understanding how to build stories that accomplish the objectives we have described.

Stories Are Fundamental to Learning

Cognitive scientists know that our brains are ideally suited for remembering many stories linked in complex webs. Individual components of stories are linked to other stories by associations such as "happened before," "happened after," "part of," "causes," "is caused by," "reminds of," and so on (Schank 1995).

Here is a simple demonstration of how good our brains are at following these links. Think of a time when you were a kid and you had ice cream. What kind of day was it? What kind of ice cream did you have? Who else was there? Who sat next to you? Where did you sit? Were you under a tree? Can you see the colors of their clothes? Hear the sounds of their voices? Feel the warmth of the day?

Or think of the day when you first learned to ride your bike. What kind of day was it? What color was the bike? Did it have training wheels? Who was there watching you? Did they clap for you? Did you lay the bike on the ground when done?

Did you notice how easy it is to remember these details, and how vivid the memories are, even though it may have been many years since you last thought of this event? And how quickly the brain moves across each link?

The neural connections in our brains continuously build and evolve as we add new stories and their connections. The brain's neural network shapes how our observer works, as discussed in chapter 4. Our stories alter our listeners' networks, changing their observers and the kinds of action they can take. This process of building and remembering stories has profound influences on our lives. Stories shape us, motivate our learning, convey our values, help us remember, help us make sense of things, and give us purpose.

The innovator's objective, through the envisioning practice, is to design a story about how the world will be once the new possibility is realized. The story should be compelling, memorable, interesting, and inspiring. This story becomes the motivation for later adoption of the new practice proposed by the innovator.

Chip and Dan Heath (2007) offer six guidelines on the qualities of stories that stick in people's minds: simple, unexpected, concrete, credible, emotional, and action oriented. While sufficient for creating memorable stories, their guidelines do not go deep enough for innovators. Innovators need stories that inspire commitment and action toward adoption. We will therefore dig deeper into storytelling principles for innovators. Although everything we say will be formulated for authors putting their stories in writing, the same principles apply for speakers giving oral stories.

Drawing Listeners In

The first order of business with an innovation story is to draw your listeners in: to engage them in a conversation about the possible future and prepare them to act on it later.

Phil Yaffe (2009), a professional writer, says that most authors face an uphill battle in doing this. They are well practiced in creating expository texts—such as memos, reports, proposals, training manuals, and research papers—whose fundamental purpose is to instruct and inform. But most readers do not want to be instructed and informed. They will not give you the time of day unless you have something interesting to say on a subject that concerns them.

Yaffe says that your first priorities are to (1) define reasons why your listeners will want to read what you will write, and (2) present these reasons as rapidly and convincingly as possible. Your listeners will be most interested if you can shed new light on matters of concern to them. You can draw them in by showing this quickly and concisely at the start of your text or conversation.

Often, you have limited knowledge of your listeners' concerns. And sometimes, the topic you want discuss will be brand new to them and you have no idea whether or not they will be interested. In either case, you have to evolve your story through a number of drafts and tellings until you achieve the kind of response you seek. If you want your story to have international appeal, you have to try it out on people from other cultures because the same narrative elicits different responses in different cultures (Rapaille 2006).

When he came to the space agency NASA's Ames Research Center in Mountain View, California, in 1983 to found the Research Institute for Advanced Computer Science (RIACS), author Peter Denning was well aware that his ability to define good research projects and find sponsors for them would depend on his ability to tell good stories. But his initial idea of what made for a good story was flawed and he had to revise it before he could be successful. He recounts his experience:

In 1984, one of our teams undertook research in a field called numerical aero-dynamics. As director, I had to tell stories that would attract good computer scientists to the team and NASA funding to support them. My conception of a good story was the *Scientific American* article. My first story was: "Aerodynamics is the field that studies how aircraft fly, in particular how air flows around and near a flying craft, providing either lift or drag. Numerical aerodynamics means that we use a supercomputer to solve the equations that tell us the rate and direction of air flow at every point on or near the aircraft. We can design aircraft completely without ever having to build a model and test it in a wind tunnel." This story was technically correct but (as I found out later) it did not engage most of my listeners. Why would a computer science researcher want to work on that? A journalist friend said, "You mean, you fly airplanes inside a computer?" Now putting it that way really got people interested. How the heck, they wanted to know, do you fly an airplane *inside* a computer? That led to a whole conversation in which they asked me to explain all the finer points. They remembered our project and thought it was really cool. I made some very good recruitments with this story. (Peter Denning, unpublished)

In our workshops, we ask our students to look up stories of great innovators and present them to the other students. Their presentations are often rather dull recitations of the innovator's resume. For example, a typical presenter might say that Thomas Edison was one of the most famous American inventors; among his inventions were the teletype ticker, the phonograph, the motion picture, and the light bulb; he did most of his work in a laboratory in Menlo Park, New Jersey; he was kicked out of many companies that he founded; he received 1,093 patents in his lifetime. All true, but the account of these facts is not very exciting, and easily forgotten. In one workshop, the presenter on Edison departed from this pattern. He appealed instead to his fellow students' imaginations:

Imagine that you awoke this morning, but your world has no electricity in it. There would be no alarm clock to awaken you; something else, like a bird chirping or cock crowing might have done that. There would be no morning radio or weather report to tell you the news or what to wear. There would be no toaster for preparing your breakfast. You'd have to start your car with a crank. There would be no telephone or cell phone to call anyone. You would do your class reports on a mechanical typewriter. You would have to remember to wind your watch. Do you picture this? Without Edison, that's the world you would be living in. Edison's greatest contribution was not the light bulb, but a complete system of electric generation and distribution to homes. Light bulbs are worthless without electricity.

After that introduction, the students were eager to discuss how Edison had created the first electric power system and how he got New Yorkers to adopt it.

Author Robert Dunham has found in his workshops and dealings with clients that every time he introduces a new concept, term, or distinction in the story he is evolving with the clients, it helps to offer a "relevance story" of why is it meaningful to them before he goes on to the detailed explanation. Dunham says:

In my teaching, coaching, and consulting I learned that, in storytelling, we need to build relevance and meaning in the listening of our audience for everything new we introduce. For example, when it came time to introduce the skill and practice of centering [discussed in chapter 12], I used to say, "This is important, trust me," and was dismayed when they did not trust me and instead started questioning why we were doing the exercise. Now I say, "Centering is the skill to put yourself in a state of choice rather than be in reaction when a challenging moment demands your leadership." With this simple relevance story, the students embrace the practice and soon discover that it is indeed true that they start having choice over their actions in demanding moments. (Bob Dunham, unpublished)

These examples show that if you do not know the exact concerns of your listeners, you can discover them through an iterative process of trial stories; and that you need to pay attention to establishing the relevance of each concept in your story that will be new to your listeners. Success becomes quite likely after a few refinements.

Direction and Flow

After you draw people in, you must show them a path to get to where you say they can go. Your story needs to convey a sense of direction toward an achievable goal.

Stephen Covey, author of *The Seven Habits of Highly Effective People* (1990), maintains that you cannot be effective at anything without a mission to give you direction. You have to know what you are trying to achieve in order to know where to devote your time and energy and to avoid being pulled off course by interesting distractions. In his Habit 2, "Begin with the End in Mind," he advocates that everyone start with a personal mission statement:

A mission statement is not something you write overnight. It takes deep intro-spection, careful analysis, thoughtful expression, and often many rewrites to produce it in final form. It may take you several weeks or even months before you feel really comfortable with it, before you feel it is a complete, a concise expression of your innermost values and directions. Even then, you will want to review it regularly and monitor changes as the years bring additional insights or changing circumstances.

I recently finished reviewing my own mission statement, which I do fairly regularly. Sitting on the edge of a beach, alone, at the end of a bicycle ride, I took out my organizer and hammered it out. It took several hours, but I felt a sense of clarity, a sense of organization and commitment, a sense of exhilaration and freedom.

I find the process is as important as the product. Writing or reviewing a mission statement changes you because it forces you to think through your priorities deeply, carefully, and to align your behavior with your beliefs. As you do, other people begin to sense that you're not being driven by everything that happens to you. You have a sense of mission about what you're trying to do and you are excited about it. (Covey 1990, 129)

Speakers with clear senses of their personal missions are the most effective innovation storytellers. They take their clarity into their stories and show their listeners that the end result is not only worthwhile but also is achievable. They communicate their personal commitments well, which earns the trust of their listeners.

The sense of direction in your story is a *flow* from the current world to the new world. There are two main flavors of flow. A "moves-toward" flow concentrates on the new world that can be achieved. A "moves-away" flow concentrates on leaving the current world behind; it says hardly anything about where to go, except that almost anywhere is better than here. Let us illustrate these two forms of flow.

Apollo was a series of human-operated spacecraft missions undertaken by the United States during the years 1961 to 1972. The Apollo program's mission was to get a man to the moon and return him safely before the end of the 1960s. President John F. Kennedy set this goal in his famous speech to the U.S. Congress on May 25, 1961:

I believe that this nation should commit itself to achieving the goal, before this decade is out, of landing a man on the moon and returning him safely to the earth. No single space project in this period will be more impressive to mankind, or more important for the long-range exploration of space; and none will be so difficult or expensive to accomplish. We propose to accelerate the development of the appropriate lunar space craft. We propose to develop alternate liquid and solid fuel boosters, much larger than any now being developed, until certain which is superior. We propose additional funds for other engine development and for unmanned explorations—explorations which are particularly important for one purpose which this nation will never overlook: the survival of the man who first makes this daring flight. But in a very real sense, it will not be one man going to the moon—if we make this judgment affirmatively, it will be an entire nation. For all of us must work to put him there. (Kennedy 1961)

NASA achieved this goal with the Apollo 11 mission in July 1969.

Kennedy's declaration of a new future of manned space exploration came when the United States was still smarting over the Soviet Sputnik successes. In his speech, Kennedy opened a path to regain national pride. Although he did not mention it explicitly, Sputnik was as on everyone's minds. Kennedy's declaration moved away from Sputnik and toward U.S.-dominated manned space exploration.

One of the most powerful declarations of all time was the United States Declaration of Independence in 1776. Our colleague Chauncey Bell, an executive consultant, analyzed the declaration and reported to us personally:

The Declaration (1,325 words) consists of three parts. The first section says "We declare our interpretation of the world, who we consider ourselves to be, and the standards to which we will hold ourselves." This section is 17 percent of the Declaration (229 words). The second section says "We make a serious complaint against those who have governed us for (1) many actions they have taken without concern for our well-being, (2) the damage and suffering produced by those actions, and (3) not listening to an acting on our proper requests. We ground our complaint." This section is 71 percent (938 words). The final section says "We declare a new order, and in support we promise our lives, our fortunes, and our sacred honor." This section is 12 percent (158 of 1,325 words). The Declaration is masterfully concrete in describing the abhorrent current situation and remarkably vague on what the new order looks like.

This is a move-away flow. Bell thinks that the majority of declarations that move people to action use move-away flows. It is much easier to say what is wrong with the current situation, and to declare escape, than it is to say what would be better.

Story Architectures

Once you decide on how to draw your readers in and what kind of story flow to emphasize, you need to choose an architecture for your story.

The prime innovation pattern (discussed in chapter 1) reminds us that innovators face many challenges coming from those whom they want to adopt their ideas into practice. The challenges can be summarized in the following questions potential adopters ask when hearing the proposals of innovators:

• Where will you take us?
• Why are we going?

- How do we get there?
- What's in it for us?
- What's in it for me?
- What do you want from me?
- Why should I trust you?

In the envisioning practice, the innovator designs stories that answer these questions and inspire people to act for adoption. These stories seldom take the form of a series of answers to these questions. Four forms in particular have been used most often:

1. Research paper
2. Transformational event
3. Life struggle story
4. Manifesto

The research paper is the least effective of these stories because it describes research in particular, usually in specialized language that is difficult for potential adopters to understand, and because it does not answer all the questions. We include it here because research papers and their derivatives come up frequently in discussions about innovation; many aspiring innovators do not realize that there are more effective alternatives to the research paper.

The transformational event story calls attention to how the proposed innovation might be a turning point in history and invites listeners to join in an important change.

The life struggle story often turns up in media articles and in personal accounts of innovators. It is not a difficult pattern to learn.

The manifesto is the most effective story form because it is directly aligned with the prime innovation pattern and it answers the adopter's questions. It is also the most difficult pattern to learn and do well with.

Research Paper

The research paper is written by a researcher or scholar to inform others in the author's professional community of a new insight, discovery, or invention. Over the years, the scholarly community has adopted a particular form for these papers (see box 6.1).

The research paper obviously is not designed to answer the questions adopters will pose. Why does it come up in many discussions about innovations? There are three main reasons.

Box 6.1
The Research Paper Form

Define the problem and the main claims about it.
Review the past literature on this and related problems.
Describe the approach used to solve the problem.
Describe the solution, along with its strengths and limitations, and present appropriate data to validate it.
Speculate about potential applications and future research questions.

The first is that many researchers start small companies to turn their results into products. Their literature about the product is written in the style they are most familiar with. They may try to popularize their story, for example, by imitating the *Scientific American* narrative approach, but they do not alter its basic structure. Geoffrey Moore (2002) demonstrated that the researcher approach sells well with early adopters and fails miserably with the majority. Many startups go under because their founders could not escape the research-oriented way in which they were trained to think.

A second reason a focus on research material arises is that when we go back over the history of successful innovations, we always try to locate the person or persons who had the idea in the first place. Those creative thinkers often were researchers and their papers earn the labels *seminal, groundbreaking,* and the like. Although there is usually no evidence that the thinker actually caused or worked for the adoption, that person often gets credit for starting the innovation.

A third reason research comes up is that the research paper as a source of innovation frequently is scorned by marketing critics who remind us that people adopt based on emotions, not on the cold scientific logic presented in those papers. In the process of telling us what to avoid, they call attention to it.

In his groundbreaking work *Science in Action*, sociologist Bruno Latour (1987) demonstrated how deeply the pattern of thinking represented by the research paper is embedded into the psyche of science. He introduced a distinction between "ready-made-science" and "science-in-the-making." Ready-made-science takes the form of facts, rules, laws, and formal models that have been thoroughly tested and accepted by the scientific community. You can trust ready-made-science. For example, Newton's law $F = ma$ is ready-made; you can trust that scientists have validated that in every instance force will be measured as mass times acceleration.

Science-in-the-making refers to the dynamic processes in which scientists invent, debate, test, validate, and accept or refute hypotheses. Only after sufficient artistry, discussion, struggling, testing, and validation will the members of a scientific community come to accept a proposed claim as the truth. This process can be chaotic, emotional, polemic, and controversial. A hypothesis survives this process by winning allies. Once it has done so, it is accepted as a fact or law of ready-made-science. Latour says, "Science is a process of constructing facts."

Latour invokes the two-faced Greek god Janus to illustrate the distinction between orderly ready-made-science and chaotic science-in-the-making. The face looking backward at what has been accomplished sees what is well known (ready-made-science); the face looking forward at the dynamically unfolding process of scientific discovery sees what is just becoming known (science-in-the-making). Table 6.1 summarizes some of the statements Latour sees coming from these two views of science.

Ready-made-science and science-in-the-making are not competing notions. They are two sides of the same thing. We cannot know science by focusing on only one of the two aspects. The same is true for innovation. When we look backward after a successful innovation, we look in the same perspective as ready-made-science. If we want to sell the unfolding future to potential adopters, we need to tell stories from the same perspective as science-in-the-making.

Fortunately, a lot is known about how to tell such stories of the unfolding effectively. That is the subject of the next section.

Table 6.1
Latour on the Two Sides of Science

Ready-made science	Science-in-the-making
Just get me the most efficient system.	Decide what efficiency means.
Nature is the cause that allowed the controversies to be settled.	Nature will be the consequence of the settlement.
People are convinced because the system works.	Convince all the relevant people that the system works.
When things are true they hold.	When things hold they start becoming true.

Transformational Event

The prime innovation pattern can be captured in retrospect by a story form called the "transformational events pattern" (Denning and Hiles 2006). The transformational events pattern explains innovations in three stages: (1) An interval of increasingly unsatisfactory ad hoc solutions to a persistent problem ("mess"), (2) an offer of an invention or a new way of thinking, and (3) a period of widespread adoption and settlement. This pattern is observable only after the fact and has been used frequently by historians to explain innovations and their impact.

Let us illustrate how historians have used the pattern. Perhaps the most famous example was Thomas Kuhn's (1962) book, *The Structure of Scientific Revolutions*. Kuhn said that a scientific theory holds sway for a long time, until a growing number of anomalies and paradoxes can no longer be ignored. Someone then proposes a new framework, removing the anomalies and resolving the paradoxes. The new framework is adopted into the thinking and social practice of scientists.

In *Innovation and Entrepreneurship* (1985), Peter Drucker employed this pattern to describe the work of entrepreneurs. He maintained that the hardest part of producing transformational change was to find the right opportunity and compose a compelling offer. He devoted half his book to a study of seven areas where opportunities are most likely to be found.

In his book *The Day the Universe Changed* (1995), from his televised PBS *Nova* series, James Burke discussed eight profound innovations in Western scientific thought during the past two millennia. Each change transformed not only social practice, but also the way that people saw themselves in relation to the universe. Burke said that his method to reveal the nature and extent of the social change was to document how people lived and worked in the fifty-year period preceding the invention, then to describe the invention and the circumstances that generated it, and then to document how people lived and worked in the fifty- to one-hundred-year period following the invention's introduction.

One of Burke's examples was the invention of the printing press by Gutenberg around 1450. The stories for the period preceding 1450 reveal a society in which almost no one could write, very few could read, and most knowledge was transmitted through oral traditions. Toward 1450, demand for written records was rising, especially among merchants; but trade was stymied because manual transcription was the only method of copying. Gutenberg's moveable-type press was a breakthrough, providing a mechanical way to make many copies cheaply. In the hundred or so years following the invention, literacy became common, literatures in many subjects formed, news sheets were started, and people relied on printed works rather than oral traditions to corroborate claims. Burke said that over a 200-year period Europe moved from an oral tradition in an illiterate society to a written tradition in a literate society.

In *They Made America* (2004), Harold Evans employed the transformational event pattern in the stories of seventy American innovators, emphasizing that adoption resulted not from good fortune but from the tireless persistence of the innovator. In the individual stories, Evans reveals the social practices of the affected community before and after the innovator's work, showing profound changes.

In *Lincoln at Gettysburg* (1992), Garry Wills studies Abraham Lincoln's famous Gettysburg Address as a transformational event in U.S. political history. Prior to this time, the United States was a loose federation of states and the federal government was weak. Lincoln proposed a new concept, that the entire nation be seen as "one from many" instead of "many ones." Lincoln's formulation became a new way of thinking about the federal government and its relationships to the state governments.

The transformational event pattern is good for historians but problematic for innovators. The innovator can certainly tell a good story about the current "mess" and propose an innovation that might resolve it. But after that, the portrayal of the proposed innovation as a transformation event, and the story about the new future that will evolve, are only speculations. The problem is that many listeners will recognize the speculation and not trust the innovator's story.

By analogy with Latour's description of science, the transformational events pattern is "ready-made-innovation" and the manifesto, described shortly, is "innovation-in-the-making."

Life Struggle Story

Robert McKee is the world's best-known and most respected screenwriting teacher. He has won many awards for writing and directing, and his students have produced hundreds of award-winning hit films. He believes that the art of good storytelling has largely been lost, as can be seen by the low quality of most films today. He has made it his mission to teach screenwriters the principles of good storytelling (McKee 1997). Others, like Jim Loehr (2007), follow his lead.

Although business leaders have different objectives than screenwriters, McKee says that the same storytelling principles will help them be more effective (McKee 2003). To illustrate, he discusses a common breakdown in fundraising:

Let's imagine a biotech startup, Chemcorp, whose CEO has to persuade some Wall Street bankers to invest in the company. He could tell them that Chemcorp has discovered a chemical compound that prevents heart attacks and offer up a lot of slides showing the size of the market, the business plan, the organizational chart, and so on. The bankers would nod politely and stifle yawns while thinking of other companies better positioned in Chemcorp's market.

Alternatively, the CEO could turn his pitch into a story, beginning with someone close to him—say, his father—who died of a heart attack. So nature itself is the first antagonist that the CEO-as-protagonist must overcome. In his grief, the CEO realizes that if there had been some chemical indication of heart disease, his father's death could have been prevented. His company discovers a protein that's present in the blood just before heart attacks occur and develops an easy-to-administer, low-cost test.

But now Chemcorp faces a new antagonist: the FDA. The FDA turns down the first application, but new research reveals that the test performs even better than anyone had expected, so the agency approves the second application. Meanwhile Chemcorp is running out of money, and a key partner drops out and goes off to start his own company. Now Chemcorp is in a fight-to-the-finish patent race.

This accumulation of antagonists creates great suspense. The protagonist has raised the ideas in the bankers' heads that the story might not have a happy ending. By now, he has them on the edges of their seats, and he says, "We won the race, we got the patent, we're poised to go public and save a quarter-million lives a year." And the bankers just throw money at him. (McKee 2003, 52)

McKee says that the successful stories follow a simple, common pattern, outlined in box 6.2. The story features a person struggling to accomplish something (protagonist) who is thwarted by opposing forces (antagonists). The protagonist's struggle to overcome the obstacles produces suspense and stokes listener interest in the outcome. Eventually the protagonist learns some truth about life. And of course the story must be believable.

In the Chemcorp example you can see how McKee applies these principles to a story about a future innovation. The innovator's struggles often sound like our own; we can empathize. Although we don't know the ending yet, we can see from the accumulation of breakdowns that the story's conclusion might not be good. We get on board to help the innovator succeed.

Box 6.2
The Life Struggle Story Form

> Focus on how and why life changes.
> Protagonist (P) has a desire, organizes life in pursuit of it.
> Antagonists intervene to prevent P's success; the accumulation of break-downs builds suspense.
> P tries to restore balance in life and deal with uncooperative reality. What resources does P muster? What difficult decisions or dilemmas does P face? How goes the struggle?
> P ultimately discovers truth.
> The story must be believable.

Box 6.3
Life Struggle Form Applied to Innovation

> Focus on bringing a future to life.
> Proposer (P) has a desire, which aligns with the listeners' (L) desires. P says life can be organized to realize the desire and shows a path.
> The path has risks and obstacles. Antagonists will intervene to block success; breakdowns will accumulate.
> In their struggle with uncooperative reality, what resources can P and L muster? What risks must they face? What difficult decisions or dilemmas will they encounter? What struggles are likely? What kind of character do they need?
> Ultimately they must discover and live with new truths.
> The story must be credible.

Manifesto

The manifesto is a structure that aligns directly with the prime innovation pattern. The essence of that pattern is that an innovator is bothered by a disharmony, puzzles over it for a long time, discovers how the current common sense enables it, proposes a new common sense that would resolve it, and commits to making the change happen. The form of storytelling about how the pattern can unfold is called manifesto because it makes a big declaration about a possible future.

We learned the manifesto structure from Fernando Flores around 1990. He advocated that entrepreneurs make a big declaration about the future they wanted to create. He advised them to (1) orient to major, chronic breakdowns that cause a lot of suffering and expense, (2) examine

Box 6.4
The Manifesto Form

Declare and articulate the cost and pain of the current situation.
Articulate the limitations of the current common sense, and its inability to deal with the issue.
Declare the possibilities opened with a new common sense, and how they will enable addressing the issue in a new way.
Make the big proposal—how the new common sense can be or is being developed to create a new domain of action and ability to deal with whole categories of issues (to enlarge the breadth and power of the innovation).
Make a specific proposal for action with the current audience—next steps—addressing concerns, risks, and benefits.

---

the history of the domain to find how the current paradigm is generating the breakdown and obscuring a resolution, and (3) offer a change of paradigm that resolves the breakdown and a means to get there. He illustrated this structure with his story of Louis Pasteur and the dying cows, retold in the prologue of this book. He encouraged one of the authors to write a manifesto about reforming engineering education, which was high on Peter Denning's mind at the time. Denning did this (1992) and used the resulting manifesto as his guide while he worked for reform of computer science education.

Manifestos are not for the faint of heart. Grounding a claim that a proposed innovation can generate a paradigm shift is not easy.

Common Story Subpatterns

Within the general structure of the story architecture you have chosen, you can employ various subpatterns. These six are common:

• *Attractive future* The story depicts a world of great attraction to the listener (best for move-toward flows).
• *Repulsive past* The story calls for escape from an undesirable world (best for move-away flows).
• *Trends* The story notes a trend in the current world, extrapolates it to the future, and speculates about the resulting opportunities.
• *Scenarios* A collection of short stories depicts alternate futures as consequences of particular assumptions.
• *New games* The story describes an attractive alternative to the current way of doing things.

• *World narratives*   The story situates the breakdown into a larger historical context.

Attractive Future

The basic idea of an attractive-future story is to depict a future in concrete terms that compel your listeners to move in that direction.

We mentioned President Kennedy's Apollo program as an example of an attractive future story. After 1972 there were no more moon missions. NASA's more ambitious space projects such as building a space station and launching a mission to Mars never won sufficient support to make much headway. NASA's space shuttle program, which was to be the workhorse for future manned space exploration, proved to be extremely dangerous—recall the *Challenger* and *Columbia* disasters in 1986 and 2003, respectively. NASA has been quietly exploring alternative—safer and cheaper—means to get materiel into space. One of these, the space elevator, started as science fiction in the 1950s and began to get serious attention in the 1990s with advances in material and power technologies. Here is what Bradley Edwards (2005; Edwards and Westling 2003), one of the chief advocates for the space elevator, said:

Rockets are getting us nowhere fast. Since the dawn of the space age, the way we get into space hasn't changed: we spend tens or hundreds of millions of dollars on a rocket whose fundamental operating principle is a controlled chemical explosion. We need something better, and that something is a space elevator——a super strong, lightweight cable stretching 100,000 kilometers from Earth's surface to a counterweight in space. Roomy elevator cars powered by electricity would speed along the cable. For a fraction of the cost, risk, and complexity of today's rocket boosters, people and cargo would be whisked into space in relative comfort and safety. . . .

It now costs about US $20,000 per kilogram to put objects into orbit. Contrast that rate with the results of a study I recently performed for NASA. . . . A single space elevator could reduce the cost of orbiting payloads to a remarkably low $200 a kilogram and that multiple elevators could ultimately push costs down below $10 a kilogram. With space elevators we could eventually make putting people and cargo into space as cheap, kilogram for kilogram, as airlifting them across the Pacific.

The implications of such a dramatic reduction in the cost of getting to Earth orbit are startling. It's a good bet that new industries would blossom as the resources of the solar system became accessible as never before. Take solar power: the idea of building giant collectors in orbit to soak up some of the sun's vast power and beam it back to Earth via microwaves has been around for decades. But the huge size of the collectors has made the idea economically unfeasible with launch technologies based on chemical rockets. With a space elevator's much cheaper launch costs, however, the economics of space-based solar power start looking good. (Edwards 2005)

Edwards's story has a strong move-toward flow with its emphasis on a future world with space elevators instead of rockets lifting payloads to orbit. Moreover, it reminds us that inherent limitations of rockets make the current space program unsustainable.

The space elevator story is a speculation now embraced by a community that has grown rapidly since 2003. The leaders of the "space elevator movement" have been sponsoring annual competitions at which entrants can demonstrate prototypes for elevators and tethers. NASA provides prize money. These competitions attract dozens of technology prototypes and over ten thousand spectators (see spaceelevator.com).

Another attractive-future example is immortality, an old, often irresistible lure. Inventor Ray Kurzweil and physician Terry Grossman, MD, spoke about this possibility:

Immortality is within our grasp.

Longevity expert and gerontologist Aubrey de Grey uses the metaphor of maintaining a house. How long does a house last? The answer obviously depends on how well you take care of it. If you do nothing, the roof will spring a leak before long, water and the elements will invade, and eventually the house will disintegrate. But if you proactively take care of the structure, repair all damage, confront all dangers, and rebuild or renovate parts from time to time using new materials and technologies, the life of the house can essentially be extended without limit.

The same holds true for our bodies and brains. The only difference is that while we fully understand the methods underlying the maintenance of a house, we do not yet fully understand all the biological principles of life. But with our increasing comprehension of the human genome, the proteins expressed by the genome, and the biochemical processes and pathways of our metabolism, we are quickly gaining that knowledge. . . . Many scientists, including the authors of this book, believe that we will have the means to stop and even reverse aging within the next two decades. In the meantime, we can slow each aging process to a crawl. (Kurzweil and Grossman 2004, 3–4)

Kurzweil and Grossman believe that, if they can keep themselves alive with aggressive nutritional supplementation through about 2025, they will find themselves in an age of advanced nanotechnology and biotechnology that can repair human aging indefinitely. They invite all of us to join them, and they provide a Web site where we can buy the supplements.

Like the space elevator story, the immortality story is speculation. Most people would say the space elevator is possible and that immortality is unlikely.

Let us give one more example, a speculation that seemed far-fetched in 1945 but has been realized in the modern Internet. Vannevar Bush, a well-known MIT scientist, was President Roosevelt's science advisor during World War II. In 1945, Bush wrote a powerful article in *Atlantic Monthly* that described a future device, called the memex, which would automate scientific record keeping and discovery. Bush's speculation foretold hypertext linking, dry-chemical copying, mass storage, and automated keyword retrieval. Many of the seeds of the modern Internet are contained in this article. Bush said:

Consider a future device for individual use, which is a sort of mechanized private file and library. It needs a name; . . . "memex" will do. A memex is a device in which an individual stores all his books, records, and communications, and which is mechanized so that it may be consulted with exceeding speed and flexibility. It is an enlarged intimate supplement to his memory.

It consists of a desk [on which the individual works]. On the top are slanting translucent screens, on which material can be projected for convenient reading. There is a keyboard, and sets of buttons and levers. . . .

In one end is the stored material. . . . [With improved microfilm,] if the user inserted 5000 pages of material a day it would take him hundreds of years to fill the repository . . . .

Most of the memex contents are purchased on microfilm. . . . Books of all sorts, pictures, current periodicals, newspapers, are thus obtained and dropped into place. . . . On [a transparent platen] are placed longhand notes, photographs, memoranda, all sorts of things. . . . The depression of a lever causes it to be photographed onto the next blank space in a section of the memex film, dry photography being employed. . . .

To consult a certain book, he taps its code on the keyboard, and the title page of the book promptly appears before him . . . . On deflecting a lever to the right, he runs through the book before him, one page at a time. A further deflection steps 10 pages at a time, and a still further deflection 100 pages. Left deflection does the same backwards. . . .

He can add marginal notes and comments, taking advantage of one possible type of dry photography, just as though he had the physical page before him. (Bush 1945)

The world pictured in Bush's story became a source of inspiration for many of the people who later worked on technologies that grew into the modern Internet.

Repulsive Past

The basic idea of a repulsive-past story is to depict the past, continuing up to the present, in an unattractive light, so that your listeners will want to move away from the current, unfavorable conditions.

Politics is a good source of examples. The United States Declaration of Independence, mentioned earlier, is one. Many political campaigns are organized around detailed complaints concerning the current situation in the nation, leading to a call for change while being vague on what the change will entail.

Trends

The basic idea of a trends story is to note a trend in the world, extrapolate it to the future, and speculate about its benefits and opportunities. You position your proposed innovation as the realization of a trend. While this is one of the easier story types, it is also problematic because trend-related forecasts are notoriously unreliable.

In *Only the Paranoid Survive*, Andy Grove (1999) said that while it is often impossible to predict which new technologies will grow up and become disruptive to the existing technologies, one of the important signs is an inflection point. An inflection point occurs when a prototype demonstrates the possibility of a tenfold or greater improvement in speed or cost relative to the best current technology ("10x"). A great way to position your proposed innovation is at an inflection point in the evolution of technology—either as the cause of the inflection point or as first-to-market advantage after an inflection point.

Gordon Moore, who cofounded the Intel Corporation with Andy Grove, noted in the 1960s that the density of transistors on silicon chips doubled about every twenty-four months at the same price. Each new generation of computer chips since the 1960s has conformed to this trend line. Although Moore's trend does not have the status of a physical law, it has become an industry goal to develop new silicon circuits that conform to it. Thus Moore's Law says that computer chip technology will cause 10x inflection every seven years.

Experts now believe that Moore's Law for silicon will reach its ultimate limits around 2020—when the width of wires is reduced to only a few atoms and electricity no longer flows on them. But other experts, such as Ray Kurzweil, claim that new technologies will replace silicon and continue the trend:

Moore's Law of Integrated Circuits was not the first, but the fifth paradigm to provide accelerating price-performance. Computing devices have been consistently multiplying in power (per unit of time) from the mechanical calculating devices used in the 1890 U.S. Census, to Turing's relay-based "Robinson" machine that cracked the Nazi enigma code, to the CBS vacuum tube computer that predicted the election of Eisenhower, to the transistor-based machines used in the first space launches, to the integrated-circuit-based personal [computers]. (Kurzweil 2000, 25)

Trend extrapolation can lead to some interesting speculations, but they are frequently wrong. In *The Social Life of Information*, John Seely Brown and Paul Duguid (2000) examined a series of popular trend extrapolations that drove the Internet boom in the 1990s and never came true. The reason they failed is that people change and adapt in response to what they see happening around them; in turn that changes the directions in which technology is advancing.

The rise of the information age has brought about a good deal of "endism." New technology is widely predicted to bring about, among other things:

The end of the press, television, and mass media
The end of brokers and other intermediaries
The end of firms, bureaucracies, and similar organizations
The end of universities
The end of politics
The end of government
The end of ethics and religions
The end of the nation-state

There's no doubt that in all these categories particular institutions and particular organizations are under pressure and many will not survive long. But the categories themselves are secure. (Brown and Duguid 2000, 16)

The claim behind the endisms was that by giving individuals direct access to information, the Internet and other forms of computing would remove the assumptions that gave rise to these institutions. Without their foundations, the institutions would collapse.

A dramatic exposé of the unreliability of long-term trend evaluation is documented by historian Dave Walter (1992) who, in *Today Then*, republished seventy-four editorials written in 1892 about the world as it would be a century later. The American Press Association invited leading authors, journalists, industrialists, business leaders, engineers, social critics, lawyers, politicians, religious leaders, and other luminaries of the day to give their forecasts of the world of 1992. The occasion was the Fourth Columbian Exhibition, a major technology fair celebrating the 400-year anniversary of Columbus's discovery of America.

Perhaps the most striking feature of the 1892 forecasts is how few actually came true. Their authors engaged in a lot of wishful thinking. Many thought railways would be the primary method of transportation, extending from the northernmost parts of Canada to the southernmost parts of South America. They thought that pneumatic tubes would be common modes of transportation for people in cities and for transcontinental mail. They thought government would be smaller and that there would be fewer class differences. Few foresaw the world wars, the communications revolution, or air transportation. None foresaw the interstate highway system, genetic engineering, mass state-sponsored education, or broadcast TV and radio—or the computer.

Innovators who want to appeal to trend extrapolation need to be very careful.

Scenarios

Scenarios are collections of short stories about possible futures, each conditioned on a specific set of assumptions. These stories allow the evaluation of the consequences of the possible alternatives. They avoid the downside of trend extrapolation.

Financial planners use scenarios to spell out how an organization would function under low, medium, and high assumptions for revenue in the next year. With these scenarios planners may specify the essential actions that will be taken under the low-income scenario, along with additional actions that can be initiated if the actual revenue turns out to be medium or high. In this way they can arrive at a plan of action that does not require them to speculate about future income. They know what they will do in each case.

Shell Oil was one of the pioneers in scenario planning for business. Its financial planners had specific plans ready in case of an OPEC oil embargo, and when the embargo actually happened in 1973, they immediately put their plan into action (Ogilvy 2002; Schwartz 1991).

Professional futurists, such as the World Future Society (wfs.org), rely on scenario building as an essential practice for preparation for the future. They say that by spelling out alternative futures, people can choose the most desirable ones and devote their energies to making them happen.

New Games

The general idea of the new games pattern is to describe an attractive alternative to the current way of doing things. The storyteller declares that the current "game" does not work well any more and that a new "game" will bring prosperity.

A good example is found in the ongoing debates about the future of the university. Some pundits of the information age say that telecommunications technology is undermining the traditional assumptions on which the university model is based. In 1995, Eli Noam of Columbia University argued that the Internet undermines the library, the physical community of scholars, and the classroom lecture by replacing them with the digital library, the virtual Internet community, and distance learning. None of these new entities requires a physical campus (Noam 1995). Tehranian (2001) disputed this, saying that Noam was blinded by information technology and therefore missed other important functions of universities that will never be replaced by networks: professional certification, moral education, and interactive teaching. In 1997, Peter Drucker surprised many people with similar criticisms in a *Forbes* magazine interview:

Thirty years from now the big university campuses will be relics . . . universities won't survive . . . totally uncontrollable expenditures, without any visible improvement in either the content or quality of education, means that the system is rapidly becoming untenable . . . higher education is in a deep crisis . . . already we are beginning to see delivered more lectures and classes off campus via satellite or two-way video at a fraction of the cost . . . the college won't survive as a residential institution . . . today's buildings are hopelessly unsuited and totally unneeded." (Drucker in *Forbes* March 10, 1997)

As of 2009, universities had not succumbed to the depredations predicted by Noam and Drucker. Yet there are some whose leaders are trying to reinvent the game of being a university. The University of Phoenix, Strayer University, and Open University are privately owned and all rely on distance learning methods in niche markets. Neumont University, a more recent entrant, offers a projects-based curriculum for learning software engineering in direct competition with hundreds of traditional software engineering programs in traditional universities. Dreyfus (2001) is not sure whether distance education can replace all university courses because learning beyond straightforward competence requires physical interaction with a teacher.

Many business authors have written about how new business designs displace older ones that have stopped producing sufficient value for their customers. (Business designs are games in the business world.) Adrian Slywotsky (1995) gives numerous examples of businesses that offered new business models, such as Starbucks or the IBM PC. Clayton Christensen (1997) gives numerous examples of how disruptive technologies started as low-end technologies and gradually moved up the value chain where they displaced high-end companies. Philip Kotler and Fernando Trias de Bes (2003) illustrate the same thing in the world of marketing with examples such as Cheerios moving from a breakfast cereal to an anytime snack and Bufferin moving from a headache reliever to heart attack preventative. In all these cases, the innovators told stories emphasizing the advantages of the new game; they drew significant numbers of people in to play.

World Narratives

The general idea of a world narrative is to create a historic summary of the current situation and then claim either that history is about to change (a paradigm shift) or that an innocuous trend or practice is about to become important.

Peter Drucker was exceptionally good at this. He distrusted trend extrapolations and was wary of forecasts beyond five to fifteen years. Instead he offered historical analyses that revealed "realities" whose consequences he could lay out for the next few years. Here is an example from his 1989 book *The New Realities;* he discusses how labor unions might respond to challenging historical forces:

The labor union can go in one of three directions. If it does nothing, it may disappear—even in a free, democratic society. Or it may shrink to the point where it becomes irrelevant. This seems to be the direction in which the British, Italian, and French unions are moving, but also most of those in the United States.

A second choice is to try to maintain itself by dominating the political power structure, having government impose compulsory union membership and such power positions for the union as "co-determination," which gives a veto power over company management. This may appear a rational course; the unions in Germany, Holland, and Scandinavia seem to have chosen it. After all, feudal knights and their descendants maintained themselves this way in power and privilege for five hundred years, even though they had lost all social function by the year 1400. But then the feudal knights had a monopoly on arms and with it overwhelming military power. The equivalent in today's society would be overwhelming voting power—and that the labor union has already lost.

There is a third choice: that the union rethink its function. The union might reinvent itself as the organ of society—and of the employing institution—

concerned with human potential and human achievement, and with optimizing the human resource altogether. The union would still have a role as the representative of the employees against management stupidity, management arbitrariness, and management abuse of power. This would be not be an adversarial relationship, but would resemble that of the Scandinavian Ombudsman. The union would work with management on productivity and quality, on keeping the enterprise competitive, and thus maintaining the members' jobs and their incomes. (Drucker 1989, 193–194.)

Another example is from Jan Carlzon, who was CEO and president of SAS, Scandinavian Airlines, in the early 1980s. He turned a failing airline prosperous in a fairly short time by offering all SAS employees a new interpretation of their work:

At SAS, we used to think of ourselves as the sum total of our aircraft, our maintenance bases, our offices, and our administrative procedures. But if you ask our customers about SAS, they won't tell you about our planes or our offices or the way we finance our capital investments. Instead, they'll talk about their experiences with the people at SAS. SAS is not a collection of material assets but the quality of the contact between an individual customer and the SAS employees who serve the customer directly. . . . [In 1986] each of our 10 million customers came in contact with approximately five SAS employees, and this contact lasted an average of 15 seconds each time. Thus, SAS "created" 50 million moments a year, 15 seconds at a time. These 50 million "moments of truth" are the moments that ultimately determine whether SAS will succeed or fail as a company. . . . We have to place responsibility for ideas, decisions, and actions with the people who are SAS during those 15 seconds: ticket agents, flight attendants, baggage handlers, and all the other frontline employees. (Carlzon 1989, 2–3)

This interpretation gave Carlzon's SAS employees a new way to look at their work as endless opportunities to satisfy customers, even with the smallest of details. Carlzon gave each individual power to influence customer satisfaction and make SAS great. This innovation turned SAS around in a few short years.

Breakdowns

There are two main obstacles to storytelling: insufficient skill and myths that impede learning the skill.

Insufficient Skill

Robert McKee (1997) says that the biggest breakdown for envisioning is lack of competence at storytelling. We generally are not good at storytelling and we do not receive much social encouragement to cultivate the skill. We tend to leave storytelling to the professionals such as journalists, novelists, screenwriters, and filmmakers. This is not wise because the storytelling skill is essential for innovators; through it they create new worlds for other people to inhabit.

In the mid-1980s, author Peter Denning was concerned that too many people saw computer science as programming. He thought that this narrow image would eventually drive prospective students away from the field. (It did, starting in 2001.) To counteract the narrow image and show computing as field of great depth and breadth, he created the Great Principles of Computing project in the mid-1990s (Denning 2003; Denning and Martell 2004). His colleagues welcomed the initiative, saying that the field had matured enough that it needed to shed its image of chasing the latest technology fads; it was time to reveal the deep, fundamental, and abiding laws on which all computing technologies are based. Denning proposed that these principles be communicated with stories rather than as declarative statements or mathematical formulas. Much to his surprise, when he asked his colleagues to contribute their stories, most asked, "What do you mean by a principle?" At first, he took this reaction to be skepticism about the project. After a while, however, he realized that the question was an honest request for an example of a story that they could imitate. Denning provided such an example about his early scientific work in computing (2005). He concluded that a significant part of the project would be commissioning good stories about computing principles.

In a management class, author Robert Dunham asked his students to write their answers to the question, "What do you care about?" He did this because he knows that effective managers and leaders have very clear commitments, and commit themselves only to what they most deeply care about. He asked the students to present their answers to their colleagues. Much to his surprise, many students were completely baffled by the question. No one had ever asked them to say what they care about. And they lacked a storytelling skill to create such a story. Finally Dunham wrote a piece about what he cares about so that they would have an example to work toward.

The corporate image is a symptom of this breakdown in the business world. It has become part of business orthodoxy that every business should develop a mission statement, a vision statement, and a values statement. Numerous Web sites provide guidance on how to do this, offering helpful books, worksheets, and software. They usually recommend a group brainstorming and consensus process to arrive at these statements. Unfortunately, most of these processes yield uninspiring results. Prominent examples such as Amtrak's "A safe team on time" or a Carmel, California, taxi company's "The honest taxi company" do not inspire much confidence in the corporate visioning process. The most inspiring vision statements come from outside this formal process. One of our favorites is Qigong Master Chunyi Lin's "A healer in every family, a world without pain" (see springforestqigong.org).

Myths
Many people get blocked from developing their storytelling skill by one or more of three unquestioned beliefs.

Myth 1: Journalist skill is needed. This belief holds that we need to have the skill of the professional journalist to be effective at envisioning. It isn't so. Many journalists lack the in-depth knowledge of your particular field and cannot speak to the breakdowns people in your field experience around them. Some of the most moving and touching stories in the world are recorded in the Jack Canfield books *Chicken Soup for the Soul* (Canfield and Hansen 2003): if ordinary people can speak so effectively from their hearts, so can you. You don't even need a written story. It is enough to invent the story in an interactive conversation with someone, and then to repeat and refine the story in subsequent conversations with others.

Myth 2: Logic-based stories sell. This belief holds that people need rational explanations of risks and benefits before they will decide to adopt something new. This belief, unfortunately, substitutes logical mental process for speaking from the heart. The rational explanation won't win many converts for your innovation. You need to engage your listeners' emotions.

Myth 3: Develop an elevator pitch. This belief holds that you have thirty seconds to get someone's attention and it is therefore worthwhile to work on a very short version of your story. This may work if you are able follow Phil Yaffe's advice (2009). More often, it does not work because you simply cannot tell your story in thirty seconds. At one of his workshops, Robert Dunham asked everyone to tell the other two members of their small groups about their "professional offer" with a time limit of one minute. He said the objective is to make your listeners want to continue the conversation. Much to his surprise, nearly everyone in the room got stuck and was unable to engage their listeners—even though in real life they were successful executives with much to offer. Peter Denning, who had been through the exercise before, was sitting in one of the groups. Another participant named Wendy turned to him and said,

"Go ahead, it's your turn, what is your offer?"

He said, "Before we get to that, let me ask: Are you interested in innovation?"

"Yes, indeed, it's a big problem for me in my business, trying to be more innovative than my competitors. I wish I could be better at it."

"I may be able to help you. I'm working on an innovation book. Want to talk more about it later?"

"Sure! But now, let's get back to our exercise. What is your offer?"

"I just made it!"

This conversation illustrates the simplicity of engaging someone in a conversation. It is so much easier than trying to compress your story into thirty seconds. Instead of "elevator pitch," think of a conversation that provokes interest in an area the person cares about and which invites a longer conversation.

What to Practice

Practice is the only way to avoid these breakdowns. Your practice should be oriented not only on building a story, but also on listening to the care, value, and mood you produce. Listen to the *reaction* as much as to your own words.

Practice both written and oral storytelling. You need to be able to write the stories; therefore you need to study the style and patterns of successful stories and learn to write them yourself. You need to say the stories; therefore you need to practice telling them, without notes, to others. In either case, your listeners' feedback helps improve your written and oral versions. Like the skill of oratory, it takes study and practice but pays off handsomely. Here are five practices that will improve your storytelling ability.

First, learn to retell stories that move people. Read to your family *Chicken Soup* stories or children's fairy tales. Include a relevant *Chicken Soup* or *Reader's Digest* story in your speeches. As you use these stories, watch which aspects of them move and inspire people. The more you do this, the sooner you will find yourself able to generate your own stories that move or inspire people.

Second, practice speaking from your heart. The logic-based story of enumerated actions, risks, and benefits, is rational but not compelling. People are moved when you connect with their emotions. One highly effective way to speak from your heart is to tell personal stories about your own struggles with some of the things you are proposing. But don't get too wrapped up in your personal stories. Your ultimate objective is to move the other person, not chronicle your own life.

Third, practice writing stories in the different patterns. Write your proposed innovation as an attractive future, a repulsive past, extrapolation of a trend, a scenario, a new game, a world narrative, and a transformation event. Then write it as a manifesto. You will be surprised at how quickly you can become facile at these patterns if you actually write them out.

Fourth, practice inventing stories through interactive conversations. Try out a piece of story with one person and watch their reaction. If it is good, use that piece again within another person, add something to it, and watch their reaction. Repeat this until you have evolved a story that works. Then write it down. As noted, this practice is a good antidote to the myth of the elevator speech.

Fifth, practice conversations for possibility. Suspend your desire to judge and request actions. Just speculate with other people about what's possible. We often get so wrapped up with the actions, we forget the power and value of speculations.

Conclusions

Envisioning is fundamentally a practice of storytelling. The innovator tells a story about the world that will be produced if people adopt the innovation. The story is vivid, engaging, compelling, and opens new actions. It provokes what listeners care about. It has a flow, either toward an objective or away from a condition. The most successful innovation stories follow a "life struggles" or "manifesto" architecture. Within the architecture, they employ six main subpatterns: attractive future, repulsive past, trend extrapolation, scenarios, new games, and world narratives. The manifesto most closely matches the prime innovation pattern.

You need to cultivate your personal skill at written and oral storytelling. A good place to start is to read stories to your children. Practice telling impromptu stories to groups you meet with. Practice story writing as a literary style. Insert personal stories, or other stories, into all your speeches. Open each meeting with a story that sets the tone. None of these things is hard. You just need to practice them until storytelling becomes second nature.

Bibliography

Burke, James. 1995. *The Day the Universe Changed*. Back Bay Books.

Bush, Vannevar. 1945. "As We May Think." *Atlantic Monthly* (July), http://www.theatlantic.com/doc/print/194507/bush. Accessed January 2010.

Canfield, Jack, and Mark Victor Hansen. 2003. *Chicken Soup for the Soul*. Health Communications, Inc.

Carlzon, Jan. 1989. *Moments of Truth*. Repr., Harper Collins.

Christenson, Clayton. 1997. *The Innovator's Dilemma*. Harvard Business.

Covey, Stephen R. 1990. *The Seven Habits of Highly Effective People*. Simon & Schuster Fireside.

Denning, Peter. 1992. "Educating a New Engineer." *ACM Communications* 35 (12):83–97.

Denning, Peter. 2003. "Great Principles of Computing." *ACM Communications* 46 (11):15–20.

Denning, Peter. 2005. "The Locality Principle." *ACM Communications* 48 (7):19–24.

Denning, Peter, and John Hiles. 2006. "Transformational Events." *Computer Science Education* 16 (2):77–85.

Denning, Peter, and Craig Martell. 2004. Great Principles Web site, http://greatprinciples.org.

Dreyfus, Hubert. 2001. *On the Internet*. Routledge.

Drucker, Peter. 1985. *Innovation and Entrepreneurship*. Harper Perennial. Repr., Harper Business, 1993.

Drucker, Peter. 1989. *The New Realities*. Transaction Publishers.

Edwards, Bradley C., and Eric A. Westling. November 2003. *The Space Elevator: A Revolutionary Earth-to-Space Transportation System*. BC Edwards Publisher.

Edwards, Bradley C. 2005. "A Hoist to the Heavens." *IEEE Spectrum* (Aug.).

Evans, Harold. 2004. *They Made America*. Little Brown.

Grove, Andy. 1999. *Only the Paranoid Survive*. Currency.

Heath, Chip, and Dan Heath. 2007. *Made to Stick*. Random House.

Kennedy, John F. 1961. "Special Message to the Congress on Urgent National Needs." Speech to the full United States Congress on May 25, http://www.jfklibrary.org. Accessed January 2010.

Kotler, Philip, and Fernando Trias de Bes. 2003. *Lateral Marketing: New Techniques for Finding Breakthrough Ideas*. Wiley.

Kuhn, Thomas S. 1962. The Structure of Scientific Revolutions. 2nd ed., University of Chicago Press, 1970.

Kurzweil, Ray. 2000. *The Age of Spiritual Machines: When Computers Exceed Human Intelligence*. Penguin.

Kurzweil, Ray, and Terry Grossman. 2004. *Fantastic Voyage: The Science Behind Radical Life Extension*. Rodale.

Latour, Bruno. 1987. *Science in Action*. Harvard University Press.

Loehr, Jim. 2007. *The Power of Story*. Free Press.

McKee, Robert. 1997. *Story*. Reagan Books (Imprint of Harper Collins).

McKee, Robert. 2003. "Storytelling That Moves People." *Harvard Business Review* (June):51–55.

Moore, Geoffrey. 2002. *Crossing the Chasm*. 2nd ed., Harper Business.

Noam, Eli. 1995. Electronics and the Dim Future of the University. *Science* 270 (Oct. 13):247–249.

Ogilvy, James A. 2002. *Creating Better Futures*. Oxford University Press.

Rapaille, Clotaire. 2006. *The Culture Code*. Broadway Books.

Schank, Roger. 1995. *Tell Me a Story*. Northwestern University Press.

Schwartz, Peter. 1991. *The Art of the Long View: Planning for the Future in an Uncertain World*. Currency Doubleday.

Seely Brown, John, and Paul Duguid. 2000. *The Social Life of Information*. Harvard Business School Press.

Slywotzky, Adrian. 1995. *Value Migration*. Harvard Business School Press.

Tehranian, Majid. 2001. The End of University *Journal of United States Distance Learning Association* (October).

Walter, Dave. 1992. *Today Then: Americas Best Minds Look 100 Years into the Future on the Occasion of the 1893 World's Columbian Exposition*. American World Geographic Publishing.

Wills, Garry. 1992. *Lincoln at Gettysburg: The Words That Remade America*. Simon & Schuster Touchstone.

Yaffe, Phil. 2009. How to Generate Reader Interest in Why You Write. *ACM Ubiquity* 10 (7), http://www.acm.org/ubiquity/volume_10/v10i7_yaffe.html.

7

Practice Three: Offering

If a man is offered a fact that goes against his instincts he will scrutinize it closely, and unless the evidence is overwhelming, he will refuse to believe it. If, on the other hand, he is offered something that affords a reason for acting in accordance with his instincts, he will accept it even on the slightest evidence.
—Bertrand Russell

Often someone is obliging enough to offer me a light, and in order to oblige him I have to fish a cigarette out of my pocket.
—Karl Kraus

Our proposed innovation begins its journey from an idea to an adopted practice when we make an offer to bring it into the world.

The act of making an offer seems simple enough. We make offers by the dozens from simple to sublime: we hold a door open for someone, extend a hand to someone in need, discuss our skills during interviews, present our projects, propose business plans, put up Web pages about our services, or market our products worldwide. So it should be equally easy to offer up our innovation.

Not necessarily. Many of our listeners will not accept our offers. Experienced sales people expect that 90 percent of their cold calls will lead nowhere. They focus on their successes and look for ways to orient their offers for higher success rates. Many innovators, however, are not trained salespeople and are not used to failure. Common reactions are to become defensive about the current offer, or to refrain from future offers out of fear of disappointment or rejection. These reactions will lead to failure of the innovation.

In 1989, Tim Berners-Lee's first offer to build a prototype of the World Wide Web (WWW) was a concept paper about applying hypertext in order to share documents in his laboratory at CERN. He was taken aback when key individuals at CERN ignored his proposal and did not even respond. His colleague Robert Caillou, a senior manager, advised him that he needed user support to get the attention of other senior managers. So he talked to various people who might be prime users of his proposed technology. He discovered ways that the technology would help them—for example, giving access to the CERN phone book and to news and discussion groups, and giving them online access to new research papers. He modified his proposal so that the first applications would be in these areas. He won enough support to get management attention and permission to build a prototype Web server and browser on a NeXT computer. The prototypes strengthened his offer by building trust in him and the value of the technology. They convinced a widening circle of users to commit to the Web.

Because of his commitment to a "worldwide Web," Berners-Lee took his offer outside of CERN. He demonstrated his prototype at a hypertext research conference in 1991. Those researchers were already staunch advocates of hypertext and it was easy for them to see the potential of hypertext links to anywhere in the Web. Soon members of that community set up their own Web servers, making offers of their own. They prototyped a World Wide Web. It started small and grew quickly.

The moral of this story is that an offer is not an event; it is a process. Offers evolve over time in conversations with many people. Berners-Lee overcame his initial failure by careful listening and improving his offer to respond to his user community. As his offer (and the prototypes reflecting it) became gradually more compelling, the set of people who wanted to participate grew. Berners-Lee eventually evolved an offer with worldwide appeal.

The offer practice prepares you for the process. We will discuss the anatomy of a successful offer—the essential ingredients and structure. We will also discuss the most common reasons that offers fail, which include conditioned tendencies such as defensiveness, confusion, and withdrawal. When you are good at the practice, you will be able to diagnose failures as missing parts of the anatomy or as conditioned tendencies, and then to focus on the process of continually improving your offer.

Anatomy of an Offer

Let us begin with the structure of an "offer." A successful offer, like a healthy body, has a definite anatomy. The more you understand the parts of an offer's anatomy, the more success you will have with offers.

The dictionary says that an offer is a proposition presented for acceptance or rejection. The kind of offer needed for successful innovation is more than a simple proposition. It is a conversational process of reaching agreements with a community of listeners who commit to a new practice and to reciprocal actions such as payment, preparation of environment, or abandonment of old practices. The offer process has four main components:

• Readiness, the innovator's preparation and willingness to make an offer
• The offer act, the actual steps and interactions of the offer
• Listener response, the assessments made by listeners that affect their willingness to commit
• Anticipating yes (meaning acceptance of the offer), the steps needed to achieve the outcome and manage the risks.

These components are repeated and refined in each cycle of an offer's evolution.

We will use the term *listener* for someone who listens to an offer, but does not necessarily commit to it, and the term *customer* for someone who commits and is expecting satisfaction in the future. A listener is a potential customer.

Readiness
The innovator (person making the offer) has to be prepared to make an offer. Preparation includes the work of the previous practices (sensing, envisioning), previous experience with offers, study of the intended audience, and analysis of costs and risks. Without such preparation, the offer will not launch, and without the launch, it will not succeed.

Being prepared is not enough. You must also have the courage and willingness to make the offer. From our work with clients, we know that self-abort-on-launch is common and that many offers are never made.

Mary was one of our students who aspired to get a PhD and become a college teacher. She admired a particular professor for his intellectual gifts and international reputation, and wished to study with him. He knew of her and told us he would be delighted to take her on as a PhD student. But she avoided talking with him about this, even keeping her distance from him in any setting where an impromptu conversation could start. When we asked why she did not approach him, she replied: "How could a man of such intellect and stature possibly want a nobody like me as a student?" So there was, sadly, no deal. Mary was prepared for PhD study, but her fear kept her from offering to be a PhD student.

The Offer Act

There are five necessities for an effective offer. Take away any one, and the offer cannot succeed.

1. *A performer*

This person proposes to produce a desirable new outcome. We will use the name "Alice" for a generic performer.

2. *Individual listeners*

Listeners are people who respond to offers by committing (thereby becoming a customer) or declining. Even if an offer is made to many, each one must decide whether to be in or out. Declines are often not explicit; they occur when listeners ignore or fail to respond to the offer. We will use the name "Bob" for a generic listener or customer.

It is surprising how many performers think they have made an offer but there are no customers, or how many customers think they have heard an offer but there is no performer. If you have published an article, a memo, a Web page, or a blog entry you probably know the disappointment of having no one respond to your written idea. You were a performer without customers. Or if you have ever developed expectations about what a spouse, a boss, or a company will do for you, you probably know the chagrin of learning that no one actually made a promise and nothing will be done. You were a customer without a performer.

3. *The performer's promise*

The promise to deliver a future of value to customers may aim at delivering a tangible result by a deadline; or it may aim at moving in a direction of importance to the customers. Good offers resonate with something deep in their customers, something they care about and are willing to commit to. The organization Mothers Against Drunk Driving (MADD) did not offer to amend drunk-driving laws; it offered to work for culture change to protect children and loved ones from drunk drivers. Google did not offer a faster search engine; it offered to organize all the world's information.

4. *A "background of obviousness"*

Performers and customers interpret the conditional promise contained in the offer relative to their own background and experience. They will assume that certain things are obvious and do not need to be spelled out. The assumption that the other party sees things the same way as oneself can lead to trouble. The performer needs to pay attention not only to what is said in the offer, but also to what is not said and is tacitly understood. Otherwise there will be misunderstandings and the offer will fail. An example is the two different meanings of *programmer* in the university and the business world. Computer science departments interpret programmer broadly, as encompassing systems architect, designer, applications analyst, algorithms analyst, tester, and validator. The business world and government interpret programmer narrowly—as someone who codes. Students considering majors hear the computer science offer of "we will make you a programmer" as "we will prepare you for a low-level job that is likely to be outsourced." It is not surprising that many qualified students decline to major in computer science.

Another example is the much-reviled Interactive Voice Recognition (IVR) system that has become the darling of businesses. Businesses like IVRs because they can eliminate as much as 85 percent of businesses' call center staff. Customers hate them. Some very fed-up customers created the Web site gethuman.com, which specifies how to reach human customer service agents at companies that would prefer to hide access. To the business, it seems that an offer to cut costs and thereby lower prices by using IVRs would please their customers. To the customers, it seems that the business does not want to talk to them directly about customer service problems. The disconnect takes a large toll on customer loyalty.

5. Action conversation

The offer conversation is an interaction between the performer and the customer. It can be represented as cycle in which the offer is made, negotiated, agreed to, delivered, and accepted (figure 7.1). An incomplete cycle is an unfulfilled offer.

Listener Response
The listener's response to an offer is crucial to the outcome. If listeners do not respond favorably, they decline the offer. The proposed innovation fails.

The performer (Alice) has the responsibility to understand how the listener (Bob) responds. We call this *listening to the listening*. Fortunately, Alice does not have to understand every aspect of a listener. What are important are Bob's assessments of value, trust, and satisfaction. Figure 7.2 depicts the relative timings of these assessments.

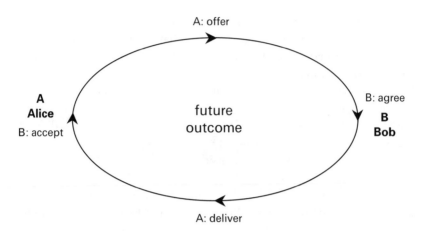

Figure 7.1
This action cycle depicts interaction around an offer between Alice (as performer) and Bob (as customer). Alice offers the future outcome; after a possible negotiation, Bob agrees; Alice delivers the outcome; Bob validates and accepts the outcome. For innovation, Alice does not actually promise the outcome; she promises her commitment to produce it. Bob agrees to the risk that Alice may fail. Alice's success depends ultimately on Bob's adopting the outcome (Practice Four) and sustaining it (Practice Five).

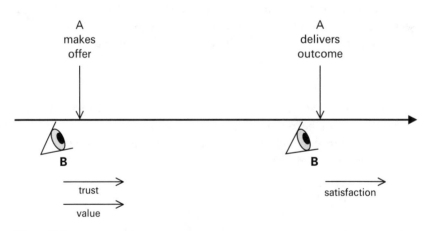

Figure 7.2
Alice (A), the performer, makes an offer, whereupon Bob (B), the customer, reacts with assessments of value and trust. Value is the belief that the offer is worth committing to. Trust is the belief that the future outcome will be delivered. When Alice delivers the outcome, Bob makes a satisfaction assessment, which is that the promised value has been delivered or exceeded. At the time of the offer, Bob trusts that he will be satisfied in the future.

Value is Bob's assessment that the offer is worth committing to: there is a net gain in sacrificing something in the current environment in favor of the new practice. Bob's value assessment is driven by his own concerns, by the prevailing concerns and moods in the community, the configuration of existing practice, the existence of alternatives, the costs, and the savings. Bob will more readily commit when he sees high value in the offer—that it promises a significant advantage over the status quo. Alice realizes that value is always in the eyes of the listener. Alice cannot be sure whether the offer is valuable until she sees how Bob reacts and until she listens to Bob's concerns. That learning process may entail several failed offers before a successful one.

Trust is Bob's belief that Alice is committed to protecting his interests and making the future outcome happen. Trust is complicated. It depends on Bob's perceptions of Alice in respect to:

• Care for his concerns and interests,
• Sincerity,
• Competence,
• Reliability in past performances, and
• Risk tolerance.

Satisfaction is Bob's assessment that the future outcome will deliver the promised value. While the final version of this assessment must await Alice's delivery, Bob will decide at the time of the offer whether there is a reasonable basis for expecting satisfaction.

In working his way to an offer that many people wanted to accept, Berners-Lee had to produce positive assessments of value, trust, and satisfaction. It took him several tries before he found a way to state the value that colleagues at CERN could understand and be willing to use on their desktop computers. His first attempt, a document sharing system, seemed abstract and did not solve any existing problem. His second attempt, providing an on-desk calendar, newsgroups, and links to new research papers, was something they wanted. At the ACM Hypertext'91 conference he demonstrated a working prototype that offered all the value that his previous conversations had shown him people would respond to. A few years later, when Marc Andreesen produced the first portable graphical browser (Mosaic), many people leapt at the opportunity to join the WWW. Not only did they see great personal value in accelerating their own research and enlarging their own knowledge, they saw big downside costs if they stayed outside the WWW network.

Through the process of interacting with listeners and customers about the offer, and revising the offer, the innovator comes to learn what potential customers value most, what they are looking for before they will trust, and what it will take to satisfy them.

Anticipating Yes

A common way to judge an offer's success is by the number of acceptances. Salespeople say that acceptance rates to cold calls are usually well under 10 percent, and so they are willing to accept rejection rates well over 90 percent. Good salespeople are able to take satisfaction in their successes and slough off the rejections without taking them personally. They say, "The market is not ready for this offer," rather than "I don't have the right personality for my customers."

An innovator's success is similarly judged by the number and extent of adoptions. The listener's decision to adopt is an initial "yes," and ongoing adoption is a sustained "yes." The practices of adopting and sustaining are discussed in later chapters. Because potential customers are most likely to decline uninteresting offers without negotiation, the negotiation phase of the innovator's offer conversation often looks like a series of repeated offers until the innovator finds one that potential customers will adopt. The offer practice therefore anticipates success in the adopting and sustaining practices, but does not include them.

The innovator as performer has to address customer concerns about two other issues on the path to adoption: how the outcome will be achieved and how failure risks will be managed. Even when the outcome is clearly stated and understood, customers want to know the expected path. This is especially true if the outcome requires significant changes of practice and it is not obvious how they will happen. What is involved to achieve the outcome? What steps must we take? How long will it take? To build trust for the offer, the innovator has to have ready answers for such questions, for otherwise the listeners will hesitate to commit.

No path is risk free. Anywhere along the way a key step may fail. Customers will want to know what kinds of risks they will face and what steps they and the innovator can take to mitigate them. The innovator must understand the nature of the risks and the problems involved in managing them. Only then can the innovator provide assurances to the customers that may lower the perceived risks below their personal thresholds of tolerance.

As with the development of a compelling offer, the process of articulating a path and ways of managing the risks is iterative. Innovators who do not have a clear articulation of path, or assurances about risks, will encounter many declines. Only by listening and refining the path and risks can they hope to get to an articulation that works.

When President John F. Kennedy proposed in 1961 the NASA program for getting a man to the moon, he explicitly acknowledged the huge risks entailed. His exact words were: "This nation should commit itself to achieving the goal, before this decade is out, of landing a man on the moon and returning him safely to the earth." The rest of his speech outlined the areas of risk and how they would be approached. Kennedy spelled out a path, said it would not be easy, and made it a priority to manage the risks.

Summary of the Offer
The fundamental offer components of readiness, the offer act, listener response, and anticipating yes are summarized in box 7.1. All these components are necessary: if any one is missing, the offer will fail.

In the light of these aspects of offers, it is easy to see why the manifesto offer form discussed in chapter 6 is so powerful. By calling attention to the "dying cows" the manifesto establishes immediate value to the listeners. By demonstrating that previous attempts to save the cows failed because of a limitation in the prevailing common sense, it offers an understanding of the source of the problem. By describing a new common sense and its possibilities for protecting the cows, it opens confidence that the new possibility will work. By describing the innovator's expertise and experience with the practice, it builds trust. And it offers an action proposal that shows how to get from the present to the proposed future and manage the risks along the way.

Breakdowns

The four components of an offer conversation are all opportunities for breakdowns. If any one of the components is missing, the offer is likely to fail. This anatomy gives you the opportunity to observe, and correct, the conditions and events that will interrupt offers. Once you know the causes of failures, you can either (1) acknowledge the breakdown and recover, or (2) avoid the breakdown by steering clear of conditions that foster it and learning skills that dodge it.

Box 7.1
Essential Elements of an Offer

Readiness:

1. The performer's preparation
2. The performer's courage or willingness to make an offer

The offer act:

1. The performer (offerer, proposer), who promises to generate the future outcome and describes the nature of actions and the level of commitment required of the listener
2. The listener (audience, customer), who commits to adopting the future outcome; how they listen
3. The future outcome, as a condition of satisfaction with a time frame
4. The "background of obviousness"—that which is not said but is commonly understood by the parties; the "common sense" that influences the alignment between performer and listener
5. The interaction: offer, negotiate, agree, promise, deliver, accept

Listener response:

1. Value: Belief that the offered outcome is worth committing to
2. Trust: Belief that the promised outcome is likely to happen
3. Satisfaction: Belief that the delivered outcome meets or exceeds the promised value

Anticipating yes:

1. Path to the outcome
2. Nature of the risks and how they can be addressed
3. Learning from failures, improving, and repeating the offer

---

A good offer always creates a breakdown for the listener. Even if the listener wants the outcome, the offer presents an interruption to the status quo that must be dealt with. Your listener's reaction can be to seize the opportunity ("I trust the performer to help me through the transition to get the outcome"), to slip into resignation ("That outcome is unattainable, I don't have the means to get it, forget it"), or to see an obstacle ("Accepting this would interfere with other commitments, leaving me worse off"). You have to listen to your listeners' reactions and help them past the breakdowns they see by showing them how they can have the outcome they value.

Box 7.2 lists common offer breakdowns. Notice that all take the form of negative assessments by the listener, which become reasons for declining. The astute innovator will anticipate these listener reactions and have

Box 7.2
Examples of Common Offer Breakdowns

The offer:

is infeasible

is too expensive

requires too much time and effort

won't integrate with current practices

promises insufficient advantage over current practice

claims satisfaction that does not match perceived value

goes too far in the future

entails risks that are too great

takes a path that is uncertain

comes from an untrustworthy proposer

comes from a proposer who is not credible

raises concerns the proposer isn't addressing

overwhelms me and I have no capacity to consider it

would establish a new order threatening my position (or power, or income)

---

good answers ready for them. Many of the listener responses reflect a mood of resignation, that is, a pessimism that worthwhile changes cannot actually succeed.

Resignation can afflict the innovator as well as the listener. This is especially common after previous failures of offers. The reaction, "I don't know why I can't succeed with my offers, I should just give up," clearly will not help the innovation succeed. In contrast, the reaction, "I see that my offer failed because an element was missing; in the future I will make sure that element is present," is part of the path to success. Developing skill with the elements of an offer can be a good antidote to resignation about making offers. After you practice post-mortem diagnosis and correction for a while, you will be able to do diagnose and correct in real time, adapting quickly to the circumstances and making successful offers.

What to Practice

The offer anatomy reveals four components to good offer practice: readiness, the offer act, listener response, and anticipating yes. It is well worth paying attention to the offers you make and diagnosing them to see what has worked and what has failed. Most people are already good at one or two of the main components and can focus their learning attention on the weaker components. Your objective is to learn offers as an embodied skill in which you attend to all the components automatically.

Practice in live conversation. The offer is not one hit-or-miss encounter; it is an ongoing process of finding the value for your listeners. Practice getting into a discussion with someone about a future outcome that you both care about. Practice making offers individually and in groups. At work, ask a group for a critique on your current articulation of an offer.

Groups are particularly effective for getting useful feedback. In a workshop, we asked people to sit in groups of three to practice talking about their professional offers and receive feedback from the others. The participants found this quite revealing because normally their listeners do not critique their statements.

In another workshop exercise, we had group members practice one element of the offer practice—communicating their expertise. Each person presented their offer and answered questions, and then the group voted on whether they accepted the claimed expertise. One of the biggest difficulties presenters discovered was that their audience did not understand either the meanings of basic terms or the standards defining expertise in their fields. They had to practice offering background information about their fields before they could get good buy-in on their claims of expertise.

You don't need to set up workshop exercises to practice. Simply engage in conversation with your audience about possibilities you see they care about.

Diagnose and assess. You'll want to review failed offers to see which elements were missing. Make special efforts to have that element present in your future offers. Try the offer again with that listener and see if by adding back the missing element you can move the conversation forward and close the deal.

Get a coach. An experienced coach or mentor can help you see aspects of your practice that you have overlooked. Their feedback and guidance can significantly improve your practice. Some people who practice offer conversations find that they are challenged by the embodied skills that are needed—for example, connecting, relaxing, staying present, coming across well, and listening well. We address these skills as part of the somatics dimension in chapter 12. Conditioned tendencies that block these skills can be devilishly hard to see on your own. If overcoming conditioned tendencies is a focus of your practice, we highly recommend finding a coach who can give you guidance and feedback on what to pay attention to.

Keep a journal. You own personal notes can be a rich source of feedback. Record your offers and your expectations of the outcomes. Later, you can compare the actual outcomes against the expected ones. Over time, you will see clearly which of your practices are paying off. You will also identify habitual patterns where your expectations are not met. You may need help from a coach to break those habits, or you may simply need to get someone else to do those things for you. Management guru Peter Drucker was a keen practitioner and advocate of journaling:

> Whenever you make a key decision or take a key action, write down what you expect will happen. Nine or 12 months later, compare the actual results with your expectations. I have been practicing this method for 15 to 20 years now, and every time I do it, I am surprised. The feedback analysis showed me, for instance—and to my great surprise—that I have an intuitive understanding of technical people, whether they are engineers or accountants or market researchers. It also showed me that I don't really resonate with generalists.

> Practiced consistently, this simple method will show you within a fairly short period of time, maybe two or three years, where your strengths lie—and that is the most important thing to know. The method will show you what you are doing or failing to do that deprives you of the full benefits of your strengths. It will show you where you are not particularly competent. And finally, it will show you where you have no strengths and cannot perform. (Drucker 1998, 66)

Drucker sees six benefits from the journaling process: (1) it reveals your strengths and allows you to concentrate on using them; (2) it reveals gaps in your knowledge and can guide you to new learning; (3) it reveals your intellectual overconfidence and allows you to overcome it; (4) it reveals your bad habits and gives you the opportunity to remedy them; (5) it reveals where bad manners are getting in your way; and (6) it reveals what you ought not to promise to do, because you seldom deliver.

Conclusions

The offer is the key step that connects the articulation of possibility with the listener's commitment to its adoption. The offer draws on your work in the first two practices (sensing and envisioning) and prepares for the next two (adopting and sustaining).

The offer itself is not simply a proposition presented for acceptance or rejection. It is a conversation. It has four components that all have to work for the offer to be accepted: readiness, the offer act, listener response, and anticipating yes. Your ability to listen to the listener's assessments of value, trust, and satisfaction, and then to adapt the offer to the listener's concerns, is the center of the practice. It involves listening for value and for what is not said but is obvious, showing a path to the outcome, and managing risks. Only when the listener trusts you to deliver a satisfactory outcome with value, will that listener commit to your offer.

In *Finite and Infinite Games*, James Carse (1986) says: "A finite game is played for the purpose of winning, an infinite game for the purpose of continuing the play." The common interpretation of offer is a finite, win-or-lose encounter. We are saying in this chapter that our offers will be much more effective when we play them as infinite games. By staying engaged with our listeners (Fisher, Ury, and Patton 1991), we will find how to get them to yes.

Bibliography

Carse, James. 1986. *Finite and Infinite Games*. Ballantine Books.

Drucker, Peter. 1998. Managing Oneself. *Harvard Business Review*. (March–April):65–72.

Fisher, Roger, William Ury, and Bruce Patton. 1991. *Getting to Yes: Negotiating Agreement Without Giving In*. 2nd repr., Penguin.

8

Practice Four: Adopting

The diffusion of innovations explains social change, one of the most fundamental of human processes.
—Everett Rogers

The resistance to change exhibited by social systems is much more nearly a form of "dynamic conservatism"—a tendency to fight to remain the same.
—Donald Schon

Adoption occurs three times in every innovation: in the mind, in the hand, and in the body. The first adoption occurs when people in a community commit to considering the idea of a new practice. The second adoption occurs when they commit to trying their hand at it for the first time. The third adoption occurs when they commit to sustain it over time. The first adoption is the outcome of the offering practice, the second the outcome of the adopting practice, and the third the outcome of the sustaining practice. We will examine now the work of the adopting practice.

It is quite common that our first innovation proposals do not sell. Tim Berners-Lee's first conception of the World Wide Web did not sell. But he did not give up. Instead, he became a student of why people at CERN (his employer) used the Internet and what value it offered them. He wanted to learn not only why his idea did not sell, but also what would sell.

He learned that the Internet delivered its greatest value when it brought his colleagues information that helped them do their jobs better. To show them that the WWW could do this better than anything in the Internet, he built a prototype browser, a mechanism that brought them valuable information instantly after a single mouse-click. He worked to overcome management resistance against such a venture in his own organization.

He persuaded programmers to build production browsers and start a network of Web servers. When he found that business leaders were not keen on the Web, he worked to make the Web a friendly place for business. When he saw that a few commercial providers wanted to appropriate the Web technology for their intellectual property, he worked hard to establish the World Wide Web Consortium (W3C) to keep the Web technology in the public domain and to encourage commercial factions and groups to cooperate on its development.

Berners-Lee's experience is typical of what all innovators face. Five key aspects of adoption are seen his story:

1. He sought an understanding of the social networks to which his potential adopters belonged. He found that each network had its own concerns. The more he understood those concerns, the better he became at answering them in his stories about the value of the Web.
2. He entered into conversations with decision makers and customers in the network, and he sought from them various kinds of commitments to participate in the Web.
3. He balanced his own natural optimism for beneficial results from the Web with potential adopters' natural pessimism over adoption costs.
4. He recruited many supporters and allies, especially among the thought leaders of communities and the executives of important organizations. They helped contain the resistance to his proposals.
5. He adapted the story of his innovation to the concerns of the different types of adopters, from visionaries (who love new technology) to the cautious majority (who want assurances that the innovation integrates sustainably into their environments).

In short, adoption is work. It does not merely involve taking a good idea and packaging it in a good story that sticks with people (Heath and Heath 2007). It also takes a lot of listening and understanding of the social network of adopters. It means establishing incontrovertible value for the innovation while also overcoming the natural resistance some elements of the community will have toward change.

Adoption is not marketing, although it is an outcome of marketing. Marketing departments tend to be staffed with people adept in the adoption practice. Marketing is a large, complex subject. The Wikipedia article on marketing (2010) says it is organized around a series of P's: product, pricing, promotion, placement, people, process, physical evidence, and philosophy. On the one hand, marketing is especially important for large-scale adoptions. On the other hand, many innovators skilled in the adoption practice have succeeded without help from a marketing department.

Adoption Models

We discussed in chapter 3 two models of the adoption process. The Everett Rogers model focuses on diffusion: "A process in which an innovation is communicated through certain channels over time among the members of a social system" (Rogers 1962). The Donald Schon model focuses on learning networks: "A process of overcoming the social system's natural resistance to change by transforming its structure, concept, and technology" (Schon 1971).

We like Rogers's emphasis on communication and Schon's on the dynamic conservatism of social groups. However, neither emphasis is sufficient to produce the objective of the adopting practice: an initial commitment to enter the practice of the innovation. We therefore offer our own anatomy of adoption, drawing on the best points of both models and focusing on the actions innovators take in their conversations.

The central idea of Rogers's model is that adoption is a communication process in a social system. Information about the innovation propagates outward from the innovator to members of the community by various community-dependent channels. The channels include word of mouth, advertising, endorsements, trade shows, professional and trade organizations, publications, feedback from other members who have tried the innovation, and peer reviews. Members fall into five categories of adoption temperament—inventors, early adopters, early and late majorities, and laggards—according to their openness to the innovation, the data they demand, and the time they take to decide affirmatively. Beginning in the 1950s, Rogers validated his model extensively for agricultural development, medical technology, and numerous industries. His work strongly influenced the principles of marketing and is taken as a classic in many marketing departments.

The central idea of the Schon model is that innovation is a change in the way a social system behaves. The change involves transformations of structure, concept, and technology. The social system is likely to actively resist the changes, a condition Schon called dynamic conservatism. Many instigators of social change resort to insurrections or revolutions to overcome the resistance. The main limitation of this model is that it does not show what conversations the innovator must enter, what

Table 8.1
Limitations of Diffusion and Learning-Network Models

Assumption	What actually happens
Innovator communicates information about the innovation.	Innovator elicits commitments to enter into the new practice.
Innovations start as ideas.	Many innovations start as practices that are later described as "ideas."
Innovations spread into the community from a source.	Many innovations arise spontaneously without an identifiable source.
People adopt by making affirmative decisions after gathering information.	People adopt by many means including impulse and imitation.
Resistance to change is inertia that can be overcome with steady pressure.	Resistance to change is active pushback from those who seek to neutralize or eliminate the innovation.

kinds of commitments to seek, and what kinds of breakdowns (aside from resistance) to overcome.

Moreover, both models are descriptive. They offer many useful ideas, but no generative framework for adoption.

Table 8.1 summarizes the central assumptions of the Rogers and Schon models and common conditions that violate them. Everything they say is true, but it is not everything the innovator faces.

Anatomy of Adoption

Our anatomy of adoption assumes that the innovator is interacting with a community (social system or network). The innovator's purpose is to induce the social network to adopt and embody a new practice. To achieve initial adoption, the innovator must initiate and guide five basic conversations summarized in table 8.2 and discussed at more length as follows.

Understand the Network

Schon's framework is a useful way to understand the community targeted for adoption. He distinguishes

- Structure (key social relationships in the community),
- Conceptual framework (principles of the community), and
- Technologies (those in use by the community).

Table 8.2
Anatomy of Adoption

Conversation	Purpose
Understand the network.	Get to know the adopting community's structure, conceptual framework, and technologies.
Listen to and interact with the network.	Discover what gets people to commit and what does not. Discover strategies to induce change.
Blend around resistance.	Translate between innovator's natural optimism about benefits and adopter's natural pessimism about costs. Find ways to address the concerns of those resisting.
Recruit supporters and allies.	Get opinion leaders to endorse you and speak on your behalf, and to help overcome resistance.
Learn what the network values.	Adapt the innovation story to reflect what you are learning. The evolving story shows each interest group in the network how their concerns are addressed.

The structure aspect includes roles, authorities, groups, reporting relationships, chains of command, consultancies, and primary working relationships. A practice called "social network mapping" is often used to reveal the structural aspect of a network. It means to understand the network as linked conversations and relationships, and thereby to identify the influence wielded by each person and role in the network. Social network maps usually reveal individuals, known as hubs and brokers, who are strongly connected to many others; hubs and brokers often have more influence than senior executives. Executives influence people by making decisions, declaring strategies, and giving orders; opinion leaders (hubs) influence by having large audiences that listen and heed them; and brokers influence by getting otherwise disconnected groups to talk with each other. Multiple maps or perspectives may be necessary to understand a network's structure: an organization chart for the reporting relationships, a social networking chart for the most common message exchanges (Barabasi 2003; Denning 2004), and a workflow chart for the main business processes (Denning and Medina-Mora 1995). In addition, it is crucial to discover the degree of leadership, power, and influence of each faction or interest group.

Understanding the conceptual framework of the network is more challenging than mapping its structure. In chapter 4 we discussed domain mapping, an effective practice for understanding a network. The practice is to determine—through conversations with people in the network or through their documents—the network's language, standard practices, breakdowns, moods, and beliefs (illustrated by Denning and Dargan 1996). What you would most like to know are the network's core assumptions, values, ambitions, and revered traditions; they are often tacit and most people are not explicitly aware of them. Such beliefs are rooted in their history: it will benefit you to read historical summaries or learn oral traditions of the community. If your innovation supports those deep beliefs, it is likely to be adopted. If your innovation challenges a deep belief, it is likely to be resisted. You want to know this as early as possible so that you can develop your strategies for meeting the resistance.

Understanding the technologies in use is often the easiest of the three aspects. The technologies are usually evident and it is usually easy to get people to talk about how they were adopted and what good they serve.

Listen to and Interact with the Network

Armed with knowledge of the structure, concept, and technologies of a network, the innovator initiates the adoption process by entering into conversations with the leaders, representatives, and members of the network. These conversations are of three kinds: listening, persuasion, and strategy.

Listening conversations include interviews, surveys, focus groups, and observation of the discussions under way in the network. These "information gathering" aspects help the innovator discern the concerns, values, and standards for commitment in the network. They lay the groundwork for the persuasion and strategy conversations. Even when those conversations are under way, we must always be listening.

A persuasion conversation aims to elicit a commitment from listeners by demonstrating the high value of the proposed change and a low-cost method to get there. The persuasion conversation is complicated by a gap between the natural tendencies of the innovator and the network members. The innovator tends to dwell on the benefits of the innovation—the various advantages that will come from the change. The network representatives will tend to dwell on the adoption costs—all the costs, tangible and intangible, that must be borne to complete the change, including money, status, power, and so on. They are the costs of the sacrifices needed to make room for the new practice.

The innovator will often benefit from an "innovation broker" or facilitator—someone who is familiar with both the innovator's and the prospective adopter's worlds. This person can help translate between the languages of the two sides, facilitating agreements.

A strategy conversation focuses on how to bring community members into the new practice. Common strategies include:

• *Directives from the top* A person in authority issues a directive that everyone in the group should learn and follow a new procedure. The directive will define the procedure and provide for training. This is a common approach in bureaucratic organizations, especially government. Unfortunately, it frequently fails if the affected constituency does not buy the rationale for the new procedure. Objectors can stall the implementation or ignore it, reverting back to the old way as soon as command changes.

• *Leadership from the top* Top leaders of the group commit to the change through their own example and enter into persuasion conversations with the group members. This approach is often used in large-scale marketing, where celebrities extol the new practice and entreat others to follow. It can be adapted to any setting in which there is no central authority to issue directives.

• *Leadership from the grassroots* The innovator finds groups representing individual community members who work on their peers for adoption of the new practice. It then becomes an easy sell to top leadership based on its popularity.

• *Pilot projects, rapid prototypes* The innovator offers a small-scale version of the innovation to help people appreciate the benefits. The prototype can be iteratively improved. Positive experience with the prototype is a strong selling point.

• *Incremental adoption* The innovator establishes beachheads of adopters within larger communities; they demonstrate the value of the innovation to everyone else.

• *Disruption insurance* The innovator develops and tests a new technology in a confined setting but does not offer it for general adoption. This is a way to develop a technology that a secretive competitor might possibly be pursuing. The innovator ensures against the possible disruption a competitor might cause by bringing the same technology to market first. Intel Chairman Andy Grove (1999) applied this principle to pursue potentially disruptive technologies in parallel with the main programs of the Intel Corporation.

• *Insurgency*   The innovator works clandestinely with others to quietly put pieces of the innovation in place, unnoticed by the mainstream, until a compelling demonstration can be made from the installed pieces. This approach is used when authorities and thought leaders are in opposition.

• *Revolution*   The innovator works publicly with a group whose intent is to overthrow the existing "order" (paradigm) and replace it with a new one. This is the strategy discussed by Thomas Kuhn (1962) for scientific revolutions.

In pursuing any of these strategies, the innovator pays constant attention to how the strategy will affect the three aspects of the network—structure, concept, and technology. Even if the strategy focuses on just one aspect, its interactions with the other two will nonetheless be important. The U.S. Navy Lt. William Sims gunnery story (see chapter 2) illustrates what happens with a strategy that focuses on one aspect alone. Sims proposed a technology and then encountered stiff resistance from leadership who thought he challenged a fundamental concept of ship society.

Blend around Resistance

In interacting with the network, the innovator will encounter both natural resistance to change and conflicts around claimed benefits and adoption costs. The innovator aims to blend with the resistance and resolve the conflict.

Blending is a leadership term borrowed from the martial arts (Strozzi-Heckler 2007). In the martial arts it means to move in alignment with the attacker's force, redirecting that force to the leader's objective. Conversationally, blending means to move to address the other person's concerns instead of resisting. If your response to an objection is, "Your objection has no basis," you are not blending. If your response is, "I see your concern and see a way to take care of it," you are blending.

On-the-spot improvisations are a form of blending. Good musicians improvise smooth transitions around their own mistakes; their listeners do not notice the faulty notes. We were once present when a businessman was making an offer of a news-clipping service to a group. He quoted a price; all the businesspeople in the audience said they could get their companies to pay. Several educators in the group said that they had no means to pay. The businessman said, "OK, I'll invent an education price," and quoted a lower rate. When the educators agreed, the businessman had sold his service to everyone in the room. His improvisation enabled him to win over the whole group.

Disguise is a form of blending. Disguise means that the new thing blends into the surroundings so that others are less likely to notice. Nature is a master of disguise—think of shrimps that blend with the colors of the ocean floors, caterpillars that resemble twigs, butterflies whose wing patterns resemble bird droppings, white polar bears that cannot be seen against the snow, tiger and zebra stripes that blend with the moving backgrounds of scattered trees, or chameleons that change their colors to match backgrounds. These disguises protect prey from being eaten and predators from being detected. Terry Pierce (2004) has found that a large number of successful disruptive innovations succeeded because their leaders disguised them as straightforward improvements to familiar things.

Apple iTunes technology illustrates a disruptive innovation that at first appeared to be a sustaining innovation. iTunes initially focused on being an online download music store that met all copyright requirements. Napster's approach of distributing copyrighted songs for free had encountered a buzz saw of resistance from publishing houses. By providing royalties to publishers, iTunes posed no threat. However, iTunes welcomed artists who wanted to publish directly without the involvement of a publishing house. iTunes's cadre of independent artists eventually grew to a significant number, raising concerns among publishing houses that iTunes was taking business from them. By that time, iTunes had become a well-established business; threats to stop using them as a distributor were counterproductive. The publishing houses now compete by offering new services attractive to artists. Imagine the resistance Apple would have sparked if they had announced iTunes as "a new paradigm of music publishing and distribution" instead of "an online music store that protects its customers from copyright infringement." Apple executed a very nice blend when introducing their innovation.

Amazon.com has accomplished a similar blend with their online book-store, which invites direct publishing by authors and tiny publishers.

Recruit Supporters and Allies

Although blending is a powerful strategy for overcoming resistance, it is not the only strategy, and there are times it may not work. Most social systems use one of two methods to resist change: dynamic pushback or apathy (noninterest). Dynamic pushback means that some subgroups of the community actively attempt to neutralize or banish the proposed innovation. Apathy means that the innovator cannot find enough people willing to listen, and therefore cannot establish any momentum behind a conversation for change.

To deal with either kind of resistance, the innovator needs allies within the network. These allies can be thought leaders or authorities who buy in to the proposed innovation and call everyone else's attention to it. They are also familiar with the concerns and methods of the active resisters, and can help contain them or win them over.

Tim Berners-Lee implemented a very nice containment strategy in the first years of the World Wide Web, when commercial companies started to vie for leadership in the new technology. With help from allies at MIT, Berners-Lee formed the W3C as an organization in which all parties who wanted to contribute to the advancement of the Web could collaborate on standards and base technologies. The only way to advance the Web was to play in the W3C game. The strategy worked. The W3C effectively contained the forces that would resist the advancement of the base technology. Companies competed based on Web products, applications, and services, but not on the base technology.

The Sims story of continuous-aim gunnery illustrates an extreme case of alliance. He got the ear of President Teddy Roosevelt, who put him in a position of authority, from which he forced the continuous-aim gunnery innovation into the U.S. Navy. Most innovators are not so fortunate.

Here is a story about overcoming apathy in a social network. In 2004, author Peter Denning proposed to the U.S. Department of Defense (DoD) that it form a W3C-like organization to help it advance the *grid* (its term for networking technology) that it needed for future defense and security operations. DoD's situation bore many similarities to the early Web, notably a proliferation of organizations that wanted to play but did not accept a common authority telling them to adopt standards for data sharing. He proposed that the DoD form its own consortium, W2COG (World Wide Consortium for the Grid). He got the ear of Admiral Arthur Cebrowski, who was head of the Office of Force Transformation. Cebrowski saw that the W2COG could help DoD in the same way W3C had helped the Web. Cebrowski began marketing the idea to his peers among agency heads. Within a month, he helped raise over a million dollars in seed funds from five agencies to start up the W2COG. On its own, it would have taken Denning's team two years to convince those agency heads to sponsor the new organization.

Learn from the Network

While engaging with the previous steps, the innovator will discover more and more about the concerns and interests of various groups of the target community. In response, the innovator will refine the innovation story (Practice Two), the offer (Practice Three), and the adoption strategies (Practice Four), so that each important constituency of the community will find something for itself in the story.

Adapting the story is a complex process because, as we have seen, there are many ways for concerns to arise and be addressed. For example:

• *Structure, conceptual framework, and technology of the social system*   We know that a change in any one of these three aspects causes changes in the others. You can learn how members of the network see these interactions and defuse the threat. If he were practicing this, William Sims would have discovered that present and former ship captains might see his proposed continuous-aim gunnery innovation as a threat to the ship's social system. He would have shown them that the gunners would remain an elite corps, as they had on the British ships that already used continuous-aim gunnery. Had Sims done this, the captains would have seen his innovation as a benefit to ships' gunners, and might have supported rather than resisted him. He would have revised his story to address the benefits not only in gunnery but also to the ship society.

• *Various interest groups and factions within the social system*   A change in the network will cause some groups to have more power and others less. The groups losing power are likely to resist. You can learn which groups win or lose in the power shifts. You might help some of the losing groups by showing them they gain something else of value or by providing something else of value. Tim Berners-Lee adapted the Web story to include the W3C, a place where potential competitors could cooperate on the advancement of Web technology. Apple adapted its iTunes story around the concern raised by Napster: they focus on how its download service meets all copyright and licensing requirements, and downplayed a possible threat to publishers when artists used iTunes instead of them.

• *The five temperaments of adopters*   We know that the people in a social group or subgroup can be inventors, early adopters, early majority, late majority, or laggards regarding their willingness to adopt and the kinds of considerations that incline them to adopt (Rogers 1962). You can learn the concerns of each group and adapt your story accordingly. For example, the story for early adopters might emphasize the novelty of the technology while the story for majority adopters will emphasize all the support services that help users. In *Crossing the Chasm*, Geoffrey Moore (2002) pointed out that many business failures result from complete ignorance of these adoption groups. The inventors and visionaries who started the company had no idea that the majority, to whom they would eventually want to sell, has much higher demands for stable supporting infrastructure than they themselves do. The founders pitched their marketing to other inventors and visionaries. When that market saturated, they could not penetrate into the majority market because they had already expended their capital and had no message for that market.

The bottom line is that adoption is a learning process in a social network. It matters to people what others are saying and doing. You will need help from the network itself to achieve adoption. Without allies—internal voices speaking on your behalf—your adoption efforts will founder. At the start of the process it is especially valuable to recruit allies who are powerful in the network. As time goes on it will become more valuable for those who have already adopted to speak on your behalf, so that others will hear positive things about the innovation from their friends.

Breakdowns   The innovator is likely to face a variety of breakdowns while seeking initial adoption. These eight are omissions of essential elements of the adoption anatomy:

- Failing to understand network structure, concept, and technology
- Failing to reconcile benefits and adoption costs
- Failing to focus on community embodiment (spreading ideas is not enough)
- Failing to blend with resistance
- Failing to recruit allies
- Failing to listen and connect with concerns
- Failing to adapt and refine the innovation story based on what is learned from the network
- Failing to have enough conversations (stopping too soon)

The other breakdowns are:

- *Inadequately articulating the value of adopting*   People will not adopt unless they see sufficient value to motivate rearranging their lives to accommodate the new practice. There is no way around this. If you do not listen carefully for people's concerns, you will not be able to tell them how your innovation will take care of their concerns.

• *Failing to anticipate different adoption rates*   People in the network take different lengths of time to commit to adoption. Their adoption times will depend on their general outlook toward change and their tolerance of uncertainty. In *Crossing the Chasm*, Geoffrey Moore has vividly demonstrated the dangers of ignoring adoption rates.

• *Forcing adoption through compulsion*   Sometimes the commander or CEO invokes the power of office to mandate a change. People go along with it because they have no choice. But as soon as the commander or CEO moves on, the mandate may end and everyone reverts to the old way. The innovation is adopted for a while, then disappears when the compelling force goes away. For innovation that lasts, you have to get the personal commitment of a substantial majority of the group.

What to Practice

The essence of good practice is to develop your skills around the five components of the learning network model, and to develop your skills to cope with the breakdowns.

• *Keep a journal*   You can record the results of your analyses (such as the structure, concepts, and technologies of a network), the strategies you decide to try, and your successes or failures. These notes can give you considerable insight about your own successes and failures, accelerating your learning process.

• *Develop good maps*   An overall map—structure, concept, technology—is a key to blending, recruiting allies, and overcoming resistance. The network's structure can be depicted by three diagrams: (1) an organization chart depicting reporting relationships and authorities; (2) a social interaction chart depicting the people with most conversational influence in the network; and (3) a factions chart depicting interest groups that will react to your innovation proposal in different ways. The network's conceptual framework can be captured by the domain mapping practice of chapter 4: you record core assumptions and principles and their origins. The network's technologies can be represented as a list of technologies you see in use, and the reasons they have been chosen.

• *Blending*   Learn the differences between the innovator's optimistic language of benefits and the potential adopter's pessimistic language around adoption costs. Learn to speak both languages and translate between them. Connect the innovation's value to the principal values in the network's conceptual framework.

• *Recruit allies* Become an astute observer of how other innovators use allies to promote their ideas and deal with resistance. Sometimes they use strategies such as pilot projects, disruption insurance, insurgency, and even insurrection as ways to achieve blends or get the change without a blend. For large innovations, these strategies often require considerable political and leadership skill. They are not for the faint of heart and you will definitely need allies to execute them.

• *Adapt the story* Innovation is a process of getting a learning network to learn something new. As the process unfolds, the innovator also learns. Adapt the story about the innovation's benefits to reflect what you have learned. If you are not adapting the story, you probably are not learning anything.

• *Build and refine the prototype* Create demonstration projects. They will show the outcomes and results in limited, more achievable settings. Capture testimonials from these projects.

Conclusions

The Rogers diffusion model and the Schon learning network model for the spread of innovations offer numerous valuable insights into how to achieve adoption. But they have some implicit assumptions that limit them in situations in which innovators frequently find themselves. For example, Rogers does not have much to say about coping with resistance, and Schon does not say what conversations the innovator should initiate. Neither is a generative model.

For our anatomy of adoption, we use a generative learning network model that blends Rogers, Schon, and language-action. This model says that the social network is an integrated system with structure, concept, and technology. The three aspects evolved together and network change incurs changes in all three. It also says that social networks have a natural tendency to dynamically resist change. Therefore innovators are always faced with overcoming active resistance to their proposals. They need allies within the network to do this. And they must learn from the network, discovering what sells and what does not, constantly adapting and improving their innovation story.

A successful initial adoption may not stick in the network. People may experience various unexpected negative consequences and decide to abandon their adoption. That brings us to Practice Five, sustaining, which is concerned with successful integration of the new practice deeply into the social network.

Bibliography

Barabasi, A.-L. 2003. *Linked: How Everything is Connected to Everything Else and What it Means for Business, Science, and Everyday Life.* Plume.

Denning, Peter. 2004. Network Laws. *ACM Communications* 47 (11):15–20, http://doi.acm.org/10.1145/1029496.1029510.

Denning, Peter, and Pamela Dargan. 1996. Action-Centered Design. In *Bringing Design to Software*, ed. T. Winograd. Addison-Wesley.

Denning, Peter, and Raul Medina-Mora. 1995. Completing the Loops. *Interfaces* 25 (3):42–57.

Grove, Andrew S. 1999. *Only the Paranoid Survive: How to Exploit the Crisis Points That Challenge Every Company.* Currency.

Heath, Chip, and Dan Heath. 2007. *Made to Stick: Why Some Ideas Survive and Others Die.* Random House.

Kuhn, Thomas S. 1962. *The Structure of Scientific Revolutions.* Rev. ed., University of Chicago Press, 1970.

Moore, Geoffrey. 2002. *Crossing the Chasm.* 2nd ed., Harper Business.

Pierce, Terry. 2004. *Warfighting and Disruptive Technologies: Disguising Innovation.* Frank Cass.

Rogers, Everett. 1962. *Diffusion of Innovations.* 5th ed., Free Press, 2003.

Schon, David. 1971. *Beyond the Stable State.* Norton.

Strozzi-Heckler, Richard. 2007. *The Leadership Dojo.* Frog.

Wikipedia. Marketing article. 2010. http://en.wikipedia.org/wiki/Marketing. Accessed January 2010.

9

Practice Five: Sustaining

Leadership is the wise use of power. Power is the capacity to translate intention into reality and sustain it.
—Warren Bennis

To live for some future goal is shallow. It's the sides of the mountain that that sustain life, not the top.
—Robert Pirsig

It takes a whole village for an innovation to be developed, launched, and adopted.
—Edmund Phelps

Sustaining is the third and final practice of the adoption triad. Sustaining is about keeping the innovation relevant and useful after adoption—integrating and fitting the new practice into the environment of the community so that it can be continued easily. The environment is likely to be a complex social system with many practices and technologies. We want the new practice to compete well for time and attention in the environment: to continue to offer more value than other options for its purpose.

Many factors figure into sustainability—for example, learnability, support, supply, maintenance, alignment, comfort, and commitment. These factors have slightly different interpretations inside the organization and outside. When an organization offers a new product, it is offering to help external customers reconfigure themselves around the new practice of using the product. And it is also reconfiguring itself internally so that it can supply, teach, support, and maintain the new product. Therefore, when we examine the sustainability factors in detail, we will interpret them for both inside and outside the organization.

We approach sustainability from a systems perspective. The environment (social system) accommodates the new practice by changing its structure, conceptual model, and technology. And the supplying organization accommodates the new environment by changing its internal structure, conceptual model, and technology. The interactions among these aspects are likely to be complex.

There is a big difference between adopting and sustaining. Adopting concentrates on getting people to commit to the practice for the first time; it succeeds if the adopters reckon startup costs to be less than the initial value received. Sustaining concentrates on helping people maintain their commitment after the initial phase; it succeeds if adopters reckon ongoing costs to be less than the ongoing value received. People will abandon an innovation if the costs of sustaining it are too high.

There is a difference between "a sustaining innovation" and "sustaining an innovation." The former refers to an innovation that is an incremental improvement over a prior practice (Christensen 1997). The latter refers to the commitment to stay with a new practice after it has been adopted. Sustaining a practice is easier if the practice is a sustaining rather than a disruptive innovation.

Sustaining does not have an objective of lasting forever. Innovations have lifetimes. Over time a practice is superseded by a superior practice. It is entirely normal that people eventually decide to give up the practice. We are interested in sustaining the practice through its normal lifetime, and not causing people to abandon it early because of inadequate support or too many negative consequences.

The Environment of an Innovation

In their book *Lean Thinking* (1996), James Womack and Daniel Jones outline how lean manufacturing techniques consistently produce a 90 percent reduction in cycle times and a 50 percent reduction in manufacturing costs, after a set-up period of a few days. Even though the results are astounding, setting up for a trial is easier than sustaining it after the initial excitement fades. To sustain it, the manufacturing workers must acquire new practices and think in new terms about their work. The authors recount how a plant in Europe installed the lean-manufacturing plant layout and processes and achieved the expected improvements in performance—only to revert in six months to their inefficient, traditional manufacturing processes. The workers and management gave up their performance improvements in order to maintain the familiarity and comfort with the old processes. Apparently there were no internal customers who demanded the new results.

This example illustrates that outstanding results achieved in initial adoption are not always sufficient in themselves to motivate people to sustain an innovative practice. To sustain an innovation, the environment (community, market, or organization) must value, enable, and support the innovation, and it must discourage or overcome resistance.

The environment of an innovation is the social system in which it is practiced. Not only do individuals need to enter into the new practice, the entire system also needs to adapt to it. The elements of the environment are summarized in table 9.1. The first three elements come from Schon's model (1971) and the rest from domain mapping (see chapter 4; Spinosa, Flores, and Dreyfus 1997). It important to remember that all these elements are mutually interdependent. An innovation can be sustained only if it is consistent with all of them.

The Internet is an instructive example. The configuration of the Internet five years before the introduction of the World Wide Web in 1994 was markedly different from its configuration five years after. The structure had evolved from government control to private collaboration. The concept had evolved from information exchange among computers to universal access to human knowledge. The technology had evolved from a handful of information-exchange protocols to a complex set of protocols for online markets. The standards had evolved from arduous manual entry of protocol commands to automated commands from graphical interfaces. The possibilities had enriched from remote access to new businesses and industries. Breakdowns were no longer simply broken connections, viruses, or intruder attacks; they included financial frauds, identity thefts, denials of service, and loss of virtual markets. The moods changed from the curiosity of technical geeks to the ambition of entrepreneurs. Tim Berners-Lee did not meticulously plan all these changes, but he did pay attention to how proposed changes in the evolving Web were compatible with the existing environments. He sustained the Web by choosing each new direction consistent with current momentum and his few general principles.

The Betamax videotape system, introduced by Sony in the late 1970s, illustrates an innovation that did not sustain. Betamax was judged by many engineers to be technically superior to VHS, which came later. But consumers were more interested in being able to record an entire show on a single cassette than in having error-free recordings. Betamax could not be sustained because it did not conform to the consumer concept of

Table 9.1
Elements of the Innovation Environment

Structure	Roles, relationships, authorities, prior commitments. Who has what powers to make decisions?
Conceptual framework	The dominant paradigm—tacit common principles, beliefs, ways of thinking, ways of interpreting, criteria for truth, common sense, philosophy, history, and values
Technology	Tools and equipment used to carry out standard practices and tasks
Incentives	Rewards, recognitions, and other inducements offered to those who engage in the new practice. Reinforcing feedback. Penalties imposed on those who do not.
Standard practices	Standard (widely accepted) ways of doing things, including habits and routines. Everyone in the community is expected to learn and do them, whether by education, training, apprenticeship, or involvement.
Possibilities	Possible new worlds (or modifications of world) accessible to those in the community. Some possibilities are seen as so wild or improbable that they are not taken seriously.
Breakdowns	Obstacles that prevent people from reaching their goals; can be chronic and persistent, or fortuitous.
Moods	Individual and group attitudes toward the future. Include positives (such as ambition, wonder, trust, resolution) and negatives (such as confusion, fear, anxiety, distrust, overwhelm). Mood affects what possibilities are visible and believable.

a video recording system; it introduced the inconvenient breakdown of changing cassettes mid-show.

Prohibition of alcohol is an innovation that had been adopted in at least seven countries in the early- to mid-1900s. These countries all ascribed many social problems to alcohol use. They all had sufficient public support to pass laws prohibiting it. But within a few years, black markets and associated crime had become such a social problem that the prohibition laws were repealed. Today, the Mothers Against Drunk Driving movement has succeeded not by banning alcohol, but by seeking penalties for those whose drunken behavior has violated social norms.

These examples show that sustaining an innovation is a complex process of bringing about a change in a dynamic system that is naturally resistant to change. The key to the innovator's success in the face of such complexity is listening. The innovator listens to the moods of a community and tries to generate positive moods by focusing on the positive possibilities that the change will produce. The innovator listens for the deep concerns of individuals within the community by paying attention not only to the words they speak, but also to their actions. Their actions reveal what they value, find comfortable, and are willing to commit to. An innovator who listens well can find a path to sustaining an innovation.

Anatomy of the Sustaining Practice

A practice will be sustained if it remains more valuable than other choices, its operating costs are lower than its returns, it does not generate undue discomfort, it is learnable, and it is reinforced by feedback. Four principles are involved in attaining these objectives:

1. *Integrating* the new practice into an existing environment;
2. *Enabling* the new practice by providing the relevant declarations and resources that create the conditions for the new practice to be started, learned, and established;
3. *Supporting* the continuation of the new practice by maintaining its value relative to other options; and
4. *Dealing with resistance* that arises as people encounter the consequences of the new practice.

These principles are applied slightly differently inside an organization than they are outside in the marketplace. An organization proposes an innovation to the market by reconfiguring itself around a new offer. An individual in the market has many competing offers and will be influenced by the style of marketing and the reputation of brands. We will not dig further into marketing and branding; they are covered well elsewhere (Kotler and Trias de Bes 2003). Our focus here is on the conversations that the innovator must generate in order for the new practice to be sustained.

Integrating
When the new practice fits with all the other existing practices, it becomes part of the fabric of thinking. It meshes with other routines. It causes little or no friction.

Marketing guru Jack Trout (2008) emphasizes the "search for the obvious"—things customers find simple, easy to understand, and evident. He is looking for a fit between what is offered and what customers perceive works in their current environment. He sharply criticizes a common attitude in business that seeks nonobvious ideas. If the proposed innovation will not obviously integrate with the current environment, it will most likely fail.

The starting point for integration is domain mapping, first described in chapter 4 and integrated into table 9.1. The purpose is to understand how the community currently constituted already works. This allows the innovator to assess the impact of the new practice on each of the aspects, and then to design actions that achieve the integration. Three areas, discussed in sections that follow, need constant attention: enabling, supporting, and dealing with resistance.

As part of the design, innovators will consider incentives for people in the organization or marketplace to join the new practice. The incentives aim to increase the value of joining and staying in. Incentives, however, have to be considered in the context of all other existing incentives. Incentives for behaviors that are no longer important should be removed. The new incentives ought not reduce the rewards from other incentives that are still important. For example, salespeople who are asked to increase customer service activities at the expense of their commissions are unlikely to support the new practice.

We cannot overemphasize that adoption is a commitment. The Womack-Jones manufacturing example given earlier illustrates what happens when the people of the organization do not commit to the new practice, and its leadership do not commit to holding anyone accountable for engaging.

Objectives with explicit, owned commitments and measures will be acted on; those without won't.

Enabling

Leadership must give permission and encouragement for individual members of the community to join the new practice. The encouragement includes investment of resources to provide learning opportunities, time for learning, incentives, penalties, and special attention during the transition.

The key conversations here include getting business executives and thought leaders in markets to back the new practice, advertize the ongoing value propositions clearly and compellingly, and recruit leaders within the community to promote the new practice. The new practice must be integrated into plans, budgets, and processes.

Supporting

The leadership must provide means to assist and reward members of the community who join the new practice. Early in the adoption, members are more likely to encounter breakdowns resulting from the unfamiliar practice; they are in special need of support and handholding during this time. Here are some important elements of a supportive environment:

• *Education and training* Community members must have the time needed to learn and embody the new practice. The learning curve must not be too steep or long.

• *Customer service* Technical support, help desks, frequent-question databases, and customer discussion groups are common ways to help customers get the support they need to sustain their practice. The customer—internal or external—holds the person making the promise for support accountable for satisfaction (Denning and Dunham 2003). Without feedback it is impossible to know whether customers are satisfied.

• *Tools* Tools support practices and enable them to be carried out. Many innovations fail because the tools are inadequate. The Web browser is an excellent example of an enabling tool. Before the browser, users had to type long series of commands to locate and fetch documents in the Internet; the browser did all that with a simple point and click of the mouse.

• *Maintenance* Tools and equipment break or become obsolete. Community members want clear and simple ways to deal with breakdowns, upgrades, supplies, returns, and replacements.

• *Emotional support* Leaders and managers acknowledge good performance and express their appreciation for work done well.

• *Value* Leaders and managers frequently articulate the value of the new practice, and track measures that enable them to assess whether the value is being delivered consistently and effectively.

• *Accommodating adoption rates* Different segments of the community have different appetites for change. Early adopters are easy to bring on board, laggards take a lot of effort. The majority is in between. Each group has concerns that must be addressed if they are to come on board and stay on board.

• *Managing moods*   Leadership pays attention to the moods the proposed changes provoke. Some people welcome change. Others find newness a source of anxiety. Leaders work with people who have fallen into negative moods by offering them new possibilities, new value, and occasionally new positions that are not affected by the change.

Dealing with Resistance

A change of practice can lead to disruptions that provoke resistance from the individuals and groups affected. The main sources of resistance are:

• *Perceptions of diminished identity or power*   Generally any change of practice will generate winners and losers. Winners get more stature or power, losers less. Strategies for dealing with resisters include (1) seducing them, by showing them that their loss is not significant or that their gain from a stronger community offsets their perceived loss; (2) containing them, by working with the supportive sectors to limit the effects of action by the resistive sectors; and (3) removing them, for if all else fails, the dissenters in an organization can be fired or transferred.

• *Reluctant bodies*   A new practice feels awkward and uncomfortable until it is embodied; some people welcome the discomfort and others cannot tolerate it for long. Some people cannot overcome old habits despite having the best intentions. Some people will not enter a new game unless they feel (not just think) there is a chance for them to win.

• *Perceived operating costs too high*   Operating costs include time, money, assets, worry, and frictions between the new and existing practices. If these costs exceed an individual's personal threshold, that individual may drop out. The same is true of groups and organizational units.

• *Threats to cherished values or beliefs*   The new practice can fail if individuals perceive that a fundamental value is at risk. For example, the residents of Ojai, California, hold dear the open-space feeling of their community, and steadfastly resist lucrative offers from developers. And the residents of California as a whole must approve tax increases by a referendum; they steadfastly refuse despite the obviously good purposes of proposed new taxes.

Summary

The four strategies and the main conversations they involve are realized in different ways inside the organization and outside. We have summarized these differences in table 9.2.

Table 9.2
Anatomy of Sustaining Practice

Principle	Innovator's conversations	In organizations	In markets
Integrating	Domain mapping and redesign.	Organization is the domain.	Marketplace is the domain.
Enabling	Declarations of commitment from people in power.	Senior managers, CEO, president	Authorities, thought leaders, celebrities, influential organizations
	Incentives that encourage staying with the new practice and discourage from reverting to the old.	Commissions, bonuses, awards, recognitions, etc.	Rebates, early discounts, risk sharing, money back guarantees, etc.
	Generate leaders for integration into the social system.	Recruit people to lead or join project teams that work on organizational change.	Recruit people to lead or join project teams that work on community change.
Supporting	Getting and keeping commitments of followers.	Clear articulation of ongoing value. Provide education, training, tools, maintenance, customer service, emotional support, and mood support.	Clear articulation of ongoing value. Provide education, training, tools, maintenance, customer service, emotional support, and mood support.
	Generate changes in organizational commitments.	Reconfigure organization roles, practices, accountabilities, and promises among business units and to customers.	Provide new support organizations and partner with existing organizations.
Resistance	Anticipate, neutralize, contain, enroll, or remove opponents.	Attend to power shifts, reluctance, perceived operating costs, and threats to beliefs. Hire, fire, win over, cajole, and contain. Maintain coherence between announced strategy and action. Manage expectations.	Anticipate power shifts, reluctance, perceived operating costs, competition, and threats to beliefs. Watch for or use (counter) insurgency, political containment, and recruitment to cause. Manage expectations.

Innovators are sometimes called on to resolve what we call *wicked problems* (Roberts 2000). These are the most difficult and often intractable problems in social systems. There is usually no agreement on exactly what the problem is: various influential people have their own interpretations that do not line up. In the preceding anatomy, the first obvious challenge will be aligning with people in power, because, in relation to a wicked problem, the people in power have no alignment among themselves. Unless the innovator can generate new alignment, the wicked problem will remain unsolved. We will discuss wicked problems in depth in chapter 14.

Discontinuation

Sometimes, after an initial trial period, many community members decide to abandon a new practice because there are many negative consequences or insufficient benefits. Prohibition of alcoholic beverages in the United States during the 1920s is a historical example; Intel's decision in the 1980s to abandon its memory chip business and concentrate on processors is another.

Sometimes an innovation does not last because it was adopted by compulsion. When the leader who imposed the change is gone, the community reverts to the older way. The Berlin Wall came down when the regime that erected it was no longer in power.

Eventually an innovation reaches the end of its useful lifetime: a better one displaces it. This is a natural process. Sometimes organizations do not let go of an obsolescent practice even when there are many signs of obsolescence. They invest considerable energy in attempting to sustain a practice that is no longer sustainable. Prior to the financial crisis of 2008 to 2009, many banks began to have suspicions that subprime mortgages and mortgage-backed securities were unsustainable, but few moved to shed those commitments.

Much has been written about the process of abandoning or discontinuing a practice after its value becomes marginal. Most companies find this is difficult to do, even when the see the costs of continuing. Among the many books addressing this concern, we particularly like these:

• Clayton Christensen (1997) discusses how an innovation in a minor market can spread into a company's major market and destroy the company's business.
• Andy Grove (1999) discusses his own paranoia about the disruptive potential of new technologies, especially those with a tenfold or better

advantage. He gave Intel disruption insurance by commissioning projects that would explore the potential disruptor and be prepared to offer it in the market if it became viable.

• Richard Foster and Sarah Kaplan (2001) describe how "creative destruction" (a term coined by economist Joseph Schumpeter) requires conscious and often hard choices. Businesses that do not engage in the "practice of hard choices" do not survive.

• Glenn Hubbard (2007) builds on Nobel Laureate Edmund Phelps's work to argue that *nondestructive creation* is a better term than *creative destruction*. *Nondestructive creation* refers to the work of entrepreneurs who deal with uncertainty, take risks, and experiment to find attractive offers. They build, grow, and extend, but do not destroy.

Breakdowns

The sustaining practice is particularly challenging to innovators because there are numerous ways it can be blocked. We have identified twenty-three breakdowns, and there are undoubtedly more. Each shows up in slightly different ways inside and outside the organization. We have summarized the twenty-three internal and twenty-three external possibilities in table 9.3. To help in understanding a table so dense with information, we offer examples from each category.

• *Integrating*   The main concern is whether the new practice fits with existing practice and beliefs. Fit is easier to establish with sustaining innovation than with disruptive. In 1993, President Clinton proposed a massive overhaul of the U.S. healthcare system to bring down costs and supply universal coverage. The proposal ran into a buzzsaw of public opposition and died in Congress. Political leaders were baffled because they thought public sentiment favored lower costs and extension of coverage to the uninsured. The problem was that the plan did not fit with the deeply held American belief in freedom of choice. Many perceived that the new system would deprive them of choices they valued. Sixteen years later, President Obama proposed an overhaul with similar objectives, and encountered the same type of public opposition.

• *Enabling*   The main concern is whether the conditions that will support adoption are in place. A common enabling breakdown in organizations, and source of many complaints, is the "unfunded mandate"— the declaration by leadership that a group should take on a new practice without additional budget or staff. A related complaint is "granting responsibility without authority."

Table 9.3
Breakdowns in Sustaining Practice

Principle	Breakdowns	In organizations	In markets
Integrating	A new practice conflicts with well-established practices and beliefs.	A new practice takes people from their comfort zones, or has no internal customer.	A new public plan violates widely held, fundamental values.
	Obsession with the new overwhelms common sense; valuable old practices are dropped.	Top-down process reengineering; may need expensive recovery to reinstate old practices.	Fads and "irrational exuberance."
	Lack of commitment to continue.	Other commitments override, conservative orientations (laggards), lack of customer demand.	Learning curve too steep or long. Too little value.
	No capacity for learning.	Time and resources not available for learning	Time and resources not available for learning.
Enabling	Declaring a new practice without providing budget or staff.	Unfunded internal mandates. Delegating responsibility without authority.	Unfunded mandates in the law.
	Cannot generate leaders.	Failure to establish project teams for internal change.	Failure to establish voices who speak for the new practice.
	Lack of alignment with people in power.	Project proposers don't get support from chain of command.	Established leaders see no value for them in the new practice; they are unsupportive.
	Contradictory incentives.	New practice reduces ability to receive incentive awards.	Too expensive. Makes the user look out of place in the community.

Table 9.3
(continued)

Principle	Breakdowns	In organizations	In markets
	People lack customer skills.	Weak leadership. No knowledge how to hold a performer accountable.	Weak leadership. No knowledge how to hold a performer accountable.
Supporting	Lack of commitment, process, or resources. Leadership does not set example.	Leadership does not supply budget or moral support for new practice. Managers who don't "walk the talk."	Politicians unwilling to live the practice they want to impose on all.
	Cannot generate followers.	Ineffective incentives, people unmoved, leadership does not display commitment.	Ineffective incentives, people unmoved, leadership does not display commitment.
	No accountability.	Team members and leaders not accountable for their promises.	Perceived lack of commitment, loss of credibility.
	New practice is unfamiliar.	High overhead to learn. No time allocated for learning. No coaches or mentors. Public exposure as a beginner.	High overhead to learn. Benefits of learning not obvious.
	New practice is uncomfortable.	Not knowing how to accept the discomfort of learning. Insufficient support for learners.	Benefits of learning not obvious. Value proposition does not justify learning.
	Local internal relationships more valuable than customers.	Group members favor prior standards and practices. No customers for the new practice.	Customers can't find performers for the new practice.

Table 9.3
(continued)

Principle	Breakdowns	In organizations	In markets
	Failing to let go of an obsolescent practice or business model.	Internal waste, uncompetitive costs, company failures.	Market migration.
	Over reliance on compulsion.	Low internal commitment (group reverts on change of leaders).	Black markets, flouting of the law.
	Lack of leadership continuity.	New leaders dump or ignore predecessor's programs.	A company makes a mistake that damages its brand name.
	Neglecting to modify organizational commitments.	Unable to support new service; wasteful old services.	Low adoption rates; customers turn to other organizations.
	Neglecting moods.	Unaware of how moods affect performance. No actions to manage mood.	No awareness of public moods or how to inspire positive moods.
Resistance	Loss of power or reputation.	Did not clarify roles and how to win in the new game. Lack of relevance.	Majority threatened by aggressive early adopters.
	Blind or ineffective at containing or seducing those who resist.	Internal subversion of leadership, votes of no confidence.	Low adoption rates.
	Manage expectations poorly.	People at cross-purposes, frustrated, resentful, leadership distrusted.	Hyped claims, poor customer service, lack of information undermine brand credibility.

• *Supporting*   The main concern is whether there are ongoing commitments and processes to keep the adoption going. In the mid-1990s, the new president of a university in which one of the authors served, declared his interest in continuing professional education and asked the new provost to take responsibility for this area. Unfortunately, the provost did not believe in his heart that continuing education was as important as the main academic mission and his support was thin in words and deeds. At the end of a year, several industry and university partners, who were encouraged by the president's words, were profoundly disappointed by the skimpy results and unkept promises, and refused further cooperation with the university.

• *Resistance*   The main concern is whether there is opposition strong enough to interfere with adoption. We knew a dean who was brought in by the president of the same university to enact a bold plan of reform for the business school. The dean articulated a set of new principles for research, curriculum, department structure, and fundraising. He was praised by the administration and outside business world for his ideas. But he did not notice that his faculty had not committed to his principles. When he began a massive reorganization to implement his ideas, the faculty pushed back and eventually rebelled with a vote of no confidence, forcing him to resign. The dean's story also illustrates the phrase "attend to power shifts" in table 9.3. He did not attend to the faculty perception of power loss when their departments were disbanded and core curricula revised. He did not support the more entrepreneurial faculty whom he intended to lead the new structure. His boss, the provost, did not support him in promoting the new plan for the school.

What to Practice

Practice observing for integration, enabling, support, and resistance—the key distinctions of the anatomy of the sustaining practice. Ask frequently: does the new practice produce continuing and obvious value? Address areas where there may be friction or a poor fit. Make sure that the key conversations, commitments, and responsibilities for integrating, enabling, supporting, and dealing with resistance are established and maintained. Using the table of breakdowns for guidance, observe how those conversations can be disrupted, and practice coping actions when disruptions occur.

Always listen. Engage in regular interviews to uncover issues or dissatisfaction that people may have with the new practice. Set up forums where people can bring up issues and management can respond. At General Electric, CEO Jack Welch established such a practice called "Work Out." At a Work Out forum session, anyone could raise an issue with management; management had to respond only with action statements or declines, not explanations.

Conclusions

The objective of the sustaining practice is to keep your innovation in play through its useful lifetime, but no longer, by maintaining its value, relevance, and adoption. To do this, you focus on four areas: *integrating the practice into the existing environment, enabling* the new practice itself, *supporting* the new practice, and *dealing with resistance.* The sustaining practice is particularly challenging to innovators because of the numerous breakdowns that can occur.

Bibliography

Christensen, Clayton. 1997. *The Innovator's Dilemma.* Harvard Business.

Denning, Peter, and Robert Dunham. 2003. The Missing Customer. *ACM Communications* 46 (March):19–23.

Foster, Richard, and Sarah Kaplan. 2001. *Creative Destruction.* Financial Times Prentice Hall

Grove, Andy. 1999. *Only the Paranoid Survive.* Currency.

Hubbard, Glenn. 2007. Nondestructive Creation. *Strategy and Business* 47, http://www.strategy-business.com/article/07203.

Kotler, Philip, and Fernando Trias de Bes. 2003. *Lateral Marketing: Techniques for Finding Breakthrough Ideas.* Wiley.

Roberts, Nancy C. 2000. Wicked Problems and Network Approaches to Resolution. *International Public Management Review* 1 (1).

Schon, David. 1971. *Beyond the Stable State.* Norton.

Spinosa, Charles, Fernando Flores, and Hubert Dreyfus. 1997. *Disclosing New Worlds.* MIT Press.

Stewart, Matthew. 2006. The Management Myth. *The Atlantic* (June), http://www.theatlantic.com/doc/200606/stewart-business.

Trout, Jack. 2008. *In Search of the Obvious: The Antidote to Today's Marketing Mess.* Wiley.

Womack, James, and Daniel Jones. 1996. *Lean Thinking.* Simon & Schuster.

10

Practice Six: Executing

Management is not about making decisions; it is about initiating and guiding conversations.

—Fernando Flores

In innovation, execution refers to the actions that convert the possibility offered into a promise delivered. Execution is essential not only for the final outcome of the innovation process, but also for all the outcomes of the individual practices. Intermediate results, such as prototypes and demonstrations, build trust in the promise and its value through evidence.

Much has been written on project management, planning, marketing, and executing. We will not repeat that here. Our focus here is on the conversational practices of execution that enable the innovator to turn offers into effective, trustworthy, delivered promises.

In innovation practice, the term *execution* actually has two related meanings: (1) the means of effecting action, or (2) a phase of the innovation process. We will emphasize the first sense. The possibility, the vision, the offer, and the adoption are all the results of successful executions in the previous practices. In other words, the execution practice creates an environment for success in the other practices.

The second sense is actually an illusion. In an ideal world, it might be possible to conceive and offer an innovation before executing the actions to deliver it. In reality, nothing is certain: we try offers and actions and we learn from our mistakes. Execution pervades the other practices. No definite phase of the innovation process is purely execution.

A prevalent notion about executing is "doing"—taking part in the activities to produce something. Our focus is on the conversations that *generate* and *shape* the doing. Those conversations define the actions to be carried out, articulate clearly the outcomes expected from them, and produce a commitment from someone to perform them. The emphasis on conversations is especially important for innovators. Innovators do not need to be expert doers of everything needed to produce the innovation. They do need to be expert in the conversations to get the right things done—to attract talent, form teams, and manage networks of conversations within the teams and with their customers.

No innovation can succeed unless members of the target community trust the innovator's ability to execute and deliver the promise. It is never certain whether the innovation will be adopted and will deliver the promised value. Community members must come to trust that the innovator can perform, manage the risks, and deliver the value. The innovator builds trust mainly by providing a track record of successful, valuable deliveries. Trust is a direct consequence of skillful execution and fulfilled promises.

Conversations and Action

In 1986, Peter Denning visited Fernando Flores in his office at Action Technologies, a software company. Denning was intrigued with Flores's work on how people coordinate action and his email system, the Coordinator. He wanted to discuss a possible collaboration that would bring the Coordinator into NASA. Flores asked questions about the computing field, the state of computing research, computing education, NASA research, and sensitivity to coordination among computing people. He asked about Denning's history, motivations for working at NASA, and assessments about the Winograd and Flores book (1986). He discussed his own history and involvement with computing. It was quite a wide-ranging conversation. After three-quarters of an hour, when Denning was starting to get fidgety because they had not yet talked about a possible collaboration, Fernando moved from a conversation for information to a conversation for possibilities. They speculated about what they could do together and what value it might bring NASA and Action Technologies. After ten minutes of speculation, Flores said, "Let us now define action. I will make two requests of my staff. I will introduce you to my head of development so that you can talk details about projects and licensing. I will also introduce you to my head of education so that you can learn about the language-action philosophy behind The Coordinator." Then he adjourned the meeting, introduced Denning to these two people, and went on to his next appointment. From this one-hour conversation a long and fruitful collaboration followed.

In this story we see how Flores, a master at management, worked in conversations to produce action and valuable outcomes. He spent most of the time on context—what was going on in Denning's world, NASA's world, his world, and the general computing world. Then, in that context, he speculated about possibilities he and Denning might pursue together. Finally, in the last minute of their time, he made declarations and requests that led to actions.

This conversation was obviously the initiation of a long process. There were many more conversations for context, possibility, and action.

This example illustrates the three kinds of conversation needed for successful execution and their purposes:

- *Conversation for context*   Clarify the environment and what we care about in it.
- *Conversation for possibilities*   Generate possible future actions and outcomes without committing to any one.
- *Conversation for actions*   Generate specific commitments to produce specific outcomes.

Figure 10.1 illustrates that action conversations depend on prior possibility conversations, which in turn depend on prior context conversations.

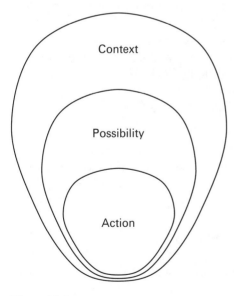

Figure 10.1
Three constituent conversations of execution.

Although the action conversations will often dominate, the context and possibilities conversations are essential.

Anatomy of Execution

The innovator is bound to deliver a promise as soon as community members accept the offer. In accepting, members trust that the innovator (and team) can actually fulfill the promise and manage the risks. They believe that the innovator is likely to fulfill even though there is a possibility of failure. In executing, the innovator initiates the right conversations involving the right people and moves them all toward completion. The innovator holds the promise and makes sure that all performers actually deliver their components. The essential elements of execution are:

1. Setting context and generating possibilities
2. Managing conversations for action
3. Managing the network of conversations to coordinate fulfillment and deal with changes and breakdowns
a. Inviting the right people to be in those conversations and establishing a network of coordination network among them. (The right people include team members with right expertise, authority figures, investors, customers, and users.)
b. Managing all conversations to keep the actions moving toward completion and maintaining awareness of the customer for every promise
c. Ensuring that all performers (including oneself) have the capacity to deliver
d. Building trust in the promise and its performers
4. Managing breakdowns, changes, and dissatisfaction

Once again, we emphasize that the innovator does not need to be the expert or the doer, but must be able to find and motivate experts and doers to join the team. We will discuss each of these in the next sections.

Conversations for Context and Possibility

A conversation for context reveals the aspects of the environment that bear on the intended outcome. A good framework for the environment has already been discussed under domain mapping in chapter 4. The innovator can engage others in conversation to bring these aspects out and to provide motivation. Context setting can take a while (as seen in Peter Denning's conversation with Fernando Flores) or it can be brief (as when a team leader speaks encouraging words about the value of a member's contribution to the team's purpose).

A conversation for possibilities generates ideas for possible action. This conversation is conducted in a mood of speculation, identifying possible future actions without judging them or committing to them. Its purpose is to generate a range of possible outcomes, especially including many that are not obvious in habitual frameworks and current constraints. To maintain the mood of speculation and generate the richest set of possibilities, the speakers willfully refrain from making feasibility assessments and commitments. An example is a "what if" conversation requested by a team member to explore a proposal. Another example is a group brainstorming session that designs goals or ways around obstacles. Winograd and Flores described it in this way:

The key aspect of conversations for possibilities is the asking of the questions "What is it possible to do?" and "What will be the domain of actions in which we will engage?" This requires a continuing reinterpretation of past activity, seen not as a collection of past requests, promises, and deeds, but as interpretations of the whole situation—interpretations that carry a pre-orientation to new possibilities for the future. (1986, 151–152)

Speculations are not limited to teams and short time spans. They can involve entire communities and can last for many years. An example is the NASA-led speculation about building a space elevator (Edwards 2003; see spaceelevator.com). As discussed earlier in this book, the space elevator is a vehicle that climbs a cable anchored to earth and to a massive geosynchronous counterweight at 22,000 miles altitude. A space elevator would transport people, payloads, power, and gases between earth and space at a fraction of the energy and cost now required for rocket launches. The ongoing speculation involves scientific analyses, engineering prototypes, and prize competitions for components of the system such as cable material, cable installation process, and elevator car design.

The generative mood of a speculation will be destroyed if participants are close-minded, inconsiderate of possible future actions, overly critical of fragile new possibilities, or too anxious to commit to a possibility. When the speculative part of the conversation is over, the next stage is to generate commitments for action. That is the purpose of the conversation for action.

An important skill of the innovator is to maintain the distinction between conversations for possibility and action, and to know when the time is right for a transition. The transition is marked by a shift of mood, from speculation to resolution. During the transition, a subset of the newly generated possibilities is selected for feasibility and further study, and then a subset of those is selected for commitments to action.

Conversation for Action

The conversation for action is one of the most celebrated conversational patterns for producing desired outcomes. This pattern was first identified by Fernando Flores in his PhD thesis at University of California, Berkeley, titled "Management and Communication in the Office of the Future" (1979). He based it on distinctions made by the linguistic philosophers John Austin and John Searle. It is a universal pattern for how two parties act together to cause a specified condition to hold in the world. In the early 1980s, Flores founded Action Technologies to sell the Coordinator, his email system that tracked conversations for action.

Although many people think the conversation for action is a technique for speaking, Flores never intended it that way. The intention was to define a universal observer who could see the exact moments at which two parties agree on the state of their coordination. The person who could observe in this way is far more likely to notice when a conversation is going off track and able to guide it back toward its final objective. It helps the person manage conversations well.

The conversation for action involves two parties, the customer A and the performer B, who work together to negotiate a condition of satisfaction (COS) that both will commit to. A diagram of four key milestones in their conversation is depicted in figure 10.2. The stages are:

• *Request preparation*   A formulates a request specifying the desired COS and presents it to B with some form of the speech act "I request" that produces in B the listening for a request.
• *Negotiation*   After a negotiation in which the two parties may modify the COS, B signifies agreement with some form of the speech act "I promise" that produces in A the listening for a commitment to produce the result.
• *Performance*   B takes whatever steps are necessary to fulfill the COS and indicates to A the outcome is available with some form of the speech act "I complete" that produces in A the listening for a delivered promise.
• *Acceptance*   A reviews the results, and upon agreeing that they have met the COS, declares completion of the transaction with some form of

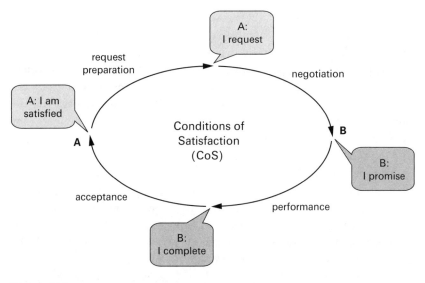

Figure 10.2
Structure of conversation for action. The outcome of value is noted at the center. The speech acts or their equivalent variations mark transition points in the conversation.

the speech act "I am satisfied" that produces in B the listening that the entire transaction is complete.

The model captures the deep structure of two-person coordinations. It reveals the moments in a conversation where the parties achieve a shared understanding of their commitments to the shared future. The speech acts are actually *listening acts* (Dunham 2009), the points at which the listener perceives an intended request, a promise, a completion, or an acceptance. Simply speaking the words dues not ensure that the other party actually heard them or interpreted them the same way as the speaker.

The real conversation, therefore, may not be so precisely structured. Some segments may be abbreviated; for example, A could say "hamburger, please" and the waiter immediately hands over a hamburger without saying a word. Moves, grunts, or gestures may be speech acts as well as words.

Winograd and Flores (1986) used the model to design a software program in which the users explicitly selected the speech acts they were currently engaged in; the program tracked the state of every transaction between two parties toward its final state. The software program is simply a tracking device for users who have agreed to a stylized form of conversation. Because it only records commitments, but does not make them, it is incapable of generating the outcome on its own. They incorporated their program into the Coordinator email software.

The purpose of the conversation for action is to enlist the performer's expertise to provide something of value missing in the customer's world. What is missing can be expressed as the COS. Because the two parties might have different interpretations of the conditions, the conversation includes a final check where the customer reviews the proposed result and explicitly agrees that it is satisfactory. Thus customer satisfaction is an essential part of the conversation. It is not a psychological evaluation; it simply means that the customer certifies that the COS are satisfied.

Notice that the customer acts from two assessments: perceived value on entering the transaction and satisfaction at the end. Value is an assessment about the future, satisfaction about the past. Customers will not enter transactions unless they expect worthwhile benefits. They will refrain if they have had prior bad experiences with the same performer.

Notice also that the two parties must trust their mutual commitments. The customer trusts that the performer has the capability to deliver and intends to do it on time. The performer trusts that the customer will accept the results if they meet the COS, and will pay for them if that is part of the deal. In most cases, trust will be based on reputation: the performer's past record of delivery and the customer's history of acceptance and payment.

The terminology of customer and performer comes from the business world. The conversation for action is much more general: it applies any time one person makes a promise to another. Thus there are many interpretations of customer, including buyers, clients, consumers, patients, patrons, purchasers, internal customers, external customers, and users—anyone whom others have agreed to satisfy. Likewise there are many interpretations for performer, including promiser, provider, professional, service provider, manufacturer, and producer—anyone who has a commitment or obligation to satisfy another.

In other words, you are a customer for a company that accepts your order, for a doctor who agrees to examine and treat you, for a professor who promises you a certain outcome from taking a course, for a lawyer who agrees to represent you in court, and even for your spouse when you say, "please pass the salt." You do not have to engage in a business transaction to be a customer.

In closing, we offer figure 10.3, which connects the conversation for action to the chain of events leading to a valued outcome.

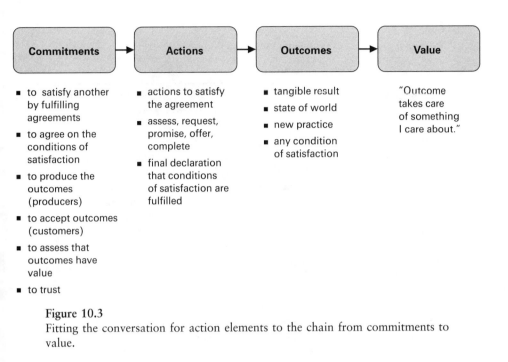

Commitments → **Actions** → **Outcomes** → **Value**

Commitments	Actions	Outcomes	Value
■ to satisfy another by fulfilling agreements ■ to agree on the conditions of satisfaction ■ to produce the outcomes (producers) ■ to accept outcomes (customers) ■ to assess that outcomes have value ■ to trust	■ actions to satisfy the agreement ■ assess, request, promise, offer, complete ■ final declaration that conditions of satisfaction are fulfilled	■ tangible result ■ state of world ■ new practice ■ any condition of satisfaction	"Outcome takes care of something I care about."

Figure 10.3
Fitting the conversation for action elements to the chain from commitments to value.

Incomplete Conversations for Action

One of the most powerful uses of conversation for action structure is to analyze such conversations for breakdowns—missing elements that prevent successful completion. Incomplete or missing conversations will breed dissatisfaction, waste, lost value, and distrust. Without mutual trust, neither party is likely to be willing to enter future transactions with the other. Table 10.1 lists seven common breakdowns in conversations for action.

A "missing customer" is the most prevalent breakdown (Denning and Dunham 2003). It occurs whenever a provider is uninformed about customer concerns or perceptions of value. The provider simply produces products that it thinks are good and that meet its own conceptions of customer "needs." In many cases the customer has no alternatives and begrudgingly accepts the products.

A prominent example of the missing customer breakdown is the widespread use of VRUs (voice recognition units) by companies. VRUs are the systems that offer callers dense trees of voice menus, with options chosen by pushing buttons or speaking their names. Most paths through the tree lead to automated subsystems consisting of a speaking software

Table 10.1
Breakdowns in Conversations for Action

Breakdown	Examples
Missing customer	Performer generates results and tries to foist them on unwilling persons (software companies are famous for this). Unclear who makes a request.
Missing performer	No one accepts request or then responds to customer (bureaucracies are famous for this). Request goes to a group without specifying anyone to agree and act.
Missing Conditions of Satisfaction (COS)	Customer and performer do not agree on COS but work begins anyway. COS are unclear or sloppy.
Missing request	Customer drops hints, issues no clear request, expects performer to read customer's mind.
Missing promise	Performer shrugs but does not make promise, customer interprets shrug as agreement. Performer says, "I'll try" instead of making a clear commitment.
Missing performance	Performer does not complete work, delivers it without notifying customer, or does not keep the customer informed of upcoming problems.
Missing acceptance	Customer does not indicate whether he or she is satisfied. The system does not provide for customers to indicate satisfaction.

agent interfacing with a database. VRU vendors promise huge savings—by routing 85 percent of calls to automated subsystems they reduce the customer service center staff to 15 percent of pre-VRU levels. Companies reason that most customers prefer the resulting lower prices and that they will adapt to automated systems, as they have to bank ATMs. But the vast majority of surveyed customers see VRUs as a service without a customer. They frequently complain of very long hold times, surly and overworked service agents, and the blatantly insincere recordings ("we are experiencing unusually high call volume, your call will be answered in the order received," and "we apologize for the delay, your business is very important to us"). Many customers, having come to believe that these companies are not interested in them as individuals, have no loyalty.

The most prominent explanations for the prevalence of the missing-customer breakdown are captured in these inconvenient truths:

• *Abstraction* Marketing departments have turned the "customer" into a behavioral profile represented by survey numbers including demographics, sales, preferences, and perceived needs. Abstract customers do not have concerns and do not care about value—they are only probability distributions.

• *Hostility toward the notion of the customer at universities* University faculty vociferously proclaim that students are not customers; the larger, noble mission of the university overrides individual desires of students for value and satisfaction in their interactions with faculty. Graduates carry this learning into the business marketplace.

• *Professional hubris* Experts sometimes consider their superior knowledge as a reason to dismiss the concerns of customers with inferior knowledge. They take their own assessments more seriously than their clients.

The missing-customer example illustrates a powerful result from being able to observe conversations for action. With the model, we can notice not only that a component of a conversation is missing, but also that an entire conversation is missing. Only then can we restore the missing component or initiate the missing conversation.

A pitfall in developing innovations is falling in love with our own ideas and forgetting to ask how they might appeal to customers. It is surprising how many aspiring innovators forget that their success depends on others making positive assessments of them and their promises.

Managing the Network of Conversations

The conversation for action coordinates two parties. Each party, however, will coordinate with others on secondary requests. Figure 10.4 illustrates the network of a typical process where a customer orders from a catalogue. Each subsidiary conversation has its own customer and performer. An entire organization can thus be represented as a network of conversations (Flores and Ludlow 1980) and managed as a network of promises (Sull and Spinosa 2005, 2007).

Managing the network of conversations has a number of aspects: inviting the right people, clarifying roles, keeping their conversations moving toward completion, ensuring capacity, managing satisfaction, managing trust, and managing breakdowns. These aspects are discussed next.

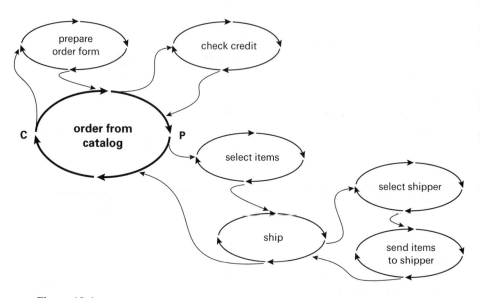

Figure 10.4
Customer C orders from a catalogue of provider P. To implement the main conversation seen by C, P manages a coordination network of loops staffed by its employees and suppliers.

Inviting the Right People to Join Your Coordination Network

You will normally want to create a team or a network of teams to help you accomplish your innovation. Your team's collective expertise can help produce the innovation when you lack key skills or have insufficient capacity. Much has been written about team formation and management; we will not duplicate that here. Good samples of the literature are Lencioni (2002) and Whitney and colleagues (2004).

In forming and managing your team, it is not necessary that you have all the answers worked out at the beginning. You are asking people to join you in an exploration, a journey of many starts and stops before you attain the goal. Your team accepts the risk of failure and the necessity of much work to overcome false starts, because they believe in the goal and in your commitment. In *Good to Great* Jim Collins (2001) says that the teams that elevated companies to extraordinary performance were passionate, willing to engage in the hard questions and conversations to resolve decisions, and fully supportive of the final decisions.

Clarifying Roles

As noted earlier, conversations for action cannot complete satisfactorily if it is not clear who is the customer and who is the performer. Customers and performers in action conversations are not just names for who speaks and listens, but roles. Each role implies skills and practices for being competent as a customer or performer. For example, a promise made by a printer assumes that the printer is competent at printing. But there is more. The individual filling roles must also be competent at the coordination required for the action conversation to be effective. Both roles call for those filling them to have a fundamental commitment to produce satisfaction of the agreements made between them. This focus— satisfying an agreement and thereby satisfying a customer—is a different focus from the common one of completing a task.

The demand for effective coordination imposes performance standards for the roles of customers and performers in action conversations. An effective customer must make clear requests, provide feedback of satisfaction or dissatisfaction to the performer, and ask to be informed of changes or breakdowns that may affect the fulfillment of the agreement. An effective performer keeps listening for the satisfaction of the customer, keeps the customer informed, coordinates changes or actions around breakdowns, and makes promises that they are competent and committed to fulfill.

Most people are not trained to be effective customers and performers by these standards. It is common that professionals are competent at the tasks they perform but not at coordinating action with their customers, or at being an effective customer for those who perform for them. We find that many leaders cause breakdowns in their organizations by being ineffective customers. Meeting the standards for being an effective customer or performer is a good focus for practice.

Managing Conversations toward Completion

Fernando Flores has said that the job of a manager isn't making decisions, it's making sure that people are in the right conversations and that their conversations and actions are all progressing toward completion.

When your network is in action, many people are working on producing outcomes in many conversations for action. As leader you watch and listen to all these conversations so that you understand where they are in their progress toward agreement and fulfillment. You facilitate them in moving toward completion by their deadlines. This may be easy for small innovation projects with small networks, but can require considerable management skill for large complex networks (see chapter 14).

As a manager, you will be the customer of many promises, especially those made by people who report to you directly. To be effective, you must be rigorous in your assessments about whether their results satisfy the agreements that you have made with them. You must be a good judge of the credibility of the promises offered to you, and not accept promises from those in whom you have little faith. You must teach your performers how to be rigorous customers of the promises made to them, and ensure they know you are rigorous in completing your own promises.

You will need to set up regular means to verify that all conversations are progressing. In a small network, this may be as simple as reading emails and injecting encouragement where needed. In a larger network, it will require more structure such as a weekly review meeting, in which each project leader assesses project status, estimated time of completion, current breakdowns, and red flags (threats that should be addressed). You may need other meetings as well such as periodic one-on-one meetings with your employees and periodic information-sharing group meetings.

It is very important to have clear purposes for these meetings, or you will wind up with people whose disdain for meetings becomes an obstacle for the project. To make your meetings effective, be very clear in advance of the conversations what will and *will not* happen, be firm during each meeting at enforcing these expectations, and make sure that the participants are competent in the conversations of the meeting. You may also need to coach your team members on the general conversational skills of negotiating agreements, grounding assessments, making clear requests and promises, listening well, and articulating conditions of satisfaction.

Ensuring Capacity to Deliver

Many people—including even the most committed and competent— often have difficulty fulfilling their promises. Their missed deadlines can create numerous breakdowns for others who depend on their results. They underestimate their capacity to fulfill their commitments. Their lack of capacity affects their reliability and credibility.

Capacity means that the person has the time, competence, and resources to fulfill all their promises. Unfortunately, many people, including many experienced people, do not have good practices for assessing the time or resources they need to fulfill their promises. They do not negotiate for what they really need and they come up short. When they get into trouble, they do not ask for help; they try to handle it alone and get deeper into the hole.

Many people say yes to too many requests, creating slates of promises beyond their capacities, and setting up their customers for dissatisfaction. They simply do not have enough hours in a week to attend to everything.

Some promises remain unfulfilled and many breakdowns result. They often wind up feeling overwhelmed, stressed, and frazzled.

The only sure way to avoid this breakdown is to learn to make honest, grounded assessments of your commitments and capacity to fulfill them. Here is an exercise we have used to help people get started in Robert Dunham's Generative Leadership Program (GLP) and Peter Denning's Sense 21 classes (Denning 2002). Build a spreadsheet listing all your commitments, their raw demand (time you need each week to attend to them properly), and their actual allocation (time you actually get to spend on them each week). Include *all* commitments in your life, not just those in your innovation project. Many who do this exercise discover that the total raw demand exceeds 168 hours a week! Moreover, their actual allocation comes to over one hundred hours a week. We have found that people with actual allocations of one hundred or more hours a week struggle constantly and feel overwhelmed.

You are in a much better configuration when your total raw demand is no more than one hundred hours a week. If you are over capacity, you need to delegate or cancel commitments, so that the ones remaining are within your capacity. If reducing your commitments means you cannot fulfill expectations, it is time to sit down with your customers and develop new strategies and new expectations. Extreme overcommitment is a sure path to failure.

You can practice this exercise frequently to track whether you are staying within capacity. When you develop enough of a feel for it, you will no longer need the exercise.

Once you have matched your commitments to your capacity, you need a practice to keep you there. It seems simple enough: say yes only to the important things, and no to the unimportant. But the truth is, many of us cannot say no. It seems as if saying no to a boss is inappropriate, or saying no to a friend will injure the relationship, or saying no to something interesting will leave us bored. Yet if we cannot learn to say no, we cannot long avoid being overwhelmed. In some cases, such as responding to the boss, saying no may not be an option; we must counteroffer with helpful actions within our capacity. Some people find it helpful to train themselves to say no by a role-playing game with a colleague: one person makes the same request over and over and the other repeatedly declines. The requester can try different approaches, such as seduction, persuasion, threats, and intimidation, to get the other to say yes. The other person develops the capacity for saying no despite the allurements and incentives of yes.

Stephen Covey (1990) defines the attributes "urgent" and "important" for events demanding your action. *Urgent* means it must be done now; *important* means it contributes to your major goals. Failure to work on important tasks leads to breakdowns that must be corrected by new, urgent tasks. People who are over capacity tend to spend most of their time on urgent but unimportant tasks and never get to the important ones. Their inattention to the important generates breakdowns that ultimately demand urgent corrective actions. Therefore, a suffocating backlog of urgent tasks can be another indicator that you are over capacity. Knowing what is important and what is urgent can be very helpful in prioritizing projects so that you remain in capacity and have enough time to work on important tasks.

In his bestselling book *Getting Things Done*, David Allen (2001) describes a method of tracking tasks with a small number of lists, files, and folders. Many people have found his method helpful for managing their personal workflows within capacity. Interestingly, his system of lists, files, and folders closely resembles the parts of a computer operating system that manage the flow of work.

Managing Trust

As an innovator, you will not get very far unless potential adopters and teammates trust you. You must pay attention to how your presence, action, and speaking produce assessments of trust or distrust. If others trust you, you can accomplish much. If others distrust you, you will accomplish little.

There can be no innovation without trust. Adopters are asked to take risks. They need to trust that the outcome will be positive and that the innovator brings the right qualities to make it happen. Trust enables people to make the commitments that mobilize action.

Trust is a bet that a person will deliver an expected outcome (Covey 2006; Fukuyama 1996; Solomon and Flores 2001; Sztompka 2000). It is based on the assessments that the person is:

- Competent and skillful
- Sincere
- Reliable
- Efficient and cost effective
- Respectful of one's interests
- Caring
- Honest

- Fair
- Just

The conversation for action is a major arena for these assessments. Many people base their assessments on how they see you perform in your conversations for action. We will not trust someone whom we think fails on any of these aspects. Simply knowing that this is how others will treat us can help us shape our own actions so that we are seen as trustworthy.

It is all too easy to grant trust based solely on a good feeling about the person. Ungrounded assessments of trust can lead to betrayals.

One of the most difficult skills to learn is how to make grounded assessments of trust in promises other people make to us. Our accomplishments depend on others fulfilling their promises. Nothing is more disconcerting than to fail to achieve an objective because we trusted someone else who did not deserve our trust. Their failure to deliver something important prevented us from delivering something we promised. This is why being a rigorous customer for all promises made to us as innovators is essential for success.

As an innovator, you have a lot to live up to, to earn the trust of your potential adopters.

Managing Satisfaction

The term *managing* is often understood as managing people, managing work, or managing tasks. In our generative interpretation, we are not managing people, work, or tasks—we are managing commitments. In fulfilling commitments, it is not enough just to get the work done; we also manage satisfaction. Managing satisfaction is the practice of regular communication with the customer, listening for potential dissatisfaction because of changing expectations about the conditions of satisfaction or the conduct of the process. If we sense potential dissatisfaction, it is time to revisit the agreement or the process, and either reaffirm its original form or change it. This practices attends not only to the fulfillment of the agreement, but also to the satisfaction of the customer and performer in the process of fulfillment. A satisfactory outcome may not sustain trust and relationship if the process of achieving it is painful and unpleasant.

Breakdowns

There are numerous ways to interrupt execution. Each of these common breakdowns disrupts an essential element of execution:

• Failing to prepare for action with conversations for context and possibility
• Failing to initiate all the conversations for action needed to complete the promise
• Any of the seven failures of conversation for action, especially missing customer
• Failing to assemble a good team that represents all of the kinds of expertise needed to complete the promise
• Failing to establish a network of conversations that coordinates all actions toward the completion of the promise
• Failing to monitor the key conversations and keep them progressing toward completion
• Failing to ensure that all performers (especially those on the team) are managing their commitments within their capacities
• Failing to be a rigorous customer of all promises made to you by your team
• Failing to build trust in yourself, your team, and your promise
• Failing to manage expectations about what will be delivered and when
• Failing to listen to and manage satisfaction through the fulfillment process
• Failing to declare breakdowns and develop recovery plans to address them

As you encounter breakdowns that block progress in your innovation, this list can be helpful to locate the source and to address it.

We noted earlier that breakdowns are more likely when we get too wrapped up in urgent actions and fail to take care of important things. Therefore we can avoid some breakdowns by explicitly asking what the most important things are for us to do, and making sure we have the capacity to do them.

A useful practice for productively anticipating breakdowns is the "red flag practice." It mobilizes the entire team to mitigate breakdowns. Under this practice, everyone on the team is expected to raise warnings about threats, actual or potential. The team can then decide which red flags require action and which can be ignored. Team members together can decide what help is needed, what promises to modify, what expectations to change. By catching breakdowns in the making, the team can mitigate or avoid them.

Another useful practice for avoiding or mitigating breakdowns is expectations management. Every promise generates an expectation in its customer about what will be delivered and when. Your trustworthiness generates expectations about how you will keep people informed and how you will treat them if there are breakdowns. The more you are aware of these expectations, the better you can modify them when needed. For example, if a delivery will be late, it is better to inform the customer and offer alternatives than to break your promise. Expectations management is part of managing satisfaction.

What to Practice

Practice the conversations for context and possibility. Do you have enough of these with people you lead? Do you use them to motivate and give meaning to actions you request? Do you use them to design resolutions for breakdowns?

Practice the conversation for action. Nothing is more powerful for bringing rigor to all coordinations. Do you make clear requests? Do your performers understand your requests? Are the promises clear? Do you work for satisfaction at the end of the conversation? Are you ever a missing performer? Missing customer? As you improve your skill, you are likely to experience a sharp reduction in the number of misunderstandings and miscoordinations. You will experience greater trust from other people, who will come to regard you as a person of your word and very reliable.

Practice approaching your projects as conversations. Which people need to be around your table to make a project work? Have you invited them? Do they all have the right skills? Can they be trusted? What conversations need to exist for you to complete your promise? Have you put responsible people in charge of those conversations? Are they progressing toward completion?

Practice making grounded assessments of team members' performance (see chapter 4). Encourage this in the team. When people are not used to making assessments of each other's performance, small breakdowns can escalate into major emergencies for the team. With practice, people get over their embarrassment about assessing each other and the team moves to a higher level of coordination. High-performance teams are constantly making assessments, always to help the team meet objectives, and they are completely comfortable doing this.

Practice checking that your commitments are within your capacity and helping others on your team do the same.

Practice noticing the expectations people in your network have, and managing those expectations. It leads to greater satisfaction.

Practice announcing and managing breakdowns. An important difference between excellent teams and mediocre ones is often their ability to do this.

Conclusions

Our approach to the executing practice is based on this overall view of actions in groups and communities:

- People are observers through language.
- People are constantly listening for care and value.
- Care and value motivate action.
- Conversation for context articulates what is valuable.
- Conversation for possibility generates possible actions of value.
- Conversation for action produces the commitment to actions of value.
- Teams, organizations, and communities are networks of commitments.
- Choices are driven by assessments of value, satisfaction, and trust.
- Breakdowns are inevitable and are opportunities to increase value.

To execute your promise of innovation successfully, you need domain-specific and conversational skills. The executing practice focuses on conversational skills that enable you to design conversations that produce commitments to actions and to put responsible people in charge of them. These skills are generative because they create action in any domain.

Your effectiveness depends critically on your skill at the conversational practices of execution. The higher your skill level in completing actions, the more trust others will grant you. The higher levels of skill require you to embody the basic actions outlined here. Practicing them regularly is very important to increasing your effectiveness. You can couple this practice with embodiment (Practice Eight) to attain the highest levels of skill.

Bibliography

Allen, David. 2001. *Getting Things Done*. Penguin.

Brothers, Chalmers. 2004. *Language and the Pursuit of Happiness*. New Possibilities Press.

Collins, Jim. 2001. *Good to Great: Why Some Companies Make the Leap ... and Others Don't*. HarperBusiness.

Covey, Stephen R. 1990. *The Seven Habits of Highly Effective People*. Free Press.

Covey, Stephen M. R. 2006. *The Speed of Trust*. Free Press.

Denning, Peter. 2002. Internet Time Out. *ACM Communications* 45 (March):15–18.

Denning, Peter, and Robert Dunham. 2003. The Missing Customer. *ACM Communications* 46 (March):19–23.

Dunham, Robert. 2009. The Generative Foundations of Action in Organizations: Speaking and Listening. *International J. of Coaching in Organizations* 7 (2).

Edwards, Bradley C. 2003. *The Space Elevator: A Revolutionary Earth-to-Space Transportation System*. BC Edwards Publisher.

Flores, Fernando. 1979. Management and Communication in the Office of the Future. PhD thesis, UC Berkeley.

Flores, Fernando, and Juan Ludlow. 1980. Doing and speaking in the office. In *Decision support systems: Issues and challenges*, ed. G. Fick and R. H. Sprague, 95–118. Pergamon Press.

Fukuyama, Francis. 1996. *Trust: The Social Virtues and the Creation of Prosperity*. Free Press.

Lencioni, Patrick. 2002. *The Five Dysfunctions of a Team: A Leadership Fable*. Jossey-Bass.

Solomon, Robert, and Fernando Flores. 2001. *Building Trust*. Oxford University Press.

Sull, Donald N., and Charles Spinosa. 2005. Using Commitments to Manage Across Unit. *MIT Sloan Management Review* 47 (Fall):1.

Sull, Donald N., and Charles Spinosa. 2007. Promise Based Management, the Essence of Execution. *Harvard Business Review* (April) 78–86.

Sztompka, Piotr. 2000. *Trust: A Sociological Theory*. Cambridge University Press.

Whitney, Diana, Amanda Trosten-Bloom, Jay Cherney, and Ron Fry. 2004. *Appreciative Team Building: Positive Questions to Bring Out the Best in Your Team*. iUniverse, Inc.

Winograd, Terry, and Fernando Flores. 1986. *Understanding Computers and Cognition*. Addison-Wesley.

11

Practice Seven: Leading

A leader is best when people barely know he exists. When his work is done they will say: we did it ourselves.

—Lao Tzu

Leadership is the art of getting someone else to do something you want done because he wants to do it.

—Dwight Eisenhower

If anything goes bad, I did it.
If anything goes semi-bad, then we did it.
If anything goes really good, then you did it.
That's all it takes to get people to win football games.

—Bear Bryant

If we don't change the direction in which we are moving, we are likely to end up where we are headed.

—Chauncey Bell

Leading is the skill of initiating possibility and action with others through conversations that evoke their commitment to a new future. It infuses all the other innovation practices, providing the actions to generate followers for the innovation.

There are many leadership styles (Bennis 2003; Greenleaf 2002; Goleman, Boyatzis, and McKee 2002; Dupree 2004). One is especially well suited for innovation. It is the style in which the leader initiates the movement and then gets out of the way of followers so deftly that they think they did it themselves. Other styles do not produce a deep individual commitment to stick with the new practice. The leaders quoted at the beginning of this chapter—a philosopher from three thousand years ago, a general who became president, a renowned football coach, and a visionary designer—all advocate this leadership style.

We call this style *generative leadership*. Generative leaders get their power from authority granted by others. They generate followers and build more power by using their power to help others take care of what those others care about. Generative leaders regard power as the capacity to persuade and influence people to commit to a new practice. Their leadership is based on care, the most important quality for a leader to develop.

In the common sense of our culture, leaders exercise power, often based on coercion or the threat of withdrawal of some perk, to mold the futures of others. A leadership style based on coercion produces compliance and submission, but leaves no foundation of commitment to sustain an innovation. Coercive leaders can sustain their power only by resorting to greater force as people withdraw their support.

Those who seek power only for the sake of power itself, power for only their own personal concerns, or power against whole communities, eventually alienate their followers. These leaders do not include the concerns of others in their view of the future and their exercise of power. Some may try to produce the appearance of concern for others, but in the end they cannot conceal their raw greed for power. Negative leaders run the gamut from Hitler and Stalin, who built visions of a future that included the destruction of whole communities, to demagogues who create power through division and hate, and to those who pursue power for their own greed.

The masterful leader of innovation is committed to a positive future for all affected by the new practice (Heifetz 2004). This leader is committed to working through the tradeoffs and challenges that designing and producing such a future requires (Drucker 2004).

Our focus here is on the conversational practices that enable the innovator to develop generative leadership skills and to generate followers who make their own commitments to support the innovation.

Innovation Leading

John Kotter, a Harvard Business School professor well known as a guru in leadership, comments on leadership so:

The pioneers who invented modern management . . . were trying to produce consistent results on key dimensions expected by customers, stockholders, employees, and other organizational constituencies, despite the complexity caused by large size, modern technologies, and geographic dispersion. . . . Leadership is very different. It does not produce consistency and order, as the word itself implies. It produces movement. Throughout the ages, individuals who have been seen as leaders have created change, sometimes for the better, and sometimes not. (Kotter 1996)

The key word is *movement,* meaning change. The movement sought by innovators is adoption of a new practice in a community. To achieve movement, innovators must produce new commitments, actions, and outcomes in the other seven practices.

Many would-be innovators believe that the prime work of innovation is the generation or discovery of novel ideas. Their leadership focuses on invention, not adoption (see chapter 1). Idea leaders promote ideas and convince people to accept them. Idea leaders change minds; adoption leaders change practices and hearts.

We do not mean to suggest that idea leadership has no place in innovation. It does. Idea leadership dominates the sensing and envisioning practices. Adoption leadership dominates the offering, adopting, and sustaining practices.

The relative importance of the two senses of innovation leadership will vary by situation. When the change of practice is small, such as when a consumer switches a different product in the same category, a good marketing campaign to plant the idea of switching may be sufficient to bring about adoption. When the change of practice is significant, marketing alone will not induce adoption.

One of the important lessons we have learned with our clients is that good ideas do not automatically sell themselves. Someone must persuade others to adopt the ideas. For example, many engineers tell us that their colleagues ignore their good ideas and allow demonstrably inferior ideas to make it into products. When we ask what actions they took to achieve adoption, they reply "none," noting their belief that ideas should be judged on their own merits and good ones do not need to be pushed. The notion of a meritocracy of ideas is quite strong and persists despite abundant evidence that other factors such as memorability, inertia, fashion, resistance, or peer pressure trump merit.

The conclusion is that idea leadership, while important, is not enough for innovation. We need to emphasize adoption leadership. Adoption leadership produces the movement needed to change the community's practices.

Anatomy of Leading

Innovation leadership relies on these seven principles:

1. Leaders look for opportunities to take care and produce value.
2. Leaders engage others with new narratives for the future.
3. Leaders make offers, take stands for their offers, and engage with disagreement and resistance to their offers.
4. Leaders inspire followers to make and sustain commitments; in so doing they build power for themselves and others.
5. Leaders initiate actions and conversations, accept the risks, and learn from the consequences.
6. Leaders build a presence, a voice, and identity to have their offers heard and accepted.
7. Leaders are continually learning and sharpening their own skills.

We have found these seven principles effective over the years: for Robert Dunham in his Generative Leadership Program and for Peter Denning in his teaching. Although all of the principles are important, the two that get the most attention are care and power (principles one and four). We have not listed "building power" as a separate principle, but rather as a consequence of inspiring others to make commitments.

Leadership and innovation are closely linked. The seven leadership principles support the leadership concerns needed to realize the desired outcomes of the other practices. The innovation practices enable leaders to bring about change, often considered to be the ultimate goal of leadership. We have come to the conclusion that the eight practices of innovation are also essential practices for leadership. That is an interesting proposition, perhaps worthy of study in another book, but beyond the scope of this book.

Let us examine briefly each of the leadership principles and its application to innovation.

1. *Leaders look for opportunities to take care and produce value.*

Leaders listen, discern, connect to the concerns of others, and sometimes provoke new concerns. They are disposed to take care of those concerns and build the capabilities of others to take care of their own concerns. They know that taking care of concerns creates value and meaning for people. To them, innovations are means to take care of concerns.

The concerns of others that leaders listen for lie in three main dimensions: self, social, and world. Self concerns focus on things a person wants for well-being; examples are health, wealth, work, career, respect, and dignity. Social concerns focus on relationships: examples are family, community, networks, membership, play, reputation, identity, profession, and power to make changes. World concerns address the entire setting in which our life of the self and social lives exist.

Effective leaders bring care and passion to their commitments. Caring moves them not just to words, but also to action. Passion adds to their presence, power, and ability to get things done.

2. *Leaders engage others with new narratives for the future.*

As they move from care to action, leaders build stories about how concerns can be taken care of in the world. Their narratives are compelling because people can see their place in the new world and can commit to working toward it. Innovators likewise build their narratives over time through interactions with members of a community (Bell 2008). They modify their stories after seeing how people react to them.

3. *Leaders make offers.*

The offer is a fundamental social act of leadership. It is an act of relationship, of proposing a shared future with another. Leaders promise to produce a new future for those who accept the offer, and invite others to accept their promise.

Leaders do not make their promises lightly. They take stands in the face of disagreement and opposition to their offers. They embody deep commitments to fulfill their promises. They are not easily deterred from their commitments: they find creative ways to keep them when confronted with obstacles.

Offers lead to an exchange of power: the leader is granted power by others in return for the promise made about the future. Through these exchanges leaders not only shift the future with others, but they also build teams, organizations, and movements as well as their own identity and power.

4. *Leaders inspire followers to make and sustain commitments.*

The leader knows that the innovation will be most successful when people own it; and once they own it, they will, as Lao Tzu predicts, forget the leader. In *Good to Great,* Jim Collins (2001) identifies "Level 5 Leaders." These leaders are not centered on themselves, but are passionate about the organization's people and its mission. For these leaders, the new practice gives the people new power and new value in their lives. Paradoxically, the leader gains power by giving it away to others.

Power is a capacity for action. Adopters of an innovation gain power from the new practice and from being part of a community that shares the new practice. Leaders get their power from one or more of these sources: wealth, know-how, control of means of production, credibility, opinion leadership, or the admiration of others. All these sources are ultimately grants from others. The one source of power not granted by others is coercive force or fear. Both the military and gangs have this kind of power. Most innovators are concerned with earning power, because they know that coerced adoption cannot be sustained without continuing force.

Leaders earn power when others grant authority based on positive assessments they have about the leader, the leader's promises, and the leader's record of fulfilling their promises. Power is granted in many ways: by the money people pay for actions, by the love and care of families and friends, by the trust earned from keeping promises, by the credibility from belonging to communities, or by demonstrated expertise.

Power is increased by numbers. A larger community of voices speaking on behalf of an idea is more powerful than a few individual voices. Leaders leverage a large network of support by building alliances with key people in the network.

5. Leaders initiate actions and conversations.

Leaders are disposed toward action. They make requests and offers and start conversations that will push the innovation forward. They know that some actions may not work out but are willing to manage the risks and take the responsibility. They see every mistake as a learning opportunity for more effective future action (Denning and Dunham 2003).

6. Leaders build presence, voice, and identity in the world.

Leaders know that their credibility is important. They need the identity and presence that produces enough trust so that others accept their offers, or at least so the leaders can engage others in conversation with them about the possibilities represented in the offers (Senge et al. 2004). Thoughtful leaders are keen observers of their own and their colleagues' presence, voice, and identity, and make appropriate adjustments in their actions.

7. Leaders are always learning and sharpening their skills.

Leaders know that innovation is a learning process for their communities. They watch how the learning is going and constantly adjust their methods for improved performance. They learn from their mistakes. They engage in practices to build their own capacities at leadership and in the fields of their expertise. They expect the same from their cohorts and followers. They practice regular self-renewal and learning (Covey 1990; Loehr and Schwartz 2003).

We close this section with table 11.1, an illustration of how Candy Lightner and Cindi Lamb exercised each of these leadership aspects in the organization they cofounded, Mothers Against Drunk Driving (see chapter 2).

Measuring Innovation Leadership

It is often said that if you want more of something, measure it. Then people can see if they are getting it and will adapt their actions to get more of it. This notion has been applied to leadership by Daniels and Daniels (2007). They said that the success of leaders is measured by what their followers do, according to four principles:

1. Followers direct their behavior toward the leader's goals.
2. Followers make sacrifices for the leader's cause.
3. Followers reinforce or correct others so that they also conform to the leader's teachings.
4. Followers set guidelines for their own personal behavior based on what the leader would approve.

These outcomes define a *charismatic leader* but not an innovation leader. The innovation leader eventually disappears from the picture. The point of innovation leadership is adoption and integration of new practices in a community, not sustaining the power of a leader. With effective innovation leadership, followers appropriate the goals as their own; thereafter they follow their own goals and they sacrifice for their own cause. They gauge their behavior relative to their new community standards, not leader teachings. Once they adopt, they no longer seek approval from the innovation leader.

The seven principles of innovation leadership are generative, observable, and measurable. They are generative because the desired leadership behavior results from following them. They are observable because we can tell if they have been accomplished; for example, we can tell if there are followers, we can count them, we can ask if they believe their leader

Table 11.1
MADD Founders as Innovation Leaders

Principle	Lightner and Lamb examples
Look for opportunities to take care	From their personal experiences, they cared deeply about the damage caused by drunk drivers.
Engage new narratives about the future	They envisioned a world with new laws reflecting low tolerance for drunk driving, new practices to keep drunks off the road, and specific goals for death and accident reductions. They collected and told inspirational stories about the tragedies caused by drunk drivers and our willingness to tolerate them.
Make offers, take stands, engage disagreement	They made offers to media and public officials to lead a movement to change things. They offered their own tragic stories to illustrate that the situation had to change. They called on others to join them. Their strong and principled stands melted the opposition.
Inspire others to make and sustain commitments	They crisscrossed the country telling their personal stories and enlisting supporters. They enlisted many volunteers into MADD and set them loose in state legislatures around the United States, eventually securing passage of tough new alcohol and DUI standards in every state. They built power for their organization by getting state legislatures to change their laws.
Initiate actions, take risks, learn from consequences	They enlisted volunteers, politicians, federal and state officials, mothers, and fathers across the country to be voices and activists for their cause. In states where they had setbacks, they regrouped and tried again.
Build presence, voice, and identity	Their organization became the world-leading voice for intolerance of drunk driving and for social practices to keep drunk drivers off the road. MADD became a formidable force for curing society of drunk driving.
Learn and sharpen	They built their organization to be one of constant renewal, with new volunteers and leadership every few years. They themselves stepped down as the leadership after five years.

cares, and so on. They are measurable because we can observe whether and how often the desired outcomes occur.

The importance of the Daniels-Daniels idea is not so much the specific measures as (1) the focus on followers, (2) the focus on outcomes they produce, and (3) the observability of outcomes. By measuring the outcomes of the eight innovation practices, we can assess the effectiveness of innovation leadership.

In addition to the outcomes of individual practices, we can measure the outcomes of the entire innovation process: magnitude of impact (sustaining or disruptive), duration of impact (months, years, generations), and size of innovation (number of followers).

Leader Virtues

Much is made in the innovation literature of the leader virtues of innovators. We list here the ones most often mentioned (Gilder 1992; Spinosa, Flores, and Dreyfus 1997). Some people mistakenly believe that these virtues generate innovation leaders. They think that successes come from exercising these virtues, and failures from lapsing in these virtues. Their belief lures them into looking in the wrong place for the sources of innovation.

The key virtues of innovation leaders include the following.

• *Care* To focus on what concerns people have and how they can be addressed
• *Persistence* The capacity to maintain the commitment over an extended period, to keep trying in the face of resistance or repeated failure
• *Humility* The capacity to put one's own opinions and interpretations aside, listen to others, and display genuine curiosity about others and the world
• *Risk tolerance* The capacity to put up with physical discomfort and anxieties accompanying risk assessments
• *Destiny* A sense that one's actions are in service to a higher good, that one is drawn into service by that good
• *Focus* The capacity to articulate the core principles for which one stands and not be sidetracked by interesting distractions
• *Value* The capacity to articulate and deliver value in one's promises
• *Courage* The capacity to face down threats and dangers even when one's well-being or reputation is at stake

• *Ethics* The capacity to act in accord with ethical principles while carrying out all actions

While these virtues are unquestionably important for supporting the leadership practices, they do not guarantee them. They are qualities and predispositions with which we do the practices. No combination of these virtues can assure that the leader has the capacity to build narratives, make offers, inspire commitments, initiate actions, or build power.

Some innovators do not display all these virtues. Some lack humility. Some lack courage. Some cannot maintain focus. Some have no sense of destiny. Nevertheless, they succeed because they are skilled in the eight practices.

We have not organized the practices around virtues because virtues are not generative; they predispose certain actions but do not produce those actions. Even if we teach you to be caring, humble, persistent, and so on, we cannot assure that you will improve as an innovator. These virtues are best treated as assessments provoked by your leadership actions. If you are not getting these assessments, you may want to review how you are performing the practices to see what is missing. Then work on building the practice.

What to Practice

The core of leadership practice for innovation is engaging in the seven principles of innovation leadership listed earlier. You can do this in two ways:

Coached study There are always things you cannot see for yourself. Ask your customers, peers, and supervisors for their assessments. Get someone to be your coach or mentor, or a group to be your personal advisory panel. Use your coaches to get regular input on how others see you.

Self study Examine your leadership actions in your innovation projects with the help of table 11.2 and the more detailed set of questions in the appendix at the end of this chapter. This will tell you where to focus your attention for the most results.

Breakdowns

A list of common breakdowns in innovation leadership follows. Each is an obstacle to one or more of the seven innovation leadership principles.

Table 11.2
Self-Study Questions for Innovation Leadership

Principle	Questions
Look for opportunities to take care	Can you state clearly what you care about? Can you state clearly what the people to whom you make offers care about? Are they clear about what you care about? What do your adopters see as value? Do you listen to concerns?
Engage new narratives about the future	Do you have a narrative about your innovation? Does the narrative address a concern and reveal value? Are people making new commitments on account of your narrative? Are you building identity with it? Are you building a team? Are you and your team effectively spreading the narrative and generating new followers?
Make offers, take stands, engage disagreement	Are you making offers? Are they seen as valuable? Are they being accepted? If not, are you listening to why not, and adjusting? Are you building satisfaction, value, identity, and power in fulfilling your offers? Do you take a strong stand for your offer? Do you productively engage with disagreement and resistance to your offer?
Inspire others to make and sustain commitments	Are people committing to your offer—and not only initially but for the longer term? Are you building power: financial, know-how, symbolic? If not, what is missing? Are you building alliances? Networks of support? Value exchanges?
Initiate actions, take risks, learn from consequences	Are you disposed to map out action plans based on commitments, organize teams, initiate conversations, and build networks? Do you make grounded risks assessments and show people that the risks can be managed?
Build presence, voice, and identity	Do you have a presence? A voice? An identity? Do people respond positively to you? If not, what learning and actions are needed?
Learn and sharpen	What are your regular practices for renewal and learning? How do you continuously improve your competence in your area of expertise and as an innovation leader? Do you learn from your mistakes? Do you encourage those around you to do likewise?

If you discover that you have any of these breakdowns, you should engage your allies, team, advisors, and coaches in conversations to identify the sources and take corrective actions. The breakdown questions in the appendix of this chapter should be of further help. The most common breakdown forms follow.

• You don't know what you care about. Others don't know what you care about. Others don't care about what you say you care about.
• You are not fully committed to what you say you care about. You don't really care if your project succeeds.
• You don't know how to listen or find out what others care about.
• You see your project as a means to help your résumé or improve your chances for promotion.
• You don't have a narrative about the future. Or you have one but others don't get it or see a place for them in it. Or you think that storytelling is a waste of time.
• You don't make offers. Or you do, but people are not committing to them. If people object, you crumble. You hide from disagreement or send others to deal with it.
• It takes a lot of wheedling and cajoling to get people to accept your offers. They don't stick with your offer, but instead drift away.
• You are indecisive. You have trouble formulating action plans.
• People don't keep their promises to you. You don't know how to tell if someone's promise is trustworthy.
• You have no team. Or you do, but it is dysfunctional.
• You have no allies.
• You have no followers.
• You have lost power.
• Your reputation does not command respect. You are not seen as credible or trustworthy.
• Your presence and voice are not engaging or compelling.

Conclusions

In many ways, leadership and innovation overlap and are expressions of the same thing—changing the future for a community. Innovators need to exercise leadership through the other practices to make them effective. Leaders are often judged by their ability to innovate in their communities.

The two most important aspects of leadership are care and power. The purpose of leadership is to help people take care of things they care about—to have a "heart of care." Power is the ability to influence people to change so that they can better take care. Power for its own sake—to control and dominate others—is a dead end for innovators.

The seven leadership principles can be practiced as conversations. They are connected with the virtues of persistence, humility, risk tolerance, destiny, focus, value, courage, and ethics. While these virtues do not guarantee effective leadership, they are worth cultivating because they enhance our leadership impact by inspiring greater trust from adopters.

In building leadership, it is crucial to avoid trying to lead for personal gains, or to try to live up to someone else's standards that are not your own. It is all about taking care of what others care about most deeply.

When you connect deeply to what you care about, and listen deeply to what others care about, you will be able to live *your* life and to generate meaning and satisfaction *with others*. There is no prize in the end but the life you live and share, the impact you have on others, and the future that you create with them.

Bibliography

Bell, Chauncey. 2008. My Problem with Design. *ACM Ubiquity* 9 (34), http://acm.org/ubiquity/volume_9/v9i34_bell.html.

Bennis, Warren. 2003. *On Becoming a Leader: The Leadership Classic*. Rev. ed., Basic Books.

Collins, Jim. 2001. *Good to Great*. HarperBusiness.

Covey, Stephen R. 1990. *The Seven Habits of Highly Effective People*. Free Press.

Daniels, Aubrey, and James Daniels. 2007. *Measure of a Leader: The Legendary Leadership Formula for Producing Exceptional Performers and Outstanding Results*. McGraw-Hill.

Denning, Peter, and Robert Dunham. 2003. The Missing Customer. *ACM Communications* 46 (March):19–23.

Drucker, Peter. 2004. What Makes an Effective Executive. *Harvard Business Review* 82 (June):58–63.

Dupree, Max. 2004. *Leadership Is an Art*. Doubleday Business.

Gilder, George. 1992. *Recapturing the Spirit of Enterprise*. ICS Press.

Goleman, Daniel, Richard Boyatzis, and Annie McKee. 2002. *Primal Leadership*. Harvard Business School Publishing.

Greenleaf, Robert K. 2002. *Servant Leadership*. 25th anniv. ed., Paulist Press.

Heifetz, Ron. 1994. *Leadership Without Easy Answers*. Harvard University Press.

Kotter, John P. 1996. *Leading Change*. Harvard Business School Press.

Loehr, Jim, and Tony Schwartz. 2003. *The Power of Full Engagement*. The Free Press.

Senge, Peter, C. Otto Scharmer, Joseph Jaworski, and Betty Sue Flowers. 2004. *Presence: Human Purpose and the Field of the Future*. Society for Organizational Learning, Random House.

Spinosa, Charles, Fernando Flores, and Hubert Dreyfus. 1997. *Disclosing New Worlds*. MIT Press.

Appendix: Leadership Questions

(These questions are taken from materials developed by Robert Dunham for his Generative Leadership Program, offered by The Institute for Generative Leadership, Inc.)

In working with many people on their leadership skills, we have found that individuals tend to focus their energy in one of these four areas:

• *Breakdowns* Events that interrupt the flow of action toward the objective. Breakdowns usually are seen as a loss of power. The skill of addressing them includes declaring them, requesting help from our communities, accepting that which we cannot change, and designing actions for resolution. The tendency in a breakdown is to take it personally, to contract, to become defensive, and to disconnect from others.

• *Accumulating power* Increasing the ability to influence others, or the number of others who are influenced. Leadership must have a purpose, a "heart of care." The skill of accumulating power includes more clearly articulating what we care about, aligning our actions with what others care about, helping others achieve more power, and rising to new standards of excellence.

• *Extending care* Reaching out to others, helping them take care of matters important to them, and putting one's personal interests aside. It helps to have a sense of larger destiny drawing one out toward others. The skill of extending care includes designing and extending offers, finding ways to invite others into more effective games, and bringing one's passion into the service of others.

• *History making* Changing practice in a community, that is, innovating. The skill of innovating has been laid out in this book as the eight foundational practices of innovators.

We offer review questions in each category to help you and your team discover actions you should discontinue and new actions that you should take.

Breakdowns

1. Have you declared the breakdown?
2. Is your declaration of breakdown effective, meaning it declares the domain and the missing action? Does it open new actions to produce a different result?

3. What is the loss of your power that has provoked this breakdown? Who else has lost power that has diminished your own? Where can you locate or produce new power?

4. What is your strategy to overcome this breakdown?

5. Are you doing more of what hasn't worked?

6. Have you made requests for help? Are you building a team? Or are you trying to solve this situation solo?

7. What is your recovery plan? Has your plan been reviewed by a competent group of advisors? Will the execution of the plan be in time? What are its risks? How are you managing the risks of your plan?

8. Are you calling on allies or building allies for your situation?

9. Are you even making offers?

10. In what domain are you making offers?

11. What is the narrative of the offers you make? Does your the narrative say why you are qualified to make the offers? Does your narrative say what your offers' impacts will be?

12. Have you listened for the value of the offers you can make?

13. Have you reviewed the value of your offers?

14. Do you have committed listeners who can provide you feedback on your assumptions, strategies, and capabilities?

Accumulating Power

1. What is your offer? What is its value?

2. To what audience do you make your offers?

3. How do you find the members of your audience?

4. What do you communicate to them?

5. How do you engage in establishing mutual commitments with them?

6. Do you have a regular practice and medium of communication with your customers, allies, and team members?

7. Do you have a strategy? Have you had it reviewed by those competent in the domain of your offer? Is the offer clear about which concerns of others it addresses? Does it build power?

8. Do you have a plan? Does it have a clear financial component?

9. Do you have a team? Are you building one? Are you effective as a team leader?

10. What are the gaps between your plan and results, and what interpretation do you have for new action?

11. Have you built alliances that generate power for you?

12. Are you clear on what you care about, and that you are not becoming a slave to accumulating power?

13. Are your offers and actions aligned with what you care about?

14. What are the gaps between your care, your offers, and your actions? What are you doing about your gaps?

15. In what bigger games are you playing *your* game? How do you relate to them? How do you build power in them?

16. Do you have the presence, identity, and trust to have your offers accepted? Your requests? Your narratives?

Extending Care

1. What are you offering to take care of?
2. What is the meaning and satisfaction to you for extending your care?
3. Is the commitment to extend your care preventing you from taking care elsewhere, so that it is a breakdown for you?
4. What is your offer around the care you extend? Are people accepting it?
5. If people are not accepting your offer, have you listened to them to find out why not?
6. How do you get your offer heard among all the competing requests and offers for people's time, attention, and resources?
7. What is the level of power you want to build, or enable a community to build in taking care beyond the accumulation of power (e.g., charities, causes, nongovernmental organizations)?
8. Do you have a narrative of your values and mission?
9. Do you have a narrative for others that invites them to join you in your care efforts?

History Making

1. Are you clear about what you care about?
2. What is the breakdown or possibility in the world you are passionate about, and committed to take care of?
3. What is your offer to the world? What world of concerns is your offer relevant to?
4. What is your narrative of the future? To whom are you speaking your narrative? What does your narrative produce in others?
5. What value is your offer to others?
6. What is the structure of power that is, or will be, opposed to your offer, and opposed to what you declare is worth caring about?
7. What is your strategy for being heard?
8. What is your strategy for building power, in the face of opposition?
9. Who are your allies?
10. What are the rules of the game that you are already appearing in? How are you going to play?
11. How are you building a public voice?
12. What is your presence and identity? Is it sufficient for your mission?
13. Do you have a plan? A team? A community of support?
14. What are others learning and what actions are they committing to in order to take your discourse forward in the world, either as speakers or actors?
15. What institutions does your innovation require to change? What is the process of change in these institutions? What is the pattern of resistance to change in these institutions? How will you deal with this resistance?

12

Practice Eight: Embodying

Somewhere out there he is practicing, and I am not. And when we meet, he will win and I will lose.
—Anonymous Coach

Body refers to the shape of our experience. We learn through our bodies, through recurrent practices.
—Richard Strozzi-Heckler

The innovator's challenge is to get the members of a community to embody a new practice. When that is accomplished, they will speak differently, act differently, feel differently, and even see the world differently. To meet that challenge, the innovator has to manage and maintain coherence among the three dimensions of every practice: language, body, and moods-emotions. This chapter is about how to achieve coherence, not only for the community, but also in the innovator's own practice.

It should be obvious that the dimensions of language, body, and moods-emotions are interconnected and mutually interacting. We just need to recall times when we said we would do something, but did not because we couldn't get our body moving or we weren't in the right mood; or times when we learned a new technique and experienced elation at our success and began speaking differently about what we can do.

It is easy to separate the three dimensions and forget their coherence. For all three, we have distinctive vocabularies and professions—notably linguists, physical trainers, and psychologists. If we are too good at the separation, we might get caught up in the language patterns behind the seven practices studied so far and be blindsided by breakdowns in body or emotional reactions. For example, we could become fixated on "offering" as a language act and forget that our offers will be listened as valuable only if they make sense to our listeners in the context of their moods, emotions, and body reactions.

In this chapter we will show not only how to be observers of these three dimensions, but also how to manage them. We will discuss a core practice called *blending* that helps us embody the sense of coherence and successfully manage change in a community.

The field we are about to discuss is large and draws on mind–body methods, psychology, biology, and neuroscience. Its name is *somatics*, a word derived from the Greek *soma*, referring to the unity of mind, emotion, and body. We will say just enough about somatics to show how to learn to blend with the concerns, listening, and intentions of the people you want to adopt a new practice. Our bodies are constantly interacting through the "body language" of posture, gestures, contractions, openness, gracefulness, energy, resistance, and the like. Somatic communication goes on even when there are no words, for our living presence always stimulates reactions in others.

There is plenty of data to support the claim that the expressive actions of the feeling and energetic body can be more important than talk. Albert Mehrabian (1971) found that in conversations in which people spoke about feelings and attitudes, listeners on average weighted body language 55 percent, emotional intonation 38 percent, and words 7 percent in assessing credibility. Although these percentages do not apply to every type of conversation, they do demonstrate that people can respond significantly to body and emotion as well as words. Allen Weiner (2007) also emphasizes how important our body is in determining how we are listened to. Paul Eckman (2007) discusses how emotions are "wired" into the body where they can be triggered by linguistic events.

Alignment of language, body, and moods-emotions is crucial in innovation conversations, where trust is a big issue and the innovator's credibility is on the line from the start. Misalignments are likely to cause innovation train wrecks.

A New Common Sense

The somatic idea flies in the face of centuries of Western tradition, inherited from René Descartes in the 1600s, which tell us that mind and body are distinct and that our actions are controlled from the mind.

Our modern culture honors the power of the mind and discounts the power of the body. We tend to ignore our bodies except when we are concerned about health, appearance, sex, sports, and fashion. Our common approach to understanding communications breakdowns is to analyze the words we spoke rather than the actions we took or the dispositions of our bodies in the communications. Our cultural common sense puts the brain as the master that reasons and decides, and the body as the servant that implements the brain's decisions. A consequence of this is that we do not see that most innovation breakdowns originate in the body in three ways:

1. *Lack of awareness*   We are unaware of signals from our listeners that reveal their real concerns, or of how our own behaviors are affecting them, and so we do not connect.

2. *Conditioned tendencies*   Some of our automatic behaviors, called "conditioned tendencies" by Strozzi-Heckler (1984), disconnect us from our listeners or push them away.

3. *Lack of blending*   We lack automatic behaviors and skills that enable us to join with others in a smooth and graceful flow in harmony with their responses.

The field of somatics, founded in 1976 by Thomas Hanna (1928–1990), has developed a different common sense that is very useful in revealing how to overcome these breakdowns and amplify the effectiveness of the other practices. Somatics is concerned with the unity of mind, body, and emotions. This field has developed these principles and a rich literature[1]:

• The mind and body are not separate, but form and act as a unity.
• The brain is influenced by experiences of signals carried by the nervous system from all parts of the body.
• Emotions and moods predispose how we think and act.
• The history of our experience and practices conditions our perceptions of the world and shapes our capabilities.

1. Selected books that address aspects of somatic practice include: *You Are What You Say*, Matthew Budd; *The Seven Habits of Highly Effective People*, Steven R. Covey; *The Speed of Trust*, Stephen M. R. Covey; *What Computers Still Can't Do*, Hubert Dreyfus; *Emotions Revealed*, Paul Eckman; *Social Intelligence: The New Science of Human Relationships* and *Emotional Intelligence*, Daniel Goleman; *Anatomy of Change* and *Being Human at Work: Bringing Somatic Intelligence into Your Professional Life* and *The Leadership Dojo*, Richard Strozzi-Heckler; *Mastery: The Keys to Success and Long-Term Fulfillment*, George Leonard; *A General Theory of Love*, Thomas Lewis, Fari Amini, and Richard Lannon; *Silent Messages*, Albert Mehrabian; *The Passions: Emotions and the Meaning of Life*, Robert Solomon; *So Smart But . . . : How Intelligent People Lose Credibility—and How They Can Get It Back*, Allen Weiner.

• Communication is not just the transfer of information—it is the inter-action of people that produces interpretations, emotions and moods, and body reactions.
• Practice is the foundation for learning and mastery.

Our own work has been inspired by Richard Strozzi-Heckler's work on leadership (1984, 2003, 2007). Strozzi-Heckler has been the leading expert in the somatics of leadership. He studied Thomas Hanna's mind–body philosophy and psychology for his PhD thesis and developed a discipline of leadership training around it. He has published numerous books on the subject. Because embodiment means that the electrochem-ical pathways of the brain and nervous system are modified, Strozzi-Heckler likes to say that "body is the shape of our experience." And because new behaviors can be learned and replace less productive behav-ior, he says that "body is a domain of action."

In this chapter we will show you a series of somatic practices that reveal and teach blending, the central somatic skill of innovators. The reason for these somatic practices is that we cannot be effective at blend-ing unless we understand it as an *experience* in our bodies. These prac-tices incorporate three basic principles:

• *Awareness creates choice*   Every practice is based on distinctions that give you choices. Initially, the distinctions may be unfamiliar; you will have to practice until you notice them and make the choices effortlessly.
• *Energy follows attention*   Focus your practice on what you want to accomplish, not what you want to avoid. If you focus too much on what you want to avoid, you will have trouble avoiding it.
• *Your body is always practicing something*   It is easy to develop unpro-ductive habits if you do not deliberately focus on the outcome that you want from the practice. You cannot cut corners or put up with unwanted outcomes, for then the sloppiness and tolerance will become part of your habit.

Before we discuss blending, we need to explain the somatics of com-munication and listening, which we will do in the next two sections.

Somatic Dimensions of Communication

Our paramount interest in innovation is listening to, and connecting with, cares and concerns of others. This is the platform for us to move in alignment with them and redirect them in a more productive direction.

We have noted many times the prevalent notion that ideas originating in the mind drive innovation. Somatic awareness discerns many challenges to this notion in the large number of oft-cited examples of body phenomena that initiated new practices—urges, hunches, gut feelings, cravings, emotional reactions, frustrations, anxieties, sensibilities, sensitivities, or spontaneous improvisations. Other body phenomena that influence innovation are connection, care, moods, defensiveness, trust, and the experience of blending.

We use the term *embodied action* for actions the body takes without thought. Practices are the most common way of accessing, developing, and expressing embodied action. Similarly, let *mind action* refer to actions generated from thought processes in the mind. Language is the most common way of accessing and expressing mind action.

Embodied and mind action are only loosely connected. In the body-to-mind direction, we cannot put into language much of what we know in our bodies, often called tacit knowledge (Polyani and Kegan 1966) and practices (Spinosa, Flores, and Dreyfus 1997). We often find ourselves utterly unable to explain how we do our skillful actions. High-end performers and masters cannot articulate what they do in a way that others can learn from them. Their talent is expressed through their embodiment, not through their language. In the mind-to-body direction, we know that talk, will power, and good intention are often ineffective at getting the body to change its habits. Just ask the smoker who cannot stop reaching for the cigarettes.

Somatic practices align embodied and mind action. Figures 12.1 and 12.2 sketch the richness of the possibilities. Figure 12.1 depicts two parties interacting to create a shared future. They interact through conversations and "structural couplings" mediated by their personal listenings. The biologists Humberto Maturana and Francesco Varela used the term *structural couplings* because biological entities interact only by stimulating one another; they react to stimuli according to their respective structures, which are a product of their individual and genetic histories (Maturana and Varela 1980, 1987).

Figure 12.2 enumerates the many aspects of personal listening. They fall along the three main dimensions of interpretations (language), body, and moods-emotions. They all affect how sensory information is filtered before being perceived, what sense we make of it, and what actions we take. To observers, our embodiment of these three aspects reveals (or "discloses") our world to others (Spinosa, Flores, and Dreyfus 1997).

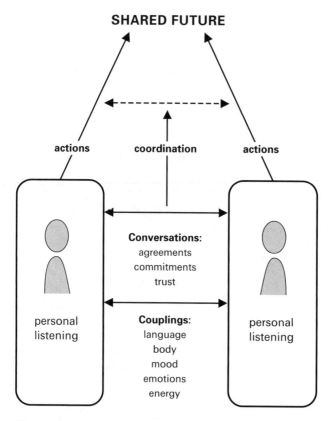

Figure 12.1
Two individuals in separate worlds (personal listenings or individual frameworks
of interpretation) take actions to achieve a shared future. They couple through
spoken language and unspoken body dispositions, energy, moods, and emotions.
They engage in conversations in which they reach agreements, make commitments, develop trust, and coordinate their actions.

Personal Listening

Let us examine more deeply the meaning of personal listening as we use
it here. Many of us were taught that good listening is a special form of
paying attention to another person's words. This teaching is misleading
in two ways: it assumes that inattention is the main reason we do not
listen well, and that words are the main carriers of the meaning we are
listening for. We have already seen that inattention is only one of many
reasons we may not listen well, and that in many conversations somatic
signals convey more meaning than words.

PERSONAL LISTENING

Interpretations	Body	Moods — Emotions
values	habits, skills, practices	joy
beliefs	awareness	care
culture	attention	wonder
standards	breath	ambition
community	energy	resolution
background	presence	————
assessments	open/closed	
personal history	center/off-center	inquiry
prior commitments	tension/relaxation	perplexity
	contraction/extension	bafflement
	grounded/ungrounded	————
	connected/disconnected	
	dynamic relaxation	apathy
	blending	confusion
		overwhelm
	————	resignation
	conditioned tendencies	resentment

Figure 12.2
A person's listening, or way of interpreting and experiencing the world, embraces three dimensions: interpretations, body, and moods-emotions. Interpretations are ways we make sense of sensory input according to our concerns. Body includes behaviors that we can train through practice (such as habits) and our automatic, first reactions to stimuli (conditioned tendencies). Moods are general predispositions toward the world; they can be energizing (such as joy), neutral (such as inquiry), or de-energizing (such as apathy). All three dimensions are connected to and influence the others; a change in one will produce a change in the others.

Neuro-Linguistic Programming offers the idea of an "internal map of reality" as a metaphor for personal listening. NLP interprets a person's brain as a complex system with filters that delete, distort, and generalize sensory input; the system uses the filtered input to update an internal representation (map) of the world. The internal map in turn influences the filters, emotional states, and action. Thus, what one interprets as having been said is the result of a dynamic, ongoing, complex feedback process. Bill Harris (2002) offered ways to help people observe and reprogram their filters and become more effective listeners and goal achievers. Of course, there is no internal map. There are only neurological structures that set up how we, as biological entities, respond to external perturbations, and learn by changing the structure of our neural couplings (Doidge 2007).

The somatic perspective goes deeper by considering the profound influence of the body (not just brain functions) in *how* we listen, make sense of the world, and interact with others. When we seek action, as we do in innovation, it is not enough to try to listen by turning off our brain filters and paying attention to what others mean by their words— we want to *"listen to their listening" in order to connect to their concerns and open them to our offers.*

As an example, consider an apparently simple request: "Come here." The words *come here* can be listened to as a command, an invitation, a playful provocation, a threat, a plea, a tease, a complaint, or plaint of despair; the differences are conveyed by the tone, posture, mood, and energy of the speaker's body. These are not simply brain interpretations because each is accompanied by a different emotional reaction and bodily sensations.

How does the speaker of "come here" tell which of these possibilities is the one actually in the listener's listening? The same question comes up with all conversational acts including requests, promises, declarations, assessments, and disclosures. What does the speaker listen for to tell if these acts actually showed up as intended for the listener? That process—listening for listening—is deeply somatic and operates simultaneously at multiple levels:

- The sounds and intonations of the spoken words
- The meanings of the words
- The unspoken concerns behind the words
- The unspoken background of practices that shape the concerns
- The primordial drives behind the concerns
- The history of interpretation and cultural practice behind the practices

The more we are aware of these levels, the better we are at identifying our listeners' real cares and concerns so that we can shape our innovation conversations to address their concerns. Our "conversation" is no longer simply an exchange of words; it is a complex set of somatic interactions. Many of these communications are very subtle. Skilled innovators have learned not only how to pick up the subtleties, but also to generate them.

Interpretations

Our interpretations are automatic. They place meanings directly on the sensory input, amplifying input judged important and discarding input judged meaningless. Interpretations may also modify the stored memory of the sensory input to more closely match the interpretation (Harris 2002).

Our interpretations are built over time in our interactions with the world and with other people. Many are acquired cultural patterns that may date back centuries or millennia (Gladwell 2008). When people speak to us, our ability to hear what they say is affected by our many automatic interpretations.

To become better listeners, we can learn to observe our own interpretations and retrain them (Strozzi-Heckler 2007). That gives us a strong foundation to listen for interpretations others make. The more we are involved with a community, the better we can learn a person's community history, interests, values, and concerns. As shown in figure 12.2, there are many distinctions that we can use to listen for which interpretations our audience is listening from. These distinctions can help us align our offers with their values and beliefs, fit their cultural norms, and avoid their taboos.

Frank Barrett and Ron Fry are pioneers with the Appreciative Inquiry process, a facilitated conversation that helps representatives of communities resolve difficult, complex problems (Barrett and Fry 2005). Prior to their workshops they conduct extensive interviews with the participants. From these interviews, they gain knowledge of community interpretations that helps them guide their workshops to successful outcomes. Since writing their book, they concluded that getting participants to start talking in blogs or wikis is even more revealing about what concerns them and how they interpret the world. The key thing for them is to observe conversations and, using the distinctions listed in figure 12.2, discover the background of interpretations in the community they are working with.

Learning to observe and listen to the background of interpretations of others is an important ingredient of blending. We all do it to some degree already, but in innovation conversations we must be good observers of the listenings of others.

Body

The body is the arena in which our intentions, interpretations, moods, and emotions play out as actions. Our experiences and skills at performing actions are embedded in the physical, chemical, and electrical structures of our bodies and nervous systems.

Richard Strozzi-Heckler (2007) says that our bodies achieve beginner's status with a skill after about thirty recurrences of a movement, advanced beginner status with three hundred recurrences, and basic competence with three thousand recurrences. These repetitions strengthen neural connections in the muscles and the parts of the brain that control them. Malcolm Gladwell (2008) says that people whose embodiment of a practice is so deep that they stand apart from most others have spent at least ten thousand hours practicing. This is an enormous amount of time that takes many years. Because the quality of the resulting skill depends on the focus and quality of the practices, it is essential to have standards for good practice from the beginning.

Modern research in brain and cognitive science explains why embodiment is so important and fundamental. Our cortex, the site of consciousness, can process sensory input at about forty events per second; in contrast, our limbic system, the site of the unconscious, can process about twenty million events per second (Lipton 2005, 166). Conscious thinking is mostly serial; unconscious thinking is mostly parallel. The body, therefore, moves our practices from conscious to unconscious performance so that they can be done far faster and better. The process of embodiment puts more and more of what we pay attention to into our unconscious. Experts and masters who fully embody a practice have no conscious awareness of how they actually perform it.

To be an effective innovator, you must embody the eight practices of innovation. Fortunately, you can achieve competence relatively quickly by aiming for Strozzi-Heckler's three thousand recurrences. If you aspire to masterful innovations, you will need much more time; we will discuss this in chapter 16.

Practice Eight (embodying) is aimed at making you a competent blender and helping you deepen your embodiment of the other seven practices by making you a better observer of their somatic aspects.

Emotions and Moods

Our moods and emotions, and those of our listeners, affect our abilities to connect and elicit commitments. We will not get far with an angry, resentful person; we may get an easy adoption from a grateful, appreciative person.

Emotions are feelings triggered by events and stories. Emotions trigger instant assessments that dispose us or indispose us toward certain actions. For example, anger can make us want to strike at people, sadness to contract, happiness to celebrate with them, and love to shower them with affection. Some emotions are cultural; the Germans experience *Schaden-*

freude, but not the English. However, most people share the same basic emotions.

In *Emotions Revealed*, Paul Eckman (2003) saw the same basic emotional expressions on faces in many cultures around the world, and found that people in different cultures recognize the same emotions. In *A General Theory of Love* (2001), Lewis, Amini, and Lannon (2001) concluded that emotions shape how we listen and respond. Marketers appeal to people's emotions all the time to get them to remember messages and buy products (Heath and Heath 2007). Emotionally charged conversation can be difficult (Patterson, Grenny, and McMilland 2002; Scott 2004; Stone et al. 2000). Skilled innovators learn how to blend with people's emotions and elicit emotions conducive to shared commitments and adoption.

Moods are predispositions toward the future. Unlike emotions, moods can last for a long time. Emotions tend to be triggered by events or situations, whereas moods precede events and color our interpretations of them. We embody tendencies toward certain moods; we can, for example, be ambitious or resigned without any triggering event.

There are three categories of moods. *Energizing moods* open possibility and stimulate action; examples are joy, wonder, resolution, ambition, serenity, gratitude, and determination. Energizing moods predispose us to a bright future. *De-energizing moods* close possibility and discourage action; examples are apathy, confusion, resignation, resentment, despair, jealousy, panic, anxiety, overwhelmedness, and boredom. De-energizing moods predispose us to a dim future. *Neutral moods* are in between; examples are inquiry, serenity, acceptance, and perplexity. Neutral moods predispose us to search for possibilities without knowing what we will find. Figure 12.2 includes a few examples of these three kinds of moods.

Moods are more difficult than emotions to observe in ourselves. Our mood just seems to be part of the reality of our world. When we are resigned, for example, we see few possibilities to change our situation and we see little point in working for change. We find it hard to step back and observe that we are in a mood of resignation. Skilled leaders read moods, blend with them, and change them. A leader can, for example, break resignation by inspiring hope or opening new possibilities for productive action.

Moods are manifested by their felt experience in the body and by their linguistic aspects. The body aspect includes postures, gestures, facial expressions, and readiness (or reluctance) to act. The linguistic aspect manifests as a story with assessments about the future; an ambitious person, for example, is full of stories about upcoming achievements, a resigned person stories of futility. These aspects provide numerous clues that a good observer can use to identify someone's mood.

As with other bodily dispositions, moods can be shifted. We do this by consciously engaging with stories, body dispositions, and practices associated with the mood we would rather be in. For example, we can listen to music we associate with the mood we want. The centering practice, discussed shortly, is very good for putting ourselves into a mood of nonreactive openness, creating an opening for a positive mood. Managers and leaders shift group moods by telling stories and getting people to engage with practices associated with the different mood.

Conditioned Tendencies

Sometimes, despite our best efforts at the eight practices, a breakdown blocks our way to the outcome. How we react strongly influences our success at resolving the breakdown. Our conditioned tendencies are the biggest sources of unproductive reactions.

Conditioned tendencies are automatic reactions to stimuli. They are patterns learned at an earlier time that show up without a conscious choice. Some are energizing, such as jumping away from a hot fire. Others are de-energizing such as tensing up and becoming confrontational when someone disagrees with you.

Joe was a client who decided to buy his first house. After a diligent search, he found a house that satisfied his long-term goals. His friends backed him enthusiastically. On the day of the closing, however, he could not bring himself to sign the papers. He broke into a sweat and sounded like he was gasping for air through his trembling voice. Afterwards he said, "I was suddenly overwhelmed with a feeling of foreboding. It happened so suddenly, I had no chance to do anything about it. It was *logical* to sign, but I could not make myself *feel* like signing." Later we learned that when Joe was a teenager, some older boys tricked him into lending them his bicycle. When it became clear they would not return it, he fought them and they beat him up. He vowed never again to allow someone to trick him out of something valuable. He developed a conditioning that kept him out of bad deals. But, years later, his conditioning from that old event prevented him from closing an important good deal.

Joe's story illustrates how a conditioned tendency can look like a skill as long as it produces positive outcomes; but it became an impediment when it prevented him from attaining his goal. His conditioned tendency always took over quickly, outside his awareness. He had no choice in how he could respond.

A couple both authors know had a period of crisis in their marriage. Liz thought Jim jealous and clinging. Jim thought Liz flirtatious with other men. Her conditioned tendency for freedom and his for jealousy had come into conflict. A counselor got them to agree to a thirty-day experiment: at social events (where these behaviors were most trouble-some to them) Jim and Liz would circulate separately and not be together at all. He would seek others to talk to, but not her. Three times during the party, at her choice, she would come to him and offer a compliment. At first they found this very uncomfortable. After a month they found they liked it so much they stayed with it. They are still together thirty years later. After that, whenever they found themselves stuck in a conflict, they would step back and define a thirty-day experiment that started with scripted behaviors and retrained their tendencies. Almost invariably the new behaviors became natural for them and eliminated the conflicts.

Liz and Jim's story illustrates how different conditioned tendencies can interact and produce breakdowns, and how they can be retrained by engaging with a new behavior until it is embodied.

As innovators, we need to be sensitive to the conditioned tendencies in ourselves and in our audience. Our own tendencies can interfere with our success in any of the eight practices. Audience tendencies can derail its members from accepting our offers.

Here are more examples that show a range of conditioned tendencies we can encounter in innovation conversations.

In the martial arts, novices almost always tense up when confronted by an attacker. Tensing up blocks effective response and lands the novices on the mat in a compromised position. The instructor tells them to relax, but they cannot. With training and practice, they gradually learn to maintain a relaxed, centered stance that enables them to move toward, and blend with, the attacker. Tensing up is a tendency hardly confined to the martial arts. Many people tense up and respond poorly in a conversation in which they think they are under attack. Somatic training can help them learn how to maintain their center and blend with the other person to take more effective action than tense resistance.

A second example is a person who comes from a family in which saying no was not accepted. Even when grown up, such individuals still cannot decline requests. They wind up feeling overwhelmed and stressed from having too many commitments. They feel intensely uncomfortable when it is time to say no. Their automatic yes avoids the immediate discomfort, but produces ongoing breakdowns for both the person saying yes, and the people who rely on the yes.

A third example is the difficulty of cross-culture negotiations. Japanese think direct eye contact is impolite; Americans think avoided eye contact is impolite. The Japanese person feels uncomfortable when talking with the seemingly staring American, and the American person feels uncomfortable when talking with the seemingly evasive and noncommittal Japanese. Their cultural conditioning makes them behave in ways that prevent agreement. The parties feel uncomfortable in a situation out of tune with their conditioning, and they cannot act effectively.

A fourth example, which Fernando Flores discovered in the late 1970s, is a tendency to accept, and act on, gratuitous negative assessments, such as being called a "pointy-headed boss" by an employee. To help overcome the tendency, Flores invented a "negative assessment exercise," in which a group of people took turns giving negative assessments and observing body reactions. Flores gave the group members a script to retrain their tendency to grant permission for anyone to make assessments. After a few repetitions of the exercise, most people learned to choose a different reaction from the original "What is wrong with me?"

A fifth example is the common inability to learn from mistakes because emotional reactions such as fear of rejection or punishment get the better of one. With practice, these reactions can be managed so that one is willing to face a mistake and learn from it (Shepherd 2009).

A sixth example concerns tendencies that can appear at the organizational level. During the 9/11 attack in New York City, the pilot of a police helicopter noticed signs that one of the World Trade Center towers was starting to crumble and issued an evacuation order. No one in the police department thought to notify the fire department of the order. As the police were coming down the stairwells, the firefighters were going up. Later, the 9/11 Commission determined that, overwhelmed by the magnitude of the disaster, individual policemen and firefighters fell back on their old conditioning, which was to communicate only with their immediate buddies and not with others. The 9/11 Commission recommended new training programs for police and firefighters in preparation for future emergencies (Denning 2006).

A powerful somatic antidote to conditioned tendencies is developing the skill known as *centering*. We'll introduce the skill of centering shortly as one of the necessary prerequisites for effective blending.

Blending

Let's turn now to blending, the essential somatic skill for innovators. We will dissect the skill into ten components, and show how to practice each, and how to integrate them into the blending skill.

In innovation, blending is the embodied skill to engage with another person in such a way that they feel connection and rapport with you, and yet no resistance or pressure from you, and together you flow smoothly into collaboration around the other person's concerns. Your energies do not clash; both individuals move together. When we blend with another person, we experience flow and engagement. It is a physical experience, not a mental assessment.

Strozzi-Heckler (2007) describes blending as moving in the other person's shoes, seeing their perspective, engaging with their interpretation of the world, feeling their feelings, and channeling their energy toward partnership and collaboration. He states: "Blending is a deep listening that produces connection." We are born with the sensibilities for doing this. We seek and cherish limbic resonance, "a symphony of mutual exchange and internal adaptation whereby two mammals become attuned to each other's internal states" (Lewis, Amini, and Lannon 2001).

When we blend, we experience a single (blended) entity rather than separate parts. In music, a chord is a resonance among a set of notes; we experience the chord as a single entity, not as separate notes playing simultaneously. So it is with innovation: when we blend with the concerns of a potential adopter, we experience the conversation as a chord of collaboration; "we" appears in place of the separate "you" and "I."

It is important that you understand *blending as an experience*. There is a whole-body "feel" to it that can be learned only by doing it. You cannot get the feel by reading about it in a book. We ask that you do the practices we will describe in this chapter and learn that feel for yourself.

If you play a musical instrument, you are familiar with the whole-body experience of blending. When you were a beginner, you learned how to read musical notation and how to place your fingers on the instrument to get each note. You learned about tempos, themes, and movements. When you first tried playing the instrument, your brain was furiously trying to remember all the rules and get your fingers into the right places so that you would hear some semblance of the music. After a while, everything you learned moved into your unconscious brain; you found your fingers automatically going to the right places, and you played music. You eventually found that you could play music without thinking at all. When you played with other people, you learned how to play chords, then pieces, and maybe symphonies together. Each of these moments was an experience of blending that probably defies description. Your whole body just did them in a smooth and coherent way.

Athletic skills are the same. As a beginning golfer, for example, you learned many components of stance and swing and struggled to get them to work as a smooth flow that hit the ball straight and far. Eventually all the components came together and you experienced the "swing" as a single, whole-body movement. Your hands, feet, and hip positions, your straight left arm, the pivoting around of your head—all those details were gone and only the swing remained. The same is true for other sports that use balls including baseball, football, soccer, and tennis.

The experience of blending is what you must aim for with innovation. All seven previous practices involve interactions with other people. The more you can organize your interactions as blends, the more successful you will be.

Somatic awareness and blending are not part of our mainstream common sense about innovation and leadership. For most of us the practices we are about to describe therefore present significant opportunities for learning, developing, strengthening, and refining our skills as innovators. Do them as you read about them: some will remind you of what you already know, others may surprise you with new distinctions.

The first step toward improving our skill at blending is to become an observer of the elements of blending. Figure 12.3 gives a map of three groups of somatic skills that combine to enable the blending skill. The foundation of awareness, attention, and relaxation gives us the capacity to center. Centering enables us to be present, open, and connected with other people. In turn, that permits us to interact with others by listening, facing, extending, and entering. We will discuss each of these elements in the sections following.

Somatic Practice

As you do any of these practices, keep in mind these guidelines:

• Reflect regularly on your practice. You can unwittingly reinforce an unproductive behavior by not being aware of it.
• Be patient. Your level of skill as an innovator will increase over time as you practice the practices and learn from your mistakes.

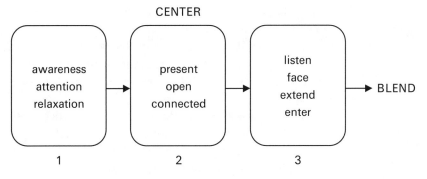

Figure 12.3
The skill of blending is enabled by three sets of component skills. Strozzi-Heckler articulates the principles that ground "leadership presence" as centering, facing, extending, entering, and blending. Presence is a quality of connection that makes other people feel included; leaders with presence attract followers.

Box 12.1
About the Boxes

In these boxes we will introduce practices that enable you to experience and practice embodied skills. Can you become proactive rather than reactive in the body domain? Can you go beyond the conditioned tendencies in your own body and in your audience to produce a positive coupling? As we examine the components of blending, we will suggest practice exercises that will help embody them. There is a pattern in these practices:

• Notice your own conditioned tendencies and what your body is doing. Practice "somatic self awareness."
• Notice the reactions you see in others. How are their reactions related to your state? Practice "somatic awareness of others."
• Notice when people's conditioned tendencies in some situations turn into resistance; for example, I insist, you withdraw. Practice blending with the resistance.

Reflection is an important part of practice. After you engage in the practice we suggest that you make notes in a journal about what you experienced, observed, and concluded. Ask someone else to give you feedback. If you can, work with an experienced coach.

• Start small. Begin with small innovations and then move to progressively larger ones as you become effective.

• Expect breakdowns. Your ability to deal with breakdowns and win adoption grows as the depth of your embodiment of the practices grows.

• Seek mentors and coaches. Work with more experienced innovators to elevate your own skill.

• Expect discomfort. It is normal to find that changes of practice motivated by new learning are uncomfortable. Keep practicing and the discomfort will fade. You can generate a productive new practice by starting with a script that leads you through the steps.

Remember that our descriptions of practices are aimed at your mind. You have to actually do the practices to get the experience into your body. You will not get far by treating these distinctions only as intellectual understandings. And since many practices involve interacting with others, you cannot really do them alone. If you try to learn them on your own, you will be unable to observe deficiencies in your own practice, and you will produce many unwanted outcomes. We therefore recommend that you find a partner or coach who can give you feedback and work with you in these distinctions.

Awareness

Awareness means that something has been distinguished in our perceptual field, giving us the potential of paying attention to it and putting it into language. Awareness is the foundation of our power to act and interact with another. To be unaware is to be blind. When we are aware of something, we have a choice in our response to it. When we are unaware, we have no choice. The realization that awareness is the foundation of all action is behind the principle "awareness creates choice."

Much of our sensory input never makes it into our perceptual field because of various filters in our brains and nervous systems. We are literally aware only of what our bodies are trained to be aware of.

We refer to an unaware person as a "bull in the china shop." To develop a new skill we must become aware of what we have previously been blind to. We have to see the china before we can hope to avoid breaking it. The most efficient and effective way to do this is to find a competent coach in the area we are learning who shows us how to make distinctions and see what was previously unavailable to us.

Box 12.2
Awareness Practice

> Develop your somatic self-awareness by spending time paying attention to what is happening in your body. What are your sensations—for example, hot, cold, tightened, contracted, or tingly? What are your moods, emotions, and automatic assessments? Are you centered or off center? Open or closed? Relaxed or contracted? Extended or withdrawn? Connected or disconnected? Blending or resisting? After you become good at noticing these things when you're alone, pay attention to what happens when you're in conversations. Don't judge, just observe. Keep a journal of your observations. At intervals make assessments of your developing capacity for somatic awareness, self-awareness, and awareness of others.

Attention

Attention means to consciously focus on something of which we are aware. It is the choice of where we place our focus from among everything we are aware of. We can only act effectively when we focus our attention productively. What we are attending to? Where does our energy need to go? Which of the many aspects of a situation are important to focus our attention on? "Energy follows attention" in consciousness, in the body, and in organizations.

The process of embodying skill includes developing attention skills appropriate to our level of learning. When we learn to drive a car, we first pay a lot of attention to our hands and feet. After we embody the skill of driving, our hands and feet become transparent in the practice, and we put our attention on safety in the midst of everything going on around us. We learn to focus on what will make our actions have the most desired impact. As our embodiment makes parts of our practice transparent and automatic, we can transfer our attention elsewhere, enabling us to develop the next level of skill.

Many guidelines for innovators call their attention to speaking and presentation, but not to how their audiences are listening and reacting to them. It is easy to develop enough skill and confidence in our speaking so that we do it as automatically as moving our hands and feet while driving. It is more difficult to pay attention to our audience and adapt to their listening, reactions, and concerns (Yaffe 2009). That is where our attention must go.

Box 12.3
Attention Practice

> Try putting your attention on areas that you normally ignore in conversations. Notice what is happening with the body, mood, and emotions of the other party in the conversation. What kinds of assessments are you having in reaction to their gestures, urges, habits, and conditioned tendencies? What are you doing with your own attention? Is it wandering? Staying focused on the other person? What is happening with your face? Your posture? Your energy? What do others respond to with their own attention? What do you call their attention to? Keep daily notes in your journal until you become good at these observations.

Relaxation and Tension

Our bodies tend to respond to each other by mirroring the energy of the other. If you are tense, the first reaction of others is likely to be tense. If you are calm and relaxed, the first reaction of others is likely to become calm and to relax.

Tension is a condition of the body in which muscles are contracted. In this state, we are less aware, less flexible, less open, less adaptable, restricted in available actions, and resistant to suggestions. Tension tends to bring our attention inward out of our contraction. When we are tense, we cannot blend with an audience because our tension inspires their tension and possible resistance, we are less able to adjust to them, and we don't appear open. In communication, relaxation is much more powerful than tension. Instead of producing a responding tension, we can practice to relax in a way to produce a responding openness and connection with others.

Relaxation often carries the connotation of sitting quietly or winding down prior to sleep. We are talking about a different kind of relaxation—the absence of tension while in action. We call this *dynamic relaxation*. It allows us to open energy, heighten awareness, focus attention, and be flexible and adaptive. It is a fundamental skill in public speaking, martial arts, building relationships, connecting, and innovation. In dynamic relaxation, we are more alert, not less, and flexible to be able to blend with whatever shows up.

Center

We are centered when our body, mind, and emotions are in a state where we can choose our actions. When we are not in a state to choose our

Box 12.4
Breath and Relaxation Practice

Our breath is the pacesetter for our body's energy and moods and our focus. The breath is the only autonomous process in our body over which we have some voluntary control. When we are tense we tend to hold our breath or breathe more shallowly and rapidly. This reduces oxygen to the brain and limits our ability to pay attention. We can calm our nervous system, produce dynamic relaxation, and enable ourselves to be readier for a wider range of action by taking slow, deep breaths, with exhalations longer than inhalations, allowing relaxation on the exhalation. Most somatic practices begin with a few deep, slow breaths with relaxation. Make a regular practice of noticing your breath and state of tension. When you notice tension, take a deep, slow breath and relax.

Box 12.5
Tension Attention Practice

Pay attention in conversations to whether you are tense or relaxed and to what degree. Where is your tension? Around your eyes? In your jaw? Your shoulders? Chest? Belly? Where is your habitual tension? Get someone else to watch you in conversations to see where you hold tension. Once you have identified the tension, take a deep breath and release the tension as you slowly exhale. You can also release the tension by simply letting relaxation flow into the area; you don't have to move or twitch. Pay attention to how others respond to your relaxation. Keep notes in your journal.

actions, we are "off center"; our reactions and tendencies choose for us. We cannot blend when we are off center. In centering we attain complete balance and focus regardless of our situation:

1. Our mind is alert, we are connected to what we care about, and we are free of distracting mental chatter.
2. Our mood is serene and open to the current situation.
3. Our physical state is dynamically relaxed, alert, balanced around our center of gravity, and ready for action.

These three aspects are mutually connected. We can center ourselves by starting with any one; the other two will follow. With practice, we can center within a fraction of a second.

Well known in the martial arts, centering is a somatic principle applicable to any human moment. The centered state is proactive and mindful.

The off-center state is reactive and mindless. Reactions that remove our choice in the moment put us in the state of being off center; anger and fear, for example, can overwhelm our bodies and sweep us into unproductive behaviors. An essential somatic skill is noticing when you are off center—and then *recentering*.

It is impossible to remain in the centered state all the time. A random thought can distract the mind. A physical blow can disrupt balance. An emotional trigger can bring up anger or fear. It then matters how quickly we notice that we have gone off center and return to center. A recentering practice can help us learn to do that rapidly. Students of the founder of Aikido, Morihei Ueshiba, told him that they saw him centered all the time. He replied that he also experienced being off center, as they did, but that he had learned to come back to center very quickly.

Box 12.6
Centering for Beginners

First enter a state of dynamic relaxation, releasing tension in your body, eventually with a single breath. Next bring your attention to the present moment, letting go of thoughts, sensations, and emotions that would distract your attention. Then let your awareness drop from your head and upper body down to your belly area, where your physical center of gravity is located, and from there connect to your entire body. Then open and extend your attention to what is around you, and connect to your care or your commitment in the moment. Remain relaxed and flexible, and move from your choice. With practice, these steps become a single act, completed within a single breath.

Box 12.7
Grab Practice

(From Richard Strozzi-Heckler): A "grab" is an event that startles you, seizes your attention, and creates an emotional reaction. You can practice a physical grab with a partner—let's call her Alice. You stand and center. Alice emits a yell ("Ha!") and grabs your wrist or forearm. Most likely this will startle you and throw you off center. Observe exactly how you went off center and then recenter. Repeat this several times. Have Alice experiment with the grab pressure. Does a tight grab throw you more than a light one? What is the right pressure to best get your attention? This exercise gives Alice the experience of getting your attention and you the experience of recentering after a grab for your attention. Discuss what you learned. Keep notes in your journal to track your learning.

Box 12.8
Recentering Practice

> After moments of intensity, breakdown, stimulation, or stress, ask yourself if you were in a state of reaction or choice. Were you captured by an emotion, mood, or conditioned tendency? Recenter. As you keep doing this, the time from the event until you recenter will gradually diminish. Eventually, you will be able to recenter rapidly enough to make centered choices in a triggering situation.

The skill of rapid centering is particularly important in moments of high stress and significant consequence—such as conflict, danger, high risk, emotional intensity, distrust, and disconnection. We need to practice centering so that we can do it automatically—within a single breath—when we do not have the time to pause and reflect, when our first action will be our only action. Stephen Covey once likened centering to autopilot—it keeps the plane moving toward its destination despite the perturbations it encounters.

Richard Strozzi-Heckler defines centeredness by calling attention to its three components: present, open, and connected. *Present* means that our attention is focused outward on other people. The most common way of being not present is to focus inward on mental activities, feelings, emotions, and concerns. We can be worrying, daydreaming, planning a schedule, thinking about email, or almost any form of "being in our heads." An innovator reciting a memorized script or "elevator speech" will not seem present to listeners.

Open means that we are receptive to what surrounds us and what others offer us; we are willing to give them a hearing. When we are closed, we are not receptive. De-energizing moods such as resignation and distrust will close us. As innovators, we want our listeners to be open to what we offer. The easiest way to generate that openness is to be open ourselves.

Connected means that we feel the presence and energy of the other, and of ourselves, and we stay in contact with them. Close somatic connection results in limbic resonance, where bodies seem to be in a shared state. We feel a sense of relationship and engagement. We are disconnected if we avoid relationship and engagement. We can be disconnected from our own bodies if we get lost in our heads and pay no attention to its sensations.

Box 12.9
Present-Open-Connected Practice

Sit with another person. For one minute both of you act out your versions of being not present with the other. Notice how it feels for you and what you notice about your partner, then discuss it. Repeat the same exercise being present, but not open. Repeat it again, being present, open, but not connected. Can you be open but not present? Connected but not open and present? Once you have practiced with a partner, observe yourself in everyday conversations, noticing when you and your partner are present, open, and connected. What happens in the conversation if either person is not present, open, and connected? Note at least one observation a day in your journal, and draw conclusions about how your ability to be present, open, and connected affects your outcomes.

We cannot blend if we are not present, open, and connected. If we experience difficulty blending, our best move is to pause and get present, open, and connected. Returning to being present, open, and connected becomes second nature with practice.

Centering is the skill that enables us to intervene in our conditioned tendencies. When the tendency takes hold, we lose our center, and with that our balance, our ability to choose, and our ability to extend and connect with others. The retraining of our conditioned tendencies consists of two parts.

1. Become an observer of the tendency by asking others what they see and by noticing what throws you off center.
2. Retrain your body so that when you notice the tendency has gripped you, you take a moment to recenter.

Once centered you can deal with the triggering event in a more productive way. In his *Anatomy of Change*, Richard Strozzi-Heckler (1984) has an excellent discussion of conditioned tendencies and how to overcome them.

Listen

Listening is the way in which individual bodies interpret what they see and hear. No two listeners are identical: they have different histories. The skilled listener produces a connection that enables sensing the concerns and care of the other. The sense is not just intellectual, but is also a felt sense of what the other cares about, of what deeply matters to them. The skilled listener connects to another's world and their experi-

Box 12.10
Simple Listening Practice

> Ask a partner to talk about something they care about. Then give your partner a summary, in your own words, of what you understood as their deep concerns and intentions. Discuss how accurate you were. Did you miss anything? Can the other person tell you what was missing? What signs did you use to "read" the other person in this deep way? If possible, get a skilled listener to do this with you. What signs did that person use to "read" you?

ence of it. Suzanne Zeman (2008) has an excellent collection of somatic exercises to improve listening.

Face, Extend, and Enter

In *The Leadership Dojo*, Richard Strozzi-Heckler (2007) outlines five elements of leadership presence: centering, facing, extending, entering, and blending. We recommend this book as a much fuller treatment of these skills than we can provide here. His distinctions are essential for observing and enhancing the embodied skills of innovation. It is important to understand that these five elements are observable somatic skills that can be developed with practice.

To *face* is to physically turn fully toward another, an audience, or a situation, and to prepare to direct our full attention and energy there. This seems simple enough—until we face a challenge. Then a conditioned tendency is likely to seize us. We will avert our gaze, turn away, go away, run away, direct attention elsewhere, procrastinate, or ignore the challenge completely. The skill is to automatically face the challenge—or to notice that we are not facing, recenter, and then face the challenge.

To *extend* is to project our attention and energy toward the challenge or our object of attention. The skill is to feel your attention and energy move toward the challenge—or to notice that you are not extending, recenter, and then extend toward the challenge.

To *enter* is to move forward into engagement with the challenge or our object of attention. We do not hang back in observation, tentativeness, doubt, or fear. We do not avoid the challenge. Entering can be the most difficult of the three skills. Can we engage productively with the challenge of distrust? Conflict? Disrespect? Skepticism? Anger? Fear? Or a host of other triggered emotional situations? When we are not entering, we recenter, extend again, and then move toward the challenge.

Box 12.11
Face, Extend, and Enter Practice

(From Richard Strozzi-Heckler). Do these exercises with a partner. Stand so that you are not facing your partner at a distance of several paces. Your partner calls your name. Center, then turn and face your partner. Extend your energy and attention toward your partner by raising your arm to a horizontal position with palm projecting energy to your partner's upper sternum. Then walk toward your partner and stop just when your hand contacts your partner's sternum below the throat. Keep your arm relaxed and pay attention to the quality of the connection. Debrief with your partner, noticing all the places where you found these moves difficult. Did you lose center at any time? Switch places and repeat. Now notice what it's like to be faced, extended to, and moved toward. Do any of these moves throw you off center? Did you recenter?

Now take this into actual conversations. When someone brings up a difficult or challenging subject, do you face it? Reach out toward it? Move to engage with it? What happens when you choose to face, extend, and enter? Do you achieve a better outcome?

Keep notes in your journal about these experiences.

Blending

Blending is the culmination and integration of the preceding practices. It is the heart of the innovator's somatic skill. It means to join the other in engagement and flow with them and their concerns without triggering defensive reactions. Blending is not agreeing, surrendering, or copying, since we hold our own center and choose to align with another for the sake of opening a shared future. It is "a deep listening that produces connection," and allows an exploration of possible shared action.

Trust

People are strongly influenced by a speaker's somatic presence when deciding to trust. Trust is especially important to innovators because the risks for adopters are likely to be (or seem) significant. What grounds do listeners have for believing the speaker is competent, sincere, committed, and reliable? What are the risks and how well can they be managed?

People trust when they *feel* like trusting. They are making a bet that under the other person's care, everything will turn out well. They rely heavily on somatic signals to decide whether to make this bet. Many will decide to trust based solely on their feelings. Others will go through the

Box 12.12
Basic Blending Practice

(From Richard Strozzi-Heckler). To experience physical blending, do this physical dramatization with a partner—let's call her Alice. Stand facing each other, centered. Alice walks toward you, right arm extended toward your upper sternum. You start walking toward her. (Do not wait until she reaches you; the practice of entering should start you moving toward her right away.) Just before Alice's arm would strike you, you make a 180-degree turn on her right (your left) and begin walking with her, shoulder to shoulder. As you complete your turn, raise your left arm and touch the back of your left wrist to her right wrist. With a little practice you will discover how to make the turn gracefully without disturbing her flow. This exercises simulates a physical blend between you and your partner, and gives an experience of what blending can feel like.

When done, discuss with your partner. Where did you have the most difficulty? Did you lose center anywhere? What does it feel like to blend? To be blended with or not? Did you remain relaxed, open, and connected?

Now translate this experience into the flow of energy you bring to your everyday conversations. Can you blend with the mood of your conversational partner? Can you feel the same sensations as when you did the walking blending exercises?

Keep a journal with one written observation each day.

Box 12.13
Intermediate Blending Practice

Once you master basic blending, try a variation. When you are walking wrist to wrist, see if you can redirect Alice's direction by gently extending energy through your left wrist to a new direction. With a little practice, you will discover that you can redirect your partner without actually exerting force on her arm, and without producing tension or pushing. Try redirections to the left and right.

Now bring this into everyday conversations. Can you blend with the mood of your conversational partner? After blending, can you redirect your partner? Can you feel the same sensations as when you did the walking blending exercises?

analysis and discover that their feelings do not support their rational conclusions. If you wish to explore this further, the book *The Speed of Trust*, by Stephen M. R. Covey and Rebecca Merrill (2006) discusses thirteen somatic practices that inspire trust: Talk straight, demonstrate respect, create transparency, right wrongs, show loyalty, deliver results, get better, confront reality, clarify expectations, practice accountability, listen first, keep commitments, and extend trust.

Blending inspires trust. Innovators who inspire trust are the most likely to succeed. Those who rely on power and authority of office, or on psychological tricks, will not be trusted and are much less likely to succeed.

Responding in Chaos

Under stress, embodiment is your *only* access to effective action.

The examples we have given illustrate how an unfamiliar, stressful situation or a reaction can bring out a conditioned tendency. Centering exercises are helpful because they teach how to maintain awareness, avoid becoming flustered, and make choices that are not limited to the conditioned tendency.

Centering is a way to cope with a conditioned tendency after it arises. To shift our response to situations that trigger the tendency, it is helpful to practice training for the stressful situation. Thus, airline pilots undergo extensive training with simulations of engine failures, severe turbulence, loss of control surfaces, loss of navigation, and much more. Lawyers condition their clients for intense cross examination by subjecting them to mock cross examinations. Military leaders use war games to simulate battle situations and train themselves to respond favorably should the real thing happen. Police, fire, and other first responders train in simulations of various emergencies so that they will respond well in the real emergency.

However, many situations are so new and unfamiliar that no strategy of prior training can be designed. Organization leaders and innovators often find themselves in chaotic situations, where the rate of unexpected and confusing events can become overwhelming. When that happens, the brain cannot figure out what to do and drops out.

When the brain drops out, the body falls back on what it knows— some embodied practice. The most common default is the hunker-down reaction in the face of uncertainty and fear. We gather in all our resources and go it alone. We stop communicating with others. If that does not ameliorate the fear, the body can itself become chaotic in a mood of panic.

Donald Schon discussed this problem as he considered whether data gathering is even a useful strategy in a complex, fast-changing situation (1971, 220). He quoted a long, graphic passage from Tolstoy's *War and Peace*, in which a commander is bombarded with new, often conflicting proposals, each demanding a quick decision. Even if the commander could have all the data about every proposal, inherent conflicts and inconsistencies would render many data useless. The commander is forced to take action and then see how things play out. The armchair critic who later determines what the commander should have done has no appreciation for the chaotic nature of the situation. Schon concludes:

The conflict of incompatible perspectives cannot be resolved by waiting to hear more of what the data say. New data may yield new perspectives, or may aggravate old differences. In one way or another, conflicts of perspective must be resolved through action. (1971, 213)

In other words, in chaos, the leader cannot hope to figure things out and plan optimally. The best strategy is to face the problem and create joint action with others.

Malcolm Gladwell (2008) discusses this in connection with air crashes. When the pilot, copilot, and flight engineer stay in conversation they are far more likely to extricate themselves from emergencies than if they fall silent. Reconstructions from voice recorders of the events preceding airplane crashes show that most were preceded by lengthy periods of silence, lack of communication, and lack of sharing information. The airlines subsequently instituted "mitigation training" to teach employees that in the cockpit they must stay in communication and be truthful about expressing concerns or demanding action. The frequency of air accidents has diminished markedly since this program went into place.

David Snowden and Mary Boone (2007) have extensively studied how to cope with complex and chaotic situations—the ones in which known solutions, approaches, and even problem definitions do not apply. In complex situations we must give up the notion that we can figure out what to do in advance. He recommends that we "probe, sense, respond," meaning to experiment and get reactions to find out what we are dealing with. For chaotic situations, where things are changing too fast and sensory data are quickly obsolete, our only choice is to stay in communication with others, to intervene to produce some area that is stable, and then move to other states where actions can be effective.

The conditioned tendency to stop communicating in chaotic situations, to apply inappropriate solutions, or to wait for more data in complex situations, can be overcome by the practices of facing, extending, and entering. A team can often do this better than any individual.

This lesson should not be lost on innovators. They often find themselves in chaotic and complex situations. They need to keep their centers and help their communities find a center of effective action.

Conclusions

All our lived experiences, interactions with others, and communications occur in our bodies, and our body reactions are the most powerful and fundamental part of our impact on others. Although the first seven innovation practices have somatic dimensions, the eighth practice is crucial for advanced skill in the other seven. It emphasizes somatic awareness, overcoming conditioned tendencies, and blending. Blending is the highest attainment of the innovator's somatic skills.

Blending is an experience, not a mental calculation. We suggested a few practices that can teach components of the experience, and then integrate them into the full experience of blending. In appendix 4 at the end of the book, we offer more examples of somatic practices that can help deepen your skill with the innovation practices of this book (from Denning 2004; Dunham 2004).

Your appreciation for your own discomfort as your body changes can help you appreciate the discomforts your adopter community will experience as they adopt your proposed new practice. Your success will increase as you learn to help them tolerate the discomfort and learn the new way.

Bibliography

Barrett, Frank, and Ronald Fry. 2005. *Appreciative Inquiry*. Taos Institute.

Budd, Matthew. 2000. *You Are What You Say*. Crown.

Covey, Stephen R. 1990. *The Seven Habits of Highly Effective People*. Free Press.

Covey, Stephen M. R. with Rebecca Merrill. 2006. *The Speed of Trust*. Free Press.

Denning, Peter. 2004. The Somatic Engineer. In *Being Human at Work*. Ed. Richard Strozzi-Heckler. North Atlantic Books.

Denning, Peter. 2006. Hastily Formed Networks. *ACM Communications* 40 (April):15–20.

Doidge, Norman. 2007. *The Brain That Changes Itself.* Penguin.

Dreyfus, Hubert. 1992. *What Computers Still Can't Do*, 3rd ed. MIT Press.

Dreyfus, Hubert. 2001. *On The Internet.* Routledge.

Dunham, Robert. 2004. The Body of Management. In *Being Human at Work.* Ed. Richard Strozzi-Heckler. North Atlantic Books.

Eckman, Paul. 2007. *Emotions Revealed.* 2nd ed., Holt.

Gladwell, Malcolm. 2008. *Outliers.* Little Brown.

Goleman, Daniel. 1995. *Emotional Intelligence.* Bantam.

Goleman, Daniel. 2007. *Social Intelligence: The New Science of Human Relationships.* Bantam.

Harris, Bill. 2002. *Thresholds of the Mind.* Centerpointe Press.

Heath, Chip, and Dan Heath. 2007. *Made to Stick.* Random House.

Leonard, George. 1992. *Mastery: The Keys to Success and Long-Term Fulfillment.* Plume.

Lewis, Thomas, Fari Amini, and Richard Lannon. 2001. *A General Theory of Love.* Vintage.

Lipton, Bruce H. 2005. *The Biology of Belief.* Mountain of Love/Elite Books.

Maturana, Humberto, and Francesco Varela. 1980. *Autopoiesis and Cognition.* Reidel.

Maturana, Humberto, and Francesco Varela. 1987. *The Tree of Knowledge.* Shambhala.

Mehrabian, Albert. 1971. *Silent Messages.* Wadsworth.

Patterson, Kerry, Joseph Grenny, and Ron McMilland. 2002. *Al Switzler. Crucial Conversations.* McGraw-Hill.

Polyani, Michael, and Paul Kegan. 1966. *The Tacit Dimension.* Routledge.

Schon, Donald. 1971. *Beyond the Stable State.* Norton.

Scott, Susan. 2004. *Fierce Conversations.* Berkeley Trade.

Shepherd, Dean. 2009. *From Lemons to Lemonade: Squeeze Every Last Drop of Success Out of Your Mistakes.* Pearson Education.

Snowden, David J., and Mary E. Boone. 2007. A Leader's Framework for Decision Making. *Harvard Business Review* (Nov.).

Solomon, Robert. 1993. *The Passions: Emotions and the Meaning of Life.* Indianapolis: Hackett Publishing.

Solomon, Robert, and Fernando Flores. 2003. *Building Trust: In Business, Politics, Relationships, and Life.* Oxford University Press.

Spinosa, Charles, Fernando Flores, and Hubert Dreyfus. 1997. *Disclosing New Worlds.* MIT Press.

Stone, Douglas, Bruce Patton, Sheila Heen, and Roger Fisher. 2000. *Difficult Conversations.* Penguin.

Strozzi-Heckler, Richard. 1984. *The Anatomy of Change.* North Atlantic.

Strozzi-Heckler, Richard, ed. 2003. *Being Human at Work: Bringing Somatic Intelligence into Your Professional Life*. North Atlantic.

Strozzi-Heckler, Richard. 2007. *The Leadership Dojo*. Frog, Ltd.

Weiner, Allen. 2007. *So Smart But . . . : How Intelligent People Lose Credibility—and How They Can Get It Back*. Wiley.

Yaffe, Phil. 2009. How to Generate Reader Interest in What You Write. *ACM Ubiquity* 10, no. 7 (June), http://www.acm.org/ubiquity/volume_10/v10i7_yaffe.html. Accessed February 2009.

Zeman, Suzanne. 2008. *Listening to Bodies: A Somatic Primer for Coaches*. Shasta Gardens Publishing.

III

Journey to Mastery

13

Building a Culture of Innovation

In the race to the future there are drivers, passengers, and road kill.
—Gary Hamel and C. K. Prahalad

The key is to accelerate the process of transformation through a culture of innovation.
—Admiral Vern Clark

Innovation cannot be managed. You have to satisfy necessary conditions for innovation to occur. To start with, you have to listen to people.
—Eric Schmidt

Few of us innovate alone. We join organizations, where we pool our skills with the skills of many others, and work collectively toward goals that no one of us could achieve alone. What are the implications of the eight practices of innovation for organizations?

We have devoted the previous twelve chapters to establishing that the eight generative practices are not discretionary. Innovations happen because people in conversations make each of the eight essential outcomes happen. Innovations will not succeed without all eight outcomes. Our main purpose in this chapter is to demonstrate that the eight generative practices are essential for organizations just as they are for individuals. Innovative organizations have embedded the eight practices into their cultures and operations.

The main difference at the organizational level is that the eight practices are no longer restricted to individuals. They are spread among many individuals and teams. Dividing them among the many has the potential of increasing the skill level of each practice, mobilizing more help and resources to make the practices successful, and bringing more observers to the act of listening to customers. Dividing them also increases the cost of coordination, which must be well designed lest it become an energy sump in the organization.

The job of the organization is to provide an efficient framework of strategic direction, support, and coordination to make a division of labor worthwhile. The framework is the way the organization selects customers, differentiates offers, configures and manages resources, coordinates, goes to market, and creates value. We call that framework the *organization design*, which extends Adrian Slywotsky's (1996) term *business design* to include innovation in government, military, and consortia as well as businesses.

Innovative organizations have learned to embody the eight practices within their organizational designs. When they pass their embodiment of the eight practices from generation to generation, the organization has achieved the much-sought *culture of innovation*. Our secondary purpose in this chapter is to show how organizations can constitute their organization designs for this to happen.

Innovation is hard to achieve if the organizational practices and individual skills are out of balance. Organizational policies that encourage and reward new product ideas will founder if the members lack the basic skills of innovation. Similarly, highly innovative individuals can be stifled by organizational bureaucracy or by a rampant culture of idea killing. We will discuss what makes for a synergy of individual skills and organization design.

The eight practices need not be explicit in the organization design. It matters only that their essential conversations are happening. In this chapter's examples of Google and the World Wide Web we will see two radically different organizations that have integrated the eight practices successfully. We have included an assessment tool in appendix 2 at the end of this book to assist you in examining your organization to see which of the eight practices are strong, weak, or missing.

Several authors have pointed out that information technologies have been driving down communication and data management costs, enabling new kinds of coordination, organization learning, and collective intelligence (Seely Brown 1997; Davenport, Leibold, and Voelpel 2006; Malone 2004; Malone, Laubacher, and Dellarocas 2009). In our view, these changes make it all the more important for leaders to see how the eight practices work in their organizations. No matter what the configurations of information technology are, those conversations must always be present and effective for innovation to succeed.

Organization Designs

An organization is a group of people who have banded together for a declared purpose, often referred to as the *mission*. Most missions concern products, services, or outcomes that the organization offers to its customers or clients. As with most everything else in this book, we interpret the work of organizations as embodied conversations. In all these conversations, people talk, discuss, commit, and act to address each set of concerns.

Fernando Flores and J. J. Ludlow (1980) introduced the idea that organizations are networks of conversations, and that certain conversations must take place for the organization to maintain its existence as an entity. For example, the constitution and bylaws are not just documents; they are also the conversations that generate the documents, as well as the constitutional conversations that subsequently live in the everyday thinking and actions of those in the organization.

We list below our interpretation of constituting concerns and conversations for any enterprise or organization. We call them *constituting* because without them an organization cannot survive as a separate entity. Departments, business units, or component organizations within larger organizations will have to address any of these constituting concerns that are not taken care of by the parent organization.

These essential conversations are most evident among the organization's leaders, who must explicitly deal with bylaws, stakeholders, business plans, marketing plans, organization charts, customer relations, performance assessments, and the like. These conversations affect the development of new offers, allocation of resources, and expectations regarding outcomes. It is a breakdown in organizational life when these concerns are not addressed effectively. If any of the following categories of constituting conversations is weak or missing in the organization or its parents, the organization will founder.

1. *Foundational declarations* This conversation addresses the nature, purpose, mission, and constitution of the organization. The essential declarations address structure, legal aspects, organizational declarations, ownership, stockholders, executives, managers, other roles, values, cultural norms, and ethics.

2. *Strategy* The conversation focuses on how the organization will approach its mission. It includes the allocation of resources, organizing around core strengths, compensating for weaknesses, analysis of threats

and opportunities, choice of market segments, choice of allies, and the distinctive value offered by the organization.

3. *Planning business or financial outcomes*   This conversation focuses on analyzing market opportunities and futures of interest, aligning the key business or financial outcomes with the strategy, stating expected returns or outcomes, and organizing the promises and roles needed to fulfill the outcomes.

4. *Action or operations planning*   This conversation outlines the promises and responsibilities for accomplishing the business or financial plan. It includes project schedules, deliverables, and milestones.

5. *Execution*   This conversation addresses the processes and practices that fulfill the promises of the action plan. It includes project schedules, deliverables, milestones, assignments of persons to roles and tasks, and performance measures.

6. *New offers or marketing*   This conversation addresses the design, development, communication, and execution of new market offers. It addresses discontinuing obsolete offers.

7. *Customer relations and satisfaction*   This conversation addresses how the organization will listen to customers and assess their satisfaction. It includes sales and maintenance of products and services, help and support services, and quality assurance. It also includes where the identity of the organization is evident to customers and their experience of that identity.

8. *Innovation and learning*   This conversation deals with the process of learning that is needed to create an innovative culture, as well as the learning that innovations require. It covers how the eight foundational practices of innovation are implemented, measured, and maintained in the organization. Its intent is to keep the business design and business model fresh, produce an adaptive organization, and monitor effectiveness at value creation.

These eight essential organizational constituting conversations are not the same as the eight practices of innovation. We will discuss the relationship between the conversations and the practices shortly.

These constituting conversations differ from one organization to the next, reflecting each organization's style. We use the term *organization design* to signify a particular realization of these conversations. Consider music distribution as an example. Some organizations follow a "publisher" design, others a "broker" design. A music publisher signs contracts with songwriters, finds artists to perform the songs, markets the recordings, and distributes royalties to artists and songwriters. A music broker allows artists to offer their songs directly to customers and takes a commission on the sales. A music publisher is a copyright administrator; a music broker holds no copyrights. Universal Music is an example of a publisher, iTunes of a broker.

The organization design itself has value. *Value migration* occurs when customers shift from organizations with low-value designs to organizations with high-value designs (Slywotsky 1996). Music distribution illustrates that the broker design is increasingly popular and is seen by some publishers as a threat to their existence.

The term *organizational model* should not be confused with organization design. An organizational model is narrower in scope, and is included in the organization design. In *The Balanced Scorecard*, Robert Kaplan and David Norton (1996) call it the "business model"; it lays out how the business handles its strategies for money, operations, customers, and growth.

The main value in interpreting an organization as a network of conversations is that the organization can change by changing its conversations, especially those that generate action. An organization can innovate a service by initiating internal conversations to produce the new service and external conversations to orchestrate adoption among its customers. It can innovate its own design by changing its constituting conversations.

Now let us look at how conversations for innovation fit into an organization and its design.

Innovation and the Organization

There is nothing in the constituting conversations that guarantees the presence of the eight innovation practices. These conversations may be missing or incomplete. The "innovation and learning" conversation might be based a faulty interpretation of innovation. We will now discuss how to enable the eight innovation practices in an organization.

In an organization, the term *innovation* can refer to three different kinds of conversation, based on who is to do the adopting:

• *External target community* These innovation conversations are directed outside the organization. They involve creating and marketing new products or services. Example: Intel created a new kind of chip, a multiprocessor architecture it described as "multicore," and worked to secure its adoption by desktop and laptop computer makers. Another example is "branding" conversations, which are marketing conversations focused on building the perceived identity of the organization in support of new offers and customer loyalty.

• *Internal target community*   These innovation conversations typically involve internal reconfigurations to achieve new or more effective operations and lower costs. The adopting community is a subset of the organization. Example: Intel developed new internal simulation, testing, lithographic, and fabrication methods for its multicore architecture. Another example is internal conversations to align the internal operations of the organization with the brand identity.

• *The organization design itself*   These innovation conversations involve the organization's design and culture. They affect both the external and internal communities, and they shift the constituting conversations and commitments. The adopting community is the entire organization. Example: In the mid-1980s, Intel abandoned its memory chip business and focused entirely on computer chips. Another example: A new emphasis on quality or customer service can require a fundamental change to an organization's frames of reference and practices.

The eight innovation practices serve all three innovation conversations.

In *The Innovator's Dilemma*, Clayton Christensen (1997) illustrates how many companies have run into serious difficulties by concentrating on the first two conversations and ignoring the third. These companies innovate their product lines and internal processes, but cede their low-end market to competitors. Later, their competitors expand and start competing directly with the companies' high end at a lower price than they are able to afford. To survive, these companies needed to rethink the entire business, not just refine their current products.

In *Only the Paranoid Survive*, Andy Grove (1996), CEO of Intel, showed that technology companies are particularly vulnerable when they are not open to innovating their own organization designs. An "inflection point" that may demand an organization redesign is the emergence of a new technology that improves over the current technology by a factor of ten ("10x") or more. The company may have to adopt completely different manufacturing and distribution processes to participate in the new technology. Otherwise, it can quickly be put out of business when someone else perfects the 10x technology.

Embedding the Eight Practices

Let us look more closely at how the eight practices can be integrated into an organization. Figure 13.1 shows that organizational and individual practices are both embedded into the organization's design. The organizational practices are all those represented by the constituting conversations. The individual practices are all the practices individuals bring, including the eight innovation practices. The organizational practices interact endlessly with individual practices. Thus, the conversations constituting the organization integrate with, and facilitate, the conversations specifically focused on producing innovations.

Table 13.1 illustrates how the eight practices can appear in organizations. If the organizational conversations do not align with the innovation conversations, there will be little or no innovation. This can happen if the organizational conversations impede, inhibit, neglect, or omit any of the eight innovation practices. It can also happen if many individuals are not skilled at the eight practices. In the first case, the organization stifles individual actions leading to innovation; in the second, the lack of individuals' skill stifles the organization's intention to build a culture of innovation.

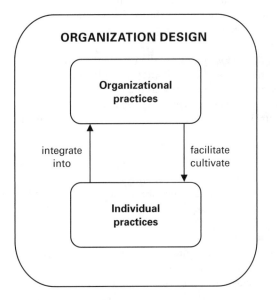

Figure 13.1
The organization design defines a context for organizational and individual practices of innovation.

Table 13.1
The Eight Practices in Organizations

Practice	Examples in Organizations
Sensing	HP and IBM maintain research labs staffed by top scientists and engineers. Google's 20 percent time policy (discussed in this chapter) involves all employees in innovation. Other organization means of sensing include brown-bag lunch seminars, suggestion boxes, water-cooler conversations, and presentations by visionary entrepreneurs.
Envisioning	Engineers speculate about potential applications of new technologies. Marketers use focus groups and blogs to discover which stories resonate best with their customer communities. Management teams engage in strategic planning exercises.
Offering	Engineers build prototypes and working models. Google strongly encourages "getting data on everything" and rapid detection of failing offers. Architects build models and virtual tours. Marketing creates new offers and communication campaigns.
Adopting	Companies start with prototype and demonstration projects. They experiment with pilot installations. They present their visions to interested communities at research and product conferences. They work for new product adoptions by the market.
Sustaining	Companies work to embed new practices in the core processes and accountable results of organizations. They write their organizational objectives to give priority to new outcomes and the practices to achieve them.
Executing	Companies work to close loops on all customer interactions. They establish networks of coordination for fulfilling complex processes and projects. They establish online order and fulfillment processes. They assemble and manage teams, carefully document project plans and milestones, and engage in six-sigma practices.
Leading	They cultivate competent team leaders who are effective at championing innovations. Executives become customers for new practices, taking stands for a new opportunities. Senior executives develop or recruit skilled leaders as executives and managers, and they encourage every individual to be proactive in exploring ideas, telling stories, making the company's offer, and achieving quality.
Embodying	Employees are offered development and education that are supported by on-the-job accountability, tools, priorities, and incentives. The recurrent actions of an organization, whatever they are, produce its embodied skills. Some companies have a policy that everyone should be really good at something. Some companies cultivate somatic awareness.

The innovation practices differ at the organizational level from their individual versions in five ways:

1. Groups or teams perform the practices. The organization will be concerned with having effective teams, team leaders, and team members (Goleman 2007; Hughes and Terrell 2007).
2. The organization provides coordination among groups so that the practices flow, align with organizational objectives, and meet deliverables (Malone 2004).
3. The organization provides many eyes, ears, and minds to increase the space of possibilities in every practice. For example: Toyota proactively solicited employee suggestions, receiving two hundred suggestions per year per employee, and used them to attain strong market leadership.
4. The organization provides more resources to explore, develop, and execute in every practice.
5. New breakdowns appear at the organizational level that do not appear for individuals. Common areas of breakdown include the coherence of roles in the organization, who has what authority, and coordination for cross-organizational actions and changes.

The Google Example

Google is admired and frequently cited as an exemplar of an innovative company in the information technology sector. Its mission is to organize the world's information and make it universally accessible and useful. Google was picked number two after Apple in the *Business Week* survey of top innovative companies in April 2008. It repeated its number two position in 2009, while Nintendo moved to number one and Apple to number three. It has been fantastically successful with this open-ended mission, announcing a new product almost every day and attracting a hundred applications for every open position. Google achieved a market capitalization of over $170 billion ten years after its founding in 1998.

Google is famous for its policy requiring all technical people to spend 20 percent of their time on projects of their own choosing. Google also asks managers to dedicate 20 percent of their time to projects that are related to but different from the core business, and 10 percent on entirely new businesses and products (Iyer and Davenport 2008). They are also famous for a massive supercomputing infrastructure, a highly automated job application process, a talent for making new products from "mashups" of existing technologies (where internal developers work with external developers to merge technologies), many on-site boutique amenities for employees, and a culture of tolerance for chaos and risk taking. Google's CEO Eric Schmidt offered this Google employee credo in *The Economist*: "Please fail very quickly—so that you can try again." These are the most visible aspects of Google's well-designed organizational culture. Let us take a closer look at the design.

Although Google has not publicly stated what its innovation strategy and approach is, Bala Iyer and Thomas Davenport of Babson College were able to deduce its key aspects from public statements, blogs, and interviews with some of its key people (2008). Google's CEO Eric Schmidt has also discussed the company's strategy (2008). The following summary is our interpretation of their findings in the light of the eight practices framework.

At the top level, Google's design is an information ecosystem. Through its basic infrastructure "platform," Google interacts with and supports work by four groups:

1. *Content providers*   They are media companies and individuals who create information, stimulate consumer interest, foster communities, and provide means to deliver targeted ads.

2. *Advertisers*   They are companies and individuals who deliver ad content to search-identified users, and generate Google's vast revenue stream.

3. *Consumers*   They are the hundreds of millions of people who visit Google every day. Their searches reveal their interests and they consume advertising targeted at their interests. They beta-test new offers, contribute ideas for improvements, and become commercial users of new products.

4. *Innovators*   They are mashup creators, independent software vendors, Google engineers, and open source communities. Working through the Google platform, they constitute a rich and diverse product development network and attract many users who want to try new products. They generate revenue and expand the value of Google tools and technology.

These diverse groups all use the Google infrastructure and can communicate with all Google users. Google has made an enormous investment in infrastructure: several scalable and interoperable data centers with a customized operating system provide millions of individual processors, support enormous databases, and give response times under a half second. This platform is enormously attractive to the companies and individuals involved in the ecosystem. Among other things they can develop their new technologies, test with real users, and transition to production without changing infrastructure.

At the next level, Iyer and Davenport find that Google employs six basic strategies for its innovation:

1. *Strategic patience*   Google takes a long view of markets and do not demand immediate returns on investment.

2. *Infrastructure that supports innovation*   Google's scalable systems enable third-party innovators to rapidly produce new products and functions.

3. *Architectural control*   Google's powerful and responsive platform is a development facility that all of the company's third-party innovators can use. Google keeps the platform useful and responsive while controlling what is in it and how it works.

4. *Innovation built into job descriptions*   Every engineer is expected to use 20 percent of his or her work time pursuing new ideas.

5. *Cultivated taste for failure and chaos*   Google encourages people to try wild ideas. As CEO Eric Schmidt stated, the only ground rule is to fail quickly, learn from it, and move on without too much waste.

6. *Use data to vet ideas*   The company's leaders encourage everyone to automate everything. New ideas are immediately tested in random user markets. Only the ones that attract users survive. Google also uses numerous internal prediction stock markets to discover which new products are most likely to succeed in the marketplace.

Table 13.2 shows how these strategies ensure individual and team skills in the eight practices.

The WWW Example

The mission of the World Wide Web Consortium (W3C) is to lead the Web to its full potential. Since its founding in 1994, the W3C has become the authoritative body on Web standards and an engine of innovation in Web technology. The W3C is not a traditional business organization. It is a consortium of companies, nonprofits, and government agencies all focused on producing standards and public-domain software for Web infrastructure. It is an example of how innovation practices can be promoted and sustained in collaboration among organizations. Its revenues come from annual dues paid by its approximately four hundred member organizations. Member organizations donate the time of their represen-

Table 13.2
The Eight Practices in Google

Practice	How Google Excels at Them
Sensing	All engineers are required to spend 20 percent of their time on new technical projects of their own choosing. Anyone in the company can submit suggestions to a company suggestion box, which is reviewed regularly.
Envisioning	All engineers build stories about how their new ideas contribute to the Google mission. Google blogs and representatives tell these stories wherever they go.
Offering	The design process stresses testing from the very beginning. Engineers set up alpha and beta tests for their new products as they are developing them. They can tell quickly if their offers of new products are going to succeed. They mount their test products, and get real customer response. They also use internal prediction markets to gauge the likely success of new products.
Adopting	Prototypes that do not attract sufficient customers are abandoned. Those that do already have a customer base when they transition to released products.
Sustaining	The practices themselves are fundamental to the culture, and the percentage of time policies for technical staff and management require sustaining actions. The sharing of the generous revenue streams and the high-performance scalable infrastructure sustain the ecology.
Executing	The robust development environment, direct access to customers on the Web, and a development process streamlined for fast internal testing and customer response enable fast innovation. The strategies of data collection and automation ensure there is plenty of data for managers to assess the effectiveness of processes.
Leading	Google engineers are held accountable and given incentives to be proactive about promoting and testing new ideas and gaining adherents to those ideas. Management is held accountable to bring new business ideas to fruition.
Embodying	The basic values and strategies of Google are embodied by the founders and senior leadership and imitated by everyone in the company. The practices and policies of the company produce recurrent engagement and skill in its innovation-producing processes.

tatives and programmers to W3C development projects of their choice. Although its members compete fiercely in the marketplace, they collaborate well in developing and improving the playing field on which they compete.

In the early stages of the World Wide Web, Tim Berners-Lee was an individual innovator promoting adoption of the Web technology. When it became apparent that industry players were starting to jockey for position to take over the Web technology and make it proprietary, Berners-Lee collaborated with Mike Dertouzos at MIT to create the W3C. He worked hard to recruit all Web-using organizations to join and participate in the creation of new standards.

The W3C's business design is an open software consortium. All its products—standards and standardized software tools—are in the public domain. Member dues pay for staff programmers to create W3C software and manage its distribution. Its internal processes implement the eight practices (see table 13.3).

Organization-Level Breakdowns

When organizations rather than individuals perform the eight practices, new breakdowns occur that will not be encountered by individuals acting alone. They are summarized in table 13.4. Many of these breakdowns are so important and pervasive that they have been the subjects of best-selling business books (cited in the table).

Table 13.4 offers a very important lesson. The eight practices framework shows clearly that breakdowns occur regularly in all the practices. It is common in organizations to respond to the most pressing breakdown and often to miss others that might be at play. Focusing on, and resolving, a single breakdown may not get your organization out of trouble because the other breakdowns remain. It is best to begin with a comprehensive analysis of your practices (see appendix 2 at the end of this book) to determine *all* the breakdowns you are encountering, and then set about resolving all of them.

Learning Network Structures

Google and the World Wide Web share a common feature: both are examples of organizations that rely on a dispersed network to help them innovate. The W3C is a consortium of diverse organizations from many industry sectors. Google manages an ecosystem of content providers,

Table 13.3
The Eight Practices in the World Wide Web Consortium

Practice	How W3C Excels at Them
Sensing	All members are encouraged to submit new ideas for consideration as W3C standards or software.
Envisioning	Proposers of new ideas must write compelling narratives about the value of the new idea being implemented as a standard.
Offering	A review committee polls the membership and selects proposals for which there is sufficient support.
Adopting	Task forces of representatives from many member organizations are established for each accepted proposal. They design and test a detailed draft standard. They use W3C programmers to help build prototypes of software tools. Their drafts are submitted to the membership, for comments and later for votes. It becomes a "W3C recommendation" on receiving a strong vote. W3C recommendations become de facto standards since all the players agreed to use them.
Sustaining	All W3C recommendations and software are maintained on the W3C Web site. New versions are issued as needed after periodic reviews.
Executing	The processes used for task forces and voting are spelled out in the W3C rules and procedures and are applied uniformly for all projects.
Leading	Individuals and small groups who advocate that the W3C take on a project must work proactively to gain support for the project and to articulate its value so that it will ultimately receive a positive vote.
Embodying	Tim Berners-Lee, the consortium manager, and his senior leaders embody the basic principles of the Web: openness, inclusiveness, no private control of any Web technology, channeling development toward improving the Web as an information-sharing medium.

Table 13.4
Breakdowns Encountered at the Organizational Level

Practice	Examples of Breakdowns and Responses to Them
Sensing	Finding new ideas before competitors do is a major problem for many companies. Drucker (1985) developed his sources model to help overcome blindness in this area. Ideation International offers searches through patent databases to help find new ideas. Senge et al. (2004) offer ways to sense new ideas before they are articulated. Spinosa, Flores, and Dreyfus (1997) address sensing "disharmonies" as an entrepreneurial skill.
Envisioning	McKee (1997, 2003) describes storytelling as a major breakdown for many businesses and lays out a framework for effective storytelling.
Offering	Many innovation offers do not focus on the value created for the listener. Kotler and Trias de Bes (2003) have written extensively on marketing and how to make good offers.
Adopting	Rogers (1962) focused on adoption, not invention, as the heart of innovation and showed how to achieve adoption in many different communities.
Sustaining	Rogers (1962) also focused on what it takes to sustain an innovation after initial adoption. Business failures kill many innovations when the business is the main sustainer. Christensen (1997) showed that low-end competitors often kill a business. Grove (1996) showed that technologies with 10x improvement potential can kill a business. Slywotsky (1996) showed that an obsolete business design can kill a business.
Executing	Deming (1982) advocated rigorous measurement and management of business processes. Hammer and Champy (1993) advocated wholesale replacement of stagnant business processes with new ones, even at great cost to the personnel of companies.
Leading	Breakdowns in leadership have often been indicted for innovation failures. Drucker (1985) said that innovation skill is part of the job description of executives. Many leadership authors such as Adizes (1992), Bennis (2003), Covey (1990), Dupree (2004) have extolled the importance of developing leaders. Deschamps (2008) examines leadership qualities of innovators.
Embodying	Strozzi-Heckler (1984, 2007) claims that many leadership failures arise from lack of embodiment of five leader practices. Many companies regret their RIFs of most experienced employees to save costs (e.g., Circuit City).

advertisers, consumers, and innovators. Both have successfully created vast learning networks.

John Hagel and John Seely Brown (2005, 2006) believe that learning networks such as these are an emerging paradigm for organizational innovation. They call these networks "creation nets." With Lang Davison (Hagel, Brown, and Davison 2008), they propose a "shaping strategy" for managing learning networks that has proved valuable to companies like Google, Salesforce.com, and Novell.

Innovation is inherently a learning process. The proposed new practice is called marginal, or edge, to distinguish it from the core of accepted practice. Innovation is often called a process of transforming the edge into the core (Spinosa, Flores, and Dreyfus 1997; Hagel and Brown 2005). A learning network is a means for achieving this. A learning network is not simply an information sharing or surveillance network; it is people acquiring practices from each other.

In times of stability, it is a good business strategy to protect intellectual property though such means as patents, copyrights, and trade secrets. A learning network extending outside the organization offers little extra value in such a situation. However, Donald Schon (1971) said that stability is an illusion. This is even truer today, because change in global markets is much faster and less predictable. Organizations that try to legislate stability by institutionalizing their structures and operating rules are among the first to encounter breakdowns when their markets change.

Some authors argue that, in times of rapid change, going to great lengths to protect intellectual property can be a poor strategy (Hagel and Brown 2005), because in such times intellectual property loses its value quickly. An effective learning network can be a more valuable asset. A learning network is essential for success in a globalized economy.

The Internet has given birth to many examples of creation nets. These include open software organizations (such as W3C, the Open Software Foundation, Linux), sharing of intellectual property (Creative Commons), sites where school kids can sign up for astronomy experiments (Faulkes Telescope) or perform lab experiments remotely (MIT iLab), and virtual communities making an ecosystem around a company (Amazon.com, iTunes, Google).

Traditional institutional architectures in business, education, government, and nongovernment organizations do not fit well with creation nets. Table 13.5 summarizes what Hagel and Seely Brown (2005) see as

Table 13.5
Differences between Enterprises and Creation Nets

	Traditional Enterprise	Creation Nets
Goals	Mixed—both innovation and routinization	Focused—new goods and services tailored to rapidly evolving markets
Scope	Few institutional participants	Multiple institutions and individuals
Location	Highly concentrated	Dispersed
Innovation approach	Sequential	Parallel
Coordination	Stage-Gate® reviews	Integration events
Governance	Process manuals	Constitutions and norms
Outcome definition	Detailed blueprints	High-level performance specs
Mobilization	Push	Pull
Feedback	Performance reviews and compensation	Appropriate and reuse

Note: The Stage-Gate® product innovation process is a business process pioneered and developed by Robert G. Cooper. See the Web site http://www.stage-gate.com/knowledge_pipwhat.php (January 2010).

the main differences between traditional enterprises and creation nets. These differences need to be taken into account when organizing a creation net.

Fernando Flores sees additional benefits from learning networks: (1) development of trust, (2) relationships across generations, (3) development of new practices, (4) development of new observers, and (5) development of new communities that include people from many locations and sectors.[1]

Toward a Culture of Innovation

We have examined a variety of ingredients that lead to a culture of innovation. We list here key questions to ask at the organizational level to make sure that these ingredients are all present in an environment that nurtures innovation. It all begins with the chief executive and senior team making the commitment to innovation as a strategic component of the

1. Private communication in June 2008.

organization's strategy. Tools such as the Kaplan-Norton balanced scorecard (1996) can help measure progress in key areas.

The following is a list of key questions for organization leaders to ask and answer as they seek to build a culture of innovation.

Enabling the Practices
- Is there an innovation game?
- Is everyone involved in innovation?
- Are all eight practices present?
- Are they supported with enough time and resources?
- Are innovation teams properly constituted with the right skills?
- Are coaches and mentors available to help develop the skills?
- Do organizational policies and procedures encourage the eight practices or get in the way?
- Does the leadership keep the value of innovation as a strategic imperative on everyone's minds?
- Are innovation projects insulated from innovation-stifling traps?[2]

Monitoring Success
- What measures are in place to tell which innovations are succeeding at adoption?
- Are innovations returning their investments?
- Are unsuccessful innovations detected quickly?

Continuous Learning
- Are there learning opportunities for individuals and teams?
- Are innovation successes and failures reviewed regularly for lessons that can improve strategy and process in the future?
- If an innovation is abandoned, can any of its components be salvaged for use in other innovations?
- Is there a path for integrating successful innovations into the organization's objectives?

2. Kanter (2006) among others discusses organizational pathologies that stifle innovation. The main ones: (1) failure to abandon projects, lines, etc. that are no longer productive (failure to exercise "creative destruction"); (2) failure to reclaim leftovers of abandoned projects for possible reuse as components of new projects (waste of good resources); (3) trying to apply business rules for stable businesses to innovation attempts (each stage of innovation may require different rules); (4) punishing or penalizing people who make mistakes or whose projects fail (no learning feedback); (5) failure to encourage people with new ideas from coming forward (no talent farming).

External and Internal Customers
• Who are the adopting communities for each innovation?
• What creates value for them?
• How is everyone listening to them?
• Are there internal representatives of external communities, who can speak to whether an innovation produces value for a community?
• Do these internal representatives have the right tools and listening practices?
• Does every team manager act as an internal customer for the promises of team members?
• Does every higher-level manager act as an internal customer for the promises of all lower-level manager reports?

Awareness of the Breakdowns
• Are individual innovators and innovator teams aware of the kinds of breakdowns they are likely to encounter?
• Are they equipped to handle the breakdowns when they occur?
• Which internal (or external) experts can they consult when a breakdown occurs?
• Do the internal customers monitor for signs of breakdowns and intervene before they hit hard?
• Does the culture encourage (or discourage) announcing and anticipating breakdowns?
• Are there signs that innovation processes have degenerated into checklists instead of outcomes generated by good practice?

Vitality of Your Business or Organization Design
• Is the organization stuck in fixed value thinking?
• Is there a person or team in the organization charged with monitoring the market value of the business design?
• Does that monitor watch for market context, market mood, shifts of value, signs of customer migration to new alternatives, and the like?
• Does the monitor see competitors nibbling at low-end markets?
• Does the monitor spot new technologies with 10X improvements?

Conclusions

The eight practices are essential for innovation, by organizations as well as individuals. They must all be present for an organization to succeed at innovation. Many organizations base their innovation strategies on faulty interpretations of innovation such as the process myth or the invention myth. That blindness leads them to weakness in, or ignorance of, some of the practices.

The organization is a community of people banded together to advance a mission beyond their individual powers. Organizations all must address eight essential organizational concerns with ongoing constituting conversations and subsequent actions that sustain them as entities. Organizations need to take extra steps to include the eight innovation practices because their constituting conversations need not include them.

New issues arise when extending the eight practices into the organization. These include collaboration, coordination, mobilization and distribution of resources, and sharing of information. The organizational and personal practices of innovation must be in balance.

New kinds of breakdowns appear at the organizational level. They can be linked to one or more of the eight practices.

The organization design itself must be constantly reviewed and assessed to make sure it is fresh, providing value, and not becoming obsolete. Occasionally, innovation of the organization design is needed.

The W3C and Google provide contemporary examples of how organizations integrate the eight practices into their business models. Although they are radically different organizations, they are successful cultures of innovation because they have embedded the eight practices deeply into their organizations.

Creation nets are a model of the learning networks used by these and other modern organizations to support their cultures of innovation.

The assessment tool of appendix 2 at the end of the book provides a means to evaluate the strength of your organization in all eight practices.

When bringing innovation into organizations, leaders have to face the complexity of the existing conversational networks, standards, and practices of the organization. We wish you well in bringing the eight generative practices to your organization, and to helping your organization create a new future for itself, its employees, and its customers.

Bibliography

Adizes, Ichak. 1992. *Mastering Change*. Adizes Institute.

Bennis, Warren. 2003. *On Becoming a Leader: The Leadership Classic*. Rev. Ed., Basic Books.

Christensen, Clayton. 1997. *The Innovator's Dilemma*. Harvard Business.

Covey, Stephen. 1990. *The Seven Habits of Highly Effective People*. Free Press.

Davenport, Thomas, Marius Leibold, and Sven Voelpel. 2006. *Strategic Management in the Innovation Economy*. Wiley.

Deming, W. 1982. *Edwards. Out of the Crisis*. MIT Press.

Deschamps, Jean-Philippe. 2008. *Innovation Leaders*. Jossey-Bass.

Drucker, Peter. 1985. Innovation and Entrepreneurship. Harper Perennial. Repr., Harper Business, 1993.

Dupree, Max. 2004. *Leadership Is an Art*. Doubleday Business.

Flores, Fernando, and J. J. Ludlow. 1980. Doing and Speaking in the Office. In *Decision Support Systems: Issues and Challenges*. Ed. G. Fick and H. R. Sprague Jr., 95–118. Pergamon Press.

Goleman, Daniel. 2007. *Social Intelligence: The New Science of Human Relationships*. Bantam.

Grove, Andy. 1996. *Only the Paranoid Survive*. Doubleday.

Hagel, John, and John Seely Brown. 2005. *The Only Sustainable Edge*. Harvard Business.

Hagel, John, and John Seely Brown. 2006. Creation Nets: Harnessing the Potential of Open Innovation. Working paper, http://johnseelybrown.com.

Hagel III, John, John Seely Brown, and Lang Davison. 2008. Shaping Strategy in a World of Constant Disruption. Harvard Business Review (October).

Hammer, Michael, and James Champy. 1993. *Reengineering the Corporation*. Harper Business.

Hughes, Marcia, and James Bradford Terrell. 2007. *The Emotionally Intelligent Team*. Jossey-Bass.

Iyer, Bala, and Thomas Davenport. 2008. Reverse Engineering Google's Innovation Machine. *Harvard Business Review* (April):59–68.

Kanter, Rosabeth Moss. 2006. Innovation: The Classic Traps. *Harvard Business Review* 84 (11):72–83.

Kaplan, Robert, and David Norton. 1996. *The Balanced Scorecard*. Harvard Business.

Kotler, Philip, and Fernando Trias de Bes. 2003. *Lateral Marketing: Techniques for Finding Breakthrough Ideas*. Wiley.

Malone, Thomas. 2004. *The Future of Work*. Harvard Business.

Malone, Thomas, Robert Laubacher, and Chrysanthos Dellarocas. 2009. *Harnessing Crowds: Mapping the Genome of Collective Intelligence*. MIT Center for Collective Intelligence Report (February), http://cci.mit.edu/publications/CCIwp2009-01.pdf. Accessed January 2010.

McKee, Robert. 1997. *Story*. Reagan Books (Imprint of Harper Collins).

McKee, Robert. 2003. Storytelling That Moves People. *Harvard Business Review* (June):51–55.

Prahalad, C. K. and Gary Hammel. 1994. *Competing for the Future*. Harvard Business School Press.

Rogers, Everett. 1962. *Diffusion of Innovations*. 5th ed., Free Press, 2003.

Schmidt, Eric. 2008. How Google Fuels Its Idea Factory. Interview in *Business Week* (April 29).

Schon, Donald. 1971. *Beyond the Stable State*. Norton.

Seely Brown, John. 1997. *Insights on Innovation*. Harvard Business.

Senge, Peter, C. Otto Scharmer, Joseph Jaworski, and Betty Sue Flowers. 2004. *Presence: Human Purpose and the Field of the Future*. Society for Organizational Learning, Random House.

Slywotsky, Adrian. 1996. *Value Migration*. Harvard Business Press.

Spinosa, Charles, Fernando Flores, and Hubert Dreyfus. 1997. *Disclosing New Worlds*. MIT Press.

Strozzi-Heckler, Richard. 1984. *The Anatomy of Change*. North Atlantic.

Strozzi-Heckler, Richard. 2007. *The Leadership Dojo*. Frog, Ltd.

14

Mastering the Mess

Success is relative. It is what we can make of the mess we have made of things.
—T. S. Eliot

The Americans can always be counted on to do the right thing, after they have exhausted all the alternatives.
—Winston Churchill

Managers are confronted with dynamic complexes of messy systems of changing, interacting problems. Managers do not solve problems: they manage messes.
—Russell Ackoff

Have you ever found yourself in a mess, a tangled social situation that is too costly to stay in and too intransigent to get out of? Messes are also called wicked problems. The people involved are frustrated because they cannot reconcile their concerns. Their search for solutions produces few results and seems open ended amid constantly shifting constraints (Denning 2007; Roberts 2000, 2001). The end state is a moving target (Reeves and Lemke 1991). Those involved cannot bring together their proposed solutions or find healthy compromises. They actively resist the proposals of others.

When messes are resolved, the people will say that a disruptive innovation has been achieved. Resolving a mess is the most difficult challenge an innovator can face, because:

1. There is no shared interpretation of the breakdown or opportunity.
2. There are multiple stakeholders with social and political reasons to resist proposed solutions.
3. It is often very difficult to get everyone in the mess to collaborate because of past resentments and distrust.

The main point of this chapter is that resolving messes is far from a hopeless task. The key is to augment the eight practices with seven "mess strategies": declare, learn, question the paradigm, blend, develop "we," lead collaboration, and make shared promises. Collaboration is at the core of these seven strategies and is essential for resolving messes.

We will investigate six main ideas in this chapter:

1. Messes and wicked problems are the most difficult in a hierarchy of difficult problems.
2. Mess resolution usually involves disruptive innovation.
3. Mess resolution can be achieved with the eight practices, with special emphasis on seven mess strategies.
4. Mess resolution can be blocked by belief in win-lose outcomes, belief in authoritative or competitive solutions, or a conditioned tendency of retreating into the known.
5. Collaboration is essential for mess resolution (and hard to achieve).
6. Information technology can help with the process using tools in the categories of exchangers, coordinators, and games.

Because of the size and complexity of messes, innovators need a skill level of at least "expert" to have reasonable prospects of success.

The Nature of Messes

Let us begin by considering messes as the most difficult category in a hierarchy of difficult system problems. We use the word *system* broadly to include social systems (e.g., a nation), life systems (e.g., an ecology), or human-made systems (e.g., the Internet), or some combination.

Problems come in four categories of difficulty (see table 14.1). The simplest are the ones where the solution knowledge already exists (Category I). The next hardest are the ones whose solutions are knowable but not yet known (Category II). When the system of interest is complex and governed by fixed (but unknown) laws, its reproducible behaviors can be discovered through experiments (Category III). When the system of interest is complex and adaptive, it tends not to have reproducible behaviors; it adjusts its responses and neutralizes repeated probes (Category IV). The last category is the abode of messes and wicked problems.

These categories blend together ideas from Kurtz and Snowden (2003) and Roberts (2000, 2001). Kurtz and Snowden discuss the notions that Category III problems may be complex natural systems governed by unknown laws waiting to be discovered, and that Category IV problems

Table 14.1
Categories of Problem Difficulty

Name	Category	Characteristics	Actions
Simple problems	I	Solution knowledge exists.	Redirect attention, apply the known solution.
	II	Design approaches for a solution exist.	Find an expert (or become one) and design your own solution.
Complex problems	III	No solution exists in any domain; system is very complex but responds the same way to repeated stimuli.	Explore for recurrent patterns by probes and experiments; design resolution around recurrences discovered.
Wicked problems (messes)	IV	No solution exists in any domain; system is chaotic and adaptive, does not repeat patterns under the same probes.	Organize collaboration in a local part of system, impose a structure, then spread the new organization to the whole.

are complex adaptive social systems. Roberts lumps our Categories I and II into a single class (known as *simple problems*) and uses the terms *complex problems* for our Category III and *wicked problems* for our Category IV. Kurtz and Snowden refer to Category IV as "chaos."

These categories represent the degree of agreement among the social power centers about the problem and its possible solutions. The simple problems are those in which everyone agrees on the problem definition and there is a power center that can implement the change. The complex problems are those in which everyone agrees on the problem definition, but there is no consensus on how to proceed. The wicked problems are those for which there is no consensus on the problem definition or on the solution approach, and partisan interests block collaboration.

These categories suggest a strategy for solving a problem of unknown difficulty. We start with the hypothesis that our problem is of Category I, and then work our way upward through the categories until we find a solution or know that we confront a mess. If our problem is Category I or II, we will discover an expert to help us. If our problem is Category III, there is no expert, but we will discover and exploit the system's recurrences for a solution. If our problem is Category IV, we will find no recurrences; we can employ the strategies discussed shortly for resolving messes.

Category III problems tend to appear around undiscovered aspects of complex systems. They demand the skills for inventing new hypotheses and validating them with experiments. Examples are an ecologist seeking an understanding of global warming, or an economist seeking an understanding of the collapse of financial markets. Kurtz and Snowden (2003) report success with large-group processes that mobilize a diversity of observers to interpret the messy situation.

Sometimes current methods and instruments are not powerful enough to discern the patterns needed to solve the problem; the solution may have to wait for a later age with finer instruments. Throughout most of the 1800s, for example, physicists hypothesized that light traveled in a medium known as *ether*. They could not verify this because they lacked the instruments to measure ether. In 1887 the Michelson-Morley experiment provided the instrument. That instrument's failure to detect any ether influenced Einstein's 1905 inspiration for relativity: he postulated there is no ether and light travels at the same speed in all frames (Einstein 1916).

Category IV problems tend to appear in conflicted social systems. As noted previously, Nancy Roberts described them as wicked problems:

Government officials and public managers are encountering a class of problems that defy solution, even with our most sophisticated analytical tools. These problems are called "wicked" because they have the following characteristics: (1) There is no definitive statement of the problem; in fact, there is broad disagreement on what "the problem" is. (2) The search for solutions is open ended. Stakeholders champion alternative solutions and compete to frame "the problem" in ways that directly connect their preferred solution and their preferred problem definition. (3) Resources and political ramifications are constantly changing. (4) Constraints constantly change as interested parties come and go. (Roberts 2001, 353)

The systems embodying wicked problems tend to resist and defy attempts at change. Change occurs only when leaders achieve consensus among power centers to enact new social agreements and new organization within the system. They seek local solutions that can be propagated to the whole.

Although we use the terms *mess* and *wicked problem* interchangeably in this chapter, there is a nuance of difference. The word *problem* carries a connotation that we can articulate the nature of the concerns and conflicts sufficiently well that we can anticipate an "answer." Messes don't have answers. With a mess, the problem is that we do not know how to characterize it as a problem. We may even disagree about whether there is a mess at all!

Candace Lightner cofounded the organization Mothers Against Drunk Driving in 1980 as a response to a wicked problem: the widespread tolerance of drunk drivers and their annual carnage. Lightner and her colleagues showed great skill in attracting media attention and in gaining the support of politicians for new laws.

The messiness of wicked problems originates with social conflicts. Lewis Perelman cites infrastructure renewal as a messy problem involving the clash of "green" and "blue" agendas (2008). Green represents the sustainability movement, which aims at environmental protection and resource efficiency; its main concerns include energy-neutral designs for buildings and other infrastructure. Blue represents the security movement, which aims to protect against attacks and disasters; its main concerns include critical infrastructure. Although blue and green approaches are laden with technologies, the technologies are neither the cause of problems nor the solution. Each perspective reaches different conclusions about infrastructure renewal and best use of technologies. The mess results from the various players holding their respective interests as the most important and failing to give any ground to other perspectives.

We acknowledge that the term *mess* is used not only for social issues, but also for intractable personal issues. It is not unusual to speak of a person's health, family relations, or finances being a mess. Such messes feature small-scale incoherencies and breakdowns, from purely personal matters to immediate relationships. Personal messes can escalate into a wicked problem if many people have the same issue; for example. the obesity epidemic is a wicked problem within the health care system. Here the innovator must show each individual how to solve their local version of the mess; for example, by joining Weight Watchers.

Messes as Social Tangles

Here are fifteen contemporary examples of messes:

- Spam
- Identity theft
- Information overload
- Struggle between open or secure Internet

- Making large software systems safe and delivering them on time
- Global warming
- Bipartisan politics
- Reforming education in public schools
- Reforming zoning laws for affordable housing
- Obesity epidemic
- Health-care cost crisis
- Poverty
- Detecting and thwarting terrorist plots
- Reconstructing society after war or disaster

The first six of these examples seem like technology problems and the last seven like social problems. However, they are all social problems. The first eight are the social consequences of pushing technology beyond its limits; their resolutions lie in the social domain. Messes cannot be resolved without untangling the social situation. The signature signs of a mess—all social—are summarized in table 14.2 (Denning 2007).

Messes and Innovation
History tells us that resolutions of messes are likely to be disruptive innovations (Christensen 1997). The reason is that the paradigm (belief system) hosting the mess does not allow the new thinking needed to resolve the mess. Only a belief-changing innovation driven by an entrepreneurial mindset will succeed. This is why many in the throes of the mess feel threatened about the prospect of a solution. The solution may

Table 14.2
Signs of a Mess

Threat	Something of great value is threatened in a (large) community; many stakeholders are involved.
No progress	Little or no progress despite huge effort; improvements haven't worked; existing solutions are ad hoc, incompatible, and ineffective.
Social paralysis	No agreement on problem statement, causal relationships, or solution strategies.
Active resistance	Multiple stakeholders have social and political means to block actions that do not support their agendas. They distrust or resent one another.
Negative moods	Frustration over disordered conditions, feeling of being stuck, confusion, discord, conflict, turmoil, controversy.

challenge everything connected with the mess, including social power structures and deep beliefs.

Figure 14.1 depicts a mess's temporal structure. The horizontal line represents time. The condition generating the mess builds in the social system and exists for a period of time. A transformational event provides the key to a resolution. The social system integrates the resolution and settles down with the mess gone. Smaller social systems resolve more quickly than bigger ones. Highly uncomfortable messes motivate quicker resolutions than less uncomfortable ones. James Burke showed that the messes and settlement periods accompanying great scientific revolutions lasted fifty to one hundred years each (Burke 1995).

There are three main observers in the mess structure. Alice (A) is embedded in the mess and lives under its mindset and rules. To Alice, the mess looks normal and impossible to change. Bob (B) is embedded in the settlement and its mindset and rules. To Bob, the settlement looks normal and the ways of the mess archaic. Chris (C) straddles the transformation and sees both the mess and the possibility of resolution. We will design a strategy for C shortly.

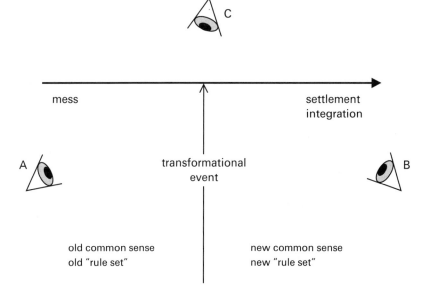

Figure 14.1
The mess and its observers. The transformational event marks the beginning of adoption of new practices that eventually resolve the mess.

Science fiction writer Arthur Clark once said: "Every revolutionary idea seems to evoke three stages of reaction: It's completely impossible. It's possible but not worth doing. I said it was a good idea all along." The three observers of the mess personify Clark's stages. Alice says, "Change is impossible." If Alice meets Chris, she will say, "Your proposed change is not worth doing." If Alice survives and becomes like Bob, she will look back and say, "It was a good idea all along."

Sometimes a chain of sustaining innovations (incremental improvements) will collectively create sufficient disruption to alter the mess. In the 1970s, aeronautical engineers sought entirely new ways of designing and testing ever larger and more complex aircraft. Their main tools were the wind tunnel and test pilot. The world's biggest wind tunnel, at NASA Ames Research Center, was extremely dangerous to operate and was reputed to consume a substantial fraction of the electricity used by the nearby city of Mountain View, California—and was still not large enough to test the new generations of aircraft. For engineers, the situation was a big mess. They could not agree among themselves how to design and test large aircraft. The solution came from an unexpected direction facilitated by the advancement of computing technology under Moore's Law. By the late 1980s, supercomputing technology enabled computer simulation of flight without wind tunnels. The Boeing 777 aircraft was a product of this advance. A ten-million dollar computer made a billion-dollar wind tunnel obsolete.

It is worth noting that a mess is not a necessary precondition for disruptive innovation. Many disruptive innovations arise from other conditions and motives. For example: (1) Someone serendipitously stumbles on something wonderful (e.g., penicillin). (2) Someone envisions a whole new potential (e.g., Alan Kay's Dynabook led to laptop computers). (3) Someone creates a new social entity that unleashes creativity and new values (e.g., MySpace, Facebook, Twitter). (4) Someone seeks a cheap way to give to the many what only the well-to-do can afford (e.g., Unix, Internet telephony, low-cost inkjet printers); according to Clayton Christenson (1997), many disruptive innovations arise from this source.

Strategies for the Mess

From the preceding description, we can see that messes may be the most challenging situations innovators will ever face. Even so, the eight innovation practices, with a few special emphases, give a way to meet the challenge.

Mess innovators will engage in the eight practices as they (1) sense opportunities to resolve the mess, (2) envision an approach, (3) offer the means to accomplish the approach, (4) get people to adopt the approach, (5) get people to stick with the approach until the resolution is apparent, (6) coordinate all the actions needed to make the approach work, (7) exercise leadership, and (8) blend with the concerns, discomforts, and resistance that people will experience.

The unique characteristics of a mess demand seven mess strategies composed from the eight practices (not to be confused with the seven leadership strategies discussed in chapter 11):

• *Declare* Begin by declaring that you see a mess and intend to do something about it. Your declaration is needed because many people find the mess to be normal and see no point in changing or fighting it. Your declaration will mobilize others who may be willing to join you in the struggle. (Part of Practice One, sensing.)

• *Learn and listen* Few people appreciate the full complexity of the mess. Most see only their parts and think of other groups as obstructionists. Do not take sides. Instead, make yourself a student of the mess; learn everything you can about what anyone has said about the mess; become an expert on it. Read what has been written, talk to people about what they know, and perform experiments. Listen to how people in the mess see their worlds, actions, breakdowns, possibilities, and concerns. When you accomplish this, you will see patterns that no one else has seen, which may help you lead the stakeholders to a resolution. Becoming an expert is challenging because many people are unable to articulate all their concerns: you must listen for what is not said as well as what is said. (Part of Practice One, sensing, and Practice Two, envisioning.)

• *Question the paradigm* The "paradigm" is the belief system in which everyone is operating. The existence of a mess is strong evidence that the paradigm is not able to resolve the problem, and in fact may be the cause. Therefore, try to identify all the assumptions in the belief system and diagnose which are questionable in the current situation. Pay special attention to anomalies; they reveal the limitations of the paradigm. Looking outside the current paradigm is quite difficult because most stakeholders don't know what "outside" looks like; they lack the language to discuss it or even think about it. Synergistically combining their multiple perspectives is the way to overcome this blindness. (Part of Practice One, sensing, and Practice Two, envisioning.)

• *Blend* This is Terry Pierce's advice (2004). Your proposed innovation to resolve the mess is certain to be resisted. Many groups in the social system have enough power to block action they dislike but insufficient power to forge consensus around action they favor. You will probably have to use politics and media to forge healthy consensus and keep large numbers of people involved in the new game until they embody it. You want a critical mass of people to buy in to the innovation before the resistance solidifies. Think of Amazon.com and iTunes as examples; they blended with the copyright protection interests of traditional publishing by looking like an online version of a conventional store, but they wound up disrupting the traditional publishing houses by allowing authors to self-publish through them. (Part of Practice Eight, embodying.)

• *Develop a "we"* Bring together representatives of all the different views and interests in the system who are willing to talk it through together. (Nancy Roberts calls this "Getting the system into the same room.") Lead them to experience solidarity by helping them generate new observers of the mess and new possibilities for resolving it. Chances are that the group will see something together that no individual saw alone. They may find a new perspective that the various power centers can accept and move with. In other words, collaboration may find a solution where serendipity, coercion, or competition cannot. (Part of Practice Three, offering, Practice Six, executing, and Practice Eight, embodying.)

• *Lead* All the declarations, learning, questioning, and thinking will come to naught unless someone steps up to lead the change. If that is not you, you had better convince someone else to do it. The primary work of the leadership is provoking people to question and learn, facilitating collaboration, and managing large-scale coordination. (Part of Practice Six, executing, and Practice Seven, leading.)

• *Produce shared promises* Lead the collaborating group to develop shared commitments and follow-up plans for coordinated action. The group will design shared promises that address the shared concerns of the group and the concerns of the stakeholders. Their design accepts limits while producing a better future for all. (Part of Practice Four, adopting, Practice Five, sustaining, and Practice Six, executing.)

These strategies are not linear "steps" to be performed. They are areas of action and skill and often are performed in parallel.

Because multiple stakeholders are involved throughout, collaboration is essential to bring all eight innovation practices to successful completion. Collaboration is a synergistic coordination in which the collaborators jointly create new observers, new possibilities, new futures, and new concerns (London 1995; Straus and Layton 2002). Everyone in the collaboration shares a commitment and orientation to take care of the concerns of all parties as best can be done. Collaboration is the only way that the stakeholders will come together, come to understand the nature of the mess, blend with the resistance, transform their thinking and practice, develop solidarity, and coordinate their resolution-generating actions.

Collaboration does not mean consensus. Consensus means to make a minimally disagreeable compromise that may be unsatisfying to many but not so bad as to provoke serious opposition. It is a lowest common denominator. Consensus narrows possibilities; collaboration opens possibilities. Consensus is an enemy of collaboration.

Obstacles to Collaboration

Although collaboration is essential to resolving messes, it is an unfamiliar practice to many people. They have to consciously choose to collaborate; and even then they may not know how. Three important reasons for the unfamiliarity are belief in win-lose outcomes, belief in authoritative and competitive political traditions, and a tendency to retreat to the known. We will briefly describe each.

Belief in Win-Lose Outcomes

Robert Axelrod, a political science professor at University of Michigan, is an international expert on game theory. He uses the Prisoner's Dilemma game to understand what disinclines people cooperate in social systems:

There are two players. Each has two choices, cooperate or defect. Each must make the choice without knowing what the other will do. No matter what the other does, defection yields a higher payoff than cooperation. The dilemma is that if both defect, both do worse than if both had cooperated. (Axelrod 1984, 8)

The Prisoner's Dilemma game is a model of many ordinary interactions. We tend to favor actions that benefit us individually and to avoid the work of arranging the more beneficial group cooperation. Traffic congestion is often aggravated by people cutting others off while trying to get to their destination faster; their small gains cause the gridlock that delays everyone. Many people insist on their SUV cars for convenience and complain about the high cost of gasoline. Small groups lobby the political system for favors for themselves and complain when overall taxes go up to pay for all the favors granted. The authors have been in simulation games where the leader offered to pay everyone in the room $100 if they all cooperate, or to pay only the first defector $500 and everyone else nothing—and there were always a few defectors.

Messes are like this. There are always a few who will not cooperate because they believe that eliminating the mess will eliminate their benefits and turn them into losers.

Belief in Authoritative and Competitive Political Traditions

The idea that a strong authority is needed to generate cooperation is as old as governments. Even today many people believe that only the strong hand of a central authority can achieve the common good.

The U.S. Constitution was founded from a deep skepticism of a strong central government. It is based in the democratic principle that government leaders have authority only with the consent of the people. In this framework, competitive political processes resolve disputes and everyone is expected to abide by the majority vote.

Our colleague, Nancy Roberts, has confirmed that these two traditions remain strong today. She tells the following story about teaching a class on "coping with wicked problems" (Roberts 2001).

Roberts begins the class by posing a wicked problem and asking everyone to propose and defend a solution. When students come together and report their proposals, the group judges no solution satisfactory. Student proposals typically involve getting an appropriately high authority to make and enforce key declarations. For example, a green infrastructure is best achieved by establishing a new cabinet-level "infrastructure czar" who can set sustainability goals, create timetables for their completion, and inflict punishments on those who do not comply.

After this failure, Roberts asks the students to try again. Once again, when they come together and report their proposals, the group judges no solution satisfactory. This time their proposals involve various forms of competition: the best proposal prevails in some sort of contest. For example, the green and antigreen advocates both present their cases to the public, which votes on referenda to adopt one scheme after a period of debates and campaigning.

Roberts sends the students back to try a third time. In their frustration over their recalcitrant instructor's demands for new effort they start meeting as a group. They discover they can invent solutions that take care of multiple concerns. Together they find a solution to the wicked problem.

Roberts notes that the students eventually got to collaboration, but not before they had exhausted the alternatives of authoritarianism and competition. These two approaches do not work because they fail to show how individual concerns will be taken care of. Roberts observes, echoing Winston Churchill, "People fail into collaboration."

The situation in the United States after Hurricane Katrina in August 2005 followed this pattern (Denning 2006). The wicked problem was to restore infrastructure in a region where most of the residents had permanently fled after the storm knocked out all power, communications, water, transportation, food distribution, sewage, and waste removal. President George W. Bush's first proposal (takeover by FEMA, the Federal Emergency Management Agency) was authoritarian. Local authorities asserting regional rights rebuffed that approach. Thereafter, the situation devolved into numerous competitions (including disputes and finger-pointing) between federal and local jurisdictions. Two years after the disaster, the region remained gridlocked by local rivalries, fewer than half the residents had returned, disaster reimbursements were held up by enormous tangles of red tape, and very little rebuilding had even started. Most of the progress that was made came from the grassroots level, from local businesses, churches, voluntary associations, and neighbors.

So the political system tried and failed at authoritarianism and competition and got stuck, while grassroots constituents fell into collaboration and made progress. The political system, in its desire to manage everything, did little to empower the grassroots organizations and people. The Katrina mess is one of many where grassroots movements have outperformed governments. There is a worldwide movement to empower local grassroots groups to provide humanitarian assistance (Hawken 2008).

We are not saying that authoritarian solutions or competitive solutions never work. Of course they do. They tend not to work for wicked problems because authoritarian solutions provoke resistance and competition produces local winners at the expense of the whole. The familiarity of these two approaches draws us to them first. Roberts is saying that when we encounter a wicked problem, our best route to a solution is to go straight to collaboration.

Retreating into the Known

David Snowden has been studying complex systems for many years. He believes they are inherently unpredictable because they have too many autonomous agents and rapidly forming and shifting alliances. His great insight is that, when faced with messes, our minds cannot fathom what will happen, and our bodies take over from their training. Instead of facing the unknown, we retreat into the known.

There are many examples of the retreat. The innovator's dilemma (Christensen 1997) is a famous one. In the face of low-end competition from a newcomer, companies shore up their strengths and ignore the competition—only to be killed later when the newcomer undercuts their high end. The 9/11 Commission cited another example. A police helicopter saw World Trade Center building starting to crumble and issued an evacuation order; in the ensuing near panic, the police forgot to convey the order to the firefighters. They retreated into their training, which was to take care of their buddies in bad situations (Denning 2006).

A less dramatic example of a retreat is the "hunkering down" tendency that business leaders warn against when times get tough—advice that is frequently ignored because the employees' bodies do not know what else to do.

The retreat can happen with moods as well as actions. In many messes, the participants have developed resentments and distrust of other groups. These moods become the known; moods of trust and cooperation are the unknown. The Middle East impasse between Israel and Palestine illustrates this.

The retreat can also happen with beliefs. When the mess challenges our beliefs, our bodies cling all the harder to them because they are familiar. If, for example, we believe that every negotiation ends with a winner and a loser, we retreat into taking strong, nonnegotiable positions that yield either win-lose or lose-lose but do not allow the other side to win (Fisher, Patton, and Ury 1992). The possibility of a win-win outcome is then an unknown (Covey 1990). If we believe it is impolite to question the direction of the group, we fall silent and the group can fall into disaster (Harvey 1996).

The only antidote for this is to train the body for engagements with the unknown. One way to do this is to involve people in group processes exploring complex issues (Kurtz and Snowden 2003). Practicing collaboration is particularly effective. We will discuss collaboration as a trainable practice next.

Collaboration as a Practice

The preceding examples illustrate that collaboration is difficult to achieve spontaneously. However, as with most everything discussed in this book, collaboration is much easier to achieve if we interpret it as a practice. We will focus on collaboration as a facilitation practice of innovators (Denning and Yaholkovsky 2008). This practice can foster collaboration among the stakeholders who have to perform any of the eight innovation practices together.

The facilitator leads the collaborating group through a conversation of five stages. The desired outcome of the collaboration is the design and production of new observers, new answers, and new actions for the group's question. Each stage has a characteristic mood; the sequence of stages brings the group to a mood conducive to the outcome. Although it is customary that the group be physically present together, an experienced facilitator can lead the conversations to successful conclusion in other settings such as Internet meetings or telephone conferences. The stages and their moods are:

1. *Declare* The facilitator declares the initial question for the group to consider. The question emphasizes new possibilities rather than current deficits. The facilitator declares ground rules for behavior. Each group member declares acceptance of the need or desire to work together on the issue, openness to the perspectives of the others, and agreement to the ground rules. Without the agreement of everyone in the group to cooperate with the process, egos can get in the way and hijack the process. The mood of this stage is possibility. Possibility overcomes resignation, a mood that blocks collaboration.

2. *Connect* The members take time to become present and engaged with each other. They tell which concerns brought them to the gathering. They state their aspirations and what is at stake for each of them. They say why they see a need for collaboration. They look for and acknowledge connections such as mutual friends, business interests, or similar education experiences. The mood of this stage is connection. Connection overcomes isolation and separation, moods that block collaboration.

3. *Listen and learn* Now the group speaks and listens, as openly as possible, to the concerns motivating each member on the issue. The goal is to expose all the concerns and learn how and why each matters to some member. Members tell stories showing how concerns of all kinds affect their worlds. Even seemingly small or petty concerns can be important. For example, in a meeting to reduce energy use, a person might explain: "Low-wattage light bulbs matter to me. My company replaced a thousand incandescent bulbs and saved $5,000 on our electric bill in the first year. That's a lot of cash for our little company. Whatever solution we come up with has to cater to the little guy." The facilitator

encourages the group to listen for unspoken concerns in the stories, and bring them to light too. The listening must be open and inclusive—seeking to gather many different perspectives, and avoid any initial judgment that one is better than another. Questions and comments are for clarification, not justification or argument. This stage is complete when no one has any further ideas to express; everyone appreciates that the group has multiple concerns to consider; many see a common core of concerns the group can work with. The mood of this stage is openness and curiosity.

4. *Promote "we"*   Members of the group continue the conversation about what matters for as long as necessary until they develop the *experience* of a "we." This is the hardest part. The early signs of group identity and solidarity are members making tentative proposals that recognize, respect, and even own the interests and concerns of the other members. A later sign is reconfiguration of concerns—for example, someone favoring authoritarian, protective, antiterrorist government might reconfigure into a concern for strong, safe, resilient community. The facilitator keeps the proposals tentative and the mood exploratory. The conversation will evolve into a shared feeling that all are in the same mess together, and by staying together we can resolve the mess. The mess may start to unravel as the members become aware of and take care of their interlocking concerns. Occasionally, the mess will evaporate in the light of the reconfigured concerns of "we." The mood of this stage is solidarity, a feeling of oneness.

5. *Design*   Now the group engages with the actual work of creating projects. Some will be variations of the tentative earlier proposals, others new. Members offer to lead projects; other interested parties join the project teams. Projects addressing multiple concerns are the most likely to attract teams. The facilitator guides members with doubts about a proposed project to question in a "we" mood of exploration, clarifying objectives and exploring consequences. For example, instead of saying, "This project cannot work," the member could ask, "In my experience the resources to do this will be considerable. Can we formulate in a less expensive way?" All proposals that attract sufficient teams can move forward for action. The group's final agreement on which projects to take forward cements its solidarity and service to a larger cause. The mood of this stage is ambition.

While these five stages of the conversation have a natural order, they are not linear. People may bounce around or some may happen in parallel.

For example, the group might reformulate the central question after listening to and learning their members' perspectives. The feeling of "we" may emerge naturally during the connection and listening conversations.

Throughout these five stages, the facilitator maintains a background mood of openness and appreciation. Openness encourages everyone to contribute ideas and disclose concerns. Appreciation invites creativity. This is the hallmark of the highly successful Appreciative Inquiry process (Barrett and Fry 2005). The contrasting mood of problem fixing tends to be narrow; it focuses on what's wrong rather than what could be; it discourages group solidarity.

The facilitator also displays all new points learned, proposed, or created on shared computer screens or wall posters. Straus and Layton (2002) found that this form of group memory helps everyone recall ideas belonging to the group as a whole.

Consider what might happen if this process were applied to Lewis Perelman's blue-green clash cited earlier (Perelman 2008). Suppose that numerous green and blue infrastructure advocates decide to collaborate together despite their clashing perspectives. Their facilitated discussion might evolve as follows. They discover that some of their members are motivated green because beloved family members succumbed to lung diseases. They discover that others are motivated toward blue, favoring security because their businesses have been robbed at gunpoint and because one of their companies went out of business in a blackout. They discover that all of them are hesitant to back a centralized government solution because of the government's poor track record; they do not want to risk locking in a bad solution. They start speculating about grassroots solutions that make it cool and fashionable to be both green and blue. They agree on committees and working groups that will sponsor contests for well-designed energy-efficient products and stimulate research into personal home power plants that don't depend on the grid being operational all the time.

Organizing Collaboration in the Mess

Let us now examine how to organize a collaboration that may resolve a mess.

First, let us acknowledge that organizing groups that have been in opposition is not an easy task. The struggles among the perspectives often lead the opposing groups to distrust and resent one another. In such an atmosphere, it is difficult get the parties talking about collaborating. They fight over choices among their separate agendas, but do not work together to create a combined agenda (Denning 2002).

Organizations such as the Charrette Institute report that grassroots demand for collaborative solutions to messy problems is on the rise. People are tired of failed public projects in parks, development, affordable housing, climate change, and infrastructure renewal. They are turning to facilitated processes that guide them to collaboration. Prominent examples include Appreciative Inquiry (Barrett and Fry 2005), Straus Method (Straus and Layton 2002), and Charrette Process (www .charretteinstitute.org). These successful methods have a common structure, exhibited in figure 14.2 (Denning and Yaholkovsky 2008).

The sponsor is a credible entity who declares the mess and convenes stakeholders to engage in a collaboration workshop to resolve the mess. The sponsor invites the design team to propose a question for inquiry and also a list of whom to invite to a collaboration workshop, often called a

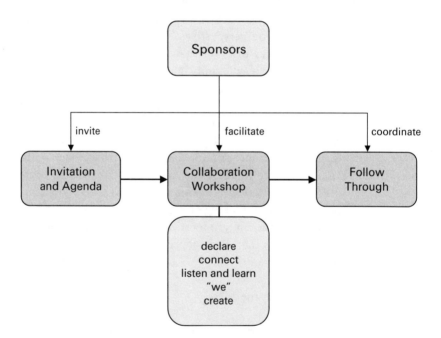

Figure 14.2
Structure of messy problem solving. A sponsor declares the mess and its intent to resolve it. The sponsor facilitates a three-stage practice where (1) a design team creates the agenda and broadly representative invitation list for (2) a facilitated workshop that fosters collaboration among the representatives, and (3) follows through with action teams carrying out projects designed at the workshop. The workshop facilitator leads the group through the five stages of collaboration.

"summit." All key players, age groups, and interests must be represented at the summit. The sponsor provides a facilitator for the summit and leads participants through the five stages of collaboration. The summit fosters a sense of community—a "we"—among its participants and designs action teams to address the mess. The sponsor coordinates the follow-through by helping the teams find people, allies, and resources.

The process of figure 14.2 is true collaboration, not consensus. The participants invent new observers and new possibilities, and they empower representative groups to pursue them.

Peter Denning applied this process to the messy problem of declining enrollments in computer science at high schools and universities. With support from the National Science Foundation, he organized the Rebooting Computing Summit in early 2009 to address this mess. He organized a design team that met for two days and created a summit theme, "the magic and beauty of computer science," and an invitation list. The three-day summit convened with 220 participants representing all sectors of the computing field—higher education, K–12 education, students from high school to graduate school, industry, government, and international. The summit attracted a large number (seventy-five) of women, who wanted to increase the enrollments of women above the dismal 10 percent common in many science and engineering fields. This was the first time that these groups were in a dialogue together. Using the Appreciative Inquiry process facilitated by its pioneers (Barrett and Fry 2005), the summit participants produced nineteen action teams and provided follow-on support through a community Web site (rebootingcomputing.org). Many of the action teams found sponsors for their projects and worked to implement their pieces of the solution.

Supporting Technologies

Over the past several decades many impressive "collaboration technologies" have become available in the Internet. They have been touted as means to achieve collaboration in the virtual settings of the Internet. They can be grouped in three main categories: exchangers, coordinators, and games, discussed in the sections that follow. We will also discuss emergent systems of practice that appear in the conversation spaces opened by these technologies, and the design considerations for technologies that support true collaboration.

Collaboration technologies for the most part are information-sharing technologies. They were not designed for the sophisticated collaboration

Box 14.1

blog	PC access
chat	personal info sharing
content streaming	photo sharing (e.g., Flickr)
corporate directories	recording
database sharing	remote blackboard
discussion board	RSS
document sharing	screen sharing
email	version control systems
file servers	remote screen sharing
instant messaging	VoIP
live presentation	VPN

processes discussed earlier, and they generally do not produce genuine collaboration. Another caveat: these technologies are only able to help users who are willing to enter the conversations they support. They will not help opposing groups who refuse to talk to each other.

Exchangers

Exchangers support the sharing and transfer of information. They are numerous and ubiquitous. The most common examples appear in box 14.1.

Coordinators

A coordinator contains a workflow representation of the network of commitments of a group and a means to observe when participants make new commitments or move existing commitments closer to completion.[1] It allows only those actions that align to the workflow. It tracks work-

---

1. Fernando Flores introduced the idea of a coordinator in his PhD thesis (Flores 1979). He cited the ATM (automatic teller machine) as an early example. It represented the workflows of deposit, withdrawal, and transfer transactions. It was easy to use because bank customers already knew the practices; they interacted with a machine rather than a teller to perform the. He also offered a much more general coordinator that represented the basic form of a "conversation for action" (CFA), which is discussed in detail in his book with Terry Winograd (Winograd and Flores 1987). He incorporated the CFA structure into an email system called The Coordinator and sold it through his company, Action Technologies. Action Technologies later developed a general method of mapping business processes, called action workflows, and tracking them with a Web-based system (www.actiontech.com).

Box 14.2

auction system	newsgroups
automatic teller machine	online payment system
business process manager	online shopping cart
classroom manager	operating system
collaboratory	project manager
concurrency controller	service-oriented architecture (SOA)
coordinators	social network systems (MySpace,
Coordinator email system	Facebook, LinkedIn, etc.)
creation net	support center
crowdsourcing	telescience (remote lab)
decision support system	travel planning and reservations system
discussion forum	wiki discussions
interactive voice recognizer	Wikipedia
Internet protocols	workflow manager
network meetings	

flows and can answer questions about workflow states. Examples of coordinators are described in box 14.2.

Games

A game is a system of interactions among players seeking to achieve a specified outcome through their play together. The players are free to make individual choices as long as they abide by the game's official rules and standard strategies. Besides sports and entertainment games, many social systems in political science, social science, economics, business, biology, ecology, computer science, and psychology have been interpreted as games. Games bring the players into a set of practices, at which they develop skill by repeated play.

Many on-line games have been developed that allow people to assume roles in the games. The current generation of these technologies is the "massively multiplayer online role-playing game" (MMORPG, or MMOG for short). A previous generation was called "multiuser virtual environment" (MUVE). Examples of these technologies are shown in box 14.3.

The list mentions "socially beneficial games," a class defined by Luis von Ahn (2006). Socially beneficial outcomes are a side effect of their regular play. At the Web site espgame.org, for example, random pairs of players test their "ESP" by guessing the keyword the other player will use to label images. Players have fun and accumulate points and national

Box 14.3

America's Army	Second Life
Active Worlds	SimCity
Dungeons and Dragons	Socially beneficial games
Flight simulator	There (there.com)
River City	Training games
Road simulator	World of Warcraft

ratings. The side effect is that the images get good keyword descriptors, which helps search engines find them. Von Ahn says that these games mobilize brains to do computations that we do not yet know how to program into computers.

Game theorists study the same kinds of games analytically. They introduce payoff matrices that award points to pairs of players according to the kinds of decisions they make in encounters during the game. They seek to discover, through analysis and simulation, which strategies produce the highest long-term payoffs for the players. Robert Axelrod (1984), for example, learned that large-scale cooperation is likely to evolve in a social system if the players use a "tit for tat" strategy when they interact; *tit for tat* means that, in your next encounter with a person, you match that person's last move of cooperation or noncooperation.

Two aspects of these games make them very interesting for innovators. First, when people join these games, they quickly become immersed in the practices of the game. The virtual world of the game becomes "reality" and they often forget they are playing in a game (Castronova 2007). This aspect of games makes them very useful for training. The players learn how to perform in the real world by developing their skills in a simulation of that world. Thus it may be possible to design games that train skills in the eight practices.

The second interesting aspect for innovators is that people tend to develop trust for their fellow community members in the game. This happens because they share in the same practices, giving them a strong connection. Thus, it may be possible to overcome trust and resentment by engaging the stakeholders into a virtual mess before tackling the real mess.

Many innovators work with a game interpretation. They begin by interpreting the mess as the result of a game. Through careful examination of the history of attempted innovations, they find the rules and strategies of the game. Then, in the question-the-paradigm strategy, they speculate about how they might change the game so that the mess will disappear. We discussed this in chapter 4 under domain mapping and in chapter 6 under manifesto. The multiuser role-playing game may be a useful tool to develop the new practice in a virtual world and then propagate it to the real world.

Emergent Systems of Practice

Each category of technology explicitly supports certain practices. Exchangers support practices for sharing and exchanging information, coordinators support the practices of a community in doing their work in specific workflows, and games support people in learning new practices in a virtual world for later transfer into the real world.

Impressive systems of practice often arise around the simplest technologies. The Faulkes Telescope Project (www.faulkes-telescope.com) provides free access to robotic telescopes and an education program to encourage teachers and students to engage in research-based science education. John Hagel and John Seely Brown (2006) see this as a fine example of a creation net, a (possibly collaborative) community that learns and invents together. Clay Shirky gives numerous examples of groups coming together spontaneously in a cause or movement using the simplest of information-sharing tools (Shirky 2008). Thus, a community practice can be harnessed and imitated even if no technology has been specifically designed to support it.

Sometimes these impressive systems are captured in a new technology. Technologies that support the work of organizations illustrate this. Initially, organizations used simple information-sharing tools such as email and online records to support their work. Workflow management systems were invented later to support standard practices, such as mapping interactions among roles and tracking the commitments made by persons in those roles. More recently, multiplayer role-playing games have been invented to enable users to practice the dynamic creation of workflows and roles.

Designing to Support Collaboration

Collaboration is an emergent practice. There is as yet no category of technology that fully supports the collaboration practice we described earlier. People learn the collaboration practice in various ways including coaching and immersion in an already collaborating community. Once they know the practice, they can carry it out with the help of exchangers, coordinators, and games.

We recommend a three-part strategy for designers of systems to support collaboration:

1. Declare the unifying principle or theme for the collaboration;
2. Interpret the social system as a network of conversations, commitments and practices; and
3. Assemble a suite of tools that enable conversations, enact commitments, and support individual practices in the network.

The users can then use the tools to participate in the process and achieve the unifying purpose.

The *collaboratory* is an example of a social process designed in this way. A collaboratory is a virtual center that supports collaborative scientific research among geographically distributed researchers (Wulf 1989, 1993). The collaboratory is envisioned as a means to solve complex natural system (Category III) problems, but not wicked problems (Category IV). Wikipedia reports at least nine collaboratories in various fields (en.wikipedia.org/wiki/Collaboratory). Some have been successful, others not. They each have a social model for their community and have selected tools to facilitate research in that community. Despite their differences of purpose, all the collaboratories employ similar technologies (Bly 2005):

- Repositories (technical papers, preprints)
- Digital libraries (access to ACM, IEEE, Wikipedia, etc.)
- Real-time communication such as teleconferencing
- Internet-connected blackboards
- Community discussion boards, RSS feeds, blogs, and wikis
- Distance learning systems
- Remote instruments
- Remote data collection and analysis
- Integration with supercomputers and grid computing

With our model of the social collaboration process for a mess (figure 14.2), we can infer the kinds of tools that would have to be assembled into a mess-resolving center. The National Charrette Institute, which has developed a suite of Web-based technology to help clients with their architectural design and infrastructure issues, perhaps comes the closest to this goal. They use:

- Repositories (articles, case studies, preprints)
- Digital libraries for easy access to existing knowledge (include Wikipedia)
- Real-time communication including teleconferencing
- Internet-connected blackboards
- Community discussion boards, RSS feeds, blogs, and wikis
- Systems to record group results at summit workshops
- Coordinator systems to track follow-on projects after the summit workshop
- Distance learning systems

The overlap with collaboratory systems is striking.

Chauncey Bell (2005) describes a coordinator system for financial management that could be adapted for supporting follow-on projects. His system recognizes three roles: proposer, investor, and manager. It provides tools that support the main actions of each role. It enables sophisticated reporting on the status of investments and the expected returns.

We anticipate that, in time, we will be able to design additional tools that will help facilitate collaboration and extend its reach into larger communities.

Limitations of This Structure

It is doubtful that the process of figure 14.2 could ever be fully automated and the facilitators sent home. The facilitator's main job is to manage the mood of the group, maintaining a sense of appreciation and moving toward the experience of solidarity (the "we"). Building computer systems that expose and monitor moods is hard. It has been done in some cases. Chauncey Bell (2005) points out that financial management systems, which record every commitment and every action leading to its fulfillment, enable auditors to make powerful inferences about participant moods and probable wrongdoing.

How far does the messy problem collaboration process scale? We know that it works for workshop-size groups (say 50–250 people). It extends to larger communities if the workshop represents them well and if the sponsors can support the follow-through teams created by the collaborating group (London 1995). What about messy problems that affect millions of people? How do we bring about enough collaboration to influence so many?

This of course is the central question in efforts to deal with large-scale wicked problems such as sustainable infrastructure, global warming, or health care. We do not yet know how to make the collaboration process scale up to enlist millions of people in a solution. Currently, problems of such scale tend to be resolved by strong leaders who combine technology with political and media savvy to inspire collaboration. For example, Candy Lightner and Cindy Lamb established Mothers Against Drunk Driving (MADD) as an international movement. Former U.S. Senator George Mitchell established the "Mitchell Principles" that created a workable framework for dialogue that ultimately led to the peace agreement in Northern Ireland. Amory Lovins, who focuses on technical facts and avoids moral judgments, has helped clients as diverse as Wal-Mart and the U.S. Department of Defense deal with energy issues.

William Maclay (introduced in chapter 2) is a sustainable-design architect. He specializes in the design of buildings and communities that impose a minimal "carbon footprint"—almost all the energy they use comes from renewable, non-carbon sources such as sun, water, and wind (www.wmap-aia.com). He uses the Charrette Process to help a local community arrive at a design for their minimal carbon footprint. He speculates that he can use existing Internet tools to scale that up to a global level. Through a Web service he would provide plans for running local Charrettes with participation from local environmental architects such as himself. As each community checks in with the adoption of its plan, he would color their zone green on a global map constructed from Google Earth. Each community could then see its efforts contributing to the whole. This approach combines exchanger tools to scale local collaborative solutions up to encompass many communities. It overcomes the mood of "we can't make a difference."

Coping with Failures

The social process depicted in figure 14.2 does not always lead to a solution of the mess. There are at least seven common failures that the participants must cope with as the process unfolds. Professional facilitators, who are trained to cope with these failures, significantly improve the odds of success. The failures are:

1. *Not developing a shared interpretation of the problem*   It is easy to blame the obvious lack of consensus on obstructionists watching for their

own interests but not the common good. But the lack of consensus on problem definition or approach is the central issue. There is no sense of a "we" to work together on the issue. It must be developed through collaboration.

2. *Falling into authoritarian or competitive approaches*   Authoritarian and competitive strategies often fail with messy problems. Without everyone's coming to a mutual understanding of all the other concerns and interests, and learning together, it is unlikely that a design will be found that wins enough acceptance to resolve the mess.

3. *Trying to do it alone*   Messes cannot be resolved without collaboration. Moreover, the action teams will require experts in various areas including technology, media, social issues, and politics.

4. *Technology-only solutions that do not address the social issues*   The mess is a social issue even if originates with technologies. Considerable collaboration building is needed to bring about social agreement.

5. *Being unprepared for resistance*   It is a mistake to discount the resistance that will surely come from stakeholders who see no benefit in the proposed solution.

6. *Demonizing other interest groups*   Groups tend to characterize their opponents in unflattering ways and accuse them of morally or ethically repugnant behaviors. Collaboration cannot occur in such an environment.

7. *Inadequate followup*   It is easy for people to fall back into their old ways of thinking after returning home from their collaboration meetings. Their home environments help sustain the old thinking. The leaders of the change movement need to find ways to keep the momentum going. They must become good at the Sustaining Practice.

Conclusions

Messes are intransigent social situations that people want to exit but feel stuck in. While some messes may be irresolvable, we can often find ways out of messes through seven basic strategies augmenting the eight practices: declare, learn, question the paradigm, blend, develop a "we," lead collaboration, and develop shared promises. Collaboration is at their core.

Collaboration is a practice of creating new observers and new possible actions together, in a mood of commitment to take care of the concerns of all parties as best possible. Through collaboration, a community creates a solution to a messy problem that takes care of all its members' concerns at the same time. Collaboration does not mean that community members give up or compromise their dearest concerns. It means they design a solution that recognizes their concerns. The process often leads to a reconfiguration of everyone's concerns. The hallmark of successful collaboration is the experience of solidarity and new energy: a "we."

Collaboration is an ideal achieved far less often than it is invoked. Many people are drawn to more familiar authoritarianism or competitive strategies—which generally do not work for messy problems. Collaboration is often confused with information sharing, consensus, cooperation, coordination, or collective action. Most "collaboration technologies" are actually tools for information sharing. The design strategy for tools is, first, understand the social process and, second, assemble a suite of tools to support the process.

As we learn more about collaboration practice and tools to support the collaboration practices of communities, we will be able to significantly scale up the known collaboration processes, perhaps even to country or global dimensions. The designs of scaled-up processes and tools will be based on deep knowledge of the practices now used by the human facilitators of today's processes.

Bibliography

Axelrod, Robert. 1984. *The Evolution of Cooperation*. Basic Books.

Barrett, Frank, and Ronald Fry. 2005. *Appreciative Inquiry*. Taos Institute.

Bell, Chauncey. 2005. Wise Organizations. In *Inquiring Organizations*, ed. James Courtney, John Haynes, and David Paradice, 229–271. Idea Publishing Group.

Bly, Sara. 2005. Special Section on Collaboratories. *ACM Interactions* 5:3.

Burke, James. 1995. *The Day the Universe Changed*. Back Bay Books.

Castronova, Edward. 2007. *Exodus to the Virtual World*. Macmillan Palgrave.

Covey, Stephen. 1990. *The Seven Habits of Highly Effective People*. Free Press.

Christensen, Clayton. 1997. *The Innovator's Dilemma*. Harvard Business.

Denning, Peter. 2002. Flatlined. *ACM Communications* 45 (June):15–19.

Denning, Peter. 2006. Hastily Formed Networks. *ACM Communications* 49 (4):15–20.

Denning, Peter. 2007. Mastering the Mess. *ACM Communications* 50 (April):21–25.

Denning, Peter, and Peter Yaholkovsky. 2008. Getting to "We." *ACM Communications* 51 (April):19–24.

Einstein, Albert. 1916. *Relativity*. Repr., Penguin Classics, 2006.

Fisher, Roger, Bruce Patton, and William Ury. 1992. *Getting to Yes: Negotiating an Agreement Without Giving In.* 2nd ed., Mifflin.

Flores, Fernando. 1979. Management and Communication in the Office of the Future. PhD thesis. UC Berkeley.

Hagel, John, and John Seely Brown. 2006. Creation Nets: Harnessing the Potential of Open Innovation. Working paper, http://www.johnseelybrown.com.

Harvey, Jerry. 1996. *The Abilene Paradox and Other Meditations on Management.* Jossey-Bass.

Hawken, Paul. 2008. *Blessed Unrest.* Reprint ed., Penguin.

Kurtz, C. F., and D. J. Snowden. 2003. The New Dynamics of Strategy: Sensemaking in a Complex and Complicated World. *IBM Systems Journal* 43 (3):462–483.

London, Scott. 1995. Collaboration and Community. A report prepared for the Pew Partnership for Civic Change (November), http://www.scottlondon.com/reports/ppcc.html.

Mothers Against Drunk Driving. http://www.madd.org.

Perelman, Lewis. 2008. Infrastructure Risk and Renewal: The Clash of Blue and Green. Concept paper, PERI Symposium, https://www.riskinstitute.org/peri/index.php?option=com_bookmarks&task=detail&id=877. Accessed February 2010.

Pierce, Terry. 2004. *Warfighting and Disruptive Technologies: Disguising Innovation.* Frank Cass.

Reeves, B. N., and A. C. Lemke. 1991. The Problem as a Moving Target in Cooperative System Design. *HCI Consortium Workshop* (January), unpublished proceedings.

Roberts, Nancy C. 2000. Wicked Problems and Network Approaches to Resolution. *International Public Management Review* 1 (1).

Roberts, Nancy C. 2001. Coping with Wicked Problems. In *International Public Management Reform: Lessons From Experience*, ed. L. Jones, J. Guthrie, and P. Steane. London: Elsevier.

Shirky, Clay. 2008. *Here Comes Everybody.* Penguin.

Straus, David, and Thomas Layton. 2002. *How to Make Collaboration Work.* Berrett-Koehler.

von Ahn, Luis. 2006. Games with a Purpose. *IEEE Computer* (June):96–98.

Winograd, Terry, and Fernando Flores. 1987. *Understanding Computers and Cognition.* Addison-Wesley.

Wulf, William. 1989. Toward a National Collaboratory. Unpublished position paper at an NSF workshop. New York: Rockefeller University.

Wulf, William. 1993. The Collaboratory Opportunity. *Science* 261 (August 13):854–855.

Wikipedia. Article on Collaboratory, http://en.wikipedia.org/wiki/Collaboratory. Accessed February 2010.

15

Social Networking and Innovation

The process of becoming an effective World of Warcraft guild master amounts to a total-immersion course in leadership.
—John Seely Brown

Remarkable innovations are coming from unmanaged social networks of people who use the Internet to communicate and coordinate. In doing so, they defy the conventional wisdom that innovation must be managed. We are interested in how participation in social networks increases the success rate of innovations.

We use the term *social networking* to mean participating voluntarily in communities of people in order to pursue shared interests. Social scientists have used this term for years to refer to the ways people develop connections in social systems and use them to build "social capital," the accumulated trust that opens action. A social network is a space of conversations, offers, adoptions, and integration of new practices. Clay Shirky (2008) argues that the Internet has expanded our awareness of social networking by providing tools to observe, measure, and track linkages, connections, and conversations. The better-known social network services include Facebook, LinkedIn, Plaxo, MySpace, Flickr, Twitter, and YouTube. Facebook had 350 million users at the start of 2010 (Giles 2010).

The dynamics of social networks affect leadership and management, the speed of adoption of innovations, and resistance to change. Internet tools and technology have intensified these dynamics in five main ways: (1) increasing the number of people who can participate in the network conversations, (2) increasing the likelihood that anomalies will be seen, (3) increasing speed at which conversations come to completion, (4) making the results of conversations widely available immediately, and (5) enabling small groups to form rapidly to complete specific actions.

Social networks have proved remarkably effective at generating innovations. Ilkka Tuomi (2003) discusses how two transformative innovations—the Internet and the Web—developed and grew exponentially in social networks. We will discuss many other examples. It is doubtful that any of these innovations could have happened without social networks.

Because participation is voluntary, centralized management processes do not work in social networks. Members of the community can choose whether to participate in an action or not. Innovation leaders are forced to become good listeners for concerns and values. The network draws them naturally toward the eight practices because there is no other way they can get results.

There are two fundamental challenges in large social networks. One is gathering a following for a proposed innovation. We call this the *attention challenge*. The network offers a community of potential listeners for many conversations and proposals, but it does not compel anyone to listen. Why will people choose to listen to your voice from among the many seeking to be heard? Innovators who cannot get people to pay attention will encounter major breakdowns in all eight innovation practices.

The other fundamental challenge is orchestrating coordination in networks with participants from very different backgrounds, worldviews, cultures, and value sets. This diversity makes it very hard for people to work in virtual teams and heterogeneous groups. We call this the *pluralistic coordination challenge*. The network leadership will need to foster a commitment to respecting and working with the differences in the ways people see things—to put the ideal of pluralism into practice. We note that the networks that produced successful open-software innovations developed excellent coordination practices that were not derailed by the cultural diversity among their participants (Tuomi 2003). For example, the Linux network relied on Linus Torvalds's "editor" role to select software modules for inclusion, and the World Wide Web Consortium (W3C) adopted a consensus voting practice to commit to new standards.

Social networking deserves careful attention because of its strong record of success with innovation. It is an active area of research and new practice, and is likely to remain so for some time. Our objective in this chapter is to show that the innovation success of social networks arises from their natural tendency to encourage the eight practices. We will comment on the consequences of social networking in business, education, system development, and leadership development.

Examples of Innovations from Social Networks

Let us begin with examples of innovations that have occurred within and on account of social networks. These examples illustrate a remarkable range.

• The most famous of the original online social communities was The Well, short for Whole Earth 'Lectronic Link. It was a dial-in service founded by Stuart Brand and Larry Brilliant in 1985. It hosted numerous groups around specific interests such as parenting or health issues. Craig Newmark's famous Craigslist got started there. Howard Rheingold, an early and active member, wrote his book *Virtual Communities* (2000) about his experiences there. Long before the term "Internet" became popular, he predicted that these "virtual communities" would become a major part of people's lives.

• Numerous companies have set up virtual communities to assist sales, spread the word about their services, and cultivate loyalty to their brands. Popular examples are the network of music publishers and artists that formed around Apple iTunes, the network of software developers that formed around Google, and the network of publishers and booksellers that formed around Amazon.com. The company ning.com generalized by providing a platform that allows any community to set up and monitor a social network. Ning hosted almost 2 million social networks for its clients at the start of 2010 (Giles 2010).

• First responders and volunteers who want to help with disaster relief and humanitarian assistance describe their work in terms of "hastily formed networks" (HFNs) (Denning 2006). Past examples were those formed to deal with the Indian Ocean Tsunami in 2004, Hurricane Katrina in 2005, the San Diego fire in 2007, and the Haiti earthquake in 2010. HFNs are social networks that are created rapidly after a disaster to mobilize everyone to help in the restoration of services and social order. An HFN is a federation of already existing networks and does not have a strong central command. Information sharing across organization boundaries has been a major obstacle to their success. Now that HFNs are recognized as an important category of networks, disaster relief experts have developed tools and training that enable setting them up quickly.

• Most of the popular Internet "social networking" sites provide simple tools that enable users to build their own networks without any effort from the site staff. For example, MySpace, Facebook, and LinkedIn provide tools to list your "friends" or "associates" and let you know about the networks that you have joined when you link to new associates. The image-sharing site Flickr lets users tag images and it automatically forms networks of the people who use the same tags for images. With these new tools, people can see the network that begins with their own connections and then ask for, and receive, help from the network.

• Clay Shirky (2008) tells the story of a woman in New York whose cell phone was stolen. She wanted to recover it because it contained important information about her upcoming wedding. Using social networking tools, she wound up mobilizing a network of local people to find the thief and eventually achieve an arrest. The police were amazed that so many anonymous people volunteered to provide information and take actions that helped recover the phone and save her wedding.

• The Internet leaders early on created a consortium called the Internet Engineering Task Force (IETF). Its volunteers represented a wide range of Internet users. Their purpose was to develop open standards for protocols and services that would allow the Internet to develop and evolve dynamically. The IETF has been a remarkably efficient means to identify problems with the Internet and reach consensus on solutions. The IETF community continues to oversee the development of standard technologies and protocols for the Internet.

• Likewise, the Web founders early on created their own open consortium to develop technologies and standards for the evolution of the Web. They wanted to keep everything in the public domain and not allow any one organization to control the base technology or its standards. Today, about four hundred organizations are consortium members, including nearly every organization with an interest in the Web technology. Members donate representatives to the consortium and volunteers for particular projects of the consortium. The consortium uses a voting process to determine which technologies and reports are considered as "consortium recommendations." The recommendations become de facto standards since all key players are members and have played a part in establishing them. The Web is in constant flux and evolution. The consortium has been effective at "going with the flowing" and is a constant source of innovations for the Web.

• Linux, a public domain imitation of the Unix operating system, was developed by a horde of programmers who contributed code modules, with Linus Torvalds integrating the best of them into new releases. Linux is widely used in Internet routers and servers. It is constantly being extended and improved by its vast community of volunteer programmers.

• Numerous open-software consortia develop software for the public domain. Well-known examples include the Internet Engineering Task Force, the World Wide Web Consortium, and the Object Management Group. A similar idea appears in the Creative Commons, a way for authors, scientists, artists, and educators to share and reuse intellectual property as long as the original author is credited.

• Learning communities form around professions and specialties. The Faulkes Telescope Project (faulkes-telescope.com) is a network that helps young people immerse themselves in the community of astronomers and learn to engage in research-based science education. LabRats (labrats. org) is a community organized to help young people learn basic practices of science. Innocentive (innocentive.com) is an "open innovation" organization that allows "seekers" to pose challenge problems and "solvers" to propose solutions, with the best solutions winning cash awards. C4I Markets (c4imarkets.com) is a service to help match resources and victims in disaster areas.

• In 2004 the U.S. Army commissioned the development of America's Army, a Massively Multiplayer Online Game (MMOG) that lets participants join together in simulated operations of the kind that soldiers would conduct. The U.S. Army values and code of honor are strictly enforced in the game. The initial purpose of the game was to help improve the retention rate in boot camp; at the time about 20 percent of enlistees dropped out, at a significant expense to the army. After the game was around for a couple of years, the dropout rate in boot camp dropped significantly because the game helped recruits judge whether the army suited them. More important for the army, a large cadre of young people discovered that army life was something that would appeal to them, and they enlisted when they reached age eighteen. In mid-2008, there were ten million registered users and about sixty thousand new users were joining every month. Many professional soldiers also play the game, not only because they enjoy the simulations but also because they have opportunity to help new recruits understand how the U.S. Army functions.

• Other MMOGs have become very popular. Second Life is a virtual 3-D world in which people can set up alternative lives and identities for themselves, perhaps as a refuge from the real world or as a means to experiment with alternative life styles. Alexandra Alter (2007) tells the story of a man who in his alter ego met and married a woman in the game. The man's wife was upset that he was spending so much time being married to a comic character instead of spending time with her. Other observers felt that the man was effectively cheating on his wife and did not understand why she would tolerate it.

• Luis von Ahn of Carnegie Mellon University devised an MMOG with an explicit, outside-the-game social purpose (2006). The game, called ESP (espgame.org), lets players earn points by guessing what their partners will choose for keywords to label images. The players are entertained and gain reputations in their gaming world, and Google gets a database of labeled images ready for effective searches. Prior to this game, it was very hard to search for images.

• Not all innovations generated in social networks have been positive. Spurred by 1990s federal policy that encouraged mortgage lenders to help all Americans own their own homes, the U.S. lending system relaxed its standards. The financial network created mortgage securities, a new kind of stock market product representing pools of risky mortgages. Eventually, in fall 2008, when the risky mortgages behind them started to fail, the securities became worthless and almost shut down the U.S. banking system. Housing prices dropped 30 percent and high foreclosure rates persisted for several years.

Many of the people in these networks were not aware they were part of an innovation. They simply joined the new practice because membership in the community was a value to them.

The Eight Practices in Social Networks

As with individuals and organizations, we find that networks that develop the eight practices will have much higher success rates than those that do not.

The aspect of social networks that makes them more likely to develop the eight practices is their volunteer nature. Volunteers will gather around people who listen well and create value for them, and will pay no attention to others. Volunteers tend to take the initiative and often ownership of certain actions, enriching collaboration in the network. They act as customers for the offers of others. They tend not to wait for direction or approval. The social network, therefore, calls people toward listening and value creation, which are essential ingredients of the eight practices. Although there is no guarantee that everyone will follow the call of the network, our experience suggests that many do. Here are examples of how this can happen:

1. *Sensing* Everyone in a network can be put on alert around a question; they quickly join their perspectives and invent new ways to approach the question. People who routinely turn to their networks to ask if anyone knows anything about a problem illustrate this nicely. With many eyes and ears attending to a problem, it is much more likely that someone will spot a marginal practice that can help solve the problem. Some pundits have touted "crowdsourcing" as an organized way to do this for focused questions, but others find its utility limited (Malone, Laubacher, and Dellarocas 2009).

2. *Envisioning* Interesting stories propagate quickly in the network; people quickly learn which stories will catch on and which will be forgotten. Viral marketing is a prominent example. Military and first-responder networks work with a "common operating picture" (a shared map) that gives everyone in the network a comprehensive way to visualize the whole network and its function.

3. *Offering* It is easy to float trial offers in the network. The members already have a connection and an openness to listening. Trial offers can be successively refined through conversations until they become strong real offers. Google's developers run constant experiments to find out which prototypes will sell; because prototypes and products share the same platform, it is easy to transition a successful prototype into a new product (Iyer and Davenport 2008).

4. *Adopting* The network is likely to contain the first adopters and to have members linked to many others who may be first adopters. Their example leads the way to broader adoption. Google explicitly cultivates inventors and early adopters along with their many users.

5. *Sustaining* The network develops support structures to keep valuable practices going. When a practice is no longer valuable or has achieved its goal, it will be quickly discontinued.

6. *Executing* The network presents many opportunities to practice effective coordination. The "common operating picture" replaces command-and-control as the main means of coordination. A person who coordinates well soon develops a reputation for effective and reliable management. Conversely, a person who does not coordinate well develops a reputation of unreliability; others will stop playing with that person. Thus, the network functions like a mirror that shows someone whether their reputation is positive or negative. It is easy to see when you need help, and equally as easy to ask for and receive help. Networks are particularly good at encouraging collaboration—the connection and solidarity is already there.

7. *Leading* Leadership is particularly important in networks. It provides an overall sense of purpose and maintains a sense of belonging and solidarity among the members. Effective leaders develop inspire-and-mobilize styles; command-and-control leadership does not work well with volunteers. The network also develops leaders by providing numerous opportunities for individuals to form and lead small groups for specific tasks. John Seely Brown and Douglas Thomas (2006) see the potential for MMOGs to be laboratories for developing and testing one's leadership skills. They tell the story of a man whom Yahoo hired after it learned that he was a master guild leader in the World of Warcraft game; he had developed the right set of skills for the job he was entering at Yahoo. Byron Reeves and J. Leighton Read (2009) see enormous potential in MMOGs for developing a wide range of business skills, including leadership, while generating a very high level of employee engagement in their work.

8. *Embodying* People operating in a completely online environment are deprived of many opportunities to observe and sense other people physically. They may come to embody habits that work online but seem weird in in-person interactions. The designers of MMOGs who hope to train users to become business savvy have a major challenge in designing their games so that the embodied skills of the players show up as useful and effective in the real world. The skill of blending—working with differences—is essential for coordination in pluralistic networks.

In a social network, these practices encounter breakdowns similar to those discussed in earlier chapters. Some breakdowns may be exacerbated by the speed of the network. For example, someone offers misinformation about you; you counteract the network's speed by moving quickly to dispel the rumor before it gets established in people's minds. Politicians are discovering this is the only effective means of combating misinformation during campaigns. Other breakdowns may be ameliorated in the network. For example, blindness may be less of a problem because more people bring more observers to a situation or question.

The dynamics of a social network are oriented around conversations. Social networks make new observers of their members, shifting them from an older information-and-tool-oriented view to a conversational view (table 15.1). The conversational view closely supports the eight practices by giving direct visibility to making commitments, taking actions, and developing new practices.

Although there is no central authority that directs the network, the people need some source of direction. Leadership must emerge from

Table 15.1
Observers of the Social Network

Information and tool oriented	Conversation oriented
Web pages	Roles
Links	Commitments
Email	Conversation space
Images	Networks of commitments
Search	Solidarity
Chat	Collaboration
Friends	Value flow
Information flow	

within the network (Denning, Flores, and Flores 2010). To enable them to take actions that contribute to the shared purpose, the leadership of a good network provides everyone with a "common operating picture," a framework that the members use to decide if a task has value in the network, and that makes a task and its results visible to everyone in the network. A military operations room illustrates this point: dozens of people are pushing markers representing ships, planes, and ground forces around on a large map of the operating arena.

Tom Malone (2004) says that the continually lowering cost of communication enables many of these features of social networks. Cheaper and faster communication makes flexible, decentralized approaches to coordination increasingly more likely to succeed. The Internet allows anyone to communicate with anyone else rapidly, it provides the means for groups to form and communicate rapidly and privately, and it provides shared distributed memory for the common operating picture. In this context, innovations seem to "emerge" rather than "get produced."

Social Network Analysis

Do not confuse "social networking" with "social network analysis" (SNA). Social networking refers to the broad range of virtual communities and their activities. SNA is an analytic approach that computes various connectivity measures of graphs (nodes and links) representing the social network and then makes inferences about the real social system (Freeman 2006; Wikipedia 2010). Here are three examples of SNA measures:

• *Degree* is the number of other persons an individual is connected to. A "hub" has the highest degree. Hubs tend to be very influential in the network; for example, opinion leaders are hubs.

• *Closeness* is the average path length from someone to all others. People with many friends in the network have the lowest closeness values.

• *Betweenness* is the number of connection paths that include a given individual. "Brokers" have the highest values. Brokers bridge between different cliques within the network and with other networks.

The Wikipedia entry for social networking lists sixteen more measures (nineteen, all told). Ronald Burt (2002) found that brokers tend to be disproportionately influential in innovation—not surprising, since brokers see into multiple communities and can spot practices in one that can be appropriated into another.

Innovators can make use of SNA to help them locate hubs and brokers in a network. These people tend to be thought of as leaders. They exercise considerable influence in the network and are good at gathering followings for ideas. They often wield more power—measured as numbers of individuals who follow—than the formal leadership.

The Attention Challenge

In the 1990s, Web pages, blogs, newsfeeds, image libraries, digital libraries, and Wikipedia were seen as extensions of traditional publishing. Most users had the impression that these new entities were the means to reach a very large audience, often faster and cheaper than with print publications. As these tools became very popular, users began to realize that whatever they had to say would be completely lost in the cacophony of everyone speaking at the same time. Consider some numbers. In 2008 there were over one billion Web pages, fewer than 10 percent of which had been located and catalogued by search engines. Keyword searches in Google typically yield hundreds of thousands or more matches; for example, the word *innovation* registers 150 million hits. Few users look beyond the first ten hits on the first page. The odds of your new Web page showing up in search results are impossibly small—Dreyfus (2001) likens a Web search to trying to find a particular needle in a huge stack of needles.

If you are a blogger, you are one of over fifty million blogs. How will anyone find yours? How will anyone learn that you have said something of value? Developing a reputation for having something interesting to say is important. Fernando Flores says he attracts people to his blog by avoiding his own opinions and drawing attention to important questions and trends; he is able to do this well because he reads about a thousand other posts daily (Lizana 2006).

Marketing experts Jay Abraham (2001), Rich Schefren (2008), and Thomas Davenport and John Beck (2001) all say that getting people to pay attention to your offers is the single most important thing in Internet marketing. They say we live in an "Age of Attention" where nothing happens unless we can draw attention to it. Simply posting a blog or a Web page is not sufficient to draw attention to something. There has to be a way of consciously building a social network around the new item.

Abraham and Schefren favor two means. One is using existing social networks to spread the word about new products. A common technique is termed *viral marketing*, in which a marketing message is spread by people as they communicate with each other on the Internet. The other means favored by Abrahams and Schefren is developing social networks in advance, for example, by offering useful items for free in return for people's email addresses. We will not go deeper here into attention-age marketing because it would take us far afield from our studies of the eight practices.

From the innovator's perspective, the goal is to locate the concerns of communities, tell a good story about taking care of those concerns, and anchor the story with a captivating image or name. One of our favorite examples of this is Bill McKibben's 350.org initiative for a worldwide movement to get carbon dioxide levels down to 350 parts per million.

Getting people to pay attention to you is a definite skill, one of listening combined with adroit blends and changes of direction. You can experiment with different messages and images, keeping the ones that attract attention and discarding the others. Many successful bloggers report that they abandoned their original idea for a blog theme after discovering that their readers more attracted to other topics and ideas.

Massively Multiplayer Online Games

Because they are increasingly important as training grounds and laboratories for innovation and leadership, we would like to say more about MMOGs. Tens of millions of people have joined the synthetic worlds generated by MMOGs, where they create and live in alternate realities (Castronova 2007; Reeves and Read 2009). Enterprise experts are studying which enterprise skills are most easily groomed in an MMOG. Does marketing of virtual products in EVE Online teach anything about marketing in the real world? Do leadership of ad hoc quest groups and guild leadership in World of Warcraft teach anything about team and organization leadership in the real world?

Online virtual games have a long history. The early MUDs (for "multiuser dungeons," ca. 1980) were extensions of the then-popular Dungeons and Dragons game into the Internet. All were based on the extremely limited text-based graphics of early computer systems. In due course they added graphical user interfaces and became known as MUVES (multiuser virtual environments).

In the 1990s the U.S. Department of Defense used *distributed simulation* to simulate war games with players participating from different commands in different locations. Many of the protocols from this research influenced the protocols in the next generation of games, the MMOGs, which used advanced 3-D graphics, sophisticated game engines, and very large user communities.

In the 2000s, MMOGs began to take on social purposes outside the games. We mentioned earlier that the America's Army game has become a powerful recruiting tool for the U.S. Army, that business leaders see World of Warcraft as a training ground for leaders who are good at generating change in social networks (Seely Brown and Thomas 2006, 2007, 2008), and that games have helped search engines become more effective (von Ahn 2006).

Because of their ability to create synthetic worlds, MMOGs have great potential beyond mere entertainment. Fernando Flores observed (in the early 1980s) that people could build compelling worlds in conversation together, with few props. He created simulation games to train people's observers in business. One of his games, offered in the early 1990s, was the five-day intensive "Business 2000." About a hundred participants were organized into ten groups at tables representing corporations. Each group's game goal was to assemble a 1,000-piece jigsaw puzzle by the end of the fifth day. This was not easy because all 10,000 puzzle pieces were mixed together and each group started with a random sack full of pieces. In a subgame that ended on the third day, the groups invented their own products made of Lego pieces; a panel of judges assigned each group's product a market value following a marketing presentation. The groups then accumulated wealth by manufacturing copies of their products. They spent the final two days scouring the market for puzzle pieces, which they bought and sold using their accumulated wealth. Amazingly, many teams completed their puzzles. All sorts of business issues came up in the game such as CEO effectiveness, bringing order from chaos, making effective decisions quickly in the face of chaos, marketing and accumulation strategies, dysfunctional teams, dealing with breakdowns, and failed individual leadership. Many players discovered their strengths and weaknesses in the business marketplace through this game play.

Flores concluded that the world-constructive power of language is so strong that our biology cannot distinguish the synthetic world from "reality." Participants took their real-world habits and conditioned tendencies into the game. They brought back new learning from the game into their businesses. Some got so emotionally involved in the game, they had trouble resisting taking grudges back into the real world.

Flores's observation makes obvious what the problem is with using cell phones while driving. The conversationalists enter a world together that does not include the driver's vehicle. So strong is the reality of the conversational world, the driver becomes oblivious to the real world and a danger to other drivers. Having a conversation with a person in the same car is less dangerous because the world of the conversation includes the conversationalists and their vehicle and the driver is much more aware of the road.

Let's illustrate ways in which social networks, and their associated synthetic worlds, are fostering significant changes in business, education, and system development.

Social Networking in Business

Businesses are finding that they can increase their business by judiciously developing social networks around their principal offers. The online bookstore Amazon.com has developed a large network of booksellers who offer books through the Amazon.com Web site store. The auction company eBay has a large network of vendors who regularly sell wares and another large network of loyal repeat buyers. Google has developed an extensive, high-capacity infrastructure that provides free computing to its users, advertisers, and developers, and enables them to mingle freely.

Many vendor Web sites offer the opportunity for customers to post reviews of products they have purchased. Technology companies incorporate user dialogue into their support databases rather than try to anticipate every question with a posted document.

John Hagel and John Seely Brown (2006) advocate that companies should host a "creation net," a social network of people who help the organization create ideas and make offers (see chapter 13). The Rocke-feller Foundation created the Web site innocentive.com, mentioned earlier in this chapter, to allow "seekers" to pose challenges that attract volunteers who answer the challenges in return for an award. This idea, sometimes termed *crowdsourcing* and *mobilizing collective intelligence*, has been used by other businesses that seek help from their communities. Crowdsourcing can work well in some situations, but is not a universal approach to innovation (Malone, Laubacher, and Dellarocas 2009).

Chauncey Bell (2005) echoes the same sentiment by advocating an ongoing practice of inquiry within organizations through internal and external networks. These practices will help make the organization wise. John Seely Brown and Douglas Thomas (2008) also cite a disposition to inquiry, often cultivated in MMOGs, as a source of organizational wisdom.

Social networks can also help an organization overcome its "stove-pipes," the tendency for organizational units to avoid communicating with each other. A stovepipe is a problem when an issue comes up whose resolution requires the cooperation of several units. Reorganizations usually do not work because they stir up resistance from those who are not interested in change. Overlaying a social network, however, is often helpful. One way to do this is with a task force team that draws from all departments with a stake in the issue. Another way is with a coordi-nating committee with representatives of all stakeholders. The point is to create a volunteer structure that spans all the units needed to address the issue, and to have actions each unit can take as its part of resolving the issue.

Social Networking in Education

For hundreds of years much schooling has been based on the principle that the teacher describes a body of knowledge that the student then applies in practice. This principle comes under frequent criticism because many students are unsuccessful at translating their descriptive knowledge into effective practice. The Internet is offering a way to change this. Communities of practice are forming around specific professions and inviting students to participate. We have already mentioned the Faulkes Telescope Project (www.faulkes-telescope.com) as an example of a com-munity of people interested in astronomy, from student novices to professional astronomers; it has attracted thousands of students to astronomy.

Other Web sites are building social networks for students. The MIT iLab (ilab.mit.edu) offers students access to robotic laboratory equipment that can be operated remotely. The Society for Amateur Scientists (sas.org) offers community services to support teachers and students in science clubs and science projects. They operate a network of clubs called LabRats (labrats.org), which as we noted earlier involves kids in science and teaches them the basics of the scientific method.

John Seely Brown distinguishes two forms of learning, which he calls "learning-about" and "learning-to-be." Learning-about means to acquire a set of rules, descriptions, and mental models for action in the world. Learning-to-be means to embody the practices of a community. The traditional approach to education moves from learning-about to learning-to-be; it is laden with unpopular breakdowns and is frequently castigated. Brown believes that this approach is contrary to most people's experience of their best learning. Most people start as a novice by involvement with a community. Their curiosity drives them to step outside to learn about something new, and then to plunge back in to the community and apply their learning. They do this repeatedly, using the reflective learning-about interludes to help them deepen their practices the next time they immerse in the network. The new social networks for students portend significant and welcome education reform.

Social Networking in System Development

System developers have been stung by the increasing frequency of large system failures. Some systems such as the replacement FAA air traffic control system, the FBI virtual case file, and the Navy Marine Corps Internet, which cost millions to billions of dollars, were abandoned because they could not deliver the functions needed. Other systems such as the Boeing 777 aircraft, the Global Position System (GPS), and the U.S. Census database system have been outstanding successes. Why do some fail and others succeed?

The critical factor is development time (Denning, Gunderson, and Hayes-Roth 2008). This is the time to deliver a system that meets the requirements set at the beginning of the development process. If development time is shorter than the time for the environment to change its requirements, the delivered system will satisfy its customers. If, however, the development time is long compared to the environment change time, the delivered system becomes obsolete before it is finished and may be unusable. In government and large organizations, the bureaucratic acquisition process for large systems can often take a decade or more, whereas the using environments often change significantly in as little as eighteen months (Moore's Law).

Evolutionary system development is an approach that produces large systems within dynamic social networks. The Internet, World Wide Web, and Linux are prominent examples. There was no central preplanning process, only a general notion of the system's architecture, which served as the common operating picture. Individuals in the network banded into small groups to quickly produce or modify modules in the architecture. They tested their modules by asking other users to try them. The systems evolved rapidly in many small increments that aligned with current perceptions of the using environment.

The traditional government acquisition process tries to avoid risk by careful preplanning, anticipation, analysis, and safeguards built into the system. In contrast, the evolutionary process embraces risk, as well as encouraging the patience to see what emerges. It works with nature's principle of fitness in the environment: components that work well survive, and those that do not are abandoned. Social networks may be the key to developing large systems in the future.

Developing Your Own Social Networks

How might you go about developing a social network to help you find attractive new offers and build an adopting community for them? Based on the eight innovation practices, we can offer some guidelines to this question.

The first step is to start a social network. Perhaps the easiest way to do this is to build an offshoot of an existing network. Abraham (2001) and Schefren (2008), mentioned earlier, emphasize the importance of the "offshoot network" for being able to respond quickly to new market opportunities. An offshoot network is formed from people already involved in other networking activities. Abraham and Schefren are constantly developing new networks and mailing lists by having people sign up for free reports. If an opportunity opens up around one of the topics discussed in a free report, they have an extensive list of people ready to contact for a new offer.

Google, as we have discussed, provides the Google infrastructure network as a common platform for all its users, developers, and advertisers. That platform makes it easy for members of the Google networks to develop new networks and to transition prototype products into regular use at any time. Offshoots are the name of the game.

On December 5, 2009, the Defense Department's Advanced Research Projects Agency (DARPA) conducted an experiment to assess the power of social networks. They launched ten red weather balloons simultaneously at undisclosed locations scattered across the United States and offered a $40,000 prize to the first team that discovered the locations of all ten balloons. The news media reported that thousands of teams mobilized. An MIT team completed the challenge in less than nine hours. The subsequent press releases (including those from balloon.mit.edu) touted MIT's hierarchical method of allocating prize money to volunteer helpers as the key to their success. However, the MIT allocation method was not new; it closely resembled well-known multilevel marketing schemes. We believe, however, that the real reason behind MIT's win was its preexisting vast network of friends and supporters. The other teams could not meet the attention challenge no matter how clever their prize-sharing schemes were. It is likely that the same people who helped MIT win would have done so even if MIT said they would donate all the prize money to charity and distribute none of it to the participants.

The moral of these stories is to work with an existing social network whenever possible. It takes a long time to develop a new social network from scratch.

When developing any social network for innovations, the eight practices are a useful guide. In chapter 12, we analyzed how Google and the World Wide Web Consortium (W3C), both innovation generators, organized themselves for the eight practices. We recommend that you do a similar analysis for your proposed network. If you are creating a generative network, how will your network facilitate each of the eight practices? If you are creating a support network, how will it help the community members as they engage with the innovation themselves? Appendix 2 of this book can help you answer these questions.

You can monitor your progress in developing your network against each of the practices and respond to breakdowns appropriately. In our previous chapters, we have described the breakdowns you will most likely encounter. You may often find yourself with ideas about possible actions but no inkling of how your network will respond to those possibilities. The best strategy is to plunge into the unknown, try out an action, and watch how the network responds. Continue to do what

succeeds and stop doing what does not. If something you offer
attracts people, do more of it. If something you offer stirs apathy or
disinterest, abandon it. Over time, you will evolve a network that functions well.

The Pluralistic Coordination Challenge

Social networks enable people from all over the world to join communities and take action together. Organizations are increasingly turning to
social networks to help them establish better connections within the
company and with customers, short-circuiting the age-old tendency for
isolated "stovepipes" (Giles 2010). The same tools that enable these
connections have also enabled increased use of virtual teams, consisting
of people in dispersed geographical locations who have different cultural
backgrounds and value systems.

Despite all the social networking tools for connections, coordination
breakdowns have become more common. Disaster-relief efforts have
been plagued with miscoordination between foreign militaries, local
governments, and nongovernment charity groups (Denning 2006).
Virtual teams have become less effective as their members are increasingly dispersed across many locations (Siebdrat, Hoegl, Ernst 2009).
Many companies have found their efforts to build bridges between
"stovepipes" come to naught. Political systems from local to national
have been tormented with increased polarization and discord. The
common factor in these cases is the different cultural backgrounds of the
participants. Their value sets lead them to different understandings of
everything from the mission that sets the context for coordination to the
simplest elements of coordinated action, such as requests and promises.

Social networking as currently practiced in the Internet is focused on
enabling connections. It does this very well and is disposing people to
be more open to connections with people in different cultures. Coordination, however, is more than connections. To foster excellence at coordination, social networks will need much more than they now have.

We believe that the solution of coordination problems in networks
depends on cultivating the ideal of pluralism. Pluralism has traditionally
been a political philosophy in which people of different backgrounds,
nationalities, cultures, and belief systems commit to working and living
together, respecting their differences, and collaborating to create value
for others. We call a network that has assimilated this philosophy a
pluralistic network.

We believe that pluralistic networks can be realized in practice. The eight practices of this book are a significant step in this direction because they focus on language action for making and coordinating commitments, building trust, delivering constructive assessments, listening for opportunities to bring value, and observing and working with moods. We have found it particularly important to help people share assessments about team performance in order to learn and improve performance (Denning, Flores, Luzmore 2010). This is part of the observing practice discussed in chapter 4 of this book.

Author Peter Denning has participated in experiments with Fernando Flores to determine whether how well the World of Warcraft MMOG can be used to develop proficiency in small, pluralistic teams. The question was whether virtual teams of people who do not know each other and who come from different professions and countries could successfully learn to be proficient leaders of small teams with the help of the MMOG. Our conclusion was that this is possible if it is embedded in a context of learning practices of coordination. The game serves as a provocateur of moods and emotions during stressful team actions, which can be observed and managed by the players with an external structure of after-action debriefs, coaching, and reflection. With that, the participants successfully transferred the learning within the game back into their real worlds (Denning, Flores, Luzmore 2010). As an example, Peter's deputy participated in the experiment, in which she discovered that she was not good at delivering assessments of other team member's performances; with the help of the coaches facilitating the experiment, she became proficient at assessment delivery. Soon after, the people with whom she worked commented on how effective she had recently become at leading teams.

Despite these positive results, and the optimism of others that MMOGs can teach leadership and management skills, we issue a major caution. We do not believe that MMOGs as currently constituted will by themselves produce better managers, leaders, or human beings. We know people who have played these games for thousands of hours and achieved peerless mastery within the game yet cannot work effectively with others in their real work lives. It is interesting to note that some movies are capable of provoking ethical self-reflection about who we are and how we create value in the world, but no game yet does this. It is possible that future games will do this, but those types of games have not been designed yet.

Conclusions

Social networks are a structure of large populations in conversation together. Their distinctive features of orientation toward volunteers, shared commitments, and rapid group formation have given some of them an edge in innovation. The edge exists because these conditions draw participants toward the eight practices. The eight practices create an observer oriented toward conversations rather than information flows and information management. Social networks are supporting new kinds of innovation in business, education, systems development, and leadership development. MMOGs have become a subject of intense research because of their potential to significantly accelerate the learning of social networking skills and innovation. You can use and experiment with social networking to develop attractive offers and get them adopted.

Bibliography

Abraham, Jay. 2001. *Getting Everything You Can Out of All You've Got.* St. Martin's Griffin. Author's Web site: http://www.abraham.com.

Alter, Alexandra. 2007. Is This Man Cheating on His Wife? *Wall Street Journal* (August 10).

Bell, Chauncey. 2005. Wise Organizations. In *Inquiring Organizations*, ed. James Courtney, John Haynes, and David Paradice, 229–271. Idea Publishing Group.

Burt, Ronald S. 2002. The Social Capital of Structural Holes. In *New Economic Sociology*, ed. Mauro F. Guillen, Randall Collins, Paula England, and Marshall Meyer, p148ff . Russell Sage Foundation.

Castronova, Edward. 2007. *Exodus to the Virtual World.* Palgrave MacMillan.

Davenport, Thomas H., and John C. Beck. 2001. *The Attention Economy.* Harvard Business School Press.

Denning, Peter. 2006. Hastily Formed Networks. *ACM Communications* 49 (4):15–20.

Denning, Peter, Chris Gunderson, and Rick Hayes-Roth. 2008. Evolutionary Systems Development. *ACM Communications* 51 (12):29–31.

Denning, Peter, Fernando Flores, and Peter Luzmore. 2010. Orchestrating Coordination in Pluralistic Networks. *ACM Communications* 53 (3) (March).

Denning, Peter, Fernando Flores, and Gloria Flores. 2010. Pluralistic Coordination. In *Business, Technological, and Social Dimensions of Computer Games.* M. Cruz-Cunha, V. Corvalho, and P. Tavares, eds. IGI Global.

Dreyfus, Hubert. 2001. *On the Internet.* Routledge.

Freeman, Linton. 2006. *The Development of Social Network Analysis*. Empirical Press.

Giles, Martin. 2010. A world of connections. Special report in *The Economist* (January 30).

Hagel, John, and John Seely Brown. 2006. Creation Nets: Harnessing the Potential of Open Innovation. Working paper (April), http://johnseelybrown.com/creationnets.pdf.

Iyer, Bala, and Thomas Davenport. 2008. Reverse Engineering Google's Innovation Machine. *Harvard Business Review* (April):59–68.

Kurtz, C. F., and D. J. Snowden. 2003. The New Dynamics of Strategy: Sensemaking in a Complex and Complicated World. *IBM Systems Journal* 42 (3): 462–483.

Lizana, Rosario. 2006. Reflections on Blogging with Fernando Flores, http://www.globalvoicesonline.org/2006/02/21/reflections-on-blogging-with-fernando-flores/.

Malone, Tom. 2004. *The Future of Work*. Harvard Business School Press.

Malone, Thomas, Robert Laubacher, and Chrysanthos Dellarocas. 2009. Harnessing Crowds: Mapping the Genome of Collective Intelligence. MIT Center for Collective Intelligence Report (February), http://cci.mit.edu/publications/CCIwp2009-01.pdf.

Reeves, Byron, and J. Leighton Reed. 2009. *Total Engagement: Using Games and Virtual Worlds to Change the Way People Work and Businesses Compete*. Harvard Business School Press.

Rheingold, Howard. 2000. *The Virtual Community: Homesteading on the Electronic Frontier*. MIT Press.

Schefren, Rich. 2008. Attention Age Doctrine Part 2. This and other free reports available at http://www.strategicprofits.com.

Seely Brown, John, and Douglas Thomas. 2006. You Play World of Warcraft? You're Hired! *Wired* (April).

Seely Brown, John, and Douglas Thomas. 2007. Why Virtual Worlds Can Matter. Working paper (October), http://johnseelybrown.com/needvirtualworlds.pdf

Seely Brown, John, and Douglas Thomas. 2008. The Gamer Disposition. *Harvard Business Review* (February), p17ff.

Siebdrat, Frank, Martin Hoegl, and Holger Ernst. 2009. How to manage virtual teams. *MIT Sloan Management Review* 50 (4) (Summer), 63–68.

Shirky, Clay. 2008. *Here Comes Everybody*. Penguin.

Tuomi, Illka. 2003. *Networks of Innovation*. Oxford Press.

von Ahn, Luis. 2006. Games with a Purpose. *IEEE Computer* (June):96–98.

Wikipedia. 2010. Article on Social Network, http://en.wikipedia.org/wiki/Social_network.

16

Dispositions of the Masters

Mastery is not a goal or a destination; it is a process, a journey.
—George Leonard

Choose anew each day your vocation. Eventually you will see unfold before you the higher purpose that uses you.
—Rev. Jim Nisbet

We are what we have practiced. We are becoming what we are practicing.
—Anonymous

The masters of a field are its most powerful performers. They make the difficult seem easy, the sweaty seem pleasurable, the complex seem simple. They bring understanding where once was confusion. Their innovations are game changing, not just game improving. They transform the discourse and practices of their field. They inspire others to their own new heights. With uncanny shrewdness the masters bring many elements together:

- They understand their communities intimately.
- They read people's deep and often hidden concerns.
- They build compelling visions that people crave to make their own.
- They create offers hard to resist in light of the community's history.
- They mobilize people around their causes without compulsion.
- They foster collaboration and work out complex political agreements.
- They seduce and contain resistance.
- They set up organizations that deliver and last.

How did Bill Gates do these things for Microsoft? Steve Jobs for Apple? Larry Page and Sergey Brin for Google? Candy Lightner for MADD? Paul McCartney for the Beatles?

When we inquire into mastery, we are often struck by the apparent scarcity of masters. Why are there so few? Their individual uniqueness does not seem to bode well for us when we admire the masters and wish we could be more like them.

Our answer to these questions is that mastery is a journey, not a goal. Bill, Steve, Larry, Sergey, Candy, and Paul were once beginners. Their path to mastery was a path of learning and development that elevated them to each next level of innovation skill, from the beginner, to the competent, to the expert, and beyond. This is a path any of us can follow. Mastery is the result of deliberate practice (Colvin 2008).

The great danger of viewing mastery as a goal is that those who achieve it seem to have something unique. Their abilities are so intuitive they are opaque, even to the masters themselves. How can we make it a goal to achieve what only one person can have? How can we learn what a master knows, if the master cannot even describe it? Michael Polyani, who called this limitation tacit knowledge, said, "We know more than we can say" (Polyani and Kegan 1966).

While we cannot say much about *what* the masters of innovation have learned, we can say a lot about *how* they learned it. That is what we mean by the journey. We will explore that path in this chapter.

What Makes Mastery?

There are several ways we might try to define mastery. These include total practice time, individual qualities, and outcomes assessments.

Malcolm Gladwell (2008) traces the histories of several people who succeeded because of their mastery of their fields. He noted that they all put in an enormous amount of time practicing. Based on studies in psychology, he cited 10,000 hours of practice as the amount it takes to achieve mastery. When Bill Joy and Bill Gates were teenagers, they immersed themselves for eight or more hours a day programming computers, accumulating 10,000 hours by age twenty-one.

The "10,000 hours rule" is hardly a definition of mastery. It is best seen as a guideline for the amount of practice but not a sufficient condition. Most of us can give examples of activities at which we have spent 10,000 hours without becoming a master. In some cases, we spent 10,000 hours practicing mediocrity! We are what we have practiced, and we are becoming what we are practicing. Thus, if we aspire to be masters, it is crucial to attend to the quality and focus of our practice.

We even hesitate to say that the 10,000 hours guideline is essential. We know many cases where good coaching put students into the right practices rapidly. The best we can say is that the guideline reminds us that it takes much time, immersion, and perseverance to become masterful.

The 10,000 hours guideline is just a beginning. It might characterize a first-degree level of performance. But as in the martial arts, there are many degrees of mastery beyond the first-degree black belt, to be attained by even larger amounts of practice. Many masters report that after immersion in their fields for an extremely long time (twenty-five years is often cited) they have "openings" that enable them to see their fields in new ways that lead to new waves of major innovations.

A second way we might try to define mastery is to list qualities and abilities that can be observed in masters. A typical list of this sort is:

· Masters amaze and dazzle people with their performances.
· They frequently mystify people with their insights.
· They offer interpretations that simplify complex situations and enable others to take useful actions.
· They rapidly see the answers to problems that baffle and stump others.
· They inspire excellent performance in those around them.
· They have innovated the discourse and practice of their field.
· They have a capacity for long-range strategic thinking and action.
· They see historical drifts and moving waves of opportunity.
· Their historical sensibility leads them see current conditions as the results of past choices, and to propose new choices for the future.
· They have a deep, resonant listening for the moods, yearnings, and concerns in their community.
· They have developed a distinctive style and way of observing the world.

Although these are signs that a person has attained mastery, they do not tell us how the person attained the relevant skills or what the person does to exercise them. So a list of qualities is not a fruitful way to define mastery. Such lists are descriptive of what we see masters produce, but are not a generative articulation of what masters do.

A third way we might try to define mastery is to examine the assessments that people make of high performers. In innovations these assessments would include that masters are:

· Able to bring about wide adoption in large communities
· Able to alter the paradigm of their communities
· Able to inspire intense mobilization around their proposals

Assessments like these call attention to the size and importance of the innovation, but not to the master. There are numerous examples of people who produced innovations that would get high marks on these assessments.

Our conclusion is that focusing on the immersion time, the personal qualities, or the results produced by the master is not a fruitful way to define mastery. A much better way is to define mastery in terms of the journey taken. It is then possible to say some significant and useful things about how mastery is attained.

Mastery Is a Journey, Not a Goal

In 1972, Hubert Dreyfus proposed a scale of learning. He said that as one gets better and better in a domain, one progresses through the stages of beginner, advanced beginner, competent, proficient, expert, and master. His purpose then was to argue that no software system could behave as an expert. He refined his argument and descriptions of the levels in his most recent book, *On the Internet* (2001), where he argued that purely online instruction might take someone to competence, but not beyond. We are less interested in his conclusions about computer-based learning than in his description of the path to mastery. His description is a tour-de-force. Of mastery he says:

When an *expert* learns, she must either create a new perspective in a situation when a learned perspective has failed, or improve the action guided by a particular intuitive perspective when the intuitive action proves inadequate. A master will not only continue to do this, but will also, in situations where she is already capable of what is considered adequate expert performance, be open to a new intuitive perspective and accompanying action that will lead to performance that exceeds conventional expertise. . . . Thanks to exceptional motivation due to their dedication to their chosen profession, the ability to savor and dwell on successes, and a willingness to persevere despite the risk of regression during learning, the master's brain comes to instantiate significantly more available perspectives with accompanying actions than the brain of an expert. Thanks to practice, these perspectives are invoked when they are appropriate, and the master's performance rises to a level of excellence unavailable to the ordinary expert. (Dreyfus 2001, 44)

In *Mastery*, George Leonard (1992) says that the experience of this learning is a series of plateaus that occur unpredictably. The jump to the next plateau feels like a breakthrough in performance accompanied by a new sense of understanding. Often there is a slight drop of performance just after the jump, but the new plateau is higher than the old. Paradoxically, the person seeking the next jump is likely to experience a long wait compared to the person who practices for the sake of the practice itself. The path to mastery is one of continued satisfaction with the play without a sense that it ever *has* to get better.

Leonard's distinction bears a remarkable similarity to James Carse's (1986) distinction between finite and infinite games. The purpose of a finite game is to achieve an objective, and of an infinite game to continue the play. The true path to mastery is an infinite game. Organizing learning as a series of finite games (quests) is a behavior of experts, not masters.

How Masters Find Innovations

What is the essence of what an innovator does along the path of learning? We find the answer in *Disclosing New Worlds*, the work of Spinosa, Flores, and Dreyfus (1997). Our summary of their work is the prime innovation pattern, introduced in the prologue and in chapter 1. It is repeated in box 16.1.

The eight practices of this book are the specific means by which the innovator carries out this pattern. A person can engage the pattern as a beginner, a competent, an expert, or a master. In Dreyfus's terms, mastery

Box 16.1
The Prime Innovation Pattern

1. Innovators find in their lives and work something disharmonious that common sense overlooks or denies.
2. They hold on to the disharmony, allowing it to bother them; they engage with it as a puzzle.
3. Eventually they discover how the common-sense way of acting leads to the disharmonious conflict or failure.
4. They design or discover a new practice to resolve the disharmony. The new practice comes from one of three sources:
a. It is already a background practice of the community, but has been dispersed and nearly forgotten. Recovering it is called *articulation*.
b. It is a marginal practice on the fringe of the community's awareness, usually resulting from an invention. Bringing it to the center is called *reconfiguration*.
c. It is a standard practice of another community, which can be mapped and adapted into the current community. Importing it is called *cross-appropriation*.
5. They make a deep commitment to getting the new practice adopted in their community.

of this pattern makes innovation intuitive and not an overt act of puzzle solving.

Is mastery an extraordinary depth in the eight practices? Or is it an augmentation of the eight practices with some others that we have not yet discovered? We interpret mastery as the learning path where the prime innovation pattern is engaged repeatedly; the engagements move the person from beginner, to competent, to expert, and eventually to master. We believe that the highest level of performance—master—expresses as intuitive performance at each of the eight practices, and in an individual style that integrates the eight practices. We do not believe there are additional practices that we have not yet discovered.

The ability to perform this pattern effectively becomes the issue in mastery. That raises three questions, which will be taken up in the next three sections.

• How deeply does one have to be involved in a community to be effective? This is the *localization* issue.
• What attitudes and moods lead to the most effective performance of this pattern? This is the *dispositions* issue.
• How does one cultivate the dispositions? This is the *learning community* issue.

Immersion and Localization

How much immersion is necessary to become effective at the prime innovation pattern?

We argue for immersion in the community one wants to change. We recommend a *practice of immersion*, which is simply to enter into the community and be fully open to whatever will happen. Allow yourself to be completely absorbed into the world of the community and flow with whatever moods and emotions it triggers. Allow yourself to acquire the community's tacit knowledge by engaging in its practices. There is no goal other than to let the community teach what it has to teach and do your best with what the community presents.

However, simple immersion is not enough. We need to be immersed while remaining sensitive to the disharmonies in the community that motivate our desire to change it. It is easy to be taken up by the immersion itself and develop a limited point of view that cannot see the need for change or the opportunities for bringing it about. We have already mentioned this in our discussion about the possibility of complex multiplayer online games (MMOGs), such as World of Warcraft, to develop leadership skills (Seely Brown and Thomas 2006, 2008). We know many expert players in World of Warcraft who are not able to transfer any learning from the game back into their real worlds. They got lost in the game without seeing the bigger possibility of learning leadership.

An effective means for retaining your sensitivity to the disharmonies is the *practice of reflection*. At intervals, you step back from the game play and, with other players and perhaps a coach, you discuss what breakdowns have occurred, what moods and emotions have been provoked, what coordination worked, what the large implications are , and what new strategies can be tried when play is resumed. You are not just interested in improving the game, but also in the possibility of changing the game itself by questioning its assumptions, point, rules, and limits.

Bringing in an outside observer, such as a good consultant or coach, can accelerate the benefits of reflection. The experienced coach is familiar with how people observe and can help you in your reflection see things about your involvement during immersion that you would otherwise miss. While perhaps unable to directly experience the disharmony, the coach can help you articulate the disharmony and the action that might resolve it.

Another accelerator for the practice of reflection is a learning community devoted to cultivating the skills of openness, connection, and blending that are needed during the next rounds of immersion. We will discuss learning communities shortly.

These two practices—immersion and reflection—make up an effective cycle for becoming masterful in the community and remaining sensitive to its disharmonies. In Silicon Valley, the immersion occurs when one sweats over the sale of a new business idea to the venture capitalists, works with lawyers to create or dissolve companies, labors long nights trying to get the technology to work, and flies to distant cities and dank motels to sell products (Metcalfe 1999). Seminars discussing the beautiful ideas and clever strategies just will not do. Moments of reflection occur in the social interactions between friends working at different companies. They step outside their experiences and compare with the others. Other moments of reflection come in interactions with one of the masters, who give them better ways to observe and offer guidance for better performance.

Which community should you immerse into? Not all communities are the same. For innovators, some communities seem to have definite advantages.

It has long been a puzzle why certain geographic localities seem to be hotbeds of innovation. What goes on in Silicon Valley, Singapore, South Korea, Taiwan, or Japan that allows their companies to consistently outperform companies from other locations?

Many authors as far back as 1890 have investigated why industries cluster (Castells and Hall 1994; Marshall 1890; Saxenian 1996; Porter 1998; Prahalad and Krishnan 2008). John Seely Brown and Paul Duguid (2000a) give a particularly good account of why innovation companies have clustered in the Silicon Valley. They analyze how people exchange knowledge (not just information) in local interactions. People doing things together communicate and learn through their coordination: they learn deep embodiment through their interactions, even though they cannot describe all that has taken place. Through shared practice, they embody tacit knowledge that cannot be described and communicated in words. This is one of the lessons of our study of the embodying practice.

A business firm is a community of practice—its members work together and constantly learn from one another. A firm is also part of an "ecology" of many firms in a region. The tacit knowledge it acquires from its regional interactions is as important as that learned within the firm. The Silicon Valley ecology grants easy access to lawyers, venture capital, business services, movers, real estate, and more. It is also blessed with a temperate climate. A firm cannot easily relocate out of the region because it then loses all its subtle connections to everything in the region it relied on for its success.

Even a relocation within the region can fail. In *Fumbling the Future*, Douglas Smith and Robert Alexander (1999) tell the story of how a team of computer system scientists at the Xerox Palo Alto Research Center (PARC) invented the first personal computer system but could not get the Xerox company to turn it into product. In the early 1990s, the computer systems research team left PARC and moved en masse over to the Digital Equipment Corporation (DEC) System Research Center in Palo Alto. Despite generous funding, they were not able to produce new innovations of the magnitude they did at Xerox in the previous two decades. Something about the Xerox environment encouraged innovation, and was not duplicated in the DEC environment. Gladwell (2008), Ogle (2007), and Stefik and Stefik (2004) all give further examples of how the environment encourages or impairs innovation.

Brown and Duguid (2000a) point out that a further factor enriching the local ecology is "networks of practice." These are networks of people in the same profession who do not work together, but share a professional identity and professional practices. Networks of practice are not the same as communities of practice because they are not localized, do not offer day-to-day friendships, and lack face-to-face interactions. Many local communities of practice can be part of a single network of practice. Lawyers, realtors, computer scientists, designers, graphic artists, and many more all have professional networks that enable to them to interact across the many companies they work in. These networks now reach far and wide in the Internet. Networks of practice create another dimension of communication within the local ecology, and many channels to expertise outside of the region.

The economist Alfred Marshall (1890) seems to have understood all this and summarized it in his view about how knowledge moves in working communities: "The mysteries of the trade become no mysteries; but are as it were in the air." Knowledge movement often seemed like a mystery because people learned from each other by doing rather than attending courses or presentations. Moreover, Marshall used the term *mystery* in the same sense it was used in the old guilds—people learned the mysteries of their trade by apprenticing to masters. Marshall thought that economic clusters formed not because communication was cheaper with neighbors, but because localization enables the mysteries to be learned by shared, interactive practice under the guidance of masters.

Our conclusion is that those who immerse themselves in a region already masterful at innovation have the best shot at becoming masters of innovation. Immersion in such a community is a way of studying with the masters.

It is sometimes argued that with the low cost and fast communications of the Internet, the importance of local communities will diminish: a worldwide virtual community could be just as innovative as Silicon Valley. Seely Brown and Duguid (2000b) chastised those making such arguments. Many had predicted that the Internet's ability to disintermediate would bring the end to the press, television, mass media, brokers, firms, bureaucracies, universities, government, cities, regions, and even the nation-state. None of these things happened then and none has happened since. The reason is clear from the preceding discussion: these entities are all communities of practice that must remain localized to retain their effectiveness and their ability to learn and adapt. Low-cost communication certainly helps, but it does not eliminate the need for local interaction.

Dispositions

What dispositions are most helpful for making progress on the path of mastery? A disposition is a predominant or prevailing tendency of one's mind and body, a natural mental outlook or mood, which inclines one to a type of action or line of thought.

Throughout this book we have inquired into the nature of the practice that enables success at innovation. We have been particularly interested in practices that individuals (and organizations) can use to attain much greater success rates by becoming skillful innovators. But it would seem we cannot do the same for masterful innovators, because they have deep, context-dependent practices that are nearly impossible to describe in a way that helps one learn them.

While we may not be able to describe *what* the master knows, we can say something useful about *how* the master learns it. We can describe dispositions that facilitate the learning.

Spinosa, Flores, and Dreyfus (1997) summarize the general idea of a disposition as a "style." They say that the innovator's disposition is a "style of history making" that inclines the person to engage with the prime innovation pattern whenever change is needed. Seely Brown and Thomas (2008) argue that a "questing disposition for inquiry" is essential for any successful learner, whether in a school or in a community of practice. Gilder (1992) argues that certain virtues, including humility, care, and commitment, create dispositions for successful entrepreneurs. Strozzi-Heckler (1993) sees conditioned tendencies as negative dispositions toward automatic actions that do not fit with the current conditions. All these authors believe that dispositions can be cultivated and sometimes trained. The idea of dispositions has already proven fruitful to help understand mastery at innovation.

Hagel, Brown, and Davison (2008) identify what they term a *shaping disposition* and argue that it is the hallmark of recent highly successful, innovative organizations. A shaping disposition leads the business leadership to a strategy consisting of a transformative view, a platform, and coordinated actions. The transformative view is a new interpretation of the world. The platform is a common operating environment (they call it *ecology*) in which new social networks can spawn and coexist with all others. The actions move toward the world envisioned in the view and demonstrate the organization's commitment. In the terms of this book, a shaping strategy is a realization of the prime innovation pattern. The "view" is the articulation of a new common sense. The "platform" is the environment that attracts potential adopters and makes it easy for them to adopt the new practice. The "actions" are the conversations that drive adoption and demonstrate the commitment of the leaders.

Throughout this book, we have discussed the various ways that innovators interpret and interact with the world. These can be summarized as a set of "innovator dispositions" as follows:

- Observing:
  - possibility and newness
  - what is needed
  - disharmonies
  - value from the eye of the customer or user
  - breakdowns, opportunities, waste, and value
  - lost values that might be recovered
  - marginal ideas that might become central
  - connections between communities
  - appropriation of practices
- Resonance with people's yearnings and deepest concerns
- Mood of inquiry and exploration through quests
- Willingness to engage over long time periods
- Willingness to experiment and get feedback
- Willingness to build networks of collaborators
- System (holistic) view
- Shaping
- Historical sensibility to how past choices shaped the present
- Moving toward the opportunities
- Engaging a learning cycle of immersion-reflection

Learning Communities

How might you practice these dispositions? Practicing them is first of all being aware that they are possible, and incorporating them into recurrent actions and practices. We have already previously discussed how to listen for concerns, make offers, and blend—practicing dispositions is the same idea. We recommend that you select those dispositions that are opportunities for you, and integrate them into your regular behaviors. Our friend Richard Strozzi-Heckler has daily practices that cultivate the dispositions he wants. He begins his day with forty-five minutes of meditation, followed by stretching, exercising, and a walk in nature. He says that by nine o'clock he has done his important practicing for the day, and is ready to engage in what the day brings.

You can go further if you are willing to engage with learning communities that cultivate the dispositions you want. You can immerse yourself into a regional community of practice that already has these dispositions. Silicon Valley is a favorite destination for those who aspire to high performance at technology innovation.

We have noted earlier that there is a danger of getting so wrapped up in the immersed world that you lose sight of the disharmonies you want to change. We therefore recommend that you do your regular reflection with an outside observer such as a good coach or consultant.

There is one other type of learning community that can be helpful. It is a community of people aiming to develop certain dispositions by practicing together without immersing into the communities they want to change.

An example of such a learning community is the Aikido dojo. When one comes regularly to the dojo, one engages in a variety of practices with others about attacks, defenses, and blends, learning to do them all well. Eventually, one learns to access a state of internal stillness while in fast-moving, chaotic situations. In this state, one deals with an attacker's moves as they come, simply by blending with the movement of the other's energy. Practice in the dojo eventually builds a disposition of internal stillness that enables one to exhibit calm and centered leadership when in the real world.

Richard Strozzi-Heckler (2007), a sixth-don (sixth-degree) black belt in Aikido, has designed a "leadership dojo" that teaches leadership dispositions though sustained involvement. His design is based on thirty years of successful practice at teaching people about the dispositions of leaders. He has trained thousands of successful leaders and coaches through the Strozzi Institute (strozziinstitute.com).

Robert Dunham, through the Institute of Generative Leadership, has designed a dojo-like community called "Company of Leaders" that teaches the practices of this book (enterpriseperform.com). His community combines leadership practices from Strozzi-Heckler's community, coaching practices from The Newfield Network (newfieldnetwork.com), and language-action practices from Fernando Flores as elements of the discipline of generative leadership.

These learning communities may accelerate the progress of serious learners to mastery in their fields by enabling them to cultivate the dispositions of innovator and leader, receive coaching not available to them in their primary communities, and attain a new awareness that helps transfer the dispositions learned.

We believe that the most effective, and possibly fastest, way to learn the practices of this book is to join a learning community of people on the same journey as you—the journey toward mastery.

Conclusions

Mastery is not a lucky accident or a rare gift; it is the product of deliberate practice. Your journey of mastery in innovation is one you can consciously design. You can design your practices, the communities and networks with which you practice, and your own dispositions toward action.

In this book we have given you the tools for these designs. We have given you the eight essential practices of innovation and shown how you can develop them as personal skills. We have shown how you can extend the eight practices into your organizations and networks. We have shown how you might organize your own journey of mastery.

And thus we come to the final sentences of this book. While the book may be over, the next phase of your journey is just beginning. We are confident that you will find good fortune, by design. Travel well.

Bibliography

Carse, James. 1986. *Finite and Infinite Games*. Random House.

Castells, Manuel, and Peter Hall. 1994. *Technopoles of the World: The Making of 21st Century Industrial Complexes*. Routledge.

Colvin, Geoffrey. 2008. *Talent Is Overrated*. Penguin.

Dreyfus, Hubert. 2001. *On the Internet*. 2nd ed., Routledge, 2008.

Gilder, George. 1992. *Recapturing the Spirit of Enterprise*. ICS Press.

Gladwell, Malcolm. 2008. *Outliers: The Story of Success*. Little Brown.

Hagel, John, John Seely Brown, and Lang Davison. 2008. Shaping Strategy in a World of Constant Disruption. *Harvard Business Review* (Oct.):1–11.

Leonard, George. 1992. *Mastery*. Plume.

Marshall, Alfred. 1890. *Principles of Economics: An Introductory Volume*. MacMillan and Co.

Metcalfe, Robert. 1999. Invention Is a Flower, Innovation Is a Weed. *Technology Review* (Nov.), http://www.technologyreview.com/read_article.aspx?id=11994&ch=infotech&a=f.

Ogle, Richard. 2007. *Smart World: Breakthrough Creativity and the New Science of Ideas*. Harvard University Press.

Polyani, Michael, and Paul Kegan. 1966. *The Tacit Dimension*. Routledge.

Porter, Michael. (1998). Clusters and the New Economics of Competition. *Harvard Business Review* (Nov–Dec):77–90.

Prahalad, C. K., and M. S. Krishnan. 2008. *The New Age of Innovation: Driving Co-Created Value Through Global Networks.* McGraw-Hill.

Saxenian, AnnaLee. 1996. *Regional Advantage: Culture and Competition in Silicon Valley and Route 128.* 2nd ed., Harvard University Press.

Seely Brown, John, and Paul Duguid. 2000a. Mysteries of the Region: Knowledge Dynamics in Silicon Valley. In *The Silicon Valley Edge: A Habitat for Innovation and Entrepreneurship,* ed. C.-M. Lee, W. F. Miller, M. G. Hancock, and H. S. Rowen, 16–44. Stanford: Business Books.

Seely Brown, John, and Paul Duguid. 2000b. *The Social Life of Information.* Harvard University Press.

Seely Brown, John, and Douglas Thomas. 2006. You Play World of Warcraft? You're Hired! *Wired* 14.04 (April).

Seely Brown, John, and Douglas Thomas. 2008. The Power of Dispositions. *ACM Ubiquity* 9, 43 (November), http://www.acm.org/ubiquity/volume_9/v9i43_thomas.html.

Smith, Douglas, and Robert Alexander. 1999. *Fumbling the Future: How Xerox Invented, Then Ignored, the First Personal Computer.* Authors Choice Press.

Spinosa, Charles, Fernando Flores, and Hubert Dreyfus. 1997. *Disclosing New Worlds.* MIT Press.

Stefik, Mark, and Barbara Stefik. 2004. *Breakthrough: Stores and Strategies of Radical Innovation.* MIT Press.

Strozzi-Heckler, Richard. [1984] 1993. *The Anatomy of Change.* North Atlantic Books.

Strozzi-Heckler, Richard. 2007. *The Leadership Dojo.* Frog, Ltd.

Epilogue: Stradivarius Street

It is the year 1720. You, a traveler, arrive in the Italian town of Cremona in search of the best violins made. You look on the street of the violin shops. At the mouth of the street, immediately to the left, you see the shop of the Guarneri family. In its window is a very large sign with majestic calligraphy: *Best Violins in All of Italy*. Farther down on the right you see the shop belonging to the Gagliano family. In its window is an even grander sign: *Best Violins in the Whole World*. Down at the far end of the street, tucked in the shady cul-de-sac, you find a small shop belonging to the Stradivarius family. In its window there is a small card. You have to lean over and squint to read the handwritten message: *Best Violins on This Street*.

The lesson is that being excellent on a global scale begins with being excellent in the neighborhood. That excellence begins with yourself. You can cultivate excellence in the way you interact with others to help them adopt innovations. The eight practices of this book are your path.

There is a second, more subtle lesson: understated excellence. Stradavarius is not pretentious. It does not waste energy trying to tell everyone it is excellent. It just goes about being excellent. And the world knows.

It is now possible to perform for your neighborhood and see the world play your songs.

Appendix 1: Eight Practices Summary Chart

The following chart summarizes the eight practices for generating innovation.

Summary of the Eight Practices

Structure	Practices	Anatomy	Characteristic breakdowns
The main work of invention	**Sensing**	Sense and articulate opportunities and their value. Locate possibilities through networks, checklists, or disharmonies.	Inattention. Blindness. Inability to notice or articulate sensations, hold the thought, or see opportunities in disharmonies.
	Envisioning	Weave vivid, concrete, compelling stories about new worlds embodying possibilities; and means to get there.	Complex, abstract, emotionless, unreal, non-credible stories; inability to design plans of action.

Table
(continued)

Structure	Practices	Anatomy	Characteristic breakdowns
The main work of adoption	**Offering**	Draw listeners into a discussion about ways to produce the new outcomes. Modify proposals to fit listener concerns. Establish trust in one's expertise to fulfill the offer.	Little awareness of and respect for customers. Inability to listen, connect, enroll, articulate value, or see people as fundamental in the process. Unwillingness to respond to feedback.
	Adopting	Achieve initial commitment to the new practice. Demonstrate value. Show how to manage risks and contain resistance. Align action plans for coherence with existing practices, concerns, interests, and community member adoption rates. Recruit allies. Develop marketing strategies for different groups. Overcome resistance.	Force adoption through compulsion. Failure to anticipate opposition and differing adoption rates of different community segments. Failure to articulate the value from adopting. Lack of enabling tools and processes for adoption.
	Sustaining	Achieve commitment to stick with new practice. Develop supporting infrastructure. Integrate new practice with surrounding environment, standards, and incentives. Assess for negative consequences. Abandon bad or obsolete innovations.	Failure to plan for support and training, to change enabling tools and systems, to align incentives with the new practices, to align political support, or to integrate with other practices and standards.

Table
(continued)

Structure	Practices	Anatomy	Characteristic breakdowns
The environment for the other practices	**Executing**	Create an environment for effective action in the other practices. Build teams and organizations. Manage commitments, resources, and capacity for reliable delivery.	Failure to manage commitments, satisfy customers, deliver on time, or build trust.
	Leading	Create an environment for recruiting followers and articulating guiding principles in the other practices. Declare new possibilities in ways that people commit to them. Move with care, courage, value, power, focus, sense of larger purpose (destiny), fluency of speech acts.	Inability to listen for concerns, offer value, work with power structures, maintain focus, operate from a larger purpose, or perform speech acts skillfully.
	Embodying	Create somatic awareness, accounting for emotion and body in the other practices, and develop the skill of blending with concerns, energies, and styles of others. Nonverbal communication. Emotional intelligence. Ascend ladder of competence. Connect. Produce trust. Develop open and inviting "presence."	Inability to read and respond to body language, gesture, etc. Inability to connect and blend. Failure to recognize and overcome one's own conditioned tendencies, to appreciate differing levels of skill and their criteria, or to practice regularly in the other practice areas.

Appendix 2: Eight Practices Assessment Tool

In this book we have mentioned several times that the eight practices framework is, in addition to being a guide to practice, a useful assessment tool. With it, we can gauge our relative strengths and identify chronic breakdowns in each of the practices. We present here a simple worksheet and assessment process that you can use to assess either your organizational or personal strength at the eight practices.

The examples given throughout the book demonstrate a variety of ways that organizations can realize the practices. There is no unique mapping from the eight practices to an organization's business model. Because the eight practices are fundamental, essential, and nondiscretionary for successful innovation, every innovative organization includes them in some way. These practices are to organizations like air and water are to our bodies: air and water do not generate our body functions, but a well-functioning body necessarily uses air and water. In the same way, a well-functioning, innovative organization necessarily accommodates the eight practices. The purpose of the assessment tool is to see how well this is happening.

The worksheet in table A2.1 is used to assess an organization's effectiveness with the eight practices. There are four steps. Step 1 is to gather and record information for the first three columns:

• In the Concerns column, record all your concerns in the area of this practice.
• In the Current Practice column, record all the ways your organization currently does this practice. Look for all organizational practices that support the innovation practice.
• In the Chronic Breakdowns column, record the breakdowns that recurrently inhibit or block your success at the practice. Look for organizational practices that interfere with the innovation practice. Record

Table A2.1
Eight Practices Assessment Worksheet

Practice	Concerns	Current practice	Chronic breakdowns	Rating	Future actions
Sensing					
Envisioning					
Offering					
Adopting					
Sustaining					
Executing					
Leading					
Embodying					
Coherence of current practice					
Coherence of future actions					

Box A2.1
Assessments to Use in the Worksheet's Rating Column

1 Blind	We have not been aware of the necessity of this practice.
2 Drifting	We are aware of this practice but have taken no actions to improve how we do it.
3 Resolving	We are aware of this practice and have already undertaken actions to improve how we do it.
4 Settled	We are satisfied with our approach to this practice.
5 Masterful	Our approach is consistently producing significant results and value.

misalignments in the perceptions of others about how this innovation practice is done.

Take your time in gathering this information. Consult with other members of the organization to get their views and to make sure you have covered everything.

Step 2 is to fill in the Rating column with one of the five numerical assessments in box A2.1.

Step 3 is to make an overall assessment of the coherence of your present approaches to the eight practices taken together. Do your practices fit together well? Interfere with one another? Are there conflicts?

Step 4 is to write down the future actions needed to achieve settlement in your approach to each innovation practice. Then make an assessment of the coherence of your proposed future actions. If their coherence is less than settled, adjust your plans. You definitely want your coherence assessment for the future to be settled.

To have a reasonable chance of success at your innovation projects, you need a score of at least 3 in every practice and a total score of at least 32.

We find that most individuals and organizations with innovation challenges have multiple weaknesses. It is not enough to focus exclusively on an obvious weak point, because you may miss other important weak points. Get the big picture and work on strengthening all your weak practices.

When you are done, you will see clearly the places where you need to focus your attention either to strengthen a practice or improve the coherence among your organizational units that implement it.

Individuals can do this exercise to assess their own levels of skill at innovation and determine where they need to get coaching.

Appendix 3: Levels of Performance at Innovation

A skill is dexterous performance of a practice. Hubert Dreyfus proposed a hierarchy of performance levels in 1972, when arguing that the common notion of "expert behavior" is not achievable by a software system.[1] In the 1980s, Fernando Flores adopted these levels to characterize every education process in every domain: education is a continuing process of learning at increasing levels of skill.[2] The highest levels can take many years to achieve. Here we apply their ideas to suggest criteria for levels of performance at innovation.

We have aggregated the seven Dreyfus–Flores levels into three for this book. The mapping between their levels and ours is summarized in table A3.1.

Recurrent practice with the eight practices of this book is sufficient to bring a person to the skillful level. In our experience, a passionate learner, who is already competent in the domain where the innovation is to be introduced, can achieve the skillful level in a year.

Recurrent practice outside the context of the community in which the innovation is to be introduced is not sufficient to attain the masterful level. Expert performance in a school or training center does not carry over to the real community. One must dwell in the community, steep

1. Hubert Dreyfus, *What Computers Still Can't Do* (first edition 1972). Dreyfus defined skill levels and argued that "experts" exhibit many behaviors not describable by rules. In contrast, software systems can only exhibit rule-based behaviors. He repeated his argument in On The Internet (2001) when considering the levels of skill that a student can achieve through online courses.

2. Fernando Flores also introduced two skill levels that are below the novice. One level down is the "blind person," who cannot see that he or she is causing breakdowns for other people on account of their own ignorance of the domain. Two levels down is the "jerk," or "pretender," who realizes this but does not care.

Table A.3.1
Mapping between the Dreyfus-Flores Levels and This Book's

Dreyfus–Flores	This book
Novice Advanced beginner	Procedural
Competent Proficient	Skillful
Expert (virtuoso) Master Legend	Masterful

oneself in its history, build diverse social networks, learn from many teachers, and repeat this many times in many communities. Mindful practice with teachers of great mastery is more effective if punctuated with periods of immersion in the community. Studying with multiple masters is essential for developing one's own unique style.

Silicon Valley in California has a reputation for being a community that spawns technology innovators. Someone who studies articles and books about Silicon Valley, and visits occasionally, will know the valley at the procedural level. Someone who lives there for a year or two, long enough to start and sell a business, will know the valley at the skillful level. Someone who has started many businesses there, has been imbued with its history, culture, and sense of possibility, has traveled widely, and has developed considerable influence will know the valley at the masterful level.

Table A3.2 suggests criteria for each of the levels of performance at innovation. For suggestive purposes only, we have included qualitative estimates of the size of the community adopting the innovation; larger communities are more complex and are more likely to require the guidance of masterful innovators. Many people do not realize that most innovations are small, involving only a few adopters. This means that you can be successful as a beginner with small groups. You do not have to be a master or legend to innovate. It also means that if you are still a beginner you cannot handle a large innovation alone—for example, founding a new business that changes the Internet.

Table A3.2
Performance Levels for Innovators

Level	Description	Learning modes	Innovator examples (typical group size)
Beginner (novice)	Just getting started in the domain. All action appears to be governed by rules defining allowable moves and strategies. Common situations are unfamiliar and are described by more rules.	Memorization, drill, and simple practice. Demonstrations of play. Practice in simple situations.	Memorizes anatomy of each practice. Follows steps of practice as a checklist. Immobilized by breakdowns. (very small)
Advanced beginner (rookie)	Recognizes common situations, which helps in recalling which rules should be exercised. Most action is deliberate application of rules or conscious recall of prior actions in familiar situations. Can perform simple actions for customers; needs supervision for more complex tasks.	Problem solving and practice with rules and strategies. Play in realistic situations with supervision. Repeated practice with common situations.	Comfortable with anatomies of practices. Recognizes common situations and immediately knows appropriate action. Copes with common, simple breakdowns. Works well with direction. (small)
Competent (professional)	Carries out standard actions without causing breakdowns. Can fulfill standard promises to customers satisfactorily without supervision. Performs most standard actions without conscious application of rules. When faced with a new situation, works out appropriate actions by application of rules.	Advanced problem solving, coaching on problem solving and projects. Extensive practice in both common and exceptional situations. Apprenticeship to more advanced professionals and teams. Membership in professional networks.	Knows all anatomies. Routinely deals with change management in moderate-sized groups with moderate complexity. Leads innovation teams. Copes creatively with breakdowns. Requires little supervision. (medium)

Table A3.2
(continued)

Level	Description	Learning modes	Innovator examples (typical group size)
Proficient (**star**)	Deals with complex situations effortlessly. Seldom thinks in terms of rules and may have some difficulty telling others what rules he or she works with. Appropriate action appears to come from experience and intuition, and is deliberately chosen. Individual performance a benchmark for others. Considerable experience and practice across wide range of situations over years of work.	Apprenticeship to experts. Coaching. Putting self into wide range of situations. Membership and contribution to professional networks. Teaches the competent.	Highly productive. Has a reputation for creative innovations. Others admire and seek to imitate accomplishments. Excellent problem solver. High individual productivity. Receives very positive assessments from customers and other professionals. (large)
Expert (**virtuoso**)	Consistently inspiring and excellent performances. Appears to solve difficult, complex problems effortlessly. Enormous breadth and depth of knowledge. Acts appropriately without thought or conscious choice of actions. Routinely forms and leads high-performance teams, admired by others as a benchmark of team performance. Performance standards well beyond those of most practitioners.	Apprenticeship to masters. Advanced coaching, development of breadth, focus on observing and adopting style of the teacher. Teaches the proficient. Years or decades of practice.	Extensive experience with large innovations. Anticipates subtle and indirect concerns and points of resistance. Anticipates and responds to customer concerns. Leads teams well. High productivity. Plans difficult innovations quickly and well, including solving some wicked problems. (large and complex)

Table A3.2
(continued)

Level	Description	Learning modes	Innovator examples (typical group size)
Master	Capacity for long-range strategic thinking and action. Sees historical drifts and shifting clearings. Has studied with many different teachers and has developed own distinctive style. Has produced innovations in the standard practices of others, has altered the course of history in the field, and knows how to do this again. Teaches others to be experts and masters.	Learning continues by working with other masters as teachers. Creates and leads professional networks. Teaches the experts.	Develops new methods and practices for innovation itself. Admired for long, historical perspectives and strategies. Deals creatively and effectively with wicked problems. (very large and complex)
Legend	Has attained high public standing with legendary status as a master and performer. Leverages public standing to achieve results that only public figures could attain. Work has widely accepted impact.	Same as for master with emphasis on public visibility.	Widely admired innovator who publicly sets the pace for everyone else. A legend's articulations shape the direction of the field. (very large and complex)

Appendix 4: Somatic Exercises

Somatic exercises are designed to build awareness, embodiment, and focus. Awareness creates choice, embodiment the capacity to perform well without thought, and focus the ability to channel energy toward outcomes one cares about.

The first section of this appendix lists somatic exercises designed for the Sense 21 project at George Mason University in the 1990s (reported in Peter Denning's chapter, "The Somatic Engineer," in *Being Human at Work*, ed. Richard Strozzi-Heckler, North Atlantic Books, 2003). These exercises aim to develop somatic sensibilities and skills in individuals.

The second section lists somatic exercises for groups. They develop members' somatic sensibilities for group and team actions.

All these exercises are adapted from exercises designed by Fernando Flores for his Ontological Design course and Richard Strozzi-Heckler for leadership training.

Exercises for Individuals

Table A.4.1
Somatic Exercises for Individuals

Value element	What is to be revealed	Somatic practices
Writing autobiography	Your life is a story and you are the author.	Write a story about yourself emphasizing events that shaped you emotionally and professionally.
Speaking autobiography	Your comportment, posture, and mannerisms reflect your history.	Speak your story to a group, then receive their assessments about congruence between the story and your mannerisms and comportment.

Table A.4.1
(continued)

Value element	What is to be revealed	Somatic practices
Centering	You can enter a state of balanced awareness of yourself and others, prepared for action.	Role-play in which you are off center in various ways; partner speaks assessments of your presence and openness.
Extending	You can focus your attention in ways that command others' attention and move them to action.	Perform immovable arm exercise; walking with intention exercise through partner barrier.
Simple blending	You are more effective if you combine your energy with the challenger's, instead of opposing or evading it.	Move toward someone advancing toward you, turning to flow with his or her momentum, interpreting in conversational space.
Distinguishing assertions from assessments	Assertions are true or false; assessments are judgments and evaluations.	Describe a table full of objects without giving any assessments. Identify assessments and assertions in newspaper articles: which sells papers better?
Grounding an assessment	People will follow if you lead with grounded assessments; most of us are inept at grounding assessments.	Present to group "I am competent at X," then receive their feedback.
Receiving a negative assessment	You have a tendency to accept the assessment and act on it uncritically.	Group forms circle, gives negative assessments to one member; recipient notices body reaction, repeats a short script to distance from the assessment with dignity.
Making a request	In asking someone to perform an action for you, you provoke body reactions in that person and yourself.	Make requests of partner with complete and incomplete conditions of satisfaction; trade assessments at end.
Declining a request	Body reactions interfere with your ability to say no.	One person repeatedly makes a request in various ways, the other declines; trade assessments at end.

Table A.4.1
(continued)

Value element	What is to be revealed	Somatic practices
Completing a workflow loop	Incomplete transactions leave both parties unsatisfied and unsettled.	Practice loops, breaking at each of the four stages; trade assessments at end.
Trust	Keeping promises builds trust; breaking promises builds distrust.	Maintain journal of kept and unkept promises and assessments provoked in others.
Distinguishing mental models from practices	Knowing a concept or principle does not enable you to act effectively.	Group and partner discussion of relation between theory of value components and ability to perform as demonstrated in prior exercises.
Mood	Mood is a pervasive interpretation about future possibilities.	Role-play with the other person posing as someone you want to make a request of or close a deal with; others observe your posture and make assessments about your mood. Practice saying characteristic conversations of various moods.
Adding value	Value is an assessment by a customer.	Make offer to partner. Ask what partner is concerned about, then make new offer. Compare assessments before and after.
Creating waste	Actions that do not add value are waste.	One partner performs actions that the other did not request or care about; trade assessments at end.
Producing an innovation	Innovation is a change of practices in a community.	Carry out a carefully structured project to design and deliver an innovation for a customer's group.

Exercises for Groups

These two exercises are based on exercises used by Richard Strozzi-Heckler.

Sensing Opportunities

This group practice helps people get somatic experience of sensing opportunities (Practice One). The group leader begins:

Folks, let's try something. Walk in the room. Random directions. Watch out that you don't crash into other people—we . . . don't want to hurt anybody. Careful, watch it. (1 min.) Now, try focusing on spaces between people. Walk into open spaces. (1 min.) Go back to crash avoidance. This time, pay attention to how the whole room is moving. (1 min.) Go back to moving into the spaces. Again, pay attention to how the whole room is moving.

(Sit down.) What did you learn about innovation from this exercise?

The group typically makes the following sorts of observations:

• To focus on avoiding obstacles impedes movement, requires lots of mental computation to watch people's paths, overall speed slow, jerky.
• To focus on space represents moving toward opportunities. Moving into them is easier and smoother. Less mental attention needed; can feel them and move toward that. Overall speed is faster, less jerky.
• Local actions affect the whole system. When everyone is acting to avoid crashes, the room feels different from when everyone is acting to move into empty spaces.
• The system accommodates local leadership actions. For example, someone extended his arms signaling he was taking space, then executed a 180-degree turn. Everyone in the neighborhood smoothly opened the space for him. Not a word was spoken.
• It's possible to open up space, not simply move into existing space. One student was trying to run instead of walk; people got out of the way, made space for him. More subtly, one can open space by extending energy into it, such as the previous person extending his arm.
• With the same group, over time, we noticed its members walked faster with practice. Initially they were tentative, slow, and plodding. With practice they could walk quite fast and never collide.

The walking practice illustrates how sensing feels. You're always moving with people and their paths are unpredictable, yet you can influence them. You move more smoothly when you look for opportunities (spaces) than when you avoid collisions. You can open up big spaces by extending your energy. The local changes you initiate propagate through the room, affecting everyone. We followed up by suggesting participants continue the exercise on their own:

You can practice this when walking on the sidewalk or in a busy hallway. Walk into the spaces. Create spaces by extending energy (imagine your energy nudging people out of the way). Learn to feel those spaces and not think about them or about collisions. Practice opening up spaces for you to walk into.

Coping with Chaos

A rondori is an exercise from the martial arts. The group forms a circle. The person in the center is "attacked" in unpredictable ways by persons from the periphery. Here, approachers extend their arms, palms projecting toward the person in the center. The person in the center is supposed to move through this chaotic maze of moving, shifting attempts to push them (gently!) off course. This continues for several minutes per person.

The person in the center usually reacts from conditioned tendencies. Some raise their hands, arms, and elbows to ward off collisions. Some get knocked around like a punch ball. Some run away from those approaching (and into others they didn't see coming). Some work the crowd like politicians seeking votes. Their mood reflects what happens to them at work or home when they are overwhelmed by a large number of events demanding attention. The observers (periphery) create stories about who these people are based solely on how they move—this one is a victim, that one is hard-edged defensive, this one loves people, that one takes care of clients.

The exercise can be repeated at intervals by the same group. Over time, as participants become more skilled with blending, their conditioned tendencies disappear and they develop individual styles of interacting with the chaos.

About the Authors

Peter Denning is a distinguished professor at the Naval Postgraduate School in Monterey, California. He chairs the Computer Science Department and directs the Cebrowski Institute, an interdisciplinary research center for innovation and information superiority. He held previous faculty positions at Princeton, Purdue, and George Mason universities, and he was founding director for the computer science research institute RIACS at NASA Ames Research Center.

In his early career he was a pioneer in the development of principles for operating systems. He made substantial contributions to performance evaluation when that industry was getting launched. He cofounded CSNET, the computer science network of the National Science Foundation, and shared in the 2009 Internet Society Postel Award for the achievement; CSNET was the first community network bridge from the original ARPANET to the modern Internet.

Denning has been an active leader since 1967 in the Association for Computing Machinery (ACM), the leading professional society for computing. He was president in 1980–1982. He was also vice president, chair of three boards, and editor of the ACM monthly magazine. He led the ACM Digital Library project that made ACM the first professional society with its entire literature online.

Beginning in the 1980s, when he was at NASA Ames, he became interested in the practices of management, leadership, and innovation. During that time he started collaborating with Robert Dunham. He studied with Fernando Flores to learn language-action philosophy and its applications to leadership, and later with Richard Strozzi-Heckler to learn the somatics of leadership and be certified as a Master Somatic Coach. When he joined the faculty at George Mason in 1991 he created a design course, known as "Sense 21," for his student engineers so that they could learn how to design systems that aligned with the interests and practices of their clients. The graduates of the course formed an alumni group that remained active for ten years after the course was first offered.

Denning has been a prolific author, publishing more than 340 articles in computer science and seven books, including *The Invisible Future* (McGraw, 2001) and *Beyond Calculation* (Copernicus, 1997).

He holds twenty-six awards, including three honorary degrees, three professional society fellowships, six technical achievements, two best-paper awards, three distinguished service awards, a hall of fame award, and several outstanding educator awards.

Robert Dunham, founder of the Institute for Generative Leadership and the consulting company Enterprise Performance, works closely with executives and management teams to produce value-creating enterprises. He also founded the Company of Leaders, a group dedicated to continued practice and learning in leadership. Since 1981 he has been developing the discipline that is now offered in the three-year Generative Leadership Program, teaching people successful practices of leadership and management. This program is based on leading-edge thinking in linguistics, biology, embodied learning, commitment-based management, communication, and coordination. The program is practice based and focuses participants on learning through application on the job with personal coaching, with the criteria for learning being measurable improvements in the performance of teams and organizations.

Prior to founding Enterprise Performance, Dunham was a vice president of consulting for Business Design Associates (BDA), an international business process redesign firm. Before that he was chief operating officer for Action Technologies, Inc., and co-holds two patents for their Action Workflow technology. Prior to that he served as vice president of system development for Motorola Computer Systems, where he directed the development of three hardware and software system product lines and delivered over one hundred and fifty software product releases to the marketplace. Early in his career, he led the on-board software development team for the Hubble Space Telescope for several years.

Dunham has trained hundreds of executives and managers. He has published nine articles on business, management, and coaching, and another thirty proprietary papers for his leadership and management development programs. His past clients include Toshiba America, IBM, Discovery Channel, Scholastic, Adobe Systems, Fidelity National, several Silicon Valley companies, and many others.

His management and leadership training programs are unique combinations of communication, language-action, leadership and management practice, and embodied learning. His programs draw on the pioneering work of Dr. Fernando Flores in language and action, and Dr. Richard Strozzi-Heckler in Somatic Leadership.

Dunham earned two degrees from Stanford University, completed three years of postgraduate work in Ontological Design, and four years in Somatic Leadership with Strozzi Institute. He is executive in residence, adjunct faculty, at Presidio School of Management where he taught in their MBA program, and currently teaches in their Executive Certificate program. He currently leads the Coaching Excellence in Organizations program offered by the Institute for Generative Leadership and Newfield Network.

Index